Rammstein on Fire

T0276960

Rammstein on Fire

*New Perspectives on the
Music and Performances*

Edited by JOHN T. LITTLEJOHN
and MICHAEL T. PUTNAM

McFarland & Company, Inc., Publishers
Jefferson, North Carolina, and London

LIBRARY OF CONGRESS CATALOGUING-IN-PUBLICATION DATA

Rammstein on fire : new perspectives on the music and
performances / edited by John T. Littlejohn and
Michael T. Putnam.
        p.   cm.
Includes bibliographical references and index.

ISBN 978-0-7864-7463-9
softcover : acid free paper ∞

1. Rammstein (Musical group)   2. Heavy metal (Music)—
Germany—History and criticism.   3. Rock musicians—Germany.   I. Littlejohn, John T.   II. Putnam, Michael T.,
1976–

ML421.R3R36 2013
782.42166092'2—dc23   2013029827

BRITISH LIBRARY CATALOGUING DATA ARE AVAILABLE

© 2013 John T. Littlejohn and Michael T. Putnam. All rights
reserved

*No part of this book may be reproduced or transmitted in any form
or by any means, electronic or mechanical, including photocopying
or recording, or by any information storage and retrieval system,
without permission in writing from the publisher.*

On the cover: Rammstein in concert at Palais Omnisports
de Paris-Bercy, 2009 (Photograph by Rémi Lanvin)

Manufactured in the United States of America

McFarland & Company, Inc., Publishers
  Box 611, Jefferson, North Carolina 28640
  www.mcfarlandpub.com

Acknowledgments

We'd like to thank all of the contributors for their interesting ideas, hard work, and patience with us throughout the process of putting this volume together. It has been a pleasure working with the world's foremost Rammstein-ologists and we hope they're as proud of this volume as we are. Thanks again!—*JTL and MTP*

I would like to acknowledge the students in his German music and culture courses at Clemson University and at Coastal Carolina University. I appreciate their great enthusiasm and I marvel at the fresh insights they bring on such a consistent basis. I'd like to thank my co-editor, with whom I've undertaken several projects, including our first paper on Rammstein in 2007. I would also like to thank Shannon, Jane, Rommie and my mom. They all know full well how I become slower and slower about returning calls when I get deeper and deeper into my writing, and they generally cut me slack about it. Of course, I especially want to thank my wife Lori; this would all be meaningless without her.—*JTL*

I would like to recognize his former students at Carson-Newman College who participated in his seminar on Rammstein during the spring of 2008 and their relation to modern German literature and culture. It was through our discussions that I began to realize that a collection of scholarly essays on this topic was sorely needed; I just never realized what potential this topic could have in the realm of academics and beyond. I would also like to thank my close friends, especially Brad "the yellow dart" Weiss, Ricky G, Zach R, Matt Davis, Ron Then and LJ, as well as my family for their unconditional love and support. Last and certainly not least, I would like to thank Jill and Abby for the constant inspiration to live life to its fullest and to follow my dreams. All of you enrich my life tremendously — thanks for having my back, y'all!— *MTP*

Table of Contents

Part III: The Elemental and the Metaphysical

Introduction: Gaining an Academic Appreciation of Rammstein

JOHN T. LITTLEJOHN and
MICHAEL T. PUTNAM

Rammstein has sold recordings to millions of people who do not understand the words the singer is growling at them. And they play with fire. These are perhaps the two facets of the band's work which most fascinate fans and scholars.

Falco hit it big with "Rock Me, Amadeus" and Nena's "99 Luftballons" still plays regularly on the radio, yet even the redoubtable Kraftwerk has failed to sell as many albums abroad. Rammstein has achieved international ticket and album sales which are staggering for a group which almost exclusively sings German texts. As of this writing, their second album, *Sehnsucht*, is the only German-language album to ever reach platinum status according to the RIAA: more than a million records sold in the United States. That number, of course, boggles the mind considering how few Americans speak German — and do so sufficiently to understand some deceptively complex lyrics.

In addition to their music, the band's play with fire has contributed greatly to their fame. The pyrotechnics in the stageshow have become legendary, with flame throwers, fire-breathing, explosions and sparks of fire. Scores — if not hundreds — of newspaper articles attest to the public's fascination with Rammstein's fiery shows. Song titles such as "Feuer frei!" ("Fire at Will!"), "Feuer und Wasser" ("Fire and Water") and "Wollt ihr das Bett in Flammen sehen?" ("Do You Want to See the Bed in Flames?") strengthen the public's association of the band with fire, as do the fiery and explosive videos, such as "Engel" ("Angel") and "Mein Land" ("My Country").

The reader must take the "play with fire" mentioned earlier figuratively as well as literally. Throughout their career, Rammstein has continually addressed taboo themes and images. Critics have, for instance, often decried the band's flirtation with fascist imagery. Perhaps the high point (or low point) of that aspect of Rammstein's infamy came when they released the video for "Stripped," which used images from Leni Riefenstahl's 1938 film *Olympia*. In addition, Rammstein has sung about such controversial or uncomfortable topics as sado-masochism, necrophilia, and cannibalism. Rammstein's evocation of taboo has on more than one occasion brought critics and even censors down on the group. Nonetheless — or, perhaps, therefore — sales and interest in the band have remained strong for almost two decades. From *Sehnsucht* up to the band's latest release in late 2011— a 14-year period in which the group released five studio albums, two live sets, and a greatest hits compilation — each one of Rammstein's albums has reached the top of the charts in their native land.

The paragraphs above appear to answer several basic questions, but these answers raise further questions still. Also, while pyrotechnics have fostered awareness of the group and garnered many fans, we can hardly consider Rammstein's use of fire on stage and in videos unique or groundbreaking. And many, many other popular music artists have broken taboos to gain infamy and sales. However, if the breaking of taboo proves an integral part of Rammstein's appeal, how can one explain the enormous sales outside of Germany and other German-speaking countries, i.e., in areas where the audience does not understand the lyrics?

One reason behind the incredible album and ticket sales may be very simple: Rammstein sounds great. Till Lindemann's words assault the listener with their deep tones and harsh syllables, and the band behind Lindemann rocks hard and plays tight together. The band's powerful, atmospheric music very quickly led to a place on movie soundtracks, beginning with David Lynch's 1996 *Lost Highway*, a film which features the songs "Heirate Mich" ("Marry Me") and "Rammstein" from the band's first album, *Herzeleid* (1995).

Rammstein could hardly count as the first German artist to reach an international audience with their sound. In the past, many culturally German composers changed Western music immensely with their sonic innovations; Beethoven, Wagner, and Schönberg are just a few names which spring to mind. More recently, Kraftwerk and Can have fundamentally influenced incalculable numbers of punk, hip-hop, electronic, and indie bands for several decades.

However, Rammstein's sound cannot be the sole component of their international success. The band sounds great, but one could not consider

Rammstein so original or compelling that it could grasp and hold such an enormous international audience for more than a decade. Obviously, the editors of this book shall not argue that Lindemann, Kruspe et al. merit a place in the Western music pantheon. Rammstein is neither a Mozart nor a Kraftwerk. Clearly definable reasons behind Rammstein's success therefore remain elusive.

In addition to the sustained support of a global audience, Rammstein has increasingly undergone the scrutiny of serious scholarship. Several Germanists and musicologists from around the world have published articles and books dealing largely or exclusively with Rammstein. One can even find multiple articles on the use of Rammstein's music in the classroom. Certainly Rammstein's adaptations or appropriations of Goethe, Brecht, and Riefenstahl work like catnip on many academics, yet even this cannot explain the many and varied scholarly treatments the band has received.

In light of the band's substantial and sustained popular success and growing scholarly interest, we heeded the call for a single volume, which would contain a number of new perspectives on Rammstein. We are fortunate that several scholars who previously published research on Rammstein have found still greater depths in Rammstein's oeuvre to examine, and have contributed new and original ideas to this volume.

Scope and Content

Patricia Anne Simpson investigates the Comic in Rammstein's stagework, music and videos in her essay "Industrial Humor and Rammstein's Postmodern Politics." She brings particular insights into Rammstein's performance of masculinity and its very different receptions in Germany and in the U.S. since the mid 1990s. She analyzes many of the more overtly political aspects in and surrounding Rammstein's works, providing astute observations into both public perception of Rammstein's supposed right-wing politics or sympathies and the song "Amerika" with its critique of U.S. cultural imperialism. Lastly, she examines the music and video for Rammstein's latest release, the single "Mein Land." Simpson demonstrates how Rammstein inhabits an ideal of a postwar innocent masculinity in the video, an ideal which has since been lost in the U.S. and which had simply been impossible because of the social climate in Germany during the first decades after World War II.

Whereas Simpson convincingly claims a postmodern position for Rammstein, David A. Robinson argues a different place for the band in "Metamodernist Form, 'Reader-Response' and the Politics of Rammstein: What Rammstein Means When You Don't Understand the Lyrics." According to Robinson, Rammstein opens their art to many interpretations by traversing the gap between modernism and postmodernism. By doing so, they can address multiple audiences with completely different political viewpoints simultaneously, while never having to commit to any one political agenda at all. Listeners are able to project their own social perspectives onto Rammstein's work, be that perspective left-wing, right-wing or even one which denies the possibility of art bearing any political meaning whatsoever.

Daniel Lukes focuses "Rammstein Are Laibach for Adolescents and Laibach Are Rammstein for Grown-Ups" on the strong influence that the Slovenian band Laibach had in the formative early phases of Rammstein. In this essay, Lukes highlights key areas where Rammstein has clearly adopted fundamental aspects of their lyrics, performance and overall persona from Laibach and ways in which Rammstein distance themselves from Laibach. What emerges from Lukes' discussion is that the relationship between these two groups was and remains incredibly complex.

Brad Klypchak, in contrast, takes a detailed look at bands that have found success following Rammstein's rise to prominence in "Über Alles: Rock Bands Following in the Wake of Rammstein." Klypchak's investigaton of Norway's Gothminister, New York's Hanzel und Gretyl, and German bands such as Subway to Sally, Extremo and Saltatio Mortis demonstrates the strong, lasting effect that Rammstein has had on these bands' lyrics and performances.

Nick Henry and Juliane Schicker, opening Part II: Rammstein, Literature and Culture, develop the conversation of personal and national identity in the works of Rammstein in "*Heimatsehnsucht:* Rammstein and the Search for Cultural Identity." Rejecting the idea that Rammstein's works bear a straightforward nostalgia for the old East Germany in which the band members grew up, Henry and Schicker argue that the band's oeuvre displays a longing for a *Heimat* which could not exist in the former East Germany and does not exist in today's reunified Germany. They contend that Rammstein, which ultimately rejects and is rejected by both the East and the West, create — and are perhaps forced to create — their own *Heimat*, a long-term process that runs throughout Rammstein's artistic work.

While Henry and Schicker look at Rammstein as a band working through its issues with the different layers of Germany, Corinna Kahnke, in "Rammstein Rocking the Republic: A Cultural Reading of Trans/National Shock 'n' Roll Circus," examines Rammstein as both a national (German) and trans-national entity. She notes that the band uses national signifiers to "play" German in a sense, and thereby reach different people in different ways. An international audience would read such play as authenticity, while the audience in their home country would understand the irony and see through it. Kahnke examines the ways that Rammstein has received such a profound and lasting reception both abroad and in a Germany which has undergone great struggles of identity for obvious cultural and historical reasons.

Karley K. Adney examines the carnival aspect of Rammstein's work, specifically in the song and video for "Mein Teil," in "A Carnivalesque Cannibal: Armin Meiwes, 'Mein Teil'" and Representations of Homosexuality." Drawing from Lois Jones and others who have described Meiwes' killing and consumption of his willing victim Bernd Brandes, Adney provides a great deal of background information and provides many reasons why Rammstein found these events so fascinating. She notes that — over and beyond Rammstein's desire to shock its audience and thereby add to its infamy — the song "Mein Teil" and its video bring to light conflicts which many gay men experience. Instead of serve as a simple *cause célèbre*, "Mein Teil" functions to enlighten people who have never had these types of struggles while simultaneously heartening those who have, letting them know that they are not alone.

Erin Sweeney Smith examines the topic of gender in "Fear, Desire and the Fairy Tale *Femme Fatale* in Rammstein's 'Rosenrot,'" the first of two essays dealing specifically with this song. Smith notes the source materials for "Rosenrot" and interprets their complex messages in order to deal with Rammstein's use of these sources. Looking at both song and video, she demonstrates how the band establishes a homosocial bond in "Rosenrot," a bond which the title character disturbs. In the video, the audience can see how she corrupts one member of an itinerant group of monks (played by the band) when his desire for her overcomes him. According to Smith, the monk has to be excised from the group after falling under the influence of this powerful female figure.

Examining different aspects of the same song, Simon Richter seeks to clarify the seminal role that 18th philosopher, collector and theorist of folk songs Johann Gottfried Herder played in the role of a "founding father" of rock and roll in his essay, "Rammstein, Johann Gottfried Herder and the Origin of Rock and Roll." Similar to Smith's essay on "Rosenrot" in the previous chapter, Richter shows how Rammstein's song and video are in many respects a musical and literary homage to Herder and his intricate role as a father of rock and roll.

Martina Lüke, in "Love as a Battlefield: Reading Rammstein as Dark Romantics," looks to the past in order to discover the roots of much of Rammstein's imagery. She contends that the band has several traits in common with writers of the Romantic period, sharing, for example, their love of such extremes as dark and light or sanity and madness. More specifically, she contends Rammstein's lyrics follow along the lines of "Dark Romanticism," a sub-movement of romanticism which she aligns closely to Gothic literature. She backs up her claim with several examples from Rammstein's oeuvre where the lyrics deal with such topics typical for Dark Romantism as sadomasochism, the *femme fatale*, and the link between love, cruelty and death.

Like Lüke, Robert G. H. Burns notes Rammstein's clear debt to the gothic in "*Liebe ist für Alle Da:* A Visual Analysis of Rammstein's 2009 Album Artwork." His essay is an extension of his 2008 article which appeared in *Popular Music*, and like that article, it examines the visual imagery in Rammstein's work. Unlike that earlier work, however, he here focuses on album artwork. This essay allows Burns the opportunity to see whether the patterns he had noted at that time remained true for the band's sixth album, which appeared a year after his article. In drawing comparisons to the photography of Jan Saudek and the paintings of Rembrandt, Caravaggio, and Thomas Eakins in his analysis of the album art of *Liebe ist für Alle Da*, the author demonstrates the ways Rammstein modified their visual aesthetic with their latest studio album.

In Part III: The Elemental and the Metaphysical, John T. Littlejohn delves into the band's underexplored thematic world which lies beneath the fascinating surface. In his essay "Fire, Water, Earth and Air: The Elemental Rammstein," he examines these four elements as they appear in the band's work. Rammstein has clearly gained riches and fame from their fiery stage show, but a thorough examination uncovers the continuous and prominent usage of Empedocles' four elements in other aspects of the band's oeuvre, from their first album to their latest release, "Mein Land." Littlejohn explores the ways in which Rammstein intensifies their use of the elements, and uncovers the ways they (with particular frequency in their videos) self-consciously undercut their elemental imagery at other times. This essay further contributes to discussions of *Ostalgie* in Rammstein's work and the band's adaptation of their German cultural heritage — two topics which have already earned serious scholarly interest in the last few years and which are further developed in other essays in this present book.

This volume concludes with Michael T. Putnam's "Discipleship in the Church of Rammstein." Although in interviews the band members of Rammstein repeatedly express disdain for organized religion, Putnam draws our attention to the oft-reoccurring themes of angels, rituals, religious ceremonies, and the afterlife throughout their music catalog. Putnam's central thesis is not that Rammstein are atheists per se, but that these religious motifs present in their music and performance convey a hope for a loving God that, in their estimation, simply doesn't exist. Putnam demonstrates that membership in the Church of Rammstein requires a focus on the here and now and strongly downplays the belief that our current situation is inferior to some afterlife as commonly portrayed in Platonic philosophy and Judeo-Christian tradition.

Part I: Experiencing Rammstein

1

Industrial Humor and Rammstein's Postmodern Politics

PATRICIA ANNE SIMPSON

When asked about their politics, the members of Rammstein, the most internationally acclaimed and most "German" band, respond in what seems to be a paraphrase of Cyndi Lauper's best known song title from 1984, but with a twist: Boys just wanna have fun. With their celebrated and reviled puns, flaming performances, and flair for controversy, the members of the band do not hesitate to reveal their leftist sympathies in interviews, confessing how upset they are when their kids come home from school having to answer the question: Do you play in a Nazi band? (Groß and Schmidt, 102).[1] The band that defined *Neue Deutsche Härte* (New German Hardness) has an East German past and a committed capitalist present. The response and reception have always struggled to pin them down (semantically), but the apparent lack of a center or core defies easy categorization. In that sense, Rammstein instantiates postmodern politics, seemingly without an ethical compass. The labile nature of their postmodern politics complicates the challenge of understanding their sense of humor, which ranges from a gleeful celebration of the shocking, the absurd, and the revolting, to performing acts of imitation with unapologetic hyperbole. Taken as a package, the men, their costumes, lyrics, and acts, push buttons the audience did not even know existed. In a socially responsible and politically aware society, Rammstein functions, in Freudian terms, as pure id.

In this essay, I explore Rammstein's postmodern politics and humor in the context of the band's German and occasionally postnational identity (Habermas). To do so, I also consider the connections between dominant national narratives and images of masculinity, as theorized by R. W. Connell (*Masculinities*), that undergird them. I also rely on Judith Butler's popularized

9

notion of gender performativity (*Gender Trouble*). With reference to Rammstein's origins, development, and performative identities, I treat the recoding of their politics and their humor in three different stages of their career. Rammstein, I argue, through a strategic use of humor, parody, and pastiche, is revising a concept of the apolitical aesthetic. In her work on parody, Linda Hutcheon writes: "Irony and parody become the major means of creating new levels of meaning — and illusion" (30). Unlike Hutcheon, I profess less interest in the formal differences among parody and other forms of imitative critique, with a focus more motivated by including a discussion of humor and politics in popular forms of parody (Hutcheon, 51). Rammstein's highly popular, postmodern music participates in a cultural tradition that would replicate beauty without political, ethical consequences. Others have noted the relationship between Rammstein's use of German romanticism, especially allusions to J. W. von Goethe and Heinrich Heine. To extend this type of genealogical reading, I want to note a specific history of theorizing humor. Rammstein's sense of humor, I claim, is performative within a cultural tradition that advances moments of defining laughter, imitation, and the comic, in Kant, Hegel, and Freud.

When the members of Rammstein assembled and began performing in the mid–1990s in Germany, the political context was dominated by the post–Unification rise in right-wing violence toward visible minorities. The East German economy had collapsed unceremoniously; unification costs sobered any residual sense of euphoria. As Torsten Groß and Rainer Schmidt dryly observe, the circumstances were less than optimal for a band that seems to be performing a high-wire act, dancing on a tightrope between the political left and right: "Es war nicht die Zeit eines Spiels mit Zitaten und Zeichen, nicht die Zeit demonstrativer Männlich- und Körperlichkeit" (97) [It was not the time for a game with citation and signs, not the time for demonstrative masculinity and physicality]. Groß and Schmidt highlight the untimeliness of Rammstein's play with signifiers, specifically deploying the language of poststructuralist theory to emphasize how out of sync the band's performance aesthetic was. In the more general cultural context of the former German Democratic Republic (GDR), the practice of poststructuralist and postmodern aesthetics implicated certain poets as Stasi informants. The presumably progressive, critical, and dissident works of writers and theorists such as Sascha Anderson and Rainer Schedlinski fell into immediate disrepute, along with the exculpatory reliance on words as mere signifiers. At the same time in the U.S., deconstruction, no matter how carefully one distinguishes it from poststructuralism, also came under attack because its foremost proponent was exposed as a Nazi collaborator in his youth (Simpson, 50). As complex as these cases are, there is a popularized sense of guilt by association when signifiers dance and political centers cannot hold. Rammstein's hermeneutic predicament replicates the moral ambiguity we see whenever there is a perceived unlinking between what people say and what they mean. Rammstein practices industrial-strength humor with postmodern politics at a time when any lack of intentionality seems inappropriate at best. The band firmly denies practicing a politics affiliated with fascism, yet the discussion persists. A longstanding debate about the relationship between their aesthetics and politics continues and continues to fascinate.

The list of Rammstein's purported infractions is long and familiar, and ultimately empowering, because their cultural crimes confer political agency on the six men from the former East. The band gleaned negative attention when it paid homage to Leni Riefenstahl's *Olympia* in the music video "Stripped" (on the DVD *Lichtspielhaus*, 2003). The release of the DVD prompted critique from the Anti-Nazi League (U.K.) and the Anti-Defamation League (U.S.); Rammstein felt compelled to justify the band's decision, and Till Lindemann defends the move adamantly. As Susan Sontag points out in her 1975 essay "Fascinating Fascism," Riefenstahl's endorsement of beauty, health, vitality "... is ... never witless...." It is Riefenstahl's role as the "priestess" of the beautiful that enables her possible "rehabilitation" in the first place. The "cycles of taste," as Sontag formulates the vicissitudes of fashion that inform our aesthetic politics, shift sufficiently in the mid–1970s to accommodate Riefenstahl's Nazi past. One could speculate that Riefenstahl turned to scuba diving and underwater beauty to continue a search, from the Alpine heights, to the horizontals of Olympic competition, to the African continent, to find finally a thoroughly apolitical world where beauty is simply there for the eyes of the intrepid observer. To some extent, Rammstein participates in a similar cycle of taste and the tasteless, or, to reformulate the categories more immediately, between the apolitical and the political. Even if the band eschews politics, their reception is highly politicized.

The band elicits criticism for its politics and its purported perversion. Occasionally, these two fronts collapse. A concert to be held in Minsk was canceled with the explication: "die sechs Deutschen könnten unter anderem 'die weißrussische Staatsordnung zerstören'" (Groß and Schmidt, 97; also Deutsche Presse Agentur [kami]) [the six Germans could "destroy the order of the state in Belarus"]. The moral guardians of Minsk, supported by the president, deemed Rammstein dangerous due to the band's alleged endorsement of violence, homosexuality, and perversion. The band now has a reputation that precedes it. Rammstein occupies a theatrical space that can best be described as performative, both in the linguistic sense of the term and in

Judith Butler's theory of gender performativity. Rammstein's music and stage aesthetic function in tandem to posit a performative politics that can be neutralized or endorsed through humor. The band members emphatically deny any sympathy with the right-wing, for example, and proclaimed their allegiance to the left in "Links 2 3 4." When they are not defending their politics, they are defending their honor, but always with a wink. The protests and their East German roots notwithstanding, the band's postmodern play with signification opens its performances to a reading of aesthetics and politics in an extra-moral sense. One strategy the band consciously employs to maintain their semantic edge involves engaging a wide audience in a hermeneutic joust. The frequent result is an industrial-strength sense of humor that defies interpretation, leaving the credulous with the question: Are they serious? In this essay, I attempt to answer the question about how the potentially comic element in the lyrics and staging contribute to a theory and practice of their version of the comic in the genre of industrial metal.

Rammstein indisputably entertains. The stage shows include some of the most sophisticated pyrotechnics and powerful deployment of theatricalized violence available in the music world today. They consciously exploit and subvert sexual politics as well. The hyper-masculinity of the lead singer, Lindemann, is often offset by the lanky keyboard player, Christian (Flake) Lorenz. Lindemann projects his voice into the hearts and minds of some dubious characters, including an infamous cannibal, a pedophile, and the voice of a beligerent America. The puns in their songs and their reticence about political clarity allow them to play with fire in a semantic sense. Lindemann goose steps across the stage, Flake appears in a dainty apron — but is Rammstein fascist or funny? Can the band be both? While they renounce fascism, their music and image appeal to an uncontainable array of fans who interpret what Rammstein brings to the stage for themselves. Anyone who has attended a concert can see that Rammstein attracts a wide range of highly committed fans who occupy all points of the political spectrum.

For many, the band's emphatic denial of fascist fantasies seems hollow. Their use of Leni Riefenstahl footage prompted accusations of sympathy with fascist politics. Yet controversy emanates from other aspects of their music as well. The 2009 release *Liebe ist für Alle Da* was "indexed" or placed on a list of effectively censored material, deemed inappropriate by the Bundesprüfstelle für jugendgefährdende Medien (Federal Department for Media Harmful to Young Persons), for example, a designation more often reserved for aggressive rap tracks and right-wing hate music. Though the decision was ultimately withdrawn, the case received intense publicity. To return to Groß and Schmidt's point about the times, Rammstein's exemplarity raises a perennial question about the relationship between politics and aesthetics, between context and texts. Does Rammstein's semantic field necessarily contract in times of political violence? It is important, I believe, to examine carefully and critically which aspects of their performance respond to the vicissitudes of the times and their contexts in order to address the question of how the process of performance and decoding impact Rammstein's reception.

The back-and-forth regarding their controversial positions certainly fuels the fire of their financial success, and only recently did the front man, Lindemann, consent to be interviewed. But keeping a curious or prurient public guessing does not constitute a political declaration of any kind. The band's record label defended the citation of *Olympia* in "Stripped" with a dismissal of accusations of neo–Nazi status: "Furthermore, Rammstein believe that good art knows no political allegiances, thus the Leni Riefenstahl footage they used for 'Stripped' is an expression of good art rather than an endorsement of Nazism" ("Rammstein Are Not Nazis"). Paul Landers' and Flake's history in the East German fun-punk band "Feeling B" confirm their credentials for humor, but also for critical and leftist politics. Laughter can be a powerful tool in the toolbox of the powerless. In recent German-language literature, it can serve as a coping strategy for those who experience social marginalization, and it also functions as a vehicle for critique (Baker). By contrast, the humor I attribute to Rammstein's performative aesthetics operates from a place of semantic sovereignty, assuming the posture of the powerful. Frequently, through the visual performances and close reading of lyrics, we can discern the shape of a critical politics through glimpses of humor and veils of signification. Rammstein's carefully coded music can also destabilize the foundations of empire.

Through the veil and smoke of postmodern and poststructuralist signification, Rammstein occasionally takes a stand. Their capacious ability to mobilize multiple meanings serves them well. While advocating the use of beautiful, if fascist-associated, art, the band positions itself on the left just as deftly. The "Amerika" song from *Reise, Reise* (2004), for example, aligns the band with those critical voices who opposed the U.S. war in Iraq, audible from the left as well as from the political center of European discourse. The song inhabits and disrupts an imperialist fantasy that transforms everyone into a citizen of the United States, its best-known consumer exports, and military-industrial complex. Soda and war inhabit a mutually complicit relationship in that presentation of U.S. foreign politics. In what many consider the extension album or related sequel, *Rosenrot* (2005), Rammstein leads off with a trenchant critique of oil consumption. Lindemann sings as if he himself were a gas-guzzling Humvee. The liner notes and CD artwork underwrite a critical view of the human factor in global warming, with views of the melting polar ice cap. From between the lines, a sense of the absurd rises and converges in their verbal and visual cues. In their recent work, "Mein Land," the band conjures issues of immigration and national identity to participate in political discourse with industrial-strength humor. Rammstein's flair for humor raises questions similar to those that hope to stabilize their politics. In discussing their humor, I both rely on that framework and shift the discourse away from the posited apolitical nature of beauty and into a different register. How do postmodern politics and industrial humor collaborate? How, if at all, do Rammstein's parodies, imitations, exaggerations, and puns function to produce humor? The short answer is through transgression: pushing the proverbial envelope and all possible buttons. The more complex response involves locating Rammstein's lyrics and performance in the context of contemporary German identity vis-à-vis the fraught past and ambiguous present.

Performing Moral Ambiguity

In postwar Germany, moral ambiguity has become mandatory. In the U.S., a series of films in which Nazi characters appear to be either sexy or sympathetic, from *The Reader* (2008) to *Inglourious Basterds* (2009), challenges our notion of good and evil. Rammstein's simultaneous foregrounding of their German national identity and the international appeal present a similar challenge. The band becomes a palimpsest for the band's projection of fantasies that involve dominance, disdain, and delight. In Groß and Schmidt's estimate, Rammstein works the ambivalence angle to the fullest. He notes as well their humor:

> Denn wie keine andere Gruppe sind Rammstein mit ihrer bewußten oder zufälligen Ambivalenz immer auch schon eine Projektionsfläche für eigene Ängste und Vorurteile gewesen, die reflexhaft abgerufen können und die keinen Raum lassen für unsubtile Formen des Humors, für die Komik der Übertreibung und den Reiz vollkommener Künstlichkeit [98].
>
> [For like no other band, Rammstein, with their conscious or accidental ambivalence, have always been a projection screen for everyone's anxieties and prejudices, which can be evoked in a reflex reaction and which leave no room for unsubtle forms of humor, for the comedy of exaggeration, and for the allure of perfect artifice.]

To get at that ambivalence effectively, I proceed with indirection. The polemic about fascism in Rammstein runs parallel to the band's emergence and rise to fame in the mid–1990s, a tense time, given the upsurge of right-wing violence and the response to neo-nationalism that characterized the political climate in the recently re-united Germany. During that period, the heavy metal group garnered popularity and gained a dedicated fan base in the United

States. My oblique approach is in part motivated by a need to sidestep the face-off about East German vs. West German vs. Pan-Germanic identities as they are perceived to be played out in Rammstein's oeuvre. Instead, I examine three formative moments that engage a more global politics of both parody and humor. First, I look at Rammstein's headlining participation in the Family Values Concert Tour from 1998. In this performance, imitation collapsed into criminality. Next, I move on to the 2004 release, *Reise, Reise*, in particular, the "Amerika" track. In this context, the globally imperial politics of U.S. preemptive war and Rammstein's response to it parody the voice of the American imperial consciousness. Finally, the national politics articulated in the lyrics that we all exist in some form of an idealized "America" transition into a simultaneous homage to and spoof of American popular culture from the 1960s. "Mein Land," I argue, reappropriates through imitation a lost sense of masculinity as it progresses from the sodomizing aggression, to the militarized imperial, to the surfing and singing though recalcitrant fun-industrial band Made in Germany. Particularly in the spoof of surf culture, we catch a fleeting glimpse of a more sinister but somewhat vulnerable aspect of Rammstein's humor.

Comic Theories: Organs, Bad Taste and Writing in Tongues

Rammstein employs parody as one articulation of the comical or humorous. Parody is closely related to performance. It inevitably involves mimesis, some act of imitation. One danger in parody issues from the performance itself: the act has unintended or uncontrollable consequences. This complex "performance" has been the subject of philosophical and psychological examination for centuries, compelling because the performative model of parody assumes a relationship between representation and reality. In Freud's cases, for example, this relationship is defined as one between words and the body. In Rammstein's performative mode, gestures and song lyrics cooperate to effect hyperbole. The element of live performance enhances the band's ability to exaggerate. By contrast, performance can undermine a text. Rammstein's stage act is all exclamation point. There is a theoretical genealogy in this type of performance, in which an attempt to posit a relationship between cognition and the body in the context of the comic or of laughter becomes legible. The reading of Freud's jokes echoes, in many ways, Kant's brief attention to laughter in the *Critique of Judgement*:

> Im Scherze (der eben sowohl wie jene eher zur angenehmen, als schönen Kunst gezählt zu werden verdient) hebt das Spiel von Gedanken an, die insgesamt,

sofern sie sich sinnlich ausdrücken wollen, auch den Körper beschäftigen; und, indem der Verstand in dieser Darstellung, *worin* er das Erwartete nicht findet, plötzlich nachläßt, so fühlt man die Wirkung dieser Nachlassung im Körper durch die *Schwingung* der Organen, welche die Herstellung ihres Gleichgewichts befördert und auf die Gesundheit einen wohltätigen Einfluß hat [72–73].

[In the case of jokes (the art of which, just like music, should rather be reckoned as pleasant than beautiful) the play begins with the thoughts which together occupy the body, so far as they admit of sensible expression; and as the Understanding stops suddenly short at this presentment, in which it does not find what it expected, we feel the effect of this slackening in the body by the oscillation of the organs, which promotes the restoration of equilibrium and has a favourable influence upon health (Knox trans., 171).]

Kant makes a fundamental connection between the response of the body and the working of the human mind. He emphasizes the play of thought and its direct effect on the body, specifically on the body's organs. In other words, the organs respond to the disappointed expectations of a joke, and the result is laughter. In Rammstein's performances, the exact opposite transpires. To break the barrier of taboos, the band sets up expectations with lyrics, almost always the product of Lindemann's creativity, with input from all band members (Groß and Schmidt, 100); even these are transgressed on stage. The healthy balance Kant describes through the movement of organs is redirected in Rammstein, as the band demolishes the convention barrier. Unsurprisingly, the violated border involves sexuality, but also politics. For Rammstein, other organs are engaged.

While Kant only briefly alights on the question of laughter, Hegel takes the discourse a step further. He does distinguish between the "laughable" and the "comic" as performative categories. The "Lächerliche" invokes or commands laughter and, as he argues indirectly, seems to belong to the inferior category that covers parody and taste. He manages to define the undefinable in laughter according to his own laws of opposition:

Überhaupt läßt sich nichts Entgegengesetzteres auffinden als die Dinge, worüber die Menschen lachen. Das Plattste und Abgeschmackteste kann sie dazu bewegen, und oft lachen sie ebensosehr über das Wichtigste und Tiefste, wenn sich nur irgendeine unbedeutende Seite daran zeigt, welche mit ihrer Gewohnheit und täglichen Anschauung in Widerspruch steht [III, 528].

[In general, nowhere can more contradiction be found than in the things that people laugh at. The flattest and most tasteless things can move people to laughter, and they often laugh all the same at the most important and profound matters if they see in them only some wholly insignificant aspect which contradicts their habits and day-to-day outlook (Bernard trans., n.p.).]

Rammstein's post-modern humor falls under the auspices of Hegelian laughter, especially if we consider the attributes of "most dull" and "most tasteless."

In a more contemporary commentary, John Morreall writes about laughter in the context of philosophy: "Not only is laughter biologically odd, but the activities that elicit it are anomalous" (2). In addition, the serious issues that the prompts of laughter exploit frequently reveal some aspect of the humorous or the absurd. Hegel's language of equation and opposition, from the silliest to the most profound aspects of human life, informs Rammstein's labile lyrics. They can tip vertiginously from the serious to the ridiculous, from parody to political commentary. In Hegel, the comic and laughable require the tension of this opposition. Hegel goes one step beyond Kant in drafting an equation in which laughter is the remainder. I read the comic in Rammstein in this sense as well. To bring this theory to bear on Rammstein, again, the oppositional force is sometimes missing; they can be all excess. On the other hand, their performance of the comical frequently implies or implicates the audience's ability to understand the larger historical context in which the comic participates and is encoded.

Freud extends the philosophical contemplation about jokes and humor, and hones in more closely on the type of performance I claim for Rammstein. In the introduction to *Der Witz und seine Beziehung zum Unbewußten (Jokes and Their Relation to the Unconscious)*, Freud quotes the poet Jean Paul Friedrich Richter twice in as many sentences to explain the connection between freedom and humor: "'Freiheit gibt Witz und Witz gibt Freiheit,' sagt Jean Paul. 'Der Witz ist ein bloßes Spiel mit Ideen.' ... Jean Paul hat selbst diesen Gedanken so witzig ausgedrückt: 'Der Witz ist der verkleidete Priester, der jedes Paar traut'" (8–9) ["Freedom produces jokes and jokes produce freedom," wrote Jean Paul. "Joking is merely playing with ideas." ... Jean Paul has expressed this thought itself in a joking form: "Joking is the disguised priest who weds every couple"] (Stachey trans., 7). In Freud's summary quotations from Jean Paul, he foregrounds three aspects of the joke: the chiastic relationship between the joke and freedom; as a "naked" (literal translation of bloß) play with ideas; and as the imposter dressed as a priest marrying couples. Of these three characteristics, the last privileges the performative power of language, and again raises the question of authority with regard to parody, specifically, to the joke. The language of concealing and revealing connects imitation to the truth. Rammstein's performances play with the freedom in humor; they exploit the dynamic between concealing and revealing through imitation.

Freud's theory of the mind clearly informs his attention to the comic, but in his elaboration on the latter, a commentary on the mimetic and humor becomes exemplary. While both involve the "expenditure" of a certain amount of energy, the comic garners attention for its duplicatory, excess investment. In one important example, he writes about the non-aesthetic category of the comical in relationship to the efforts of a child learning to write:

> Komisch ist es dagegen, wenn das Kind beim Schreibenlernen die heraus-gestreckte Zunge die Bewegungen des Federstiels mitmachen läßt; wir sehen in diesen Mitbewegungen einen überflüssigen Bewegungsaufwand, den wir uns bei der gleichen Tätigkeit ersparen würden. [*Der Witz*, IV, 177].
>
> [On the other hand, it is comic when a child who is learning to write follows the movements of his pen with his tongue stuck out; in these associated motions we see an unnecessary expenditure of movement which we should spare ourselves if we were carrying out the same activity (*Jokes*, 235).]

In this passage, Freud finds the comic in the mimetic act of a child writing with the tongue along with the pen, describing an excessive expenditure of energy. This excess is itself expressed in the tautology of "Mitbewegungen" ("associated motions") and "Bewegungsaufwand" ("expenditure of movement"): two movements, the one the copy of the other. In addition, the word *überflüssig*, literally "overflowing," implies an excess of fluid, an excess of corporeal ink, the substitute for which is bodily fluid; a coincidence of the acts of writing with a pen and salivating mimetically. Here Freud links the act of writing to the comic mimesis of "writing" with the tongue. In this example, Freud specifies the economy of exaggerated humor Rammstein enacts on stage. The imitation, with excess, especially with bodily fluids and mime, defines the post-modern performance of the band. In my close readings of Rammstein's sense of the comical and the political, I will highlight the aspects of mimesis, the juxtaposition of the serious and the absurd, and excess-parody to underscore the methods of their madness. Rammstein's humor, as I read it, functions as the product or remainder of an analog event, a reenactment of sorts, the replication of which highlights the absurd, irrational, and unconscious aspects of contemporary life. Their parodies are edgy and ambiguous enough to be mistaken for the real deal. While their intention remains elusive, their performances invite careful examination.

Criminal Mimesis

While the mid–1990s may not have been the right moment for Rammstein's play with signifiers in the recently united Germany, the timing was right in the U.S. The American audience, distanced spatially from the neo–Nazism of the post–Wall era in Germany, and also from the acts of violence that reached a peak at the same time, supported the band during the Family Values tour in 1998. Korn, the American nu metal band, envisioned and organized a concert tour that included different genres: nu metal, heavy metal, and rap. Rammstein was just launching in Europe, and this tour and the resulting CD and DVD releases vaulted their own *Sehnsucht* into platinum sales in the U.S. Again, American popular culture in general remains insulated from the prominent politics of many European groups. In the U.S., Rammstein's controversies tended to be of a sexual nature. The concert in Worcester, Massachusetts, included a performance of the song "Bück dich" (Bend Down). The track does not appear on the 1999 CD, on which Rammstein is represented solely with "Du hast." Even to view one video version of the live performance on YouTube, you have to sign in and read the consent material because of the questionable content. On stage, Till Lindemann, shirtless and buff, leads Flake Lorenz around by a leash. The lyrics are unambiguous, asserting that the face of an individual means nothing. This declarative is repeated incrementally, suggesting that the singer finds nothing of interest in the same "face." As the song approaches a high point, Lorenz bends over, Lindemann opens a panel in the seat of his partner's pants, and exposes a dildo connected to a hose. They simulate sodomy, and the hose ejaculates to excess. Once it is exhausted (and another band member takes a drink), Lindemann makes the sign of the cross and turns away from the spotlight.

Sontag's foundational essay on the relationship between fascist aesthetics and an exculpatory fascination with the creation of beauty bravely concludes with a frank discussion about the eroticization of politics. As the focus is fascism, the sexual frisson it creates can only be categorized as sadomasochist. Her comments were informed by the contemporary trend for fascist fashion, inspired in part by the popularization of punk apparel, among other forces.[2] But Sontag's insight goes beyond the influence of public taste and to the heart of Rammstein's mimesis, their frictional appeal, and their criminalized reception in the U.S. She writes:

> And sadomasochistic sexuality is more theatrical than any other. When sexuality depends so much on its being "staged," sex (like politics) becomes choreography. Regulars of sadomasochistic sex are expert costumers and choreographers; they are performers in the professional sense. And in a drama that is all the more exciting because it is forbidden to ordinary people [n.p.].

The homoeroticism and sadomasochism of the staged relationship is precisely that: choreographed. The performance replicates and exaggerates in true ejaculatory fashion the drama that is always extraordinary. The enactment, the fictional performance, was guilty of excessive verisimilitude. Lindemann and Lorenz were arrested for indecency and spent a night in jail. In this performance, the excess (of fluid) affixes a signature on the humor, but the imitation of anal intercourse was too literal for the American authorities.

Living in "Amerika"

My second example complicates the straightforward act of mimesis and its criminalization. One major controversy did surround the release of *Reise, Reise* in 2004, though it could be argued that the thematic content of some songs encode an appeal to right-wing musical trends. The translation of the title song, Reveille, or the morning call for the German navy, narrates the exigencies of life for a sea voyager. The overt reference to air travel is obscured in the more existential concept of the journey and the fight for survival at sea as conveyed in the lyrics. At the same time, images of the strong Viking hero dominated much hate music in order to circumnavigate the censors in Germany. While the similarity may appear contingent, one might speculate about an intentional play with particular signifiers. This issue coexists with the dominant disruptive moment of "Mein Teil" (My Part/Portion), a ballad projecting the voice of Armin Meiwes and the cannibalism story that attracted so much shocked and prurient attention. This song also garnered the band a Grammy nomination for best metal performance (Ferguson, 82). These extremes flank the politics of another song, "Amerika," on the same CD. This emphatic anti-love song situates Rammstein at a different end of the political spectrum. The album, which contains arguably three love songs as well, reached number one in the charts in Germany, Austria, Finland, Switzerland, and Russia, and hit number two in France and Sweden.

The song "Amerika" ostensibly attacks the cultural hegemony of the United States, but the indictment goes beyond the dominance of products. The serious element of the song and the illuminated American flags used to light the stage show (2005 in Wuhlheide, for example) contrast sharply with the absurdity of Lindemann's allegories in the lyrics. In performance, the bright presence of the American flag on stage indicates not a mimetic moment, but an ironic one instead. This marks a departure from Rammstein's modus operandi. Lindemann sings in the voice of both the "I" of American dominance and the "we" of universal American subjects and submission. While the refrain indeed indicts commercialism and popular culture, from Coca-Cola, the Wonderbra, Disney, and Santa Claus, the individual stanzas reference political imperialism in sinister ways. We can easily imagine Santa Claus invading Africa and a phalanx of Disney characters storming the Bastille. (We can try not to envision the projectile quality of the Wonderbra!) The absurdity of the images, however, also sharpen the profile of Rammstein's point: American commodities have saturated the European cultural and collective imagination.

With great velocity, the semantic valence shifts from parody to propaganda. If the world wants to dance, America will lead, even if an individual nation tries to stand alone. The crucial line proclaims: "I" will protect "you" from any possible misstep. This tutelary relationship invokes the rhetoric of military superiority and arrogance in the politics of preemptive declarations and acts of war. This aspect of Rammstein's song aligns their politics with the European political voices that criticized the Bush administration's decision to wage war in Iraq. To put it quite bluntly: Rammstein, in this anti-love song, manages to create an interpretive context in which the aesthetic and economic totality of Disneyland and Santa Claus are implicated in a non–German totalitarian politics.

"Mein Land"

The most recent retrospective release includes the new single "Mein Land" (My Land or Country). It is challenging to imagine a more ambivalent statement of petulant, proprietary, postnational, colonial, and anti-immigrant politics than this song and its official video (dir. Jonas Åkerlund). The enormous investment in fun and frolic belies the subtext of the retro aesthetic of the official video. Filmed in Southern California, the visual appearance, attire, and attitude consciously reference the globally available commodities of surf culture, but at the same time add a national inflection to the purportedly universal availability of beach masculinity, the pursuit of leisure and fun, and the entitlement to the ocean and shore themselves. And there is a parody of / homage to David Hasselhoff and the role of Mitch Buchannon from *Baywatch*, whose title logo exerts influence over the Brechtian inscriptions that appear over the images. Taken with its lyrics, Rammstein's mimetic enactment of U.S. beach culture, which culminates in a metal beach party, transforms into an act of reverse cultural imperialism.

The video aesthetic references the surfer films and Beach Boy sounds of the early 1960s. In the "Making of" video, Christoph Schneider talks about the 1950s feel, while Oliver Riedel notes that they grew up with the idea of Hasselhoff and the popular culture of the California beach dream. The interpretation of American beach culture does not necessarily adhere to any strict historical frame of reference. This Rammstein beach party is staged, without fidelity to detail, in that era. The popular culture of the time period has its own political unconscious, which I locate, taking some liberty, in 1964. While the Beach Boys released the album *Shut Down 2* that year, the larger political arena in the U.S. was less committed to the manifesto of fun. In 1964, the U.S. declared war on North Vietnam and President Johnson signed the Civil Rights Act after a wave of violence. If popular culture provides a distraction from the anguish of domestic and foreign politics, beach apparel and surf music certainly did their part. In the arena of popular culture, as well, the Beatles appeared on *The Ed Sullivan Show*; "I Want to Hold Your Hand" quickly overtook the clean-cut popularity of surfing masculinity. Whether Rammstein and their director intended these references or not, the compensatory relationship between the pastimes of beach culture and the despair of racism and war highlights what seems like a lost moment in the American masculine imaginary.

The relatively carefree quality of The Beach Boys' music, problematic as I am casting it in light of tensions within the public sphere, reinforces an image of postwar American masculinity that inflects the victorious, somehow well-meaning image of Anglo-American military masculine models. The men of Rammstein, having been "born into" socialism, to paraphrase the poignant title of Uwe Kolbe's poetry volume from 1975, resist the type of "Ostalgie" or nostalgia for the East that some scholars have identified in their work, but nonetheless would have cut their teeth on resenting the capitalist West, especially the dominant model of U.S. teenager leisure culture (Littlejohn and Putnam). Yet through the spoof we can detect a sense of longing for a masculine innocence not available to postwar Germany. In spite of the official narrative of resistance in the East, with its allegiance to the victorious and glorious Red Army of the Soviet Union, all capitalist and fascist evil was not confined to the former West. Rammstein does not participate in that narrative of purported German innocence, but seeks it elsewhere. But the visual imagery sets multiple engines of signification in motion. This is impure parody.

Their staging of the retro–American dream, or one popularized version of it, opens the door to parody, crosses the threshold, but also clearly breaks ranks with the mimetic imperative. We can perhaps witness some sense of almost stereotypical German longing for sunny climes and warmer shores, familiar not only from the cultural tradition of travels to Italy, but from the exile culture of Germans on the West coast during and following the Second World War. In the impressive travel statistics to foreign shores, Germans lead the way. But the lyrics also echo colonial ownership and imperial impulses, along with a sense of longing for a home. This work instantiates para-parody. In the video, we see a bit of Rammstein "unplugged": with the exception of Till Lindemann's heavy-metal eyes, most of the band is filmed with limited facial make-up. Paul notes the spray-on tan he had to endure to project an image and protect his pale Berlin complexion. Lindemann and others express, though only behind the scenes, their trust in the director but their uneasiness in the Hawaiian shirts and bathing suits. In the video, the bikini-clad "girls" dance the Twist and the Swim, along with a modified Pony. They represent more diversity than one would find in any period film of the 1960s. In other words, there are too many obvious references to different times and cultural categories than there would be in a straightforward parody. The direction is extremely deliberate. In a moment of disconnect, eight surfboards serve as the writing tablet for the song title, "M-E-I-N L-A-N-D." And the lyrics expose moments of isolation, homelessness, and an aggressive proprietary relationship to the waves and the sand. Through a megaphone brightly, Lindemann inquires where some people are going. The answer is directional: from the east to the south; the south to the west; the west to the north. The itinerary is disrupted by a colonizing moment. To summarize the meaning of the stanza, Lindemann sings about a man running with a flag in his hand, with the clear intention of staking a claim. The refrain, however, insists on ownership of the country. The narrative voice proclaims, presumably to the oncoming runner: You are here in my country, my waves, my beach.

Lindemann, who is responsible for nearly all Rammstein's lyrics, excels at invoking an almost mythical realm in which we can visualize an almost Aguirre-like figure crossing borders and taking all necessary and meaningless risks to claim territory for the crown by planting a flag (in Aguirre's case, in the Amazon, just before he and his entire crew die). Despite the ambiguity, the rhetoric of anti-immigration politics, which have a stronghold in Southern California as well as in Germany (and elsewhere), manage to penetrate even the most apolitical filters. Who is the invader? Who is the conqueror? Who is the expelled? These questions defy easy answers, but the lyrics raise them nonetheless.

The song lyrics develop the narrative of a lone traveler who has exhausted himself in search of a home, a place where he is welcomed and invited to stay, but that never happens (never and nowhere). There is tension between the image of the wandering, migrating non-citizen in search of a home and that of the colonizer in search of a place to plant his flag. The lyrics invoke both those seeking refuge and those seeking to seize the power of ownership. A visual cue in final section of the video, in which Rammstein reemerge for a carnival-like party with fighting girls, full black leather costumes, heavy make-up, and flaming instruments, not least a fire-breathing lead singer who resembles the Joker and wears zombie contact lenses, opens a brief window for reading the whole performance as a commentary on national identity, on the clash of flags.

Before moving to the more ominous reading, the humor deserves attention. The beach party itself, with its retro image, green screen surfing shots, and Hasselhoff homage, is a labor of fun. The color scheme contrasts sharply with the band's previous palettes, dominated by blacks and dark neutrals.

The coy sexuality and shots of shimmying "girls" and "boys" are disrupted by the insertion of happy text, following the convention of 1960s surfer films, but also acknowledging a Brechtian practice of epic theater and the intentionally disruptive use of placards or text, with the beach as the proscenium arch. The obsession with women's breasts and butts continues. At one point, male hands squirt some liquid substance onto one of the dancer's chests, then the mostly off-camera "he" proceeds to massage in the foam, which could be either a condiment or sun-tan lotion — with special attention to the cleavage. Just another day at the beach! But in this deliberately imperfect parody, the humor works in both directions.

The mood shifts abruptly when the lyrics announce the end of this road. Lindemann, wearing the red shorts and carrying the small kickboard — in the historically conflated image of Beach Boys and *Baywatch*— runs down the beach, as if on the way to a rescue. The bridge changes the tone and timbre of the performance. Gesturing at the sky, he sings about a voice through the light, tearing the horizon apart. He poses the rhetorical question: where are you going when there is no where to run here, with the exculpatory justification that there nothing, no space, remains. The lyrics here indicate that nothing is without cost, but idiomatically signifies the occupation of a particular space, such as a seat in a restaurant or a train. The ambiguity in the phrasing adds another dimension to the lyrics, attributing both political and economic unaffordability to the topography of the beach.

We are back in the brutal, maniacal space of Rammstein world. The heavy-metal clothing donned, the make-up in place, the women fighting; this is familiar territory. Throughout the frantic show, the dance around flames seems more threatening for the opposition it sets up with the beach-party atmosphere, even though the scene is still the sandy shore of Southern California. Before the final stanza, we catch a glimpse of one dancer passing in front of the camera, wearing the German flag. A moment later, Lindemann brings it all home with three crucial words: "vertrieben," "vertreiben," and "vergessen" (driven out, my country, banished, and forgotten). These words alternate with the repetition of "Mein Land" (My Country). The juxtaposition of the past-participle of the verbs opens a significatory space in which the possessive adjective and noun function both as subject of the action and the object or receiver of the action. The absence of any clarifying prepositions, conjunctions, or even endings sustains both ambiguity and anguish, with the former saving the latter from any sentiment.

The nuts and bolts of the language assume historical significance in this context. Many fans and critics have commented on the appropriateness of the German language to the cadences of heavy metal. Even band members talk about it in semi-serious terms. Some have accused Lindemann of Hitler-izing the pronunciation of his "r" (he rolls it with gusto), but others attribute that trait to his youth in Mecklenburg. The band, in a behind the scenes video about "Mein Land," notes that they filmed the video during a concert tour. While my previous discussion of the Beach Boys' 1964 album inserted the release into a reluctant political climate, Rammstein's final stanza invites a painful chapter of German national history into the bonfire of the beach-carnival. Who or what is has been expelled and forgotten?

In this closing stanza, the connections among a parody of surf culture, a spoof on American leisure, and a problematic sense of ownership participate in a political commentary on a history that is closer to "home." The mention of the word "vertrieben" (i.e., driven off) triggers an associative process that references the history of Germany's lost provinces and the expulsion of ethnic Germans from Silesia and Pomerania. Until quite recently, the plight of the "Vertriebene" and any discussion of their losses were taboo in the German public sphere. In other words, there could be no discussion of German victims when the Germans had started, applauded, and sustained the war. The horrors of the Holocaust and the "final solution" as a unique and uniquely German crime against humanity were constitutive elements of postwar German democracy and recovery. Personal trauma had to yield the right-of-way to national tragedy and accept the blame for global guilt.[3]

The debate about German war crimes and trans-generational guilt became a mainstay of the 1968 generation, which, in general terms, accused their fathers and defined themselves in opposition to that profile. The student rebellion, the women's movement, and the cultural radicalism of the 1970s created a partially shared history between East and West, though teenage revolt was criminalized in the East. More recently, the specifically German and unique crime of the Holocaust became the focal point of a heated debate about its status generations after the events. This discourse took the form of the "Historikerstreit" or historians' debate in the 1980s, demonstrating the ability of this hot-button issue to dominate even the popular press. It is difficult to imagine a similar historical debate headlining the *New York Times* or *Washington Post* in the U.S. Along with the revisiting of the historicity of the war, the question of Germans as victims lost some of its taboo. It came to the foreground in discussions of W. E. Sebald's writing about the bombing of Dresden, for example. Though others, artists such as Gerhard Richter among them, and filmmakers, among them Helga Sanders-Brahms and her depiction of German women as rape victims, had previously opened the debate, these works did not gain the momentum and jump tracks from the cultural realm to the public sphere. Only recently has there been a more widespread and morally defensible consensus about the victimization of Germans. And in the context of enormous and complex moral and ethical issues, any stance seems controversial. Rammstein footnotes a huge history in the final few lines of this "beach party" song.

In the "Making of" documentary, the band members and dancers, along with the director, comment on the contrasts between the "happy" colors and mood of the daytime party and the dark excess of the night. The strategy behind the band's and the director's plan is clearly one of supplement. Interviewed on camera, Lorenz notes that the visual construct adds another level to the lyrics, which, if they were simply illustrated, would yield boredom. Immediately following his comment, Christoph Schneider lends insight into the creative process, but also gives us a glimpse of the controversy quotient: "We are aware that the lyrics are provocative. We spent a lot of time discussing the lyrics." Lindemann ducks a direct answer, mentioning that he is no longer sure about the original idea, that the creative process was all part of a development over a 5–6 year period. Åkerlund, who directed other Rammstein videos, "Pussy" and "Mann gegen Mann" among them, openly discusses the origin of the lyrics and his concept: "Till told me that when he wrote the music he was on a beach when he came up with the idea for the lyrics." He immediately thought of the Beach Boys' image with Rammstein superimposed over it. There is a sense of glee in the sharing his vision of "Rammstein in matching shirts," and he comments that this is in line with "Rammstein's sense of humor and sense of wit." Another band member, Richard Z. Kruspe, more accurately recalls the inspiration, remembering that Till surfed on the very beach where they are shooting about five years ago, and that he had an encounter with some local "top dogs" (*Platzburschen*). Flake imagines an eternal wanderer, while Landers, the most forthcoming, talks about the abstract idea of a person without a passport, an alien trying to gain admittance to earth, and no one lets them in. He connects the dots, suggesting the plausible association between immigration politics in Germany and the "keine Ausländer" mentality. Landers declares himself on the side of abstract interpretation, but with the knowledge that for many, Rammstein singing "my country" amounts to too much: "Wir können damit leben, weil wir Ärger mögen" [We can live with that, as we like trouble].

Conclusion

Slavoj Žižek concludes his tour-de-force, *Living in the End Times*, with a reading of Rammstein's performance idiom and the undecidability of their politics. He writes about what Rammstein "does to totalitarian ideology: it de-semanticizes it and shows up its obscene babble in its intrusive materiality" (385). Žižek reads Rammstein with support from Lacan, arguing that the over-identification with "sinthomes" disrupt ideological identification (385). He explains a very different type of political enlightenment through exposure to Rammstein's musical universe: "Rammstein undermine totalitarian ideology not with an ironic distance towards the rituals they imitate, but by directly confronting us with its obscene materiality and thereby suspending its efficacy" (387). It is hard to argue with Žižek's conclusion, but there is, I would contend, some "ironic distance" in the "Mein Land" performance, inserted by the glimpse of the German flag. Also, the grammatical ambiguity of the final lines suggest a reading that situates "Mein Land" as the object of the past participle verbs, indicating a land that no longer exists. Rammstein possibly comments on the increasingly unstable status of Germany in the era of globalization. The German flag may set all sorts of signifiers in motion, but on a practical level, it covers up a topless female dancer, who subsequently teases the camera with it in the fourth of five frames to bare her breast to the audience. The German flag reveals and conceals. The element of humor can mask the irony in their work; it can create the ironic distance from the material Žižek mentions above. This performance also opens up the possibility of parody not only of the surf culture portrayed with such glee in the first part of "Mein Land," but also of the heavy-metal, overtly Germanic and carnival-esque dystopia in the conclusion. Rammstein may be engaged in the act of imitation to un-man fascist ideology, but that is not always the intended or obvious target. Here they are also using the national flag to flash, exposing themselves as well.

In discussing the controversy surrounding their use of Riefenstahl footage, Lindemann defends the decision years after the fact. When asked if it was not perhaps a bit naïve to include the imagery, Lindemann replies: "Das mag sein, aber wenn man seine Naivität verliert, zieht man ein Korsett an, aus dem man so schnell nicht mehr herauskommt. So kann sich Kunst nicht entfalten" (Groß and Schmidt, 102) [That may be, but if you lose your naiveté, you are putting on a corset that you cannot remove again so easily. Art cannot develop like that]. Performing politics with a sense of art and humor is a Rammstein specialty. Additionally, the polyvalent nature of their texts, which are sometimes stabilized, sometimes undermined by their techniques of mimesis — with or without excess, word-play, and indirect reference — contributes to their uncanny ability to mobilize multiple, sometimes contradictory, signifiers and political messages. In their artistic relationship to the U.S., Rammstein has mimicked sodomy and done (modest) jail time. They have aligned themselves with the most committed voices against American imperialism. Finally, they have taken over the beach party and exposed the darker side of a naïve American surfer masculinity. In so doing, they also reveal a German historical unconscious, perhaps affiliating themselves with a politics of forced migration, population displacement, and tragedy — or not. Åkerlund, in reviewing his work with the band, mentions the various characters they play in the videos, but also claims pride in one of a live performance: "Their best characters are when they are Rammstein." The director is referring to the work. Their stage presence, the construction of their erotic, martial, and heavy identities articulated and performed along with their winking, punning, and parading extremes. Together, these modes comprise the role they inscribe for themselves into music history. In any case, Rammstein will have the last laugh.

Notes

1. Translations, unless otherwise noted, are my own.
2. The occasion for Sontag's article is twofold: she was reviewing Riefenstahl's *The Last of the Nuba* along with Jack Pia's *SS Regalia* (New York: Ballantine, 1974).
3. In an informal discussion with two representatives of a generation that came of age during the war era in Germany, one man articulated the problem to me in this way: "Even therapists would say, 'How can you have problems with your father after Auschwitz?'"

Works Cited

Baker, Julia K. "Smiling Bonds and Laughter Frees: Marginal Humor and Mod Strangers in the Works of Hung Gurst and Wladimir Kaminer." *Finding the Foreign*, ed. Robert Schechtman and Suin Roberts, 46–57. Newcastle: Cambridge Scholars, 2009.

Butler, Judith. *Gender Trouble: Feminism and the Subversion of Identity*. New York: Routledge, 2006.

Connell, R. W. *Masculinities*. London: Polity, 2005.

Deutsche Presse Agentur (kami). "Weißrussland erklärt Rammstein zum Staatsfeind." *Welt-Online*, 22 February 2010. http://www.welt.de/vermischtes/article 6504380/Weissrussland-erklaert-Rammstein-zum-Staatsfeind.html, accessed March 8, 2012.

Ferguson, Tom, ed. "Rammstein's Grammy Nom Fires Up Universal." *Billboard* 118, no. 6 (11 February 2006). http://books.google.com.au/books?id=-hQEAAAAMBAJ&pg=PA82#v=onepage&q&f=false, accessed March 5, 2012.

Freud, Sigmund. *Jokes and Their Relation to the Unconscious*. Trans. James Strachey, introd. by Peter Gay. New York: Norton, 1960.

_____. *Der Witz und seine Beziehung zum Unbewußten*. Frankfurt a/M: Fischer, 1940.

Groß, Torsten, and Rainer Schmidt. "Rammstein: Die grosse Oper." *Rolling Stone* (Germany) 206 (December 2011): 96–107.

Habermas, Jürgen. *The Postnational Constellation: Political Essays*. Ed., trans. and introd. Pensky. Cambridge, MA Press, 2001.

Hegel, G. W. F. *Aesthetics: Lectures on Fine Art*. Trans. T. M. Knox. Oxford: Oxford University Press, 1975.

_____. *Vorlesungen über die Ästhetik. Werke in 20 Bänden*, 3 vols., Band 13. Frankfurt a/M: Suhrkamp. 1986.

Hutcheon, Linda. *A Theory of Parody: The Teachings of Twentieth-Century Art Forms*. New York: Methuen, 1985.

Kant, Immanuel. *Kant's Critique of Judgement*, 2d ed. Trans. and introd. J. H. Bernard. London: Macmillan, 1914. http://oll.libertyfund.org/?option=com_staticxt&staticfile=show.php%3Ftitle=1217& Itemid=27, accessed November 19, 2012.
_____. *Kritik der Urteilskraft*, Werkausgabe Band X. Frankfurt a/M: Suhrkamp, 1974.
Littlejohn, John T., and Michael T. Putnam. "Rammstein and Ostalgie: Longing for Yesteryear." *Popular Music and Society* 33, no. 1 (February 2010): 35–44.
Morreall, John. *Comic Relief: A Comprehensive Philosophy of Humor.* Foreword by Robert Mankoff. Malden, MA: Wiley-Blackwell, 2009.
"Rammstein are not Nazis." Antimusic. http://www.rocknworld.com/news/oct98/14.shtml, accessed October 20, 2012.
Simpson, Patricia Anne. "Entropie, Ästhetik und Ethik im Prenzlauer Berg." *Machtspiele. Literatur und Staatssicherheit,* ed. Klaus Michael and Peter Böthig, 50–59. Leipzig: Reclam Leipzig, 1993.
Sontag, Susan. "Fascinating Fascism." *New York Review of Books* (6 February 1975). http://www.nybooks.com/articles/archives/1975/feb/06/fascinating-fascism/?page=1, accessed March 20, 2012.
Žižek, Slavoj. *Living in the End Times.* London: Verso, 2011.

Discography

Rammstein. "Mein Land." *Made in Germany.* Universal Music. CD. 2011.
_____. *Reise, Reise.* Republic. CD. 2004.
_____. *Rosenrot.* Republic. CD. 2006.

Filmography

Rammstein. "Bück dich." Live performance, 1998. http://www.youtube.com/watch?v=t z_IRfcRklM, accessed March 20, 2012.
_____. "Making of Mein Land." Part 1. http://www.youtube.com/watch?v=720mPh6F3 Zk&feature=related, accessed March 20, 2012.
_____. "Making of Mein Land." Part 2. http://www.youtube.com/watch?v=yWJZV1IK p2w&feature=related, accessed March 20, 2012.
_____. "Making of Mein Land" (vimeo). http://www.youtube.com/watch?v=Vj5VUl7F Yb0, accessed March, 25 2012.
_____. "Mein Land." Official Video. http://www.youtube.com/watch?v=NNNR8UX7o Kk, accessed March, 20 2012.

2

Metamodernist Form, "Reader-Response" and the Politics of Rammstein: What Rammstein Means When You Don't Understand the Lyrics

DAVID A. ROBINSON

Since 1994 the German band Rammstein have excited international audiences with their epic style of *Neue Deutsche Härte* (New German Hardness) industrial metal — selling over fifteen million records worldwide.[1] While the complex word-play of Rammstein's songs is well-noted, guitarist Richard Kruspe admitted, "99 percent of people don't understand the lyrics,"[2] so for those with little understanding of German the extra-lyrical elements of their songs and performance must appeal. These elements of Rammstein's work — their music, their image in art and advertising, their live performances, and their music videos — will be examined here in order to address the questions of how Rammstein can be interpreted when focusing on their extra-lyrical content, and why they can appeal to audiences across the political spectrum.

Rammstein's heavy music, use of violent, militaristic and hyper-masculine imagery, and referencing of Nazi-era themes — such as Leni Riefenstahl's film *Olympia*— have fuelled speculation that Rammstein have fascist sympathies. Yet left-wing supporters such as anarchist musician Alec Empire, while admitting that Rammstein's music does appeal to the far-right, insist that "they're not a fascist band at all."[3] Thus, this essay will address the interpretative malleability of Rammstein's songs with reference to Reader-Response Theory, and argue that Rammstein occupy a metamodernist space (oscillating between modernist desire for a teleological metanarrative and ironic post-modernist critique), which contains moments of each political position that an audience can embrace from their own perspective. Thus Rammstein can appeal pan-politically to those seeking an escape from social alienation through transgression, and audiences who desire a rebirth of ideology amidst neoliberalism's "End of History." The first part of this chapter will provide a detailed description of Rammstein's musical style, art and performance, in order to draw out key themes and cultural tropes they reference. The second part will then analyze how Rammstein can be read by different politically orientated interpretive communities.

Describing Rammstein

For Rammstein fans with little understanding of German (or those who fail to engage their song lyrics analytically) extra-lyrical elements of their songs and performance must appeal. Rammstein's music, artwork, performances, and music videos will be examined here and their main features and themes described, highlighting the band's references to industrial and technological motifs, science-fiction and cyber-punk, gothic and horror themes, and social transgression. Rammstein are the most popular band within the genre of *Neue Deutsche Härte*, which generally "layers distinctive German vocals, heavy metal rhythms, and techno motifs with electronic, industrial, and Gothic influences."[4] Karen Collins writes that the broader field of industrial metal originally drew on the sounds of "mechanical and electric machinery, and later advanced to synthesisers, samplers and electronic percussion ... commonly built around 'non-musical' and often distorted, repetitive, percussive sounds of industrial machinery."[5] Rammstein's music blends these hard drum and guitar sounds — which could be said to reflect "feelings of alienation and dehumanisation"[6] — with melodies prominently utilizing minor, diminished and augmented tones, with drawn-out chord progressions, thus evoking feelings of melancholy, tension and longing which are then emotionally resolved within the song. This is accompanied by sections of electronic beats, and synthesizer riffs and interludes — which often add a gothic or science fiction flavor to their songs. Overlaying this music is singer Till Lindemann's deep and resonant voice, with its harsh timbre, "guttural German and much commented upon rolling R's,"[7] which varies between songs from a virtually operatic style to a severe bark. A number of songs, such as "Engel" and "Nebel," also feature melodious female vocals.[8] Together these sonic elements create a grand musical style spanning from ballads like "Ohne Dich," to storms of electro-metal fury such as "Weißes Fleisch."[9] All together, these works form a repertoire that can cathartically arouse and exorcise one's anger and angst, or take the listener on an emotional journey reminiscent of that described by Oscar Wilde when he wrote, "After playing Chopin, I feel as if I had been weeping over sins that I had never committed, and mourning over tragedies that were not mine."[10]

Still images and artworks related to Rammstein help to create an interpretive atmosphere for the listener — posters or album covers sometimes constituting the first visual impression a potential consumer receives. Though only hinting at the style and substance of Rammstein's oeuvre, still images do point towards major themes repeated throughout the band's work. Rammstein's industrial style begins with their logotype and insignia: the solid, all-capitalized name creates a bold, hard impression in customized typescript resembling the "Franklin Gothic Heavy" headline, with a thick equilateral cross as its "T" (a symbol that seemingly references the Slovenian industrial musicians Laibach); and the chunky but futuristic insignia layers the Rammstein "R" over an enlarged "T"— both logotype and insignia often appearing in sharp contrast to their background, usually in white, red or steel grey against black. Rammstein's imagery reflects this hardness of attitude and style: from the picture of the band members' imposingly muscular torsos on their first album *Herzeleid*, which led to them being derided as "poster boys for the master race"[11]; to publicity shots of them in fascistoid uniforms; pictures of singer Lindemann wearing skinhead-style jackboots and suspenders; and the single covers for "Asche zu Asche" and "Feuer Frei!" which respectively feature a burning microphone, and a pistol aimed at the viewer.[12]

Other images draw out Rammstein's specifically industrial and technological motif, with many portraying the band in various warehouse and factory settings. The cover of the band's fourth album *Reise, Reise* features the image of a flight recorder from a crashed aeroplane, and the cover of the fifth album *Rosenrot* pictures the icebreaker USS *Atka* crashing through Antarctic ice.[13] More self-consciously sci-fi images include: depictions of the band in a retro-futurist power plant; as astronauts on the moon in the "Amerika" music video; and Lindemann wearing a metallic exoskeleton with built-in flamethrowers, from Rammstein's live performances. This last image also points towards Rammstein's subversion of the body, and focus on the processes of life and death — which in turn merge into more gothic themes. The *Herzeleid* cover's glorification of the masculine body is paralleled by the cover of the recently released *Made in Germany 1995–2011* compilation, which features life casts of the band members' faces — and more graphically by a special box-set of *Liebe ist für Alle Da* that featured phallic sex-toys cast from the band members' genitals.[14] Meanwhile, their second album *Sehnsucht* pictured their faces being tortured by cyber-gothic metallic masks.[15] Rammstein's imagery seeks to violate the body's impermeability through its exploration of both life and death. Death is courted by images such as lead guitarist Richard Kruspe in an electric chair on the "Engel" single cover, and Lindemann pointing a gun into his mouth on the "Amerika" single[16] while the cover image of the album *Mutter*, which portrays the peacefully suspended body of a fetus in-utero, also challenges the body's boundaries.[17] Most controversially, Rammstein's sixth album *Liebe ist für Alle Da* depicted the preparation for, and aftermath of, the band butchering and eating a naked woman on a dining table.[18] This final example of transgressing bodily boundaries also links with images transgressing social boundaries. Images of general social transgression include the band appearing in guises referencing organized crime, such as costumes imitating the films *Reservoir Dogs* and *Goodfellas*, as well as appearing dressed as women, and being pictured *as* naked women.

However, the *spectacle* of Rammstein really consolidates in their remarkable stage shows. Bruce Tucker writes,

> Extramusical contexts partially displace attention from the performance of the music to the performance of the performance.... They are differing domains of discourse — visual, textual, iconographic, dramaturgic — that, taken together, orient the performance as one that is simultaneously mythic and historical, ritualistic and open-ended, all-inclusive but undertaken from the perspective of a particular time and place.[19]

Rammstein's shows are aggressive and hyper-masculine, but also contains elements of pantomime storytelling and humor. Show director Gert Hof, who passed away in 2012, had "been described as the male version of Riefenstahl, and his lighting design, known for its excess, provocation, and spectacular pyrotechnics, [was] compared to the work of Albert Speer."[20] These stage shows emphasize industrial and technological motifs, cyber-punk themes and social and bodily transgression. I will describe here some common features of these shows, referring to the performances *Live Aus Berlin*, recorded at Berlin's Kindl-Bühne Wuhlheide in 1998, and *Völkerball*, recorded at Les Arènes de Nîmes, France, in 2005.[21]

Rammstein's sets establish the industrial pathos of their performances. A steel cage design dominated the *Live Aus Berlin* set, surrounded on three sides by four-story scaffold platforms slung with lighting equipment. These both exposed backstage workings, in a kind of Brechtian insight into the show's production, and reflected the impression of a prison compound or large-scale mechanical workshop. Tubes projected from the stage like a cross between industrial piping and batteries of naval cannons. The *Völkerball* stage was two levels, which band members periodically travelled between on moving platforms on robotic arms. The ground-level background wall embodied a futuristic technological style, with Rammstein-design "T"s pulsating with electricity. On the second level drummer Christoph Schneider sat in front of a huge industrial fan, and a dense wall of lights reached-up for several stories. The ground-level wall featured an automatic door opening onto center stage, allowing singer Lindemann to disappear between and during songs for costume changes. Whether intended or not, this door and its curtains at times resembled female genitalia, thus creating an impression of Lindemann being reborn onto the stage in different guises from the womb of this industrial complex. Both shows involved intense flashes of light, and plumes of steam, sparks and flames. Smoke pervaded the stages. For the Berlin show the stage was predominantly shadowy, with periods of eerie fluro-green, blue and red light, with black outs between songs; while the *Völkerball* performance remained much lighter throughout, though it contained similar elements. During both performances large spotlights intermittently strafed the sky, stage and audience.

For *Live Aus Berlin* the band members' make-up and costumes reflected science fiction themes — most wore luminous silver eye make-up, lipstick and hair-color — and guitarist Kruspe wore inhuman contact lenses. Band members had a variety of padded black and silver costumes, Lindemann's initial costume including arms coated in serrated black rubber. For the *Völkerball* concert the band adopted darker, more gothic costumes: Kruspe wearing a black pseudo-baroque jacket; keyboardist Christian Lorenz and guitarist Paul Landers wearing lederhosen; and singer Lindemann wearing a leather tunic. Band members wore dark make-up and lipstick, and had exposed skin smothered in dark grease. During these performances the guitarists periodically acted as automatons, remaining expressionless and as motionless as possible, or moving in a jerky, unnatural manner. Lorenz has an ongoing role playing a jester/mad scientist-style character, including interludes of crazy dancing and adopting roles in pantomimes with Lindemann. The band's props and costumes are also used as extensions of the pyrotechnics show, with drum sticks, guitars, microphones, shoes and clothing having flares attached, or being set on fire. Lindemann has variously shot sparks and flares from archery bows, pistols and blunderbusses. In Berlin Lindemann fired a hand-held flame thrower out over the audience, while in Nîmes the band adopted cyborg imagery: wearing flame-throwing facial masks and Lindemann donning an upper-body exoskeleton with steel talons and flamethrowers welded to each hand. Most impressively, on the *Liebe ist für Alle Da* tour Lindemann emerged in huge angel wings that shot flames from their tips. In addition to this cyborgism, Rammstein's on-stage performances transgress other bodily and social boundaries. During the *Live Aus Berlin* concert Lindemann flagellated himself with a cat o' nine tails, and later pounded his head with the microphone — seemingly causing a bleeding head wound. Controversially, during the song "Bück Dich" Lindemann simulated sodomy with Lorenz using an artificial penis, which then sprayed liquid across the stage and into the audience for the duration of the song. Similarly, during *Völkerball* Lindemann emerged during the song "Mein Teil" (the subject of which is cannibalism) dressed as a blood-covered butcher, with Lorenz in a cauldron. During the act Lindemann sang into a giant butcher's knife and blasted the cauldron with a flamethrower. This transgressive tradition continued on the 2011 *Made in Germany* tour, with Lindemann using a large cannon resembling male genitalia to fire foam into the audience, simulating ejaculation.

Cultural critics, such as Daniel Bartetzko, have emphasized the militaristic nature of Rammstein's stage shows, saying, "Between Leni Riefenstahl and Blade Runner, the impressions fall all over each other, but they can be reduced to the formula: sex and violence."[22] The description "storm of steel" has been used (recalling Ernst Jünger's reactionary First World War memoir), and with Rammstein's apparent technological fetish raises similarities to the proto-fascist Futurist movement's aesthetic, which prophesized that art would "act as an incendiary device, upholding the new values of speed, destruction, and violence necessary for a new age of ... national grandeur,"[23] its leader F.T. Marinetti declaring, "There is no more beauty except in strife; no masterpiece without aggressiveness."[24] Rammstein's imagery could alternatively be said to reference the modern genre of "cyberpunk," which is "associated with technophilia, computer and hacker culture, smart drugs, and dark futuristic narratives.... Combined with this technophilia is ... punk; rebellious, nihilistic and street-smart, what Gibson refers to as the cognitive dissident."[25] Contrary to the Futurist ideology, cyberpunk shares the Dada movement's desire to "expose the dangers of the growing technologization of society ... to confound the Futurists' metronomical sense of rational order with chance, 'unreason,' illogical nonsense, and a mimicry of automatism which allowed the subconscious (the irrational) to take over."[26] Rather than glorifying technology, cyberpunk reflects "alienation, and exposes a growing dehumanization through a 'technocolonization' of the body."[27] Ken McLeod argues that futuristic or alien metaphors can also be used in rock music to create pluralistic spaces outside of bourgeois normality, by portraying "a transcendent form of Other capable of challenging simplistic binaries of male/female, black/white or rich/poor.... The musical power of the disenfranchised ... often resides in their ability to articulate different ways of construing the body, ... [and] the potential for different experiential worlds."[28]

Thus, Rammstein's referencing of cyberpunk, and social and bodily transgression, could be said to both critique society by embodying social alienation, and articulate potentialities outside of social norms. Being in the performance space then allows audience members "to experience the pleasures of transgression ... in a relatively safe, secure and autonomous environment."[29] While Rammstein conjures dark images and narratives, "inherent in nearly all dystopias is a critique of the socio-economic system prevailing within that narrative: ... [and] the resistance represents a utopian sentiment within the dystopian one ... a hope for change."[30]

With 24 singles released there is insufficient space here to analyze each of Rammstein's music videos, but I will highlight some themes and refer to specific examples during later analysis. While the medium of video could allow Rammstein to expand on their technophilia in spectacular ways, their music clips instead place more emphasis on the gothic, along with social transgression. These gothic themes are most deeply developed in clips such as "Du Riechst So Gut '98,"[31] which depicts the band as wolf-men who follow the scent of a woman through a forest to a manor (filmed in the neo-gothic Babelsberg Palace near Berlin), finding her amidst a masquerade ball and seducing her. While in "Sonne" the band are portrayed as dwarves in a version of Snow White, where they work as miners to feed her drug habit of precious metals; and in "Rosenrot" the band are medieval religious pilgrims who stay in a pagan village where Lindemann's character is seduced by a local girl, induced by her to murder, and then burned at the stake.[32] McLeod sees broad similarities between modern depictions of fairy tales and monsters — which represent the alien "other" — and later science fiction and cyberpunk, as their "mystery and associated feelings of awe and quasi-spirituality ... deflect the often darkly rational, scientific, and sometimes militaristic notions of progress that have characterized much of late twentieth- and early twenty-first-century life."[33]

Social transgression is the focus of a number of clips like "Du Hast" and "Ich Will," which depict the band as criminals ("Du Hast" uses a *Reservoir Dogs* style, while "Ich Will" portrays them as bank robbers)[34]; while other clips use sexuality as the field of social transgression — "Mann Gegen Mann" featuring a writhing mass of muscular naked men, and the uncensored version of "Pussy" shows band members having sex with German porn actresses, showing full intercourse and ejaculation.[35] However, Rammstein's most controversial videos are those touching on political ideology, with the "Stripped" video using footage from Leni Riefenstahl's 1938 film *Olympia*, and the video for "Links 2-3-4" seemingly referencing her 1935 film *Triumph of the Will*[36] — the imagery of which David Bathrick claims works as "an iconic language to connote some form of absolute political evil."[37] While the use of Riefenstahl's

Olympia footage for "Stripped" provoked accusations of Rammstein promoting neo-fascism, or of cheap sensationalism, Valerie Weinstein argues the clip has critical elements, and depicts "an antimodern desire to escape society as well as the ideological manipulations of the media."[38] The video for "Links 2-3-4" was supposedly a political reply to this controversy, featuring lyrics that reference SPD leader Oscar Lafontaine's book *The Heart Beats on the Left*—but the continued use of a "fascist aesthetic" (of ants in Nazi-esque parades and military formations) raised concern.[39] Further interpretations of these shall be advanced below.

Interpreting Rammstein

With Rammstein's complex style and subject matter in mind, the interrelated questions under consideration are how Rammstein can be interpreted when focusing on their extra-lyrical content, and why they can appeal to audiences across the political spectrum. I argue Rammstein's broad appeal is facilitated by the character of their artistic form, which I shall describe as "metamodern"—not "ambiguous," but oscillating between a "modern enthusiasm and a postmodern irony."[40] Thus Rammstein's performance contains moments of each political position that an audience can embrace from their own perspective—which I will explore with reference to Reader-Response Theory. My analysis will focus on three political subjectivities: the post-ideological liberal center, who are drawn to Rammstein for their spectacle and benign transgressions; the radical and neo-fascist right, who see in Rammstein a glorification of masculinity, militarism and authoritarian permissiveness; and the center-to-far left, who interpret Rammstein as attacking both capitalist modernity and right-wing politics through over-identification and irony. Moreover, Rammstein's epic musical style actually has a teleological "feel," thus providing a screen onto which audiences can project their own meta-narrative in opposition to the detotalization and indeterminacy of postmodern capitalism, which has generated "a new depthlessness to culture and a weakening of public and private historiocity."[41]

Associated with Enlightenment thought, modernism understood the self as distinct from an objective and knowable world.[42] Ideologically, modernism fostered ideas of reason, progress and grand social narratives, along with the idea that people could harness "the power to change the world that is changing them, to make their way through the maelstrom and make it their own."[43] Frederic Jameson theorized from the 1970s that a new postmodernist period arose as the cultural logic of late capitalism,[44] and over the decades since we have experienced "technological revolution and the global restructuring of capitalism ... moving the world into a postindustrial, infotainment, and biotech mode ... organized around new information, communications, and genetic technologies."[45] Postmodernism involved "the overturning or erosion of master narratives,"[46] and was increasingly characterized by a postmodern irony "encompassing nihilism, sarcasm, and the distrust and deconstruction of grand narratives, the singular and the truth."[47] Pastiche thus became a dominant cultural paradigm, which is empty of political content and "enables us to evade any truth-telling of a determinate kind."[48] However, some scholars now highlight an emerging trend of what they term "metamodernism," "opposed to both modernism and radical forms of postmodernism."[49] Vermeulen and van den Akker argue that "new generations of artists [are] increasingly abandon[ing] the aesthetic precepts of deconstruction, parataxis, and pastiche in favor of aesth-ethical notions of reconstruction, myth, and metaxis."[50] This metamodernism is "characterized by the oscillation between a typically modern commitment and a markedly postmodern detachment."[51] "It oscillates between a modern enthusiasm and a postmodern irony, between hope and melancholy, between naïveté and knowingness, empathy and apathy, unity and plurality, totality and fragmentation, purity and ambiguity. Indeed, by oscillating to and fro or back and forth, the metamodern negotiates between the modern and the postmodern."[52] I argue that Rammstein's work is characterized by this metamodern oscillation, both seriously and ironically engaging with their subject matter and narratives.

While Rammstein's work itself oscillates in meaning, all texts are open to differing interpretations by their audience. Advocates of Reader-Response theories have long argued that "meaning has no effective existence outside of its realization in the mind of a reader."[53] The meaning of a text is never completely within the author's control: "A text can have meanings that its author is not aware of.... [I]t can have meanings that its author did not intend."[54] And even the author's intention itself may be indeterminate, or draw on cultural symbols that themselves contain ambiguity: "if social intentionality may be essentially indeterminate, then that indeterminacy will be reflected in the individual intentionality of a particular person at a particular time."[55] Indeed, in the case of authors using metaphor and irony, the author is specifically *dependent* on extra-textual information from the audience's social context to convey the author's intentions.[56] So, as Stanley Fish argued, "the place where sense is made or not made is the reader's mind rather than the printed page or space between the covers of a book."[57] Thus Reader-Response concepts have become ubiquitous throughout literary theory. It is widely accepted that "readers make meaning: readers — and not only authors — engage in an active process of production-in-use in which texts of all kinds — stories, poems, plays, buildings, films, TV ads, clothes, body piercings — are received by their audiences not as a repository of stable meaning but as an invitation to make it."[58] Music and images are especially open to varied interpretations as they are semantically underdetermined, so meaning arises from, "the contexture of interpretation, the capacity to draw together a variety of semantic sources — tropes, tones, phrases, images, ideas into a sustainable discourse ... [music is] integrated with, not remote from, the general atmosphere of meaning in daily life."[59] Thus it is important to note that interpretations "are shaped and even constrained by cultural and economic conditions. Readers make meaning, but not in conditions of their own choosing."[60] Audiences constructing meaning are "part of interpretive communities and are involved in collective cultural imagining and reimagining."[61] In this case I focus on political alignments as interpretive communities.

The two major divisions emphasized here are on one hand between the post-ideological liberal center, who consume the spectacle of Rammstein's art without consciously interpreting its political content, and audiences on the ideological "extremes;" and on the other hand between those "extremes" of right- and left-wing ideological audiences. To begin, I argue that the "post-political" liberal individuals seek out Rammstein's performance to fulfill the dual function of experiencing enjoyment (or *jouissance* in Lacanian terminology), as encouraged by the hegemonic consumerist culture, and simultaneously to participate in transgression as a temporary escape from social alienation. The context for this "post-ideological" audience is the postmodern society and its organization in what might be termed "technocapitalism," "characterized by a decline of the state and enlarged power for the market, accompanied by the growing strength of transnational corporations and governmental bodies and the decreased power of the nation-state and its institutions."[62] In this context Cold War-era ideologies were abandoned, and all mainstream political parties embraced neo-liberal economics: "The effect was ... to take the politics out of politics: given that everyone who mattered accepted liberal capitalism, political debate could only centre around minor technical issues and the presentation of personality."[63] This then gives rise to a 'technoculture' in which critical analysis is increasingly replaced by technocratic "one-dimensional thought."[64] The technoculture is dominated by the mode of "entertainment," and "[t]he capitalist economy thrives on megaspectacles of consumption."[65] This,

> society of the spectacle attempts to make it appear that a life of luxury and happiness is open to all, that anyone can buy the sparkling objects on display and consume the spectacles of entertainment and information. But in reality only

those with sufficient wealth can fully enjoy the benefits of the capitalist spectacle, whose opulence is extracted out of the lives and dreams of the exploited.[66]

In this society, Aldous Huxley said "people exchange freedom for 'fun.'"[67] Fredrick Jameson observed that people lost an understanding of the world's totality, and were, "no longer able to make any felt connection between the concerns of private life, as it follows its own course within the walls and confines of affluent society, and the structural projections of the system in the outside world, in the form of neo-colonialism [and] oppression."[68] And capitalist corporations work hard to maintain this disconnection, using global consultancy firms such as McKinsey & Company to manage public relations and propagate narratives promoting neoliberal capitalism.[69]

Slavoj Žižek argues that in this technoculture the apparently liberating nature of hedonism becomes repressive as "permitted *jouissance* necessarily turns into obligatory *jouissance*."[70] Society no longer demands "sacrificial devotion to a cause but, in contrast to previous modes of ideological interpellation ... [to] enjoy!"[71] The Frankfurt School saw the "culture industry" as serving capitalism "not merely by making so much money, but by distracting people, convincing them to put their energies into dancing all night or taking drugs, rather than getting interested in trying to change the manifest injustices in our world."[72] The music industry thus serves the roles of producing products for consumption, and social regulation. Music *is* big business, and control is highly centralized — the industry is dominated by a handful of major corporations including Universal Music Group, Sony Music Entertainment, Warner Music Group and EMI Group, which produce more than 80 percent of popular music.[73] Thus, the argument about Rammstein's style and content is often that it is driven by commercial priorities, "because for German bands success in the international music market requires that musicians exploit their German 'difference' ... produc[ing] a caricature of the 'ugly German' that frequently crosses the boundaries of political correctness and good taste."[74] Music is one sector of "a larger symbolic economy ... one of the many sites of exchange through which the defining signs of a culture circulate;"[75] so even Rammstein's art is penetrated by the hegemonic logic of the culture — in this case the society of the spectacle, embodied in Rammstein's exhilarating music, outrageous themes and impressive stage shows.[76]

"Advanced Capitalism ... produces amongst some ... a sense of moral emptiness and a need for the recreation of human community."[77] Thus, in consuming Rammstein's spectacle the additional element sought by the audience is an escape from social alienation via Rammstein's social transgressions. Keith Kahn-Harris notes, "Transgression is one way of surviving the fraught experience of modernity. It is one of the few sources of almost unrestricted agency ... allow[ing] individuals to feel utterly in control, utterly 'sovereign' over their being through practices that resist instrumental rationality."[78] However, "whereas pre-modern societies contained spaces for transgression, such as the carnival, transgression has been pushed to the margins of society in modernity ... [or] assimilated to the point where it is no longer transgressive."[79] Thus, Karen Bettez Halnon argues, the

> heavy metal carnival breaks through the noise of commercial culture by raising the transgression ante to the extreme and challenging nearly every conceivable social rule governing taste, authority, morality, propriety, the sacred, and, some might say, civility itself.... Understood from the inside as carnival ... metal is a dis-alienating, liminal utopia of human freedom, creativity, and egalitarianism. ... a critical source of positive meaning for its audiences' everyday life needs.[80]

So the participants' catharsis arises from transgression of society's commercialized norms, and the extremity of transgressions is driven by the constant commercialization of transgressive forms, as youth cultures are "culturally mined" and "rebellion [has become] the zeitgeist of capitalist marketing ideology."[81] In addition to the acts of transgression in Rammstein's performance, I believe the cultural tropes Rammstein references also strike a critical chord with audiences. McLeod has argued that use of futuristic themes "often represents a neo–Gnostic withdrawal from the world and its institutions — an artificial escape from social reality, from commitment, from one's self, and into a utopian future."[82] Rammstein's referencing of cyberpunk and gothic themes is thus a form of cultural resistance to the instrumental rationality of technocapitalist culture; while industrial sets and musical style create a material embodiment of capitalist exploitation and attendant social alienation, which may have been more tangibly apparent in earlier industrial society.

However, Raymond Williams argued decades ago that political hegemony is "more substantial and more flexible than any abstract imposed ideology.... alternative meanings and values, ... alternative senses of the world, ... can be accommodated and tolerated within a particular effective and dominant culture."[83] Žižek also highlights that "what may [appear] as 'radical critical stance' or as subversive activity can effectively function as the system's 'inherent transgression,'"[84] and in the case of Rammstein it might be argued that their transgressive performances are systemically incorporated both because they are profitable, and because they are cathartic for young, socially alienated people who might otherwise direct their anger and energy into *resistance* against the political order. The actual conformism of heavy metal is noted by Kahn-Harris, who says that belonging to such a "transgressive community" allows members to "[enjoy] the mundane comforts of modernity without alienation and disempowerment."[85] Indeed, when analyzed some of Rammstein's transgressive performances are not as transgressive as they initially seem — for example, Lindemann's simulated sodomy of Lorenz in the *Live Aus Berlin* performance, or their more recent music clip for *Pussy*, which features real sex with German porn actresses.[86] There is little chance that most of the audience have not at some point seen such real acts in private, and, as Feona Attwood notes, "porn has turned chic and become an object of fascination in art, film, television and the press. Porn *style* is also now commonplace, especially in music video and advertising, and a scantily clad, surgically enhanced 'porn look' is evident, not only in the media, but on the streets."[87] And indeed young people increasingly create their own pornography, as "in our media-saturated, celebrity-obsessed culture, putting oneself into the frame of representation is becoming a means of existential assertion."[88] In the case of the song "Mein Teil," the references to cannibalism followed from the *real case* of a German man imprisoned for life for cannibalism, which sparked public debate about whether someone could consent to their own murder.[89] And while the song "Ich tu dir weh" was banned for its sado-masochistic content, is the public's latent sadism not an unspoken element of the popularity of modern crime dramas' voyeuristic attention to details of sex crimes and murder?[90]

Ideologically transgressive elements of Rammstein's performance bring us to our next audience: the political far-right. While the post-ideological liberal center may deny that Rammstein's performances are politically significant, Žižek notes that "What the new populist Right and the Left share is just one thing: the awareness that *politics proper is still alive*."[91] Critics of Rammstein believe that "recalling a historically fascist look or sound has the potential to inspire contemporary neofascists,"[92] and indeed their "Storm of Steel" aesthetic does appeal to the right-wing.[93] For decades hard and heavy music has attracted alienated urban youth, who "attempt to establish a 'defensively organized collective' around a mythic image of proletarian masculinity, ... embracing, and even ... [amplifying] the prejudices of the parent society."[94] In Britain, "observers of the radical right emphasize the key importance of concerts as sites of recruitment in a scene otherwise lacking in structure, and like to refer to music as 'Gateway Drug #1' for bringing youth into 'the violent milieu.'"[95] Rammstein has been particularly criticized for their music videos referencing Riefenstahl, such as "Stripped" using from her *Olympia* footage.[96] The "Stripped" video begins and ends with scenes of neo-classical architecture and statues — recalling the Nazi penchant for their grand form, which Albert Speer incorporated in designs such as the New Reich Chancellery in Berlin. Athletes are shown in scenes of Athenian-style physical competition, and their bare bodies are the focus of the piece. Footage of sports such as fencing, rowing and diving is presented, along with athletes performing exhibitions in unison — Riefenstahl originally idealizing the athletic Aryan physique.[97] Despite any claims denying ideological significance, "the right-wing youth magazine Sigill praise[d] Rammstein's video as 'a symphony for eye and ear' that belongs to a 'conservative cultural avant-garde'"[98] — and ideology is in the eye and ear of the beholder.

Rammstein claimed "Links 2-3-4" was a riposte to this right-wing interpretation of "Stripped," but "Links 2-3-4"'s imagery has in itself been said to reference her 1935 film *Triumph of the Will*.[99] Military marching and rhythm are a core structure of the song, and when performed live the call and response from Lindemann to the crowd — "Links ... Hey!" — echoes the sound of "Sieg Heil!"[100] The video also revolves around a military theme: ants within an anthill are attacked by giant bugs, which initially kill many of the ants. One ant addresses the other ants from atop a tall pillar, in a format that recalls the Nuremburg Rallies, inspiring them to unite and attack the bugs in military formation — swarming and killing them.[101] The attack of the (foreign and racially Other) bugs is reminiscent of the fascist ideological core, in which internal "political struggle is naturalized into ... racial conflict, the (class) antagonism inherent in the social structure is reduced to the invasion of a foreign (Jewish) body which disturbs the harmony of the Aryan community."[102] There are clues within the video referring to the satirical/critical nature of this imagery (which I shall refer to below), but "in the end, the ambiguity and irony of the juxtapositions in 'Links 2-3-4' allow different publics to construe this number differently..."[103] The song "Amerika" is another political piece by Rammstein, featuring sections in English. Primarily referring to cultural homogenization under the United States' global hegemony, the song's politics can be read equally as progressive criticism of capitalism and consumerism by radical audiences, or by conservatives as an attack on decadent democratic modernity and a call to preserve national identities.[104]

While it might be argued that Rammstein's style embodies anarchic resistance to authority and transgression of conservative mores, rather than a desire to submit to (right-wing) authoritarian order, in fact, Žižek argues that

the cliché about "escaping from freedom" into a totalitarian haven is profoundly misleading. Nor is an explanation found in the standard Freudo-Marxian thesis according to which the libidinal foundation of totalitarian (fascist) regimes is the "authoritarian personality" — i.e. someone who finds satisfaction in compulsive obedience. Although, on the surface, the totalitarian master also issues stern orders compelling us to renounce pleasure and to sacrifice ourselves in some higher cause, his effective injunction, discernible between the lines, is a call to unconstrained transgression. Far from imposing on us a firm set of standards to be complied with, the totalitarian master suspends (moral) punishment. His secret injunction is: "You may."[105]

Frederick Jameson concurs, Ian Buchanan explaining his position that

[Nazism's] transformations were inherently paradoxical: subservience to the general order of the regime was won by promoting disorder at every other level — you can do what you want, you can rape, kill and maim the enemy in whatever obscene fashion you like, just so long as you give your allegiance to the regime, was Nazism's basic message.[106]

And any observer of skinhead culture — with its violence, *basse couture* and hard-living — can recognize this libidinal economy of their cultural group. The excesses of spectacle that appeals to audiences of the liberal center, as a product of normal technocapitalist performance, are difficult to distinguish from the elements of Fascist pageantry and aesthetics of the past.[107] Thus in style, performance and symbolic content, there are many elements of Rammstein's art that can be interpreted positively by a right-wing audience.

Left-wing audiences, then, can appreciate Rammstein for the transgressive and utopic elements of style, cultural tropes and subject matter that alleviate social alienation, as previously discussed. However, additionally the left can interpret Rammstein as having politically radical messages embedded in their performances. As mentioned, "Amerika" has a quite explicit message against American cultural hegemony, and also links their commercial power to war. Another example of this critical agenda is the music video for "Mann Gegen Mann," which primarily consists of a homoerotic mass of writhing muscular men,[108] which James Little argues "aimed to directly confront homophobic attitudes in an explicit [way] ... undermin[ing] the ideology ... that drives neo–Nazi groups throughout Europe."[109] While Rammstein's general aesthetic is the militaristic, hyper-masculinity that much of the left find offensive, Žižek argues that Rammstein engages in

an over-identification with [fascist] *sinthomes* [knots of *jouissance*] which undermines ideological identification ... the unleashed brutality of Rammstein ... undermines the system not through some critical-utopian vision but through the obscene brutality of the immersion it enacts. One should therefore resist the ... temptation to reject as ideologically suspect the music of Rammstein with its extensive use of "Nazi" images and motifs — what they do is exactly the opposite: by pushing their listeners into a direct identification with the *sinthomes* used by the Nazis, by-passing their articulation in Nazi ideology, they render palpable a gap where ideology imposes the illusion of seamless organic unity. In short, Rammstein *liberates* these *sinthomes* from their Nazi-articulation: they are offered to be enjoyed in their pre-ideological status as "knots" of libidinal investment.... Rammstein undermine totalitarian ideology not with an ironic distance towards the rituals they imitate, but by directly confronting us with its obscene materiality and thereby suspending its efficacy.[110]

This over-identification is the key to deciphering the music video for "Links 2-3-4," which includes symbols connected to the band Laibach (from whom Rammstein borrowed their 'T' symbol). Laibach use an "aggressive inconsistent mixture of Stalinism, Nazism, and Blut und Boden ideology"[111] in their work, which critiques totalitarian politics through over-identification. Symbols of the band appear in video, such as the "T" shape of the anthill and marching ant formations, a range of symbols that appear on the ant's film screen, and in the final ant formation — which resembles Laibach's "cog" design.[112] For the left, this critique through over-identification is the true political content of Rammstein's work. The over-identification only works, however, in the metamodernist form: it is not merely irony, it actually contains a commitment to articulating the overt message. This is also the key to the music video for "Pussy," which effectively criticizes the commodification of sex, and over-sexualization of the media by over-identifying and taking the process to its logical conclusion: open pornography.

Finally, I argue that the form of Rammstein's music that evokes feelings of melancholy, tension and longing, and energetically resolves them within their songs, is a perfect screen onto which audiences can project the essence of their own teleological metanarrative, which is often consciously disavowed because of society's hegemonic neoliberal ideology. The ideological context that developed after the Cold War was described by Francis Fukuyama's theory of "The End of History," in which "liberal capitalism was the only rationally acceptable socio-economic framework for a modern society."[113] The dominant paradigm became that, "not only did capitalism ... resolve all its social and cultural contradictions and deliver a society as good as can be wished for, it also triumphed over all the alternative systems and extinguished the need for ideology."[114] Thus all remaining problems merely had to be addressed via technocratic governance "within narratives of potential change that reside comfortably within the exploitative framework of capitalism."[115] The flip side of this was "the liberal democratic blackmail that rejects any commitment to radical emancipatory politics as inevitably leading to violence and terror."[116] Thus, in post–Cold War technocapitalism no intellectual space remained for a different emancipatory project for society: "this notion of history dialectically progressing toward some predetermined Telos had ended because humankind had realized that this Telos had been achieved (with the 'universalization of Western liberal democracy')."[117] Vermeulen and van den Akker argue that the metamodern discourse reopens space for teleological thinking, without teleological belief. Metamodernism "acknowledges that history's purpose will never be fulfilled because it does not exist. Critically, however, it nevertheless takes toward it as if it does exist ... the metamodern discourse consciously commits itself to an impossible possibility."[118] The metamodernist form can thus be infused with a new emancipatory telos — and experiencing Rammstein's music allows individuals to subjectively *feel* their own teleological metanarrative, without its full intellectual articulation.

Conclusion

With "its ability to mediate the social — temporally, spatially and bodily — music is a powerful site of struggle in the organization of meaning and lived experience."[119] Thus, the meanings of Rammstein's music are part of society's overall political fabric, and important for the maintenance of fans' own political subjectivities. Rammstein have thrived by pushing boundaries and creating controversy — making them politically contentious — but in doing so their true political messages have remained veiled. I have argued that this stems from their work's metamodern form, which oscillates between a modernist commitment and postmodern irony. Rammstein's performance contains moments of each political position that an audience can embrace from their own perspective — technocapitalist spectacle and social subversion, neo-fascist machismo and radical critique. For those don't understand Rammstein's lyrics, there is even further underdetermination of their work's meaning, allowing greater scope for the audience to construct their own interpretations. Moreover, Rammstein's epic musical style has a teleological "feel," thus providing a screen onto which audiences can project their own metanarrative: Rammstein's music invites us to dream our own stories of love, pain, anger, struggle, loss, and redemption. Today, in our post-ideological society, perhaps this is the most subversive and important element of Rammstein's work.

Notes

1. Valerie Weinstein, "Reading Rammstein, Remembering Riefenstahl: 'Fascist Aesthetics' and German Popular Culture," in Neil Christian Pages, Mary Rhiel, and Ingeborg Majer-O'Sickey, eds. *Riefenstahl Screened: An Anthology of New Criticism* (New York: Continuum, 2008), p. 131.

2. *Grand Rapids Press*, July 22, 1999.

3. "Atari Teenage Riot's Alec Empire Questions Rammstein's Sincerity," *MTV.com*, August 1998, accessed October 10, 12 at http://www.mtv.com/news/articles/1425050/atari-teenage-riots-alec-empire-questions-rammsteins-sincerity.jhtml.

4. Weinstein, "Reading Rammstein," p 131.

5. Karen Collins, "Dead Channel Surfing: The Commonalities between Cyberpunk Literature and Industrial Music," *Popular Music*, 24, no. 2 (May, 2005), p. 166.

6. Ibid.

7. Weinstein, "Reading Rammstein," p. 132.

8. Rammstein, "Engel," *Sehnsucht*, 1997, Motor Music Records/Slash Records, track 2; Rammstein, "Nebel," *Mutter*, 2001, Motor Music Records, compact disc, track 11.

9. Rammstein, "Ohne Dich," *Ohne Dich*, 2004, Motor Music Records, compact disc, track 1; Rammstein, "Weißes Fleisch," *Herzeleid*, 1995, Motor Music Records, compact disc, track 3.

10. Lawrence Kramer, *Interpreting Music* (Berkeley: University of California Press, 2011), p. 57.

11. Rammstein, *Herzeleid*, 1995, Motor Music Records, compact disc.

12. Rammstein, *Asche zu Asche*, 2001, Motor Music Records, compact disc; Rammstein, *Feuer Frei!*, 2002, Motor Music Records, compact disc.

13. Rammstein, *Reise, Reise*, 2004, Motor Music Records/Republic Records, compact disc; Rammstein, *Rosenrot*, 2005, Universal Music Group, compact disc.

14. Rammstein, *Made in Germany 1995–2011*, 2011, Universal Records, compact disc; Rammstein, *Liebe ist für Alle Da*, 2009, Universal Records/Vagrant Records, compact disc.

15. Rammstein, *Sehnsucht*, 1997, Motor Music Records/Slash Records, compact disc

16. Rammstein, *Engel*, 1997, Motor Music Records, compact disc; Rammstein, *Amerika*, 2004, Motor Music Records, compact disc.

17. Rammstein, *Mutter*, 2001, Motor Music Records, compact disc.

18. Rammstein, *Liebe ist für Alle Da*, 2009, Universal Records/Vagrant Records, compact disc; Sean Michaels, "Rammstein Album Ban Reversed," *The Guardian*, 16 June 2010, accessed July 10,2012, http://www.guardian.co.uk/music/2010/jun/16/rammstein-album-ban-reversed.

19. Bruce Tucker, "Narrative, Extramusical Form, and the Metamodernism of the Art Ensemble of Chicago," *Lenox Avenue: A Journal of Interarts Inquiry* 3 (1997), p. 34.

20. Weinstein, "Reading Rammstein," p. 132.

21. Rammstein, *Live Aus Berlin*, 1999, Motor Music Records, DVD; Rammstein, *Völkerball*, 2006, Universal Music Group, DVD.

22. Daniel Bartetzko quoted in Weinstein, "Reading Rammstein," p. 132.

23. Anne Bowler, "Politics as Art: Italian Futurism and Fascism," *Theory and Society* 20, no. 6 (December 1991), p. 763.

24. Emil Oestereicher, "Fascism and the Intellectuals: The Case of Italian Futurism," *Social Research* 41, no. 3 (Autumn 1974), p. 525.

25. Collins, "Dead Channel Surfing," p. 165.

26. Ibid., p. 167.

27. Ibid., p. 172.

28. Ken McLeod, "Space Oddities: Aliens, Futurism and Meaning in Popular Music," *Popular Music* 22, no. 3 (October 2003), p. 339.

29. Keith Kahn-Harris, *Extreme Metal: Music and Culture on the Edge* (Oxford: Berg, 2007), p. 157.

30. Collins, "Dead Channel Surfing," pp. 171–172.

31. Philipp Stölzl, dir., "Du Riechst So Gut '98," May 1998, Universal Music Group, music video.

32. Jörn Heitmann, dir., "Sonne," January 2002, Universal Music Group, music video; Zoran Bihać, dir., "Rosenrot," November 2005, Universal Music Group, music video.

33. McLeod, "Space Oddities," p. 337.

34. Philipp Stölzl, dir., "Du Hast," April 1997, Universal Music Group, music video; Jörn Heitmann, dir., "Ich Will," August 2001, Universal Music Group, music video.

35. Jonas Akerlund, dir., "Mann Gegen Mann," February 2006, Universal Music Group, music video; Jonas Akerlund, dir., "Pussy," September 2009, Universal Music Group, music video.

36. Weinstein, "Reading Rammstein," p. 130.

37. David Bathrick, "The Afterlife of Triumph of the Will: The First Twenty-five Years," in Neil Christian Pages, Mary Rhiel, and Ingeborg Majer-O'Sickey, eds., *Riefenstahl Screened: An Anthology of New Criticism* (New York: Continuum, 2008), p. 74.

38. Weinstein, "Reading Rammstein," p. 135.

39. Ibid., pp. 139–142.

40. Timotheus Vermeulen and Robin van den Akker, "Notes on Metamodernism," *Journal of Aesthetics & Culture*, 2 (2010), p. 8.

41. Adam Roberts, *Frederic Jameson* (London: Routledge, 2000), p. 123.

42. Stephen M. Feldman, "The Problem of Critique: Triangulating Habermas, Derrida, and Gadamer Within Metamodernism," *Contemporary Political Theory*, no. 4 (2005), p. 296.

43. Marshall Berman, *All That Is Solid Melts into Air: The Experience of Modernity* (London: Penguin, 1988), p. 16.

44. Ian Buchanan, *Fredric Jameson: Live Theory* (London: Continuum, 2006), p. 73.

45. Steven Best and Douglas Kellner, *The Postmodern Adventure: Science, Technology, and Cultural Studies at the Third Millennium* (New York: Guildford, 2001), p. 1.

46. Roberts, *Frederic Jameson*, p. 115.

47. Vermeulen and van den Akker, "Notes on Metamodernism," p. 4.

48. Buchanan, *Fredric Jameson*, pp. 94–95.

49. Feldman, "The Problem of Critique," p. 296.

50. Vermeulen and van den Akker, "Notes on Metamodernism," p. 2.

51. Ibid.

52. Ibid., pp. 5–6.

53. Jane P. Tompkins, "An Introduction to Reader-Response Criticism," in Jane P. Tompkins, ed., *Reader-Response Criticism: From Formalism to Post-Structuralism* (Baltimore: Johns Hopkins University Press, 1980), p.ix.

54. Monroe C. Beardsley, "The Authority of the Text," in Gary Iseminger, ed., *Intention & Interpretation* (Philadelphia: Temple University Press, 1992), p. 27.

55. Michael Krausz, "Intention and Interpretation: Hirsch and Margolis," in Gary Iseminger, ed., *Intention & Interpretation* (Philadelphia: Temple University Press, 1992), pp. 152–153.

56. Daniel O. Nathan, "Irony, Metaphor, and the Problem of Intention," in Gary Iseminger, ed., *Intention & Interpretation* (Philadelphia: Temple University Press, 1992), p. 185.

57. Tompkins, "An Introduction to Reader-Response Criticism," pp. xvii.

58. Patricia Harkin, "The Reception of Reader-Response Theory," *College Composition and Communication*, 56, no. 3 (February 2005), p. 413.

59. Kramer, *Interpreting Music*, p. 68.

60. Harkin, "The Reception of Reader-Response Theory," p. 419.

61. Molly Abel Travis, *Reading Cultures: The Construction of Readers in the Twentieth Century* (Carbondale: Southern Illinois University Press, 1998), p. 6.

62. Best and Kellner, *The Postmodern Adventure*, p. 212.

63. Alex Callinicos, *An Anti-Capitalist Manifesto* (Cambridge: Polity Press, 2003), p. 3.

64. Best and Kellner, *The Postmodern Adventure*, p. 216.

65. Ibid., pp. 227–228.

66. Ibid., p. 231.

67. Ibid., p. 241.

68. Buchanan, *Fredric Jameson*, p. 79.

69. Kanishka Chowdhury, "Deflecting Crisis: Critiquing Capitalism's Emancipation Narrative," *Cultural Logic* (2011), p. 1.

70. Slavoj Žižek, *The Parallax View* (Cambridge: MIT Press, 2009), p. 310.

71. Slavoj Žižek, "Multitude, Surplus, and Envy," *Rethinking Marxism*, 19, no. 1 (January 2007), pp. 52–53.

72. Roberts, *Frederic Jameson*, p. 37.

73. Brian Longhurst, *Popular Music & Society* (Cambridge: Polity Press, 2007), p. 27.

74. Weinstein, "Reading Rammstein," p. 131.

75. Kiernan Ryan, "Introduction," in Kiernan Ryan, ed., *New Historicism and Cultural Materialism: A Reader* (London: Arnold, 1996), p. xiv.

76. John Brannigan, *New Historicism and Cultural Materialism* (Basingstoke: Macmillian, 1998), p. 27.

77. Robert J.S. Ross, "From Antisweatshop to Global Justice to Antiwar: How the New New Left Is the Same and Different from the Old New Left," *Journal of World-Systems Research*, 10, no. 1 (Winter 2004), p. 316.

78. Kahn-Harris, *Extreme Metal*, p. 158.

79. Ibid.

80. Halnon, "Heavy Metal Carnival and Dis-alienation," p. 34.

81. Ibid., p. 45.

82. McLeod, "Space Oddities," p. 353.

83. Raymond Williams, "From Base and Superstructure in Marxist Cultural Theory," in Kiernan Ryan, ed., *New Historicism and Cultural Materialism: A Reader* (London: Arnold, 1996), p. 23–24.

84. Slavoj Žižek, "Badiou: Notes from an Ongoing Debate," *International Journal of Žižek Studies*, 1, no. 2 (2007), pp. 5–6.

85. Kahn-Harris, *Extreme Metal*, p. 159.

86. Jonas Akerlund, dir., "Pussy," September 2009, Universal Music Group, music video.

87. Feona Attwood, "Introduction," in Feona Attwood, ed., *Mainstreaming Sex: The Sexualization of Western Culture* (London: I.B.Tauris, 2009), p. xiv.

88. Simon Hardy, "The New Pornographies: Representation or Reality?," Feona Attwood, ed., *Mainstreaming Sex: The Sexualization of Western Culture* (London: I.B.Tauris, 2009), p. 13.

89. Rammstein, "Mein Teil," *Reise, Reise*, 2004, Motor Music Records/Republic Records, compact disc, track 2.

90. Rammstein, "Ich tu dir weh," *Liebe ist für Alle Da*, 2009, Universal Records/Vagrant Records, compact disc, track 2.

91. Slavoj Žižek, *In Defense of Lost Causes* (London: Verso, 2008), p. 270.

92. Weinstein, "Reading Rammstein," p. 132.

93. Ibid.

94. Timothy S. Brown, "Subcultures, Pop Music and Politics: Skinheads and 'Nazi Rock' in England and Germany," *Journal of Social History*, 38, no. 1 (Autumn, 2004), p. 162.

95. Ibid., p. 171.

96. Rammstein, "Stripped," *Stripped*, 1998, Motor Music Records, compact disc, track 1.

97. Phillip Stölzl and Sven Budelmann, dirs., "Stripped," August 1998, Universal Music Group, music video.

98. Weinstein, "Reading Rammstein," p. 134.

99. Rammstein, "Links 2-3-4," *Links 2-3-4*, 2001, Motor Music Records, compact disc, track 1.

100. Rammstein, "Links 2-3-4," *Völkerball*, 2006, Universal Music Group, DVD, track 2.

101. Zoran Bihać, dir., "Links 2-3-4," May 2002, Universal Music Group, music video.

102. Žižek, *In Defense of Lost Causes*, p. 261.

103. Weinstein, "Reading Rammstein," p. 144.

104. Rammstein, "Amerika," *Amerika*, 2004, Motor Music Records, compact disc, track 1.

105. Slavoj Žižek, "'You May!'" *London Review of Books*, 21, no. 6 (18 March 1999), pp. 3–6, accessed at http://www.lrb.co.uk/v21/n06/slavoj-zizek/you-may, on July 10, 2012.

106. Buchanan, *Fredric Jameson*, pp. 73–74.

107. Žižek, *The Parallax View*, p. 310.

108. Jonas Akerlund, dir., "Mann Gegen Mann," February 2006, Universal Music Group, music video.

109. James Little, "Philosophico-Musical Vision: Badiou, Žižek, and Music," *International Journal of Žižek Studies*, 5, no. 2, pp. 3–4.

110. Slavoj Žižek, *Living in the End Times* (London: Verso, 2011), pp. 385–387.

111. Slavoj Žižek, "Why Are Laibach and NSK Not Fascists?," *Retrogarde Reading Room*, accessed at http://www.reanimator.8m.com/NSK/zizek.html, on July 10, 2012.

112. Zoran Bihać, dir., "Links 2-3-4," May 2002, Universal Music Group, music video.

113. Callinicos, *Bonfire of Illusions*, p. 2.

114. Buchanan, *Fredric Jameson*, p. 82.

115. Chowdhury, "Deflecting Crisis," pp. 3–4.

116. Robert Sinnerbrink, "Goodbye Lenin? Žižek on Neoliberal Ideology and Post-Marxist Politics," *International Journal of Žižek Studies*, 4, no. 2, p. 4.

117. Vermeulen and van den Akker, "Notes on Metamodernism," p. 5.

118. Ibid.

119. Robin Ballinger, "Sounds of Resistance," in Louise Amoore, ed., *The Global Resistance Reader* (London: Routledge, 2005), p. 430.

Works Cited

Akerlund, Jonas dir. "Mann Gegen Mann." February 2006, Universal Music Group, music video.

_____. "Pussy." September 2009, Universal Music Group, music video.

"Atari Teenage Riot's Alec Empire Questions Rammstein's Sincerity." *MTV.com*, August 1998, http://www.mtv.com/news/articles/1425050/atari-teenage-riots-alec-empire-questions-rammsteins-sincerity.jhtml (accessed September 15, 2012).

Attwood, Feona. "Introduction." In *Mainstreaming Sex: The Sexualization of Western Culture*, ed. Feona Attwood, xiii–xxiv. London: I.B. Tauris, 2009.

Ballinger, Robin. "Sounds of Resistance." *The Global Resistance Reader*, ed. Louise Amoore, 421–436. London: Routledge, 2005.

Bathrick, David. "The Afterlife of Triumph of the Will: The First Twenty-five Years." *Riefenstahl Screened: An Anthology of New Criticism*, ed. Neil Christian Pages, Mary Rhiel, and Ingeborg Majer-O'Sickey, 73–97. New York: Continuum, 2008.

Beardsley, Monroe C. "The Authority of the Text." In *Intention & Interpretation*, ed. Gary Iseminger, 24–40. Philadelphia: Temple University Press, 1992.

Berman, Marshall. *All That Is Solid Melts Into Air: The Experience of Modernity*. London: Penguin, 1988.

Best, Steven, and Douglas Kellner. *The Postmodern Adventure: Science, Technology, and Cultural Studies at the Third Millennium*. New York: Guildford, 2001.

Bihać, Zoran dir. *Links 2-3-4*. May 2002, Universal Music Group, music video.

_____. "Rosenrot." November 2005, Universal Music Group, music video.

Bowler, Anne. "Politics as Art: Italian Futurism and Fascism." *Theory and Society* 20, no. 6 (December 1991): 763–794.

Brannigan, John. *New Historicism and Cultural Materialism*. Basingstoke: Macmillian, 1998.

Brown, Timothy S. "Subcultures, Pop Music and Politics: Skinheads and 'Nazi Rock' in England and Germany." *Journal of Social History* 38, no. 1 (Autumn 2004): 157–178.

Buchanan, Ian. *Fredric Jameson: Live Theory*. London: Continuum, 2006.

Callinicos, Alex. *An Anti-Capitalist Manifesto*. Cambridge: Polity Press, 2003.

Chowdhury, Kanishka. "Deflecting Crisis: Critiquing Capitalism's Emancipation Narrative." *Cultural Logic* (2011): 1–14.

Collins, Karen. "Dead Channel Surfing: The Commonalities Between Cyberpunk Literature and Industrial Music." *Popular Music* 24, no. 2 (May 2005): 165–178.

Feldman, Stephen M. "The Problem of Critique: Triangulating Habermas, Derrida, and

Gadamer Within Metamodernism." *Contemporary Political Theory* no. 4 (2005): 296–320.

Hardy, Simon. "The New Pornographies: Representation or Reality?" *Mainstreaming Sex: The Sexualization of Western Culture*, ed. Feona Attwood, 3–18. London: I.B. Tauris, 2009.

Harkin, Patricia. "The Reception of Reader-Response Theory." *College Composition and Communication* 56, no. 3 (February 2005): 410–425.

Heitmann, Jörn dir. "Ich Will." August 2001, Universal Music Group, music video.

_____. "Sonne." January 2002, Universal Music Group, music video.

Kahn-Harris, Keith. *Extreme Metal: Music and Culture on the Edge*. Oxford: Berg, 2007.

Kramer, Lawrence. *Interpreting Music*. Berkeley: University of California Press, 2011.

Krausz, Michael. "Intention and Interpretation: Hirsch and Margolis." *Intention & Interpretation*, ed. Gary Iseminger, 152–165. Philadelphia: Temple University Press, 1992.

Little, James. "Philosophico-Musical Vision: Badiou, Žižek, and Music." *International Journal of Žižek Studies* 5, no. 2 (2011): 1–14.

Longhurst, Brian. *Popular Music & Society*. Cambridge: Polity Press, 2007.

McLeod, Ken. "Space Oddities: Aliens, Futurism and Meaning in Popular Music." *Popular Music* 22, no. 3 (October 2003): 337–355.

Michaels, Sean. "Rammstein Album Ban Reversed." *The Guardian*, June 16, 2010, http://www.guardian.co.uk/music/2010/jun/16/rammstein-album-ban-reversed (accessed September 15, 2012).

Nathan, Daniel O. "Irony, Metaphor, and the Problem of Intention." *Intention & Interpretation*, ed. Gary Iseminger, 183–202. Philadelphia: Temple University Press, 1992.

Oestereicher, Emil. "Fascism and the Intellectuals: The Case of Italian Futurism." *Social Research* 41, no. 3 (Autumn 1974): 515–533.

Rammstein. "Amerika." *Amerika* 2004, Motor Music Records, compact disc, track 1.

_____. *Amerika*, 2004, Motor Music Records, compact disc.

_____. *Asche zu Asche*, 2001, Motor Music Records, compact disc.

_____. "Engel." *Sehnsucht*, 1997, Motor Music Records/Slash Records, track 2.

_____. *Engel*, 1997, Motor Music Records, compact disc.

_____. *Feuer Frei!*, 2002, Motor Music Records, compact disc.

_____. *Herzeleid*, 1995, Motor Music Records, compact disc.

_____. "Ich tu dir weh." *Liebe ist für Alle Da*, 2009, Universal Records/Vagrant Records, compact disc, track 2.

_____. *Liebe ist für Alle Da*, 2009, Universal Records/Vagrant Records, compact disc.

_____. "Links 2-3-4." *Links 2-3-4* 2001, Motor Music Records, compact disc, track 1.

_____. "Links 2-3-4." *Völkerball* 2006, Universal Music Group, DVD, track 2.

_____. *Live Aus Berlin* 1999, Motor Music Records, DVD.

_____. *Made in Germany, 1995–2011* 2011, Universal Records, compact disc.

_____. "Mein Teil." *Reise, Reise*, 2004, Motor Music Records/Republic Records, compact disc, track 2.

_____. *Mutter*, 2001, Motor Music Records, compact disc.

_____. "Nebel." *Mutter*, 2001, Motor Music Records, compact disc, track 11.

_____. *Reise, Reise*, 2004, Motor Music Records/Republic Records, compact disc.

_____. *Rosenrot*, 2005, Universal Music Group, compact disc.

_____. *Sehnsucht*, 1997, Motor Music Records/Slash Records, compact disc

_____. "Stripped." *Stripped*, 1998, Motor Music Records, compact disc, track 1.

_____. *Völkerball*, 2006, Universal Music Group, DVD.

_____. "Weißes Fleisch." *Herzeleid*, 1995, Motor Music Records, compact disc, track 3.

Roberts, Adam. *Frederic Jameson*. London: Routledge, 2000.

Ross, Robert J.S. "From Antisweatshop to Global Justice to Antiwar: How the New New Left Is the Same and Different from the Old New Left." *Journal of World-Systems Research* 10, no. 1 (Winter 2004): 287–319.

Ryan, Kiernan. "Introduction." *New Historicism and Cultural Materialism: A Reader*, ed. Kiernan Ryan, ix–xviii. London: Arnold, 1996.

Sinnerbrink, Robert. "Goodbye Lenin? Žižek on Neoliberal Ideology and Post-Marxist Politics." *International Journal of Žižek Studies* 4, no. 2 (2010): 1–20.

Stölzl, Philipp dir. "Du Hast." April 1997, Universal Music Group, music video.

_____. "Du Riechst So Gut '98." May 1998, Universal Music Group, music video.

_____, and Sven Budelmann, dirs. "Stripped." August 1998, Universal Music Group, music video.

Tompkins, Jane P. "An Introduction to Reader-Response Criticism." *Reader-Response Criticism: From Formalism to Post-Structuralism*, ed. Jane P. Tompkins, ix–xxvi. Baltimore: Johns Hopkins University Press, 1980.

Travis, Molly Abel. *Reading Cultures: The Construction of Readers in the Twentieth Century.* Carbondale: Southern Illinois University Press, 1998.

Tucker, Bruce. "Narrative, Extramusical Form, and the Metamodernism of the Art Ensemble of Chicago." *Lenox Avenue: A Journal of Interarts Inquiry* 3 (1997): 29–41.

Vermeulen, Timotheus, and Robin van den Akker. "Notes on Metamodernism." *Journal of Aesthetics & Culture* 2 (2010): 1–14.

Weinstein, Valerie. "Reading Rammstein, Remembering Riefenstahl: 'Fascist Aesthetics' and German Popular Culture." In *Riefenstahl Screened: An Anthology of New Criticism*, ed. Neil Christian Pages, Mary Rhiel, and Ingeborg Majer-O'Sickey, 130–148. New York: Continuum, 2008.

Williams, Raymond. "From Base and Superstructure in Marxist Cultural Theory." *New Historicism and Cultural Materialism: A Reader*, ed. Kiernan Ryan, 22–28. London: Arnold, 1996.

Žižek, Slavoj. "Badiou: Notes from an Ongoing Debate." *International Journal of Žižek Studies* 1, no. 2 (2007): 1–15.

_____. *In Defense of Lost Causes*. London: Verso, 2008.

_____. *Living in the End Times*. London: Verso, 2011.

_____. "Multitude, Surplus, and Envy." *Rethinking Marxism* 19, no. 1 (January 2007): 46–58.

_____. *The Parallax View*. Cambridge: MIT Press, 2009.

_____. "Why Are Laibach and NSK Not Fascists?" *Retrogarde Reading Room*, http://www.reanimator.8m.com/NSK/zizek.html (accessed September 15, 2012).

_____. "'You May!'" *London Review of Books* 21, no. 6 (18 March 1999): 3–6. http://www.lrb.co.uk/v21/n06/slavoj-zizek/you-may (accessed September 15, 2012).

3

Rammstein Are Laibach for Adolescents and Laibach Are Rammstein for Grown-Ups[1]

DANIEL LUKES

"Our activity is above direct involvement. We are completely apolitical. We are not interested in actual political problems."[2]

"We've never written a political song in our life, and we probably never will"[3]

"Every kind of music is political. Laibach is just aware of it and openly admitting that"[4]

The relationship between Laibach and Rammstein is a dialectical one, which no serious interrogation of either band can, at this point, ignore. The bands share a musical and aesthetic palette, and an affiliation with a totalitarian aesthetics produced through a performance of Germanicity. The link between the two groups opens a space from which it is possible to identify ongoing conversations on the intersections between power, ideology, capitalism, and popular culture, specifically pop and rock music. How the two groups — one wildly successful on the global mainstream rock stage as well as the goth/industrial music scene which spawned it; the other a darling of critics, intellectuals, and assorted cultivators of angst — connect and intersect provides the semblance of a debate; one that hangs between Laibach's rigidly constructed identity as embodiment of critique, and Rammstein's identity as globally successful German rock band and brand.

The relationship of (strangely un-anxious) influence between Slovenian avant-industrial collective Laibach and German industrial metal band Rammstein offers a fruitful perspective through which to examine each band's articulations of aesthetic totalitarianism. Laibach explicitly foreground the political and historical elements of twentieth century central Europe's genocide and war-torn narrative, and legacy drawn between Fascism and Communism, even going as far as creating their own "state" and respective ministry of culture (*Neue Slowenische Kunst* translates to New Slovenian Art). For Laibach, industrial and martial music offer the opportunity to subvert, critique, and satirize what they perceive as the totalitarian impulse at the heart of the nation state and global capital alike. Their knowing, satiric covers of "innocent" pop songs (Europe, Opus, The Beatles), seek to bring out ideological mechanisms all too often disavowed in capitalist entertainment. Rammstein, by contrast, hark back to pre-national "Romantic" states which precede the sarcasm of Laibach's sardonic engagements. Where Laibach emphasize the collective and the aesthetic (the uniform, the flag), Rammstein present apolitical versions of the human body, as a fleshly canvas through which to enact individual, cyclical, and primordial dramas of endurance, will, violence, pain, and love. For Rammstein, the totalitarian hypermasculine body, maternal amniotic, and child-like innocence, are recurring signifiers employed in order to assemble seemingly timeless morality play spectacles of good, evil, lust, pain, and joy. Ones that offer a backdrop to their industrial metal pop songs which refuse to "mean" more than what they embody: a cathartic spectacle of fleshly absurdity and decadent *Lustmord*. But also ones which are envisaged through a de-politicizing deployment of Laibach's totalitarian aesthetics.

The two bands thus complement each other dialectically, a situation Laibach have explicitly acknowledged in interviews, seeming even grateful to Rammstein for providing the id to their super-ego. As they (collectively) comment: "Laibach does not believe in originality and we don't consider ourselves as sole authors and owners of our own ideas. Therefore, Rammstein could not 'steal' much from us. In a way, they have proven once again that a good 'copy' can make more money on the market than the 'original.' Anyhow, today we share the territory: Rammstein seem to be a kind of Laibach for adolescents and Laibach are Rammstein for 'grown-ups.'"[5]

Though the debt Rammstein owe to Laibach is largely musical and aesthetic, rather than ideological, conceptual, or political, and concerns a specific blend of barked dictator-style vocals and martial, march-influenced drum beats, rhythms and staccato metallic riffs, we seek here to investigate, following the work of Jacques Attali, how music is never "just music," but productively revelatory of the ideological maneuvers it seeks to enact, play down, and disavow.

Money/Capital

Canonical readings of Laibach, spearheaded by Alexei Monroe and his seminal and necessary monograph *Interrogation Machine: Laibach and NSK*

(2005), emphasize the band's role as critics of the system, whether that system be the totalitarian regime in power during the time of their formation — the regime of Marshal Josip Broz Tito —or the pro–Western system of international global capitalism and the persistence of nationalistic politics at the heart of the fragmentation of the Socialist Federal Republic of Yugoslavia and the Yugoslav Wars between 1991 and 2001. Critical and intellectual appraisals of Laibach's early work, including a younger Slavoj Žižek, discuss Laibach as an ironic commentary on the totalitarian regime, which throws back in the face of totalitarianism its own underlying beliefs. By offering a more exaggerated version of totalitarianism's own aesthetics and ideological modes, Laibach lay bare the lie of a power system that professes to be for the people but in fact is for an elect/unelected few: Laibach "demask and recapitulate,"[6] critiquing power, raising anti-authoritarian consciousness, laying bare the ideological pulse hidden beneath the face of official culture. In the wake of Throbbing Gristle, early pioneers who birthed the industrial movement —"Industrial Records" was how they christened their own record label — Laibach cast the pop group as paramilitary avant-garde art collective: by founding NSK (*Neue Slovenische Kunst*) in 1984, Laibach actualized for themselves a ministry of art and aesthetics, taking care of theatrical performances and figurative art. What is often forgotten however, in critical engagements with the band's ideological actions and maneuvers, is that Laibach is primarily a popular music band, though their activities cross over into contemporary performance art. Comparing their activities with Rammstein — a rock band that draws from theater and the avant-garde in places, may hopefully shed light on paradigms articulated by both bands' intersecting careers.

A phrase by Françoise Thom is very instructive when thinking of the methodology of influence between Laibach and Rammstein: "Communist power has understood that in order to get rid of an undesirable object, it is better to counterfeit it rather than simply suppress it. For the copy destroys the real object more surely than physical demolition should" (Monroe 228).[7] This is arguably Laibach's own technique towards the pop culture artifacts they engage with: to pass themselves off as a copy of something in order to destroy the unchallenged face of its integrity. Monroe enters into fascinating close readings of Laibach's albums, and their clever and de/reterritorializing use of cover songs: displacing the authenticity of the original with something more troubling, they suggest objects which have come loose and lost their place. By pulling out the button and cutting the string, Laibach threaten to unravel the whole coat of pop music, and its role in maintaining institutionalized power: "A group from an obscure Slav nation who did not even sing exclusively in English sold back to the West its own supposedly global, borderless product with a distinctive and unapologetic national element" (232).

Monroe's analysis of the relationship between "authentic" Western brand product and cheaper Eastern copy is configured as a praise of Laibach who have managed to impose themselves in the West as a brand: "Laibach's ideological problematization of the consumption of pop-cultural history has no obvious Western counterpart" (233). They have, as it were, invented their own subgenre: subaltern totalitarian industrial. Elsewhere Monroe commends Laibach's use of merchandising as yet another avenue through which their comparison between product fetishism and totemic totalitarianism takes place (186–7). Though in spite of "the conceptual depth behind ... these mere products" (186), what makes Laibach's use of merchandise qualitatively different from say, that of Kiss, who also adopt the symbolism of the army (Kiss Army) to rally and promote unity among fans, is not entirely apparent. If anything, it is their merch which fingers Laibach as a conventional pop/rock band. Laibach thus exist in an ambiguous relationship to capitalism which seemingly cannot help but co-opt them. If, as Thom states, communism seeks to get rid of an undesirable by replacing it, then capitalism seeks to multiply a desirable object by replicating it and mass-producing it. Rammstein are the mass-market Laibach, who are themselves already a brand and proliferator of products on the market: where the latter cultivate intellectual appraisal in small circles and underground elites and scenes, Rammstein court the stadiums of Western Europe and North America. Their sound is bold, brash, slick and polished, a "totalitarian" and capitalist improvement on the over-intellectualized old model: brawn over brain, tabloid present over historical past.

The cover song is the form of copy that Laibach trade in. Their covers, which they occupy with the finality of an invading army, are Laibach's calling card. Not only through covers have Laibach critiqued the West, but through covers they have engaged and conquered it. This is how the West was won, in their case: by creating demand for a product and fulfilling that demand, the product being a critique of Western pop's inability to go beyond a certain point of self-criticism within the bounds of the pop song itself. Laibach erected a new type of pop song: able to see into and beyond itself further than it had previously been able to do. There is little doubt that had Laibach remained an experimental industrial crew obsessed with noise, harshness, and industrial replications of factory and totalitarian sonics, there is no way they would have reached the audience or had the career they have had. Laibach's artistic legacy is their ability to reinterpret, to "retroquote" (Monroe 30). They are thus of a movement which seeks not to destroy but to further canonize pop music, by making it more self-aware. Laibach's covers of songs such as "One Vision" (which they rename "Geburt Einer Nation"— Birth of a Nation), "Sympathy for the Devil," "Jesus Christ Super Star," Europe's "The Final Countdown," and — a song that would be otherwise have been lost in the graveyard of one hit wonders, Opus' "Life Is Life,"— seek and find meaning in cultural productions otherwise dismissible as trivial. Laibach function as an archival, even anthropological attempt to restore significance to cultural productions ignored at our peril. They are a cultural studies department in the guise of a rock band: no wonder they are a hit among academics.

The cover is also an opening to both bands' relationship with Nazism, the Nazi aesthetic, and Nazi-Kunst — specifically the latter. Rammstein have covered a few songs, including Kraftwerk's "Das Modell" and The Ramones' "Pet Sematary," but it is their 1998 cover of Depeche Mode's "Stripped" that brought them much in the way of international attention. Along with a suave beefing up of the original song, which acquires in the honeyed jowls of vocalist Till Lindemann a slow-burning erotic quality — the Rammstein vocalist is never as compelling as when he plays vulnerable — the song was accompanied by a video montage of Leni Riefenstahl's 1938 film *Olympia* with its idealized athletic Aryan bodies. Here Rammstein made their appearance, as if caught in the act of grabbing the bull of their perceived Nazi aesthetic tendencies by it horns: tendencies that had arguably been actively stoked and courted by the band themselves. The very aestheticization of politics, the commingling of aesthetics and politics that Nazism achieved and employed, is precisely that which causes "cautious" over-reaction in well-meaning anti-fascists,[8] who see political deviance where there is perhaps merely aesthetic, or better yet, commercial provocation. From a commercial point of view, the "Stripped" Olympia video was a brilliant move, putting Rammstein on the global (and English-speaking) map as incendiarists and provocateurs, whilst also making them more accessible to Anglophone markets.

A partial reworking of Laibach's long-developed aesthetic performance of totalitarianism, Rammstein's totalitarian aesthetic also represents a manner of successfully commercializing Nazified Germanicity on a global scale. As Monroe amply documents, Laibach's relation to Germanicity is a relation to national identity and ideologies and practices of domination and war: the name "Laibach" is a German name for the town of Ljubljana, which goes back to 1144, and reappears again with the Nazi Wehrmacht. Both bands represent and embody the paradox of a Germanicity from which it seems impossible to remove the taint of Nazism. Yet both arguably profit from this ideological process: the issue of how to conceive of Germany outside of Nazism. Both bands interrogate, in their own ways, the matter of a Nazism without end: the ironies of "never again" repetitions of the concentration camp and eugenicist notions of bodily perfectibility. As Monroe notes: "Laibach's fusion of the dynamics of the totalitarian rally and the rock concert suggests that totalitarianism is a contemporary force rather than a historical phenomenon, and that popular music has an inherent totalitarian potential that various regimes use for their own ends" (184–5).

Current trends in both literature, art, and critical theory find much mileage in stressing continuities between fascist and totalitarian regimes and contemporary global neoliberal capitalism: Agamben's hook in his most notable book, Homo Sacer, is the j'accuse that the "camp" remains the paradigm of contemporary modernity, from Guantanamo Bay detention camp to the Yugoslav War prison camps to the refugee camps across the globe. Agamben's move posits itself as a counterpoint to dominant strands within the memory and trauma studies field and industry, which insists on the exceptionality of the Holocaust: a movement viewable as contributing towards the giving of ideological carte blanche to the abuses of the Israeli state. The exceptionality or not of the Nazis is the bone of contention between two recent hit novels; Laurent Binet's *HHhH* (2009) and Jonathan Littell's *The Kindly Ones* (Les Bienveillantes 2006), to which Binet's book acts as a necessary footnote and foil. Binet animalizes Nazis à la Orwell or Spiegelman (Bormann and Göring are "fat pig[s]"[9]; Heydrich, nicknamed "The Goat" as a child, also has a "horsey face"; Himmler is "a little hamster in glasses" [Binet "28"]), characterizing them as psychopathic murderers, and pathologizing Nazism as an aberration. Littell by contrast takes the time and effort to imagine the normality of Nazis. Men — mostly men — with thoughts, ethical dilemmas, conscripted into a system of career and officialdom, where the most bizarre sadistic acts are rationalized according to the good: the state, the people, and their quality of life.[10] Littell traces the every day life of fascism and the fascism of everyday life, making a compelling argument that you, the reader, might not have behaved differently than they did. Of Eichmann, Littell's narrator Maximilien Aue says:

> A lot of stupid things have been written about him: he was certainly not *the enemy of mankind* described at Nuremberg ... nor was he an incarnation of *banal evil*, a soulless, faceless robot, as some sought to present him after his trial. He was a very talented bureaucrat, extremely competent at his functions, with a certain stature and a considerable sense of personal initiative ... as a middle manager he would have been the pride of any European firm ... he could just have easily done something else.[11]

Of another officer, the narrator says, "[H]e wasn't the only one, this man, everyone was like him, I too was like him, and you too, in his place, you would have been like him" (Littell 783). It is obvious which one is the more controversial literary success story.

Violence/Power

Laibach's aesthetic political enterprise hinges on the Shakespearian dictum that things are not always as they may seem: power has a vested interest in reproducing itself through frontal fictions that disavow the inner workings of the machine. The Eastern Bloc, represented in such a film as Florian Henckel von Donnersmarck's *Das Leben der Anderen* (2006), is portrayed as a universe defined by dichotomy: public/private, official/underground, secret/imposed, a life of wire-taps and betrayal, actions and words reported to a secret police force in the function of a corrupt and unaccountable authority. But the dichotomy between the repressed East and the free, liberated West is a lie, argue Laibach, and one through which the West disavows and furthers its own authoritarian abusive power structures. It does so, argue Laibach, following Adorno, Althusser, and Žižek, among others, partly through popular culture, with pop music playing a blandishing role, lulling the masses into the rhythms of work and play, making capitalism comfortable and sweet to swallow.

Emmanuel Malchiodi deconstructs Katy Perry's use of candy and sexuality in the name of commerce, making the Laibachian connection between the ideological modalities adopted by fascist regimes and those adopted by us, free non-fascists: "I love her music, referring to it on a regular basis as the equivalent of Nazi marching songs but for consumerism. Basically, you're supposed to put on one of her songs, march right down to the mall, and purchase as many fluorescent colored Miami shirts as you can from American Apparel."[12] From a linguistic point of view, pop music rallies the shock troops of linguistic Anglo-Imperialism: in the liner notes of *Volk* (2006), their album of reinterpretations of national anthems and patriotic songs, Laibach quote Michael Stewart, British Secretary of State for Foreign Affairs in 1968: "Pop culture has done more for the expansion of English language dominance in the world than the British Empire did. The Beatles and The Rolling Stones are our most effective weapon of colonization."[13] Rammstein's use of the German tongue is a direct affront to the pop market as tool for global domination of English language, and their success in Anglophone countries is a performative validation against Anglophonic hegemony (even though the function this success may perform is that of exception proving the rule). *Süddeutsche Zeitung Magazin*'s recent cover story of the band on their latest U.S. tour, is proud to present them as "Deutschland's biggest misunderstanding — and at the same time Deutschland's largest culture export."[14] In this regard, Rammstein are a major player for contemporary Germany and new conceptions of Germanicity, the band's international rise paralleling Germany's top dog status and clout in the European Union, under Chancellor Angela Merkel.

Pop music lulls the masses, but in our postmodern world in which part of every alert citizen's ideological lifeworld is a paranoid awareness of the ubiquity of power and its breaches, pop must incorporate its own critique: the most common way this occurs is in the form of nods to social utopianism. Swedish quartet Ace of Base, themselves a cloned reproduction of ABBA, played this note on their 1993 hit "Happy Nation": to a droning Enigma-esque choral Latin mantra the physically "perfect" (and related) two woman (a blonde and a brunette), and two man (a slim and buff type) pop group extolled the virtues of a perfect society with lyrics that describe living in a happy nation, where understanding, and the dream of human perfection and the social good have arrived, and mankind has found salvation in brotherhood. A mournful note of doubt arrives at the end of the song indicating that they've "gone too far."[15] A nod to the excesses of totalitarianisms which went beyond, to define a limit case for the acceptability of human behavior in the twentieth century. I would await the Laibach cover of this song if it weren't already so Laibachian.

Laibach's sonic methodology is to introduce violence — sonic violence — into the structures of a previously familiar, commonly recognized-as-pleasing piece of music, in order to show the violence that was already inherent within it, but which the music was itself employed in disavowing. Music thus becomes both an expression of and a metaphor for power which hides its own mechanisms. Jacques Attali has written on music as a form of ideological inculcation in the service of power. *His Noise: The Political Economy of Music* (1977) traces a genealogy of music through the politics of how music is separated from noise: the legislation of sound, and noise into sound and music. For Attali music is both a product of power and a tool in the service of the power that seeks to define it through legal and economic regulation. Attali identifies three stages in the history of music, "three strategic usages of music by power"[16]:

> In one of these zones, it seems that music is used and produced in the ritual in an attempt to make people *forget* the general violence; in another, it is employed to make people *believe* in the harmony of the world, that there is order in exchange and legitimacy in commercial power; and finally, there is one in which it serves to *silence*, by mass-producing a deafening, syncretic kind of music, and censoring all other human noises.[16]

"What is called music today is all too often only a disguise for the monologue of power" (9), Attali states, arguing that contemporary music reconfigures modernity's industrial noise into pleasing sound: the incessant buzzing and endless hum and rumble of the city, the whirr of machines, the hum of traffic. Music conspires to "make repetitive society tolerable" (118).

Attali is writing just before industrial music puts a critique of pop music into a practice: one which forges a conscious response to pop's numbing effects, out of the very materials of machinic and industrial noise that pop seeks to make pleasant; the alienating and dehumanizing factories that pop presents itself as opioid antidote to. The extent to which collaborationist pop then folds industrial music's critique back into its lulling function is one of the major points debated in this essay in the confrontation and dialogue between Laibach and Rammstein.

Laibach's early works grind and pummel martial and patriotic music, their latter releases teutonize classics of the Western canon and campy pop hits: Nazifying them, Laibach ramp up the camp, revealing and critiquing both the originals' camp and that which that camp provided cover for, the mechanisms of power. In many ways Laibach paved the way for Rammstein: by the time of Rammstein's arrival, their crunchy, martial industrial metal would resonate as familiar; in dialectic and capitalist fashion, Laibach would then reap the rewards of Rammstein's popularization of that sound. Pop's aptitude for fagocitation ingests and reconfigures the fringes of noise genres: noise, industrial, metal, hardcore, punk, electronics. Where Laibach's sound is a gallery of depths and surfaces, trap doors, citations and file cabinets, Rammstein offer a smooth surface defined by the riff. Rammstein's riff sound is a polished version of *Psalm 69*–era Ministry (1991), specifically the songs "N.W.O." and "Just One Fix," which remain the de facto blueprint for the industrial metal genre. Rammstein's *Herzeleid* (1995) presents a crisp, compressed, compact version of this foundational riff, enriched by Till Lindemann's emphatic, clipped vocal. The "Herzeleid" title track is a masterpiece of such compression, even featuring a Hitler-esque vocal explosion half way through the song: the track builds majestically, constructing from the inexorable grind a climactic keyboard-tinkering pinnacle during the bridge. "Herzeleid" takes Ministry's juggernaut riff in the service of political outrage, and gently presses it into pop song format, a song about heartache ("Herzeleid"). The album's artwork appears to acknowledge this very process by representing Rammstein as a boy band, with naked, oiled torsos, stylized haircuts, and posing in front of a torrid flower — a Gerbera daisy: a hothouse exoticism dominates the cover, which is complemented by negative icy blues in the booklet. The band poke fun at themselves as a pop band as a way of admitting their pop credentials. Rammstein's pitch-perfect calibration on this matter has generated dividends; they are a band who have been embraced by the mainstream without losing their scene credibility, and their success is due to their songwriting prowess as much as it is to the acuity with which they've known how to present and market themselves. Rammstein have learned from Laibach, and have perfected their lesson, modifying their style and adapting it to a mass audience, reducing their political component and largely replacing it with depoliticized case studies of sexual perversion, unrequited love, and occasional comedy.

In Laibach, violence is ubiquitous, a state function, the modality of power and biopolitics, the methodology of resistance: the iconic cover of live album *Ljubljana–Zagreb–Beograd* features early frontman Tomaž Hostnik, posing in an officer's uniform onstage with blood dripping down his chin due to projectiles thrown from a hostile crowd in 1982 at the New Rock Festival at Krizanke. He would commit suicide in December 1982.[17] For Rammstein violence is an event, an anecdotal and heavily romanticized one at that. The band's lyrical, conceptual, and visual treatment of violence draws from the tabloid imaginary, as does their name: a unique and tragic anecdotal event involving fiery death, but devoid of political ramifications. "Mein Teil" is exemplary of this approach: a song invested in recreating the sick scenario of a sexualized murder; a Weimarian case of *Lustmord*, and an exotic perversion. As in *Silence of the Lambs* the spectator is rendered privy to a *Grand Guignol* tale of sadism and murder: that this case is consensual squares the seductive and fatal non sequitur of its narrative logic; the story can only flow into the ritual of catharsis, encapsulated within the form of the pop song. Rammstein's depoliticization of Laibach's message thus involves the process of configuring violence not as general and ubiquitous, but specific and localized, subject to episodic and specific narrativization and theatrical representation.

Sex/Eros

In the section he calls "Die Liebe Ist die Grösste Kraft" (Love Is the Greatest Power) (72–4) Monroe pinpoints a major element he argues differentiates fascist from capitalist regimes' employment of ideology: contemporary corporate capitalism is more "fun." Where, in totalitarianism, desire is strictly produced as a channeling of duty and love towards the state or its embodied figurehead, in capitalism's dispositions of apparent choice and freedoms, it is "love" that represents the ultimate node around which pop ideology composes itself. Laibach's totalitarianization of Queen's "One Vision," and their relationship to Queen in a larger sense, provide an axiomatic example of Laibach's satiric methodology, and the points they wish to make about what the two systems have in common. "The Concert as Totalitarian Spectacle" understands the structural similarities between the two types of event — suggested by Pink Floyd's *The Wall*, which features a rock concert as fascist rally — and the desire for annihilation of the individual self in the "oceanic" feeling induced by a crowd focusing on one central figure onstage, the lead singer or dictator[18]:

"Laibach view Freddie Mercury as a highly successful politician able to command mass audiences" (Monroe 186).[19]

> Despite the ambivalent sexual persona of Freddie Mercury, Queen were the most successful of all stadium rock groups, and their fans' mass devotion to him exemplified the rock star as *Übermensch*. Laibach retroactively transformed *One Vision* into or revealed it as Fascistic hymn to power, an effect amplified by the bombastic militaristic arrangement and harsh German vocal. The opening bars set a militant, uncompromising tone that creates the uncanny impression that the song is the natural expression of Laibach's *Weltanschauung*. The lyrics have obviously sinister connotations when they are sung in German by a group such as Laibach: "One man, one goal, one solution." After exposure to Laibach's intervention, Queen's song loses its innocence and apoliticality. Laibach are not ascribing any specific hidden agenda to Queen ... but amplifying or "making strange" the structures of unquestioning adulation (and obedience) common to both totalitarian mass mobilization and capitalist mass consumption [Monroe 228–9].

The only detail I would quibble with here, and it's a significant detail, is Monroe's idea of Queen's success achieved "despite" Freddie Mercury's ambivalent sexual persona. It would seem to me that this aspect of Mercury's performativity is on the contrary quite central to Queen's aesthetic: his moustachioed sexy housewife drag in the video for "I Want to Break Free" (1984) finds extension throughout Queen's oeuvre, considerably informing their appeal. Monroe's refusal to engage with Mercury's queer sexuality is Laibachian in its mirroring of the band's tendency to downplay and sublimate sexuality, and castigate sexual deviance as a trope of decadent capitalism. This condemnatory equation of sexual deviance with the excesses of Western capitalism constitutes, for example, Laibach's dissociation from Throbbing Gristle (TG).[20] Within the logic of Laibach's strategy of adapting and configuring their aesthetic from a bricolage of the frontal, surface elements of aesthetic totalitarianism, it makes total sense that sexuality would appear in Laibach only in the form of an ideological sublimation: women, if they appear at all, are as chaste and loving mothers and daughters, or adoring sirens of the regime.[21] Sex for Laibach is an eros, sublimated and employed in the upkeep of the totalitarian state.[22]

Freddie Mercury's moustache, an unfashionable insignia on an '80s pop star, exoticizes, eroticizes, and queers Stalin's totalitarian one: the rock star as sexually ambiguous dictator. By eroticizing totalitarian tropes, pop music renders them palatable, desirable, and "fun." Laibach's work is then to de-eroticize Queen, to subtract its erotic and queer qualities and "straighten" them out: their cover functions as a de-eroticization of the song, transforming Queen's vibrant, bouncing, flowing and euphoric grooves into a martial, robotic, clanging, pained and disciplined onslaught. Frontman and singer Milan Fras' face, put in prominent and dominant position within Laibach's videos, reclaims Mercury's moustache as a totalitarian one, performing a knowingly absurd form of de-campifying camp: a totalitarian aesthetic produced through an overcoming of the sexual ambiguity, or outright gayness of Queen. It is this state of tension, between totalitarian repression and an acknowledgment of how the West softens fascism by sexualizing, queering, and feminizing it, which then Rammstein exploit as if it were a Trojan Horse in Laibach's armament: re-sexualizing the de-sexualized, and giving prime place to the homoerotic element of fascism that Laibach, in order to remain "in character," must refuse to openly engage. If, in Laibach "the state is idealized, and takes the place of the traditional love-object in the pop song" (Monroe 219), then in Rammstein the repressed traditional love object returns with a vengeance, a writhing and sprawling polymorphous perverse; one that finds expression through and beyond a totalitarianizing aesthetic. If Laibach is the adult citizen who has sublimated erotic drives into state duty, Rammstein is the rebellious, sexually-obsessed and unfulfilled adolescent.

Looking for a hook by which to promote an unlikely rising star, and a problematic one due to their foreignness, U.K. rock magazine *Kerrang!* settled on sexual perversion as the audience's designated "in" to the alien world of Rammstein. Their coverage emphasized notions of specifically German sexual permissiveness, cast as perversion, that the band themselves capitalize on. Two *Kerrang!* cover stories pressed primarily on this button. April 21, 2001's cover story featured a photoshoot of the band in S&M gear, latex and eyeliner, with guitarist Richard Z. Kruspe clad in a dog collar/leash/gag, union jack draped around his nether regions, and a light blue contact lens in left eye. The cover promised a peek "Inside the world's most perverse band!" The photoshoot for the October 23, 2004, Rammstein issue featured the band in drag, dressed in vintage women's military uniforms. This time the cover promised "Murder! Drugs! Cross-Dressing!" and a companion article on "the 20 most outrageous bands ever!"

Rammstein's Germanicity as sexual permissiveness, has allowed them to follow three interconnecting strands of sex and eros: self-contained narratives of perverse and sadistic Weimarian *Lustmord*, seen through a contemporary tabloid mentality ("Mein Teil," "Wiener Blut"); eros as Romantic longing and unrequited love often accompanied by seductive and siren-like female backing vocals; and finally the comic lust and pornography of "Pussy," the "Mein Teil" and "Mann Gegen Mann" videos, and performative aspects of the band such as Till Lindemann's onstage "sodomy" of keyboardist Christian "Flake" Lorenz and "ejaculation" onto the audience.[23] Rammstein construct a fleshly canvas of the militarized male body onto which to drape individual dramas of lust and loss: beneath the baggage of history and politics, Till Lindemann's lyrical narratives probe the mysteries of the flesh, biologically intended. The human is animal above and beneath all ("Tier"). The cut-up cadavers floating in amniotic formaldehyde of *Mutter*'s artwork belie a romantic vision of humanity, doomed to repeat its oedipal and ancestral dramas which are due to human nature, not political destiny. The specter of Nazism is close by. The prism of the Nazi sadist, through which Rammstein implicitly represent unregenerate and patriarchal masculinity, is comparable to the one that provides the narrative core to Stieg Larsson's *Män som hatar kvinnor* ("Men who hate women": translated into English as *The Girl with the Dragon Tattoo*, 2005), where the Nazi is also child abuser and serial murderer, and whose corruption trickles down into the world of contemporary finance. The success of Rammstein's aesthetic no doubt in part owes a debt to their ability to capitalize on the Nazified male body as central repository of all our worst fears about the links between violence and masculinity.

If Laibach begets Rammstein, what or whom does Rammstein beget? Slavoj Žižek argues that Rammstein's music "de-semanticizes" totalitarian ideology, showing "up its obscene babble in its intrusive materiality."[24] By erasing the ironic distance between fascist tropes and our own Western post-war congenitally anti-fascist sensibility, Rammstein, according to Žižek, neutralize fascism by emphasizing its own absurdities. But Žižek's distinction "between an appeasing techno (which clearly does 'operate within the system') and the unleashed brutality of Rammstein which undermines the system not through some critical-utopian vision but through the obscene brutality of the immersion it enacts" (Žižek 386) bears some scrutiny. Perhaps the Slovenian philosopher is over-estimating the extent of Rammstein's sonic *Sturm und Drang*, which coming in the wake of Metallica's mainstream success, finds the bourgeois household now friendly and receptive to the heavy metal riff, previously thought of as sonic embodiment of the anti-social. Rammstein may be "for adolescents," but their fanbase includes many adults.

The post–Rammstein rock scene includes such similar-sounding *Neue Deutsche Härte* bands as Oomph!, Eisbrecher, and Megaherz, Norway's Gothminister and The Kovenant, and Finnish band Ruoska. Within the goth-industrial scene, in the wake of Laibach and the industrial and neo-folk genre, which deepened and cultivated punk's use of the swastika into a World War II/Nazi aesthetic (NON/Boyd Rice, Death in June, Current 93 and Sol Invictus), military attire has become de rigueur, with countless bands adopting gothic variations of military and World War I and II clothing and hairstyles. Contemporary EBM and industrial bands adapt and domesticate Laibach and others' adoption of world war, Nazi and totalitarian aesthetics, generally emptying them of all political content, and reverting to the "empty" signifier that Dick Hebdige sees in punk's use of the swastika.[25] American industrial metal duo Hanzel und Gretyl base most of their output around a concept of pseudo–Nazi imagery and sound: clipped, staccato riffs of the Ministry school, to which are set barked Germanic vocals, which further twist and empty of their political commentary Laibach's barked Germanisms. H&G turns out corny, yet kitschily effective puns and constructions ("Third Reich from the Sun," "SS Death Star Supergalactik," "Verbotenland") on their 2003 album — what else?—*Über Alles*. For Hanzel und Gretyl, any political critique is entirely subsumed in a Nazism that has become pure aesthetic, with no pretensions to making any statement on Nazism beyond one of camp fetish fashion. Unlike *Star Wars*, which still offers room for ideological readings, here Nazism is enjoyed for its aesthetic value alone, with H&G's female lead singer (Vas Kallas) building on "Stalag" exploitation sex fiction for their Nazi-kitsch schtick. Austrian EBM act Nachtmahr, a project of L'Âme Immortelle's Thomas Rainer, furthers the process of absorption of totalitarian kitsch into a mainstream "appeasing techno" goth/industrial sound. The lyrics to Nachtmahr's "Can You Feel the Beat?" (2011) trace an undisguised correlation between the activities of an international music act, touring, releasing records, garnering fans across the globe, and an invading reich.[26] Another song waxes lyrical about "Mädchen in Uniform," and Nachtmahr's artwork and photoshoots frequently present an erotic Nazi aesthetic: one which "playfully" configures Nazism as just a bit of bedroom fun, or cultural light BDSM. Aesthetic Nazism lives on in the goth scene as a sexual fetish: the world of leather, latex, and domination that Rammstein have also made their dungeon playroom.

Travel/Occupy

In "Stripped: Pop und Affirmation bei Kraftwerk, Laibach und Rammstein" Ulf Poschardt groups Kraftwerk and Laibach together as politically-informed, critical and ironic groups against Rammstein, for whom he reserves a more negative judgment calling their music and aesthetic empty, trivial, and cynical "Marketing-Kindergarten."[27] Springing from the post-war late '60s environment of Willy Brandt's anti-fascistic politics Kraftwerk articulate a commentary on perceptions of Germanicity abroad. Concerned as they are with the impact of technology on daily living, travel is one of the primary avenues through which "Powerstation" (which is how we could translate "Kraftwerk") direct their technical music. Modes of transport come under specific scrutiny: the car (1974 album *Autobahn*, which also contains a critique of Germans favorably-inclined to Nazi-constructed motorways); the train (1977 album *Trans-Europe Express*); and the bicycle (1983 single "Tour de France," which captures a snapshot of the mass media sporting event). *Trans-Europe Express* chugs and puffs to the rhythm of the train, casting a sly, ironic glance at peace-time commercial travel around Europe: post-war prosperity and the soft invasions of transnational commerce and the enlargement of the growing European Union. The protagonists of *TEE* are suave and dapper young businessmen for whom Europe is an idyllic playground: the lyrics of "Europe Endless" describe a crystal world of in which "Life is timeless" and parks, hotels and palaces, avenues and promenades make a picture postcard life of "Elegance and Decade." The title track describes a "Rendezvous on Champs Élysées," then a departure from Paris in the morning with *TEE*, a late night café encounter in Vienna, another shift back to Düsseldorf, and a meeting with those Anglophone symbols of trans–European sophistication: Iggy Pop and David Bowie. International pop stands as a symbol for growing postwar international capitalism under the English tongue, but behind the glossy surface dark shadows lurk: the history of the train as a mechanism for genocidal transportation to KL (Konzentrationslager), a one-way journey to death. *TEE*'s booklet interposes soft-focus images of the band members dressed as suave and dapper European cosmopolitans with harsher black and white images endowed with a distinctly World War II flavor: in one of them the band are posing on Gleis (Platform) 17 of Düsseldorf station; Gleis 17 in Berlin's Grunewald station is where many of the city's Jews were deported to concentration camps from.

For the international market, Kraftwerk perform a kind of exaggerated Germanicity, a robotic stiffness which parodies the clichéd image of the German abroad, between mad scientist and robot. Lester Bangs' 1975 feature on the band gives band leader Ralf Hütter the opportunity to describe the cultural manifestations of the German World War II defeat, which involve a supplanting of the Germanic with U.S. culture: "After the war," said Hütter, "German entertainment was destroyed. The German people were robbed of their culture, putting an American head on it. I think we are the first generation born after the war to shake this off ... we are the first German group to record in our own language, use our electronic background, and create a Central European identity for ourselves."[28] This specific German identity is one that is based on an internalization and critique of post-war Nazified perceptions of Germany, ones which Rammstein are still grappling with forty years later, though within a different political and economic context: that of global market capitalism.

Laibach, who have released two *Trans Slovenia Express* compilation albums of Slovene artists covering Kraftwerk, in 1994 and 2005, which examine "the broader framework of Slovenian vs. Trans-European cultural identity,"[29] and bring back into the present the historical baggage Kraftwerk seek to look beyond: for Laibach, transit within Europe means war and occupation. They give their tours such names as "The Occupied Europe Tour" (1983) and "United States of Europe" (1987). For Laibach war and totalitarianism are not a historical past, but, from the vantage of their viewpoint in the Balkans, first a prediction for the future, and then a reality of the present. Nationalism is not a problem of image on the international scale, but the bloody pretext for war: Laibach's 1994 album *NATO* is a cutting critique of the failures of Western involvement in the Yugoslav wars, its liner notes starkly mocking the body's determination to "safeguard freedom, common heritage and civilization" and its resolution to "promote stability, security and well-being in the North Atlantic area."[30]

If for Kraftwerk travel is a matter of pleasurable commerce and reconstruction, or the healthy recreationism of a nation-binding sport such as the Tour de France, for Laibach travel is mobilization, onslaught, marching armies and stomping boots, characterized by the siren, the loudspeaker, and that familiar "sound of the 1930s: the ominous drone of a propeller aircraft" (Monroe 237). WAT's 2003 album *Now You Will Pay* forces into a pounding martial techno number a guttural prediction of what awaits the West, comfortable in the self-imposed illusions of its arrogant dominance: with gutturally intoned lyrics Fras announces, "Barbarians are coming / Crawling from the East / (With their) eyes wide shut / And nostrils full of longing / Epic and powerful / Wild in a group.... They'll come out of nowhere / They'll enter your state / The nation of losers / The tribe full of hate / With knives in their pockets / And bombs in their hands / They'll burn down your cities / And your Disneylands."[31] Laibach's 2006 album *Volk* furthered the band's theme of international nationalisms, seeing Laibach, in collaboration with Slovenian band Silence, cover and rework national anthems and patriotic songs, adding lyrics sung by Milan Fras which function as a critical commentary on the patriotic sentiments expressed in the original songs. Listening to this album is an uncanny experience, especially where another pop band has previously harnessed a national anthem, such Pet Shop Boys' cover of The Village People's "Go West," which incorporates elements of the Soviet national anthem, and whose accompanying video combined Soviet with U.S. symbolism. On "Germania," Fras describes the German condition as one defined by a fall and a search for redemption based in the abandonment of the idea of the nation. After the unspeakable, in which Germany has fallen as only angels can, the nation is instructed to go find its peace, go home and grow its tree, and think no more of victory, defeat, shame, or Fatherland, but rather Unity, Justice and Freedom for all. This is the lesson Germany must learn, now and in the future.[32]

Kraftwerk's *TEE* flows gently to the lulling rhythm of the train: Laibach's "Young Europa Pts 1–10," from their 1993 album *Kapital*, a largely instrumental album and "statement on the new world order, commenting on the transition of Slovenia's (and the rest of Central and Eastern Europe's) economies from command to market,"[33] illustrates how this beat offers a lulling trance-effect: "Come, be with me" repeats a seductive female voice. For Laibach the fetishization of global capitalism under the guise of sexy cosmopolitanism involves a disavowal of its politics of violence and inequality: we travel to forget ourselves as we establish our supremacy as Westerners. Perhaps because they deal with it first-hand as an international touring band, travel is one of the fields in which Rammstein are at their least apolitical: on the topic of travel, Rammstein have something political to say, perhaps, initially at least partly due to their own history as East Germans first "looking in" to the West, and then becoming Westerners. Rammstein's growing openness to the topic of internationalism coincides with their growing success on the international stage. Their first three albums articulate a Teutonic and martial industrial sound involving lyrical and subject mutter very much founded on a primordial, a-national yet Germanic romantic self, beset by agonies and euphorias of emotion and sexuality. The exception, *Sehnsucht*'s title track, with its Orientalist melodies and its gaze at global nature, from Africa to Mexico, anticipates the conceptual opening up at the level of location, travel, internationalism, that will occur on the band's second trio of albums. *Reise, Reise* (2004), bearing out the "Travel, Travel" connotation of the title, references the city of Moscow and the continent of (North) America, the globally-roaming figure of the "Dalai Lama," and features lyrics sung in Russian and a French song-title "Amour." The album's artwork features battered and twisted metal of an aeroplane crash and a damaged black box, referencing a 1985 Japanese airplane crash, and was recorded between Malaga in Spain and Stockholm. After the self-imposed Germanicity of the band's earlier output, the internationality of its gaze and scope on *Reise, Reise* is refreshing, and contains following Kraftwerk, a latent political message regarding Germany and the rest of the world, namely "We come in peace." And we come as Germans, not Nazis.

Rosenrot (2005) keeps this momentum going: the artwork features a U.S. icebreaker ship photographed in Antarctica, and the album features an ode to petrol ("Benzin"), that oily facilitator of movement, and a track with

Spanish lyrics "Te quiero Puta!" *Liebe ist für Alle Da*, (2009) reprises the band's growing international, universalist gaze ("Love Is There for Everyone"), with "Pussy," a "sequel" to "Amerika," for its self-consciously pop song styling with English lyrics and an eye on Anglophile pop markets, "Frühling in Paris" and "Wiener Blut" (Viennese Blood/Spirit), a song whose title references a waltz written by Johan Strauss II to celebrate the marriage between Austro-Hungarian Emperor daughter Archduchess Gisela Louise Maria and Prince Leopold of Bavaria in 1873 (which Laibach covered on their 1986 album *Krst pod Triglavom*). Rammstein's latest release, a best-of collection, is tellingly titled *Made in Germany* (2011). Rammstein, with its "R" cross, is presented as internationally-recognized brand, in the wake of other German brands: Volkswagen, Mercedes-Benz, Audi, Adidas. A position anticipated by Rammstein's satiric performance as fat auto-industry businessmen in their 2005 video for "Keine Lust." If Laibach is a totalitarian state, Rammstein has become a multinational corporation.

The German export to the U.S. who arguably paved this part of the way for Rammstein is KMFDM. Self-referential as product to a point beyond parody, the primary function of KMFDM's aesthetic is to explicitly transform totalitarian symbology into capitalist branding. The band as product relentlessly reference themselves in songs, beating the political slogan into commercial brand that the band is "Better Than Best"[34] sings Sascha "Käpt'n K" Konietzko on "Megalomaniac" in his trademark Dalek voice. Rammstein's U.S. career opens on a similar note, with the eponymous "Rammstein" song, that appears in David Lynch's *Lost Highway* soundtrack, and which repeats the band's name over and over, to a menacing industrial metal stomp, impressing the brand name in the listener's consciousness.[35] Laibach's "Tanz Mit Laibach" (Dance with Laibach) can be read as a parody of this type of song.

Rammstein's relationship with explicit politics is almost non-existent, their lyrical narratives emanating from an apolitical, male-gendered self. The song "Links 2-3-4" penned to answer their critics who aligned them with right wing and neo–Nazis, explicitly positions the band and its heart as beating on the left, yet provocatively does so to a rhythm which mimics martial marching, as if to half take the partly-forced confession back. The song is arguably a reactive damage-limitation exercise which seeks to performatively clear of political content the band's performance of Teutonism. Where Laibach play up Germanic Nazi aesthetics through a filter of aesthetic fiction, Rammstein do so also but only to the point at which they are obligated to disavow the political component of these very aesthetics, without having ever explicitly discussed Nazism in the first place. Yet, the song, which seeks to extinguish it, cannot help but re-affirm exactly that very political content, acknowledging its presence through denial. For their part, Laibach refuses to engage the logic that would compel the statement "We are not Nazis," except when they make such a statement as "We are fascists as much as Hitler was a painter"[36]: to do so would be to accept the dichotomy between Nazi/non–Nazi, which reduces Nazism (and by extension all totalitarianism) to an easily dismissed demonic other, a position that their entire oeuvre seeks to deconstruct, showing instead how totalitarianisms proliferate and persist in the "post-totalitarian" world of nation state and global capital alike. Rammstein by contrast, as a band courting the mainstream, must play the "We are not Nazis" game, paying, with "Links 2-3-4" reluctant yet necessary lip service to the mainstream position that demonizes Nazism as exceptional historical other,[37] the great Satan that must be sent behind ("Vade Retro").[38] It is the price Rammstein have chosen to pay for the aesthetic Teutonism that has been their fortune. What may still irk is the suspicion that "Links 2-3-4" represents a careerist capitulation, a mea culpa designed to let the band off the hook: now that we have gotten out of the way a statement about where our political allegiance really lies, we can continue to employ totalitarian aesthetics with impunity. Arguably, these are the rules of the market, in which totalitarianism is channeled through pop music by means of its disavowal. Finally, if Rammstein were to explain their aesthetic totalitarianism as critical of political/ideological totalitarianism, that would involve an admission of its presence in the first place, of which Rammstein's entire aesthetic relies on a disavowal. It's there, but only acknowledged through denial.

That said, *Reise, Reise*'s "Amerika" holds the honor of being the band's mostly explicitly political song: a fairly unequivocal critique of American imperialism, and a rare moment in which Rammstein can be heard channeling both Laibach's sounds and critical, ironic spirit. When Lindemann sings that he no longer sings in his native language, but rather in English, between stating that this should not be confused to be a "love song," he is also channeling Kraftwerk's position on the American replacement of lost cultural Germanicity: the pressure for German culture to Americanize. Yet through its light mockery of the U.S. which Rammstein identify with some of its more famous brands, symbols and mascots (Coca-Cola, Mickey Mouse, Santa Claus, and the White House), the song itself embodies the affirmation of Rammstein itself at the level of internationally-recognized German commercial brand. At the very moment in which Rammstein mock the USA as a corporate product and brand, they impose themselves as German product and brand. The Fatherland has been replaced by capital, given form and fetishized at the level of brand product.[39] The irony present in *Made in Germany*'s title may well call attention to the band's success as brand, but it also arguably provides a compelling piece of evidence that Rammstein's critique of America does not extend to capitalism itself, and that Rammstein to some degree represent a capitalist co-option and re-absorption of Laibach into the capitalist system. An unresolved problem, I might add, that Laibach themselves never adequately confront, and one that plagues all economically successful pop bands that preach an anti-capitalist message. To their credit, Rammstein bring out Laibach's own commercialism and status as a commercial pop band and brand, one which Laibach and their supporters have been guilty of disavowing, in their zeal to brand themselves as satirical intellectual avant-garde free of monetary taint.[40] Within the economy of exchange between the two groups, this particular debt settlement seems only fair.

The Jonas Åkerlund-directed video for the song "Mein Land," which Rammstein specifically recorded for the best-of collection, looks again to the U.S., and transfers its gaze to an American beach circa 1964. Its beach movie and *Baywatch* parody accompanies a song whose lyrics read like a mocking impersonation of a nationalist protesting that this is "my land." Disagreement among commenting fans illustrates the ambiguity of Rammstein's way of positioning themselves regarding political issues. Conscious artistic ambiguity? Or a form of please-all superficiality? The Germanized beach setting itself is no innocent one: the German tourism industry, targeting, among many places, Mediterranean Spain where many Germans holiday and retire, embodies the latest wave of a globalized, "soft" imperialism, which anticipates and accompanies North/South economic disparity and domination within the European Union.[41] By this token, Rammstein's "fun" sound and jokey image act as correlative rather than critique of German economic ascendancy and prosperity. The chalky, ghostly death masks the band members are represented through in the Made in Germany artwork conjure up deathly versions of that outmoded nationalist art form: the marble statue; and together with the dates "1995–2011," may suggest a commentary on the death of nationalism. Germany as an imperialist nation is a thing of the past, of history. Now we come in peace, and, in fun. That more colorful, vibrant, and acceptable replacement of violent invasion: international capital made fun by tourism and travel in the sun. But when the sun goes down, as this video shows, the demons come out. Or, as Laibach might put it: "Nazi-fascism under the guise of democracy is *the rule of financial capital itself.*"[42]

Conclusion: Aesthetic Debts/Dancing with Dogma

Compared with Laibach's categorical statements and pronouncements, Rammstein are a generally non-political band, their lyrical and conceptual concept occurring within an elaborately constructed and self-enclosed theatrical world. Laibach comment on the real, but so do Rammstein: they go about it in different ways, and according to different aesthetic parameters. Both are bands that play pop music: both incorporate extraneous texts and paradigmatic networks into their productions. One is more politically aware and engaged than the other. For Laibach, political engagement is their raison d'être: for Rammstein, politics is an occasional interest. Not every rock band must necessarily engage in saving the world. The dialectic between politically-aware bands and the bands who depoliticize them, or offer depoliticized, corporate, safe versions of their aesthetics, is one of contemporary rock music's defining dynamics: first Rage Against the Machine, then Limp Bizkit; first Ministry/Skinny Puppy and then Nine Inch Nails (who have recently become politicized); first Nirvana and then Nickelback and so on.

The relationship between Laibach and Rammstein is an ongoing one recently thanks to a Laibach remix of "Ohne Dich" on *Made in Germany*'s special edition bonus remix disc. In their interpretation, "Mina Harker's Version," Laibach pare down and emphasize the song's balladic nature, putting lead vocals in the mouth of female singer and Laibach collaborator Mina Špiler, and changing the lyrics to Milan Fras' contributions, that existence is no longer possible without him. As in the interviews which give this essay its name,[43] Laibach like to link themselves with Rammstein in an ironic and positive way, and this remix performs a similar function, hopefully also working as a "gateway drug," which introduces Rammstein fans to Laibach. It is a clever way for Laibach to position themselves not just as historical precursors to Rammstein, but also as contemporaries. And above all an act of good grace, through which Laibach take the high road, but also through which they position themselves in a place of intellectual superiority: unlike Skinny Puppy's Nivek Ogre, who has spent much of his career complaining about the unpaid aesthetic debt he believes is owed to him by NIN's Trent Reznor and Marilyn Manson, Laibach have turned their relationship of influence on Rammstein into a victory, not a defeat.

Partly fan-financed Finnish-German-Australian 2012 B-movie-style comedy science fiction film *Iron Sky*, for which Laibach wrote and performed the soundtrack, features a Nazi colony living on the moon since World War II, and cut off from communication with the Earth. It's tag-line? "We Come in Peace." The film's female protagonist, Renate Richter (Julia Dietze) is a blonde Nazi lunar schoolteacher who teaches a ten-minute edit of Charlie Chaplin's *The Great Dictator* (1940) to her students under the illusion that it is a genuine Nazi propaganda film. Her co-protagonist James Washington (Christopher Kirby), an African-American athlete sent to the moon under a presidential campaign publicity stunt, captured then "aryan-ified" by the moon Nazis, will disabuse her of her error by taking her to a full-length showing of the film on Earth. A knowing, if lightweight piece of camp, which delights in jokes offering American imperialism as a continuation of Nazism, *Iron Sky*— in the long tradition of cinematic Nazi comedy film (from *The Great Dictator* and Ernst Lubitsch's *To Be or Not to Be* [1942] to Mel Brooks' *The Producers* [1968] and *To Be or Not to Be* remake [1983]) reiterates the ongoing flipside to tragic cultural workings-through of Nazism: the comedic world of dancing Hitlers and "Hitler Discovers" memes. Laibach's "Tanz Mit Laibach" (2003), which reprises D.A.F.(Deutsch Amerikanische Freundschaft)'s "Der Mussolini," altering the names of Hitler and Mussolini to Chaplin's Ado Hinkel ("Adenoid Hinkel" in the film) and "Benzino Napoloni,"[44] provides one among many keys to Laibach's adoption of comedy as aesthetic, political, ideological tool. Though their grim countenances may suggest otherwise, humor is the prime key to unlocking Laibach's world: "a deep vein of black irony and absurdism ... aware of striking ludicrous poses, and ... often apparently trivial musical material" (Monroe 52), a form of "militant irony,"[45] enriched with Dadaist and surrealist tendencies. Where Laibach use irony, satire, and parody to make ideological points, Rammstein are Laibach's "tragedy" (the tragedy of modernity's recurring totalitarianisms) repeated as farce, their ability to "laugh at themselves" central to their brand success. A laughter that simultaneously protests and transcends Nazified notions of Germanicity by poking fun at the Nazi German male without quite acknowledging that fact. Though a more fully-fledged collaboration might have to wait — perhaps in perpetuity, the two bands' recent encounter in the form of "Ohne Dich/Mich," suggests that both, for the benefit of music fans the world over, are in their different ways having mutually infectious and proliferating last laughs.

Notes

1. Walt Miller, "Laibach," *Industrial Nation.* #20. 29. I have been unable to find interviews in which Rammstein explicitly discuss Laibach or their aesthetic debts to them. A request to Rammstein's management for a short interview on the topic of Laibach did not receive a response. I would like to thank Jonathan Selzer and Avi Pitchon for their insights regarding this article.

2. *Laibach: A Film from Slovenia*, dir. Peter Vezja, 1993, AKA Bravo.

3. Matt Potter, "Rammstein," *Kerrang!* 1028, 23 October, 2004, 37. It is Christian "Flake" Lorenz speaking.

4. Miller, 28.

5. Daryl Litts, "Interview: Laibach," *Legends Magazine* 139, January 2004, http://www.legendsmagazine.net/139/laibach.htm

6. Alexei Monroe, *Interrogation Machine: Laibach and NSK* (Cambridge: MIT Press, 2005.), 39 et passim. Monroe's book is the fourth volume of the Slavoj Žižek-edited series

"Short Circuits." Žižek also supplies a foreword: "They Moved the Underground." Here Monroe is quoting NSK, *Neue Slowenische Kunst* (Los Angeles: Amok, 1991);: 21 It is a book-length manifesto of Laibach and satellite art collectives.

7. Françoise Thom, *Newspeak: The Language of Soviet Communism.* (London: Claridge Press, 1989), 91.

8. See the recent, and highly ironic, case of Russian baritone Yevgeny Nikitin being forced out of the 2012 Bayreuth festival due to his youthful Nazi tattoos.

9. Laurent Binet, *HHhH*, trans. Sam Taylor (London: Harvill Secker, 2012), "136" (there are no actual page numbers in this novel).

10. In the cut *HHhH* pages on *The Kindly Ones*, Binet critiques this move as one which places the novel "in the lineage of Hannah Arendt," arguing that a novel is not the ideal venue to demonstrate the Arendtian thesis because of its reliance on invention. The cut pages were published in 2012 at http://www.themillions.com/2012/04/exclusive-the-missing-pages-of-laurent-binets-hhhh.html.

11. Jonathan Littell. *The Kindly Ones*, trans. Charlotte Mandel. (New York: Harper Perennial, 2009), 569–570.

12. Emaniel Malchiodi, "Katy Perry, What the Hell?!?" *Florida Geek Scene*, http://www.floridageekscene.com/music-reviews/katy-perry-what-the-hell/ (retrieved 21 July 2012).

13. Laibach, "Volk," Mute, 2006, booklet.

14. Alexander Gorkow. "Wer Zu Lebzeit Gut Auf Erden. Rammstein — Mit Deutschlands größtem Kulturexport auf Tour in Amerika." *Süddeutsche Zeitung Magazin.* 6. Juli 2012. p3.

15. Ace of Base, "Happy Nation." *Happy Nation*, Festival, 1992.

16. Jacques Attali, *Noise: The Political Economy of Music*, trans. Brian Massumi (Minneapolis: University of Minnesota Press, 1985), 19.

17. Information for this section gleaned from http://www.gla.ac.uk/~dc4w/laibach/hostnik.html (retrieved 21 July 2012).

18. Marilyn Manson has also picked up this thread, in such videos as "The Beautiful People" (1996), "Arma-Goddamn-Motherfuckin-Geddon" (2009), and the "Guns, God and Government" tour (2000–1).

19. Here is it worth noticing that Rammstein's live performances do not tend to posit as constant focus point the lead singer, but instead offer a variety of vignettes involving various members of the band. Leo Bersani's notion of a masochistic aesthetic is one that is defined by repetition, a mobility of "de-narrativization," and "a self-reflexive discourse, in filmic terms, which repeats and deflects narrative violence in formal recognitions." A representation is created in which "the violent story never enjoys the status of a privileged mode of disruptiveness." Instead it is flanked and tempered by a "subversive passivity," that encourages a competition between "psychic dislocations of mobile desire and a destructive fixation on anecdotal violence" (Leo Bersani. *The Freudian Body: Psychoanalysis and Art.* [New York: Columbia University Press, 1986], 54–75). In other words multiplicity of effect and narrative neutralize and disperse the sadistic instinct of the spectator.

20. "The influence of mysticism, degenerate and avant-garde and structural materialism (which inspired groups such as TG and PTV) have incubated confusion. The engagement of these groups in terms of their programs has remained at the level of romantic existentialism. Laibach, on the other hand, stands in the midst of life and is pragmatic. Our motto is based in reality, truth and life. From this standpoint, every comparison of Laibach with the specified groups is meaningless" (NSK. *Neue Slowenische Kunst*, 45).

21. See the Opus Dei artwork, in which the women and children appear with blacked-out eyes, while the male patriarchal ruler watches over them grimly. The band have employed female vocalists, and currently make use of two female drummers/percussionists: Eva Breznikar and Nataša Regovec. Avi Pitchon writes: "Nowadays, Mina Spiler is almost

a 50 percent–50 percent equal to Milan as a frontwoman. Her sexuality is icy and employs uniform and revolutionary fetish, highlighted by her use of the megaphone. Previously to Mina's prominence, two interesting items — when the band introduced the drummer girls, they printed a tight-fit shirt with the cross in front, and the following writing on the back: "yes, we are men, but we love our women." In one photoshoot of the band with the drummer girls, one of them is crouching on all fours, and wears a horse's saddle on her back!" (email exchange with the author, retrieved 7 September 2012).

22. An early pronouncement designates the division Germania as responsible for "the emotional side, which is outlined in relations to the general ways of emotoinal, erotic, and family life" (NSK, *Neue Slowenische Kunst*, 19).

23. Which in 1998 in Worcester, Massachusetts caused the two to be arrested and charged with lewd and lascivious behavior.

24. Slavoj Žižek, *Living in the End Times* (London: Verso, 2010), 385.

25. Dick Hebdige, *Subculture: The Meaning of Style* (London: Routledge, 2006), 116–117.

26. Nachtmahr, "Can You Feel the Beat?" *Semper Fidelis*, Trisol, 2011.

27. Ulf Poschardt. "Stripped: Pop und Affirmation bei Kraftwerk, Laibach und Rammstein," *Jungle World* 20, 12. (May 1999), http://jungle-world.com/artikel/1999/19/30872.html (retrieved 26 July 2012).

28. Quoted in Poschardt.

29. Scott Lewis and Natalie Gravenor. "Laibach." Trouser Press. http://www.trouser-press.com/entry.php?a=laibach (28 July 2012).

30. Laibach. "*NATO*," Mute, 1994, booklet.

31. Laibach. *WAT.* Mute. 2003. "Now You Will Pay."

32. Laibach, "Germania," *Volk,* Mute, 2006. German consciousness as a question posed to Germany is present here and also in German-origin industrial band KMFDM: their second album is titled *What Do You Know, Deutschland?* (1986) and features a stylized painting of a drum-beating uniformed tough on its cover.

33. Lewis and Gravenor, "Laibach."

34. KMFDM, "Megalomaniac," *SYMBOLS*, TVT/Wax Trax!, 1996.

35. The band name also appears in the lyrics of *Herzeleid*'s opening track "Wollt Ihr das Bett in Flammen Sehen?" and *Liebe ist für Alle Da*'s opening track "Rammlied." "Wut will nicht sterben," a 1999 song by German rock band Puhdys, features guest performances by Lindemann and Kruspe, and a reference to Rammstein.

36. NSK, *Neue Slowenische Kunst*, 58.

37. Avi Pitchon writes that "'Links 2-3-4' has an extra dimension, and that is a critique of the left of being not really different than the right, especially considering the fanaticism and paranoia of German antifas. I think Rammstein were addressing the totalitarian tendency of the German left in its demand to have a pop band publicly allign itself with the correct camp" (email exchange with the author, retrieved 9/7/12).

38. Both Laibach's *Rekapitulacija* (1980–1984) and *Nova Akropola* (1985) feature songs on the Vade Retro theme, "Vade Retro" and "Vade Retro Satanas," respectively.

39. On their 2011 U.S. tour Rammstein avoided playing the song "Amerika," perhaps conscious that Americans in the audience might sing the song back to them and enjoy it devoid of its satiric content. By the time of the 2012 U.S. tour, the band have incorporated the song into their setlist as an encore.

40. Laibach's statement that "[a]nyhow, today we share the territory," offers as good an acknowledgment of their status as commercial entity as we get from them.

41. Rammstein guitarist Richard Z. Kruspe's 2007 English-language solo project was released under the name *Emigrate*: its self-titled album features artwork which weaves an altered metal star of David into its visions of futuristic factories, deserts, wires and dystopian interiors. The band's first single was "New York City," where Kruspe moved for a while.

"'I underwent therapy there,' he confesses. 'I was having panic attacks. But you know what? I thought it was the band, but it was New York City. That's what gives you the panic attacks.'" Matt Potter. "Rammstein." *Kerrang!* 1028. 23 October 2004. 36. Kruspe also says about the U.S.: "I was in a real rock 'n' roll band when I started.... Playing real American-style rock 'n' roll. And then, when I went to America, I realised that it was all nothing but a lie for me to be playing that! That's when I got interested in the kind of music Rammstein plays."

42. NSK, *Neue Slowenische Kunst*, 57.

43. Such as Sophie Albers' "Laibach ist Rammstein für Erwachsene" (2004): *http://www.netzeitung.de/entertainment/music/315256.html* (retrieved 26 July 2012). Of the song, Iwan Novak says, "Nachdem wir den Rammstein-Song gehört haben, dachten wir, es wäre schön mit einer Sängerin. Weil es ein Liebeslied ist, haben wir dann Mann und Frau gemischt. Ursprünglich haben wir auch die Stimme des Rammstein-Sängers gelassen. Wir fanden die Dreierbeziehung spannend. Aber wir wurden gebeten, sie herauszunehmen" [After having heard the Rammstein song, we thought it would be nice with a female singer. Because it is a love song, we mixed men and women. Originally, we also left the voice of the Rammstein singer. We found the three-way relationship exciting. But we were asked to remove them].

44. The reason for this switch is — ironically — a commercial one: "As for the single, we wanted to quote original DAF lyrics, but they wouldn't give us their permission, so we had to search for alternative options at the very last moment because the song was already recorded and mixed. We had to run an additional vocal recording and we didn't want to change the song completely; in the end we decided to use Chaplin's Adenoid Hinkel and Benzino Napolini so we weren't quoting DAF and could still mention more or less the same historical characters." Avi Pitchon. "Post Modern Post Mortem," *Terrorizer* 114 (November 2003), 41.

45. Monroe is quoting Erika Gottlieb's formulation for George Orwell's 1984 in her *The Orwell Conundrum: A Cry of Despair or Faith in the Spirit of Man?* (Ottawa: Carleton University Press, 1992).

Works Cited

Albers, Sophie. "Laibach ist Rammstein für Erwachsene." Netzeitung.de. 6, December 2004. http://www.netzeitung.de/entertainment/music/315256.html
Attali, Jacques. *Noise: The Political Economy of Music.* Trans. Brian Massumi. Minneapolis: University of Minnesota Press, 1985.
Bersani, Leo. *The Freudian Body: Psychoanalysis and Art.* New York: Columbia University Press, 1986.
Binet, Laurent. *HHhH.* Trans. Sam Taylor. London: Harvill Secker, 2012.
Gorkow, Alexander. "Wer Zu Lebzeit Gut Auf Erden. Rammstein — Mit Deutschlands größtem Kulturexport auf Tour in Amerika." *Süddeutsche Zeitung Magazin.* 6 July 2012.
Hebdige, Dick. *Subculture: The Meaning of Style.* London: Routledge, 2006.
Lewis, Scott and Natalie Gravenor. "Laibach." Trouser Press. http://www.trouserpress.com/entry.php?a=laibach.
Littell, Jonathan. *The Kindly Ones.* Trans. Charlotte Mandel. New York: Harper Perennial, 2009.
Litts, Daryl. "Interview: Laibach." *Legends Magazine* 139, January 2004. http://www.legendsmagazine.net/139/laibach.htm.
Malchiodi, Emaniel. "Katy Perry, What the Hell?!?" Florida Geek Scene. http://www.floridageekscene.com/music-reviews/katy-perry-what-the-hell/
Miller, Walt. "Laibach." *Industrial Nation* 20.

Monroe, Alexei. *Interrogation Machine: Laibach and NSK.* Cambridge: MIT Press, 2005.
NSK. *Neue Slowenische Kunst.* Los Angeles: Amok, 1991.
Pitchon,Avi. "Post Modern Post Mortem." *Terrorizer* 114 (November 2003).
Poschardt, Ulf. "Stripped: Pop und Affirmation bei Kraftwerk, Laibach und Rammstein."
    Jungle World 20, no. 12 (May 1999).
Potter, Matt. "Rammstein." *Kerrang!* 1028. 23 October, 2004.
Žižek, Slavoj. *Living in the End Times.* London: Verso, 2010.

4

Über Alles: Rock Bands Following in the Wake of Rammstein

Brad Klypchak

Following instances of innovation those in the music industry, be it labels, aspiring bands, or journalists, tend to replicate certain markers which designate the innovation as distinctive. Subsequently, the markers of innovation become the center point for all further discourse, and normative bounds delineating the innovation as a categorical construct emerge. Given the unexpected success of both Rammstein's "Du hast" single and *Sehnsucht* album in North American markets, a climate of contextual openness toward non–English hard rock emerged. Amidst this trend, a formulaic expectancy of Rammstein-esque comparison also arose. I aim to specifically address three distinct instances where artists following Rammstein's breakthrough reflect varying degrees of the band's stylistic elements while also being compartmentalized into arguably well- or ill-fit comparative frames. Be it Norway's Gothminister, New York's Hanzel und Gretyl, or a collective of German bands including Subway to Sally, In Extremo, or Saltatio Mortis, the sonic, lyrical, or performative elements are clearly visible when viewed through a Rammsteinian lens.

While each instance carries its own specific points of connection to Rammstein, the breadth of influence gives rise to particular discourses. One centers on constructs of authenticity and mimicry. A second engages the distinction between parody and trangsressive performative art. Lastly, as rock music has traditionally been conveyed in the English language, the collection of artists embracing their native speech in lyrics challenges the perceived (in)accessibility to North American audiences and critics. Through examining the performers and their artistic outputs, as well as the journalistic coverage of those performances, I seek to highlight ways in which artists following in

Rammstein's wake illustrate not only the group's overall influence as an innovative band, but also the larger contextual impact on hard rock music industry
practices and criticism following the band's breakthrough in popularity.

Establishing Rammstein as Archetype

Much like Vayo describes the band Neu!'s public recognition in relation
to the 70s Krautrock movement as carrying "only ancillary interest due to
their relative anonymity within that larger genre, a mere historical footnote
familiar only to music fanatics and Germans of a certain vintage" (622), bands
caught in the post–Rammstein wake also lack large scale recognition from the
mainstream, particularly beyond European boundaries. This can be partially
attributed to the contextual climate of the music industry, both in terms of
production and publicity, where the negotiation between global and local is
often proved fractured rather than encompassing. For example, Silvia Martinez
Garcia, in an examination of metal and music genres, notes how non–English
language use is a limiting barrier for Spanish and Catalan bands of the 1990s.
According to Garcia, when acts retained their native language they removed
themselves from moving beyond local and into larger discursive considerations
since "the venues, radio stations, production companies, etc., do not consider
them as a part of their world" (102). Similarly, in the introduction to his
overview of Latin rock, Ernesto Lechner notes, "*Rock en español* is too idio-
syncratic a musical expression for massive consumption in the English speaking
world. True, many of the genre's best bands are still starving as a result of
this, but at least their artistic vision is generally not compromised" (xii).

To both Garcia and Lechner, language choice presents the key barrier to
the potential for widespread acceptance. As such, language has indirectly fostered the contextual climate of musical otherness. Simon Frith in "The Discourse of World Music" goes so far as to cynically point out that, "world
music ... [is] assigned to their own shop display ghetto" (306). Though Rammstein and the post–Rammstein acts feature significations familiar enough to
Western expectation to remain in the rock bins, the artists are still considered
an ill-fit within the structures of 1990s rock genres. To emphasize non–English
lyrics is, according to Edward Larkey, to forego applying "a sign of artistic
prowess and intent, demonstrating global competitiveness and legitimacy,
particularly in the rock genre, where its use dominated" (4–5). With regard
to non–English recordings Rebecca Romanow convincingly argues that, "The
West listens to this music purely in the context of its production by the Other,
of its non–Western status, and of the impossibility of world music ever seriously competing with or eroding the financial and cultural success of American

and British bands" (6). Thus, language choice is a factor that severely limits music featuring non–English lyrics' acceptance in large markets.

In *Performing Rites*, Simon Frith describes the process of establishing genre within music discourse as fueling expectations in musical worlds. Be it through constructs of performance, perceived authenticity, taste, or other such mechanisms of critical judgment, the tendency toward scripting musical perception into familiar narratives is paramount for record label promotion. Subsequently, the music critic evaluating and contextualizing the products is confined by the same process which in turn mediates the development of both performer and audience. The effect of this process, in other words, is that the resulting commodity system features music critics and the recording industry recursively producing a version of music for the listener as well as a version of listener for the music.

When writing on the rock press, Hélène Laurin notes the institutional consistency seen within traditional rock journalism wherein "more prestigious, more influential, and more symbolically powerful" (54) publications have come to shape the expectations, both in terms of style and content of reviews as journalism and the ongoing discourse surrounding rock musical taste. At the time of Rammstein's emergence in North American markets, entities like *Rolling Stone*, *Billboard*, *Spin*, and *Melody Maker* held considerable sway in influencing rock's cannon. For Laurin, the cultural capital garnered by those critics arbitrating taste fuels the recursive process. She points out that when readers assimilate the values critics are professing as important, "rock writers have the symbolic power to 'knight' and 'un-knight' particular recordings, musicians, scenes, and phenomena" (56; see also Fenster).

As Keith Negus describes the music industry of the 1990s, "musical genres are formally codified into specific organizational departments, narrow assumptions about markets and 'targeted' promotional practices" (28) wherein new music acquisition, development and promotion are based on "'intuitive' assumptions ... informed by gender, class, and racialized divisions" (21). Innovation, be it genuine or perceived, occurs within the formulaic constructions of the genre world and, as a result of prevailing assumptions, is commonly constricted into discursively-derived expectations. Rammstein's unexpected prominence within the North American marketplace in the late 1990s highlighted both the novelty of their foreign identity and the relative systemic under-preparedness within the existing genre world to accommodate such an anomaly. Ulrich Adelt attributes Rammstein's success to the ease with which German stereotypes could be perpetuated, describing them as "technically versatile, cold-blooded, and aggressive" (288). Adelt specifically highlights "Till Lindemann's old-fashioned Bühnenaussprache vocals (a 'stage pronunciation' easily associated with the Nazi stereotype)" (288) and the band's use of Leni Riefenstahl visuals (Nazi Germany's most well-known filmmaker) as fostering the very "intuitive" assumptions of which Negus spoke (see also Daniel Lukes' essay in this volume).

As an example, consider how Wolfgang Spahr of *Billboard Magazine* represents Rammstein just prior to the 1999 U.S. release of *Sehnsucht.* Quotes include:

> Iron hard industrial metal music and blunt lyrics....
>
> ... young generation trying to escape gray everyday life ... by seeking uncompromising lyrics and hard music....
>
> ... a group you either love or hate, particularly in view of their controversial lyrics dealing with love, violence, and death. This is all backed up by a strong sound forcing more sensitive souls to flee....
>
> ... their latent, sadomasochistic, down-to-earth 'we're-someone-to-reckon-with' type of rock, including a strict dress code....
>
> ... their pyromaniac message goes beyond simply clothing themselves in macabre violence.... [56].

Additionally, the same *Billboard* article raises the portent of right-wing extremism on two separate occasions. While qualifiers mentioning Rammstein's denial of right wing political views are included in the article, they are only done so after the stereotype is consciously invoked. Finally, the article frames the spectacle of the pyrotechnic live show through violence with allusions to the air show tragedy from which the band's name derives and comparisons to bomb explosions.

As Frith describes his past as a rock critic he says "press handouts weren't just designed to sell a sound to me, but also to persuade me to write about a record or artist in the right way, in the right discursive frame" (1998, 61). Keeping the *Billboard* article in mind, it seems a core set of such frames are carried forth. While Rammstein's later recordings drifted considerably from the "iron hard industrial" of "Du hast," the initially-developed impressions were inescapable. Chuck Eddy's *Rolling Stone* review of *Sehnsucht* relishes in the markers that inform future framings:

> A sextet of east german (*sic*) sexual-torture fanatics that has been accused of luring the youth of Europe toward communist bliss..., Rammstein have secured Top 10 spots across the continent this fall in part by regularly setting themselves on fire in concert. Their guitars grind like an overbearing ear-bleed machine, locking into Sehnsucht's electronic ticktock rhythms with icy Aryan precision. The Uberserious guttural delivery of ex–Olympic swimmer Till Lindemann lends the band a melodramatic sense of melody as muscular as it is mannered. He rolls hard consonants, hiccups like Falco, begs us auf Deutsch to bend over and punish him like a certified son of "Sprockets." Haunted opera-diva counterpoint, morose Moorish gargling and cathedrals of synthesized strings waft out of the

blustering abyss, making Sehnsucht a soundtrack less for World War III than for its desolate aftermath [62].

The band, and those following in their commercial and critical wake, are discursively lumped into the parameters of the past in which the tones, tempos, and titles are signified as Rammsteinian, or as another *Rolling Stone* piece called *Sehnsucht*, "a Pantera-obsessed Kraftwerk cranking out postindustrial guitar metal with Wagnerian drama" ("Rammstein" 2). Once bred into the genre world of promotion and criticism, a discursive typography becomes increasingly hard to resist or ignore.

Though Rammstein entered the mainstream's view with the success of "Du hast," very little mainstream coverage has been afforded acts like Gothminister, Hanzel und Gretyl, or In Extremo. While still limited in its capacity to generate global exposure, the rise of alternative press outlets since the time of Rammstein's emergence, particularly those found on the internet, has mitigated the importance of a band's being prominent in mainstream rock press coverage. As Laurin argues, the internet and its "abundance of 'self-defined' rock writers" have come to challenge "the foundations of the rock writing profession" (55), and editorial choices have come to reflect a far wider reaching scope of rock-based cultural capital claims. In terms of mainstream versus scene-specific press coverage, more global outlets like *Billboard* or *Rolling Stone* become far less significant a trend-setting force within subcultural scenes (like that of metal or its assortment of subgenres) than those concentrating on a scene's specific niche.

That being noted, the core formulaic tenets of rock criticism as a whole still persist whether the source is mainstream or subcultural. The writer still aims to establish one's informed expertise in both analyzing and contextualizing the performance in accordance to one's own judgments of good taste and all that goes into that judgment: a band's perceived skill, authenticity, innovation and creativity, dedication, degree of subcultural representation, etc. Recalling Frith's genre-developing discursive frames, none of this occurs within a vacuum and presumptive patterns of where arbiter expectations presently come from largely rely on its precedents. For those bands following in Rammstein's wake, this pattern exhibited within rock criticism practices becomes imminently apparent. In what follows, I offer examples of how rock criticism, much of it internet-based, has employed and adapted these recurring discursive tendencies.

Empire of Dark Salvation— Gothminister, (In)authenticity and the Comparison Game

Originating in 1999, Norway's Gothminister is essentially the outlet for Bjorn Alexander Brem. Taking the role as frontman, composer, and studio instrumentalist, Brem guided Gothminister into the German goth scene. After a series of singles and demos, the full length *Gothic Electronic Anthems* (*GEA*) saw its 2003 release. By Brem's own admission, the band advanced considerably by the time of the release of 2005's *Empire of Dark Salvation* (*EDS*). Two years later, Gothminister played their first live dates in the U.S. in support of the *EDS* record, marking their first direct contact with American audiences and generating a modicum of coverage of the band from more internationally-driven publicity outlets. In terms of music, album art, and visuals on stage and in videos, Gothminister weave a combination of vampiric and gothic imagery to songs featuring industrial percussive rhythms layered with power chord distortions, a practice which has continued through the 2008 *Happiness in Darkness* (*HiD*) release and 2011's *Anima Inferna* (*AI*).

Though most mainstream rock journalism outlets skipped over the band, those who did offer criticism of the band's first two releases problematized the offerings as being derivative in both tone and tactic:

> *Release Magazine* (review of *GEA*): This is not anything new or original though, just pretty well done. The minister himself really excels in looking übergothic all the time, almost to the point that it becomes funny.... Try this album if you like Rammstein, Deathstars or perhaps if you just are after some flashy gothic imagery [Carlsson].

> *Spike Magazine* (review of *EDS*): Funhouse Frankenmetal and synth-washed Type O Negative me-tooing played by alien vampire S&M Berliners using mid-tempo Megadeth lines to shove low-voiced tales of like totally ominous foreboding down the throats of the eternally dag-nabbed ["Gothminister"].

> *Release Magazine* (review of *EDS*): Rammstein. The Sisters of Mercy. Rob Zombie. Pain. And a whole bunch of other heavy goth rock/industrial bands and the likes. That is where Gothminister has found his inspiration, and that is what we think we hear in his music when we like it. And, sure, Gothminister does a good job copying his heroes. But a fake song is a fake song is a fake song [Malmstedt].

Given the array of name-dropped artists within these reviews, the convention of connecting to established genre narratives seems well represented here. While both of the *Release* reviews note achievement, any credit is immediately revoked as the band infringes too closely to where rightful influences and authenticity are presumed.

As Allan Moore's survey and deconstruction of authenticity in rock music attests, there are a variety of potential qualities which come to represent who is deemed "authentic" ranging from being able to perform with virtuosity, to being driven by artistic intentions rather than extrinsic, commercial ones (selling out), to the degree to which the performance on- and offstage reflects and adheres to subcultural expectations. Frith in *Performing Rites* offers his version of authenticity as a "perceived quality of sincerity and commitment ... as if music can be heard as 'false' to its own premises" (71). Taken in light of genre worlds and the discourses from which they arise, to perform in such a way as to miss connecting with the touchpoints of genre (or, depending on its subcultural proximities, whatever fragmented subsets arising within the larger-framed classification) is to risk perceived inauthenticity. When considering Gothminister, the critical ears heard the markers of Rammstein via vocal choices, percussive rhythms, and guitar tones, but heard them too ingrained to the construct of Rammstein to merit "true" innovation or authentic creativity. That the songs are delivered in English by a Norwegian, feature far more prominent synthetic/electronic tones, and conform more closely to the bounds of goth/dance than metal are qualities which all get diminished across these reviews. Rather, what stands prominent is the perceived proximity to the archetype, the "real" songs from Rammstein versus the "fake" Gothminister ones.

As Gothminister's career continued, later records like *Happiness in Darkness* and *Anima Inferna* were more often compared to the whole of the Gothminister catalog than to being referenced in relation to other acts. In part, this might be attributed to reviewers finding need to establish the historical lineage of the band and simultaneously prove their own authoritative mastery within the "knowledge fight" (Laurin, 55) of rock criticism. Also, the ongoing diversification of rock subgenres coincided with the expanding specificity of niche-targeted outlets reviewing online. Instead of a more myopically concentrated construct of what rock entails, the fragmentation into various scenes and styles opened far greater discursive comparisons in which the aesthetics of goth or industrial metal or darkwave might be selectively applied. Nonetheless, some blog reviewers still drew upon Rammsteinian resemblances:

Side-line Music Magazine (review of *HiD*): Again, there are not so much (sic) new elements used and the eyewink to bands like Rammstein, Rob Zombie and Kmfdm (sic) is still highly recognizable, but the chemistry between all ingredients is very catchy and well produced.... In general we can say that Gothminister sounds heavier than ever before, as well as for the guitars as for the voice, while the main inspiration, the dark side, still stays the same [Sideline].

Metal Storm (review of *AI*): Those familiar with Gothminister know what to expect: beat-driven, gloomy music that makes you wonder if you should be headbanging or dancing. Harsh industrial riffs pound on while the background symphonics gently invoke the sense of dread, doom, gloom and similar goth shenanigans.... Just be prepared for the inevitable: as all fairly shallow music, it looses (sic) its effect after many listens and should be enjoyed in smaller doses [Slayer666].

AModelofControl (review of *AI*): So how does their fourth album stack up in the face of this? Well, absolutely nothing has changed, from the very first second of opener Stonehenge (not a Spinal Tap cover, sadly). It is melodic, mildly catchy goth-metal riffage, but ultimately almost indistinguishable from everything that has come before. And I could swear that I've heard The Beauty of Fanatism and the (dreadful) balladry of the title track before, too [Williams].

Despite the years of additional exposure to similar musical outfits and the ongoing development of distinctive subgenre aesthetics, some rock critics still retain the same authenticity concerns as expressed when Gothminister first emerged. The relative predictability across the whole of the Gothminister catalog becomes cited as key problematic point. Curiously, the seemingly contrarian stance of problematizing repetition in music so strongly linked to industrial, a music which in its own evolution has celebrated the relentless rhythm of the mechanical, is faulted for Gothminister, yet is seemingly acceptable for those historical predecessors alluded to. This may partly be explained by the critic's contributory role as rock historian. Mark Fenster offers that a key responsibility of the rock critic is "to legitimate and canonize" so that the extending discourse of "good" music can be shared, referenced, and applied (87). In terms of the symbiosis between artist, industry, and consumer, a narrative of musical history becomes not only a grounding point for cultural and/or subcultural authenticity claims, but also can serve as a means to further ingrain the particular signifying codes and their respective meanings to future generations of consumers, performers, and critics alike.

Blut! Zex! Fire! Hanzel und Gretyl

Given the ways in which the early career of Gothminister was critically received, one might expect a parallel reaction toward Hanzel und Gretyl (HuG). Formed initially in 1993 after Betty Kallas' previous performance art/metal persona, Venis Penis Crusher, and her band Cycle Sluts from Hell fell by the wayside, Hanzel und Gretyl introduced two new stage identities, Vas Kallas and her counterpart, Kaiser von Loopy (Rob Lupie). In its earliest iterations, HuG utilized some German significations, but for the most part, stuck to more science-fiction/post-apocalyptic eccentricities to complement their "Machines Good, People Bad" ethos. However, by their third release (and notably after having toured with Rammstein in 1998), the full transformation into their German-immersed personas had manifested itself. Here, HuG presents a far closer association to Rammstein — the industrial foundation of the music prevails and lyrics are prominently delivered in German. If anything, HuG increasingly foregrounded the elements emphasized in reviews of Rammstein's releases, drifting away from the electro-space dance of 1997's *Transmission from Uranus* and towards the more consciously industrial-driven releases of 2003's *Über Alles* (*ÜA*), 2004's *Scheissmessiah!*, and 2008's *2012: Zwanzig Zwölf* (*ZZ*). Lyrical and visual themes across these later records emphasize imagery of World War II and the Third Reich (for example, the lightning bolt/Schutzstaffel "ss" incorporated into the titular font of *Scheissmessiah*'s album art or the war eagle atop the helmet Kaisar von Loopy wore on stage) as a means of provoking reaction via lingering unease with Germanic significations in post–World War II America. Frequent, repeated references to fire and sex are reminiscent of Rammstein's penchant for pyrotechnics and sexual entendre, and the band pushes ever further into something they deem "more German than German," the phrase even serving as a tagline for the band's 2011's concert tour.

In terms of critical response to HuG, music journalists invoke a slightly differing set of authenticity-grounded arguments predominantly tied to the sheer spectacle of HuG's performative choices. In large part, how the music critic interprets the Germanic significations influences the way the narrative is spun, though elements of prevailing genre framings certainly recur:

Sea of Tranquility (review of *Scheissmessiah*): Marilyn Manson meets latter-day Theatre of Tragedy by way of an introduction from Rammstein on *Scheissmessiah*, the fourth album from the cyber/industrial-metal maniacs Hanzel Und Gretyl ... much of the music here begins to repeat itself early on [Popke].

Metal Sucks (review of *ÜA*): The concept of another Rammstein strikes me as kinda silly, because, well, we've already got Rammstein. As far as industrial metal songs sung in German go, Rammstein fill that niche rather nicely. But here we've got Hanzel Und Gretyl — a band from New York City, no less, singing in faux German accents — doing the exact same thing. Only their songs aren't as catchy, outrageous or hilarious [(Neilstein].

AllMusic (review of *ÜA*): Now, these two do know how funny they are, right? Really, one must assume that they do, because the alternative assumption — that the lederhosen, the affected German accents, and the tasteless flirtations with Nazi themes are actually meant as some kind of serious musical or cultural statement — is simply too horrible to contemplate. Luckily, song titles like "S.S. Deathstar Supergalactik," "Mein Kommandant," and, most painful of all, "Third Reich from the Sun" make it pretty clear that they are dealing in a sort of high-camp make-believe here. (They're obviously only pretending to be German — actual Germans would know how to pronounce the word "über.") Close your eyes and go along with the charade, though, and you'll find yourself caught up in the music, which is a genuinely well-thought-out fusion of techno and industrial sounds with lots of guitars and tight, crunchy beat.... If they'd just outgrow the leather-fetish Nazi stuff, Hanzel und Gretyl could probably go places [Anderson].

Spike Magazine (review of *ZZ*): Slowly but surely, more acts are partaking of the noxious Hitler-doom atmosphere first stolen and transmogrified from Skinny Puppy's genius by Marilyn Manson, ie KMFDM, Combichrist, half of what

Dancing Ferret Records is releasing, etc.... Hanzel adds the destructive coldwave sounds of machines assembling terminator robots to their angry, megaphoned German gibbering ... they're content to bellow long and madly over their Pro Tools Panzer tanks, comfortable as they are in their noise-metal skin [Saeger].

Sound + Noise Presents (show review): it feels contrived and the music is boring because in all honesty, I would rather be listening to the group that made it famous. Its (sic) hard to let Hanzel und Gretyl go on their own merit, because the entire set I couldn't stop thinking about how much I would rather be at a Rammstein show [Behr].

Village Voice (review of *ÜA*): Young, fast, and scientific, Hanzel und Gretyl's ersatz Kraut-rock makes dance-metal out of the goose step and sieg heil. *Über Alles* is a rock opera aimed at our SS troops on the stairway to the stars; the Baron von Strucker comic-book-Deutsch lyrics make everything *ganz klar* to even those without a Cassell's German-English dictionary.... The greatest appeal of the act is in its *krank*— that's *ill*— talent for making Teutonic exhortation into a rhythm instrument [Smith].

For a critic like the Village Voice's George Smith, faux-ness amounts to parodic worthiness and the performative morphs into creative camp. To Smith, the "kraut-rock" significations ironically mock the stereotypical solemnity which Nazi Germany (and its contemporary neo–Nazi offshoots) have come to represent. While tapping into the most popular Germanic musical representation of its time, HuG's appropriation of Rammstein's musical and performative essence revels within the very notions that Rammstein needed to discursively distance themselves from: a question of political affiliations and the threat of fascist allegiance. Flaunting the issue by hyperperforming it (more German than German after all), HuG could be construed as dissolving rock criticism's commonplace reliance on authenticity by rewriting it through postmodernly performative art. While HuG's music may certainly sound like and appear to be a derivative knock off, the band's claim to creative license resulted in a new discussion about cultural perceptions of Germanity.

On the other hand, less convinced critics like *All Music*'s Ryan Anderson see the signifiers as gimmicks, drawing attention problematically away from the music and its relative worth. For those critics, claims of artistic license or high-minded conceptual underpinnings are less important than a perceived connection to the overarching qualities ascribed to "good" music. Returning to Allan Moore's notion of authenticity, should Kallas' and Loopy's personas and their collective performances read as contrived, their first person authenticity is sacrificed. Moore suggests the first person authentic "arises when an originator (composer, performer) succeeds in conveying the impression that his/her utterance is one of integrity, that it represents an attempt to communicate in an unmediated form with an audience" (214). In the case of HuG, by aping Rammstein's original utterance of integrity so closely without aspiring to add anything more musically, the band provided their detractors with a basis for their respective condemnations.

The harshest criticisms come from those who find only spectacle in the performance and, in some instances, see that spectacle as being solely and blatantly derivative. Reliance on gimmick, technological apparatus, and/or spectacle versus demonstrating "true musicianship" is routinely offered as a sign of rock inauthenticity (see, among the many, Jones and Featherly; Moore; Walser; Frith 1998; Laurin). As suggested in the review excerpts above, pilfering "edgy" ideas from Marilyn Manson or Skinny Puppy draws derision, but to do so ham-fistedly is unforgivable. The novelty of singing about blood, sex, fire, and shit in pseudo–German wears off quite quickly, and without something else to offer an audience base, negative comparisons to established innovators (like Rammstein, Manson, and Skinny Puppy) are inevitable. Regardless of how ironic the ploys of perversity and potty-mouthing might attempt to be, to fail to deliver something authentically creative garners the harshest of condemnations: being called boring and repeatedly so.

Aus der Asche: Mittelalters in the Mix

The final artists to be considered are those who are the most sonically and stylistically removed from Rammstein's genre world. Yet, as a result of these acts recording and releasing material in German during the period when Rammstein's global popularity first surged, bands like Subway to Sally, Saltatio Mortis, and In Extremo found themselves initially framed within the oversimplified confines of Rammsteinian discourse. For audiences outside of native German speakers, the incongruence of hearing vocals conveyed auf Deutsch in the late '90s and early 2000s necessitated some sort of convenient interpretative base. At that time, many within the recording industry still clung to ideologies of Anglicizing as a primary means for broaching international markets. Beyond the anomalous one-hit crossovers (Nena, After the Fire, Falco, Peter Schilling — many of which were released in English-translated versions too) or the more underground niche (the whole of the Krautrock movement, Kraftwerk in particular), American audiences had severely limited discursive narratives to apply to such happenings. Rammstein's success offered a contemporary point of reference — regardless of how well- or ill-fit.

Of the three artists to be covered in this section, In Extremo achieved the greatest degree of access to North American consumers and press outlets. When Metal Blade Records distributed three of In Extremo's records, 1999's *Weckt die Toten*, 2000's *Verehrt und Angespien* (*VuA*), and 2002's *Sünder ohne*

Zügel (*SoZ*), the band experienced unprecedented access to American audiences without needing to alter or adapt their artistic content. Performing compositions derived from minstrel songs of medieval times, In Extremo featured "authentic" medieval instrumentation (most notably bagpipes and other horns) intermixed with the more contemporary metal tones of electric guitar, bass, and drums. The native language of the originating song was generally maintained—mostly German, but also ranging from Latin, to French and Italian, and to Icelandic and Scandinavian dialects. When the American music press finally discovered the band, critics more often than not praised the innovation, but also commonly made connection to the band's nationality and/or their German musical brethren:

> *Spin* (review of *VuA*): ...(What is it about Deutschland rockers and flames?) The result is something akin to Ozzfest crashing the Renaissance Fair.... [Kenneally].

> *Brave Words and Bloody Knuckles* (review of *SoZ*): What In Extremo's latest, *Sünder ohne Zügel*, does put forth is a strange amalgam of Irish Celtic bagpipes, Rammstein-like military riffing and clean vocals a la Die Toten Hosen (fellow Germans, though Hosen are punks). So, for a nation supposedly filled with boring thinkers, this is a pretty multi-dimensional release, combining a lot of odd influences into a sound that's highly listenable.... Evidently, the fact that this is sung entirely in German might have something to do with the reason I can't appreciate this release ..., but it is admirable that In Extremo has chosen to face the international market on its own terms. However, bis die Nacht zerfallt? Muss wie Luft vergehen? Sunder Ohne Zugel? How the hell should I know? [Perri].

> *San Francisco Weekly* (review of *VuA*): Sure, the group smells like high concept. But In Extremo is only the latest in a long line of rock bands overseas that've adapted the form to fit their own cultures. As Einstürzende Neubauten demonstrated, rock's traditional instrumentation can be replaced or supplemented by any number of objects and machines. The stomping uber-industrial march of Hungarian totalitarian-rock pranksters Laibach proved the sounds of ancient culture can be updated and blended with contemporary styles. And the flame-drenched spectacle of German industrial-metal barbarians Rammstein drove home the point that the consonant-crunching and growl-rich sound of Germanic languages perfectly matches the barre-chord crunching and snarling rhythms of speed metal ... the jaw-dropping harmonica solo in the group's anthem, "In Extremo," and the deft layering of bagpipe arpeggios over a descending guitar riff in "Ich Kenne Alles," demonstrate the band's unique musical prowess [Clifford].

> *Rough Edge* (review of *VuA*): In Extremo mix instruments that one doesn't normally think of when one thinks of hard rock into a brutally hard rock delivery that can't help but bring the music of Rammstein to mind. Of course, it doesn't help that not a single word In Extremo sings is in English which is the most obvious comparison one has to make with Rammstein. How else do Rammstein and In Extremo differ? Rammstein take more of the steamhammer approach, blasting their musical notes with near nuclear velocity. In Extremo, on the other

hand, take a more artistic approach, using bagpipes, glockenspiel and other such non-metal instruments and twisting them into a hard rock sound.

It works and it works well. In Extremo are extremely talented musicians and their combination of musical genres is nothing short of stunning [Bolton].

What proves most interesting is that once the notion of German vocals is negotiated, elements of the music, the skill with which it is performed and the novelty of instrumentation and composition become the critical focus.

Moving into the 2000s, the internet as independent distribution and publicity outlet also began impacting the critic's engagement of the genre world process. With the major labels veering away from metal by the mid–1990s, metal returned to its modest, scene-based roots. In particular, independent labels reclaimed their prominence in the metal scene, and the opportunity for metal acts to artistically experiment was rekindled. The emerging success of labels like Germany's Nuclear Blast and Century Media paved the way for other European labels like Peaceville, Listenable, Black Mark, Candlelight, Spikefarm, and Napalm. Given the sheer number of functioning labels in Europe, experimentation in European metal thrived throughout regional "underground" scenes, and these labels significantly increased the number of outlets for up and coming acts. Forgoing the energies required to cater to a less-than-receptive American market, bands and labels established new strategies for negotiating the musical marketplace, specifically by focusing their attention locally. For Subway to Sally, In Extremo, and Saltatio Mortis, this has proven successful as all three have placed records on the German charts. Specifically, four Subway to Sally releases broke into the German top 10 as did five In Extremo albums (two of which, 2008's *Sängerkrieg* and 2011's *Sterneneisen*, reached number one).

Though international fame like that experienced by Rammstein would certainly be welcomed, independent European music labels presumed if a record managed to capture attentions across the Atlantic, it would do so without the need for any sort of alteration beyond translated lyrics in the record's liner notes. As a result, a diverse range of locally-focused releases became seen as commercially viable. One such subgenre of metal, folk metal, saw bands adapt the traditional music styles of their respective native regions in conjunction with the aesthetic forms of metal. Much like what is expressed in the In Extremo review excerpts above, new genre frames began to emerge and discourses of "folk metal" and "mittelalter rock" afforded more specific aesthetic connections to be explored. As these discourses expanded and became more collectively defined, the reliance upon more generalized German referents was relinquished in favor of more targeted comparatives and/or markers of subgenre authenticities.

Side-line (review of Saltatio Mortis' *Wer Wind Sæt*): When we think of Napalm Records we directly think of metal music, but a few bands like Saltatio Mortis are the exceptions to the rule. This band remains a kind of offspring between softer metal influences and rock-folk music. The mixture will be highly appreciated by the lovers of Letzte Instanz, In Extremo or yet Tanzwut. Saltatio Mortis possibly influenced a lot of bands (and probably some of the aforementioned names) gaining a serious recognition in their genre [Side-line].

All Music (review of Subway to Sally's *Foppt Den Dämon*): effortlessly merge the diverse influences like Brian May, Jethro Tull, Kansas, and Horslips with '90s progressive metal. It must have been a formula that both the band and BMG approved of due to the similarity of their three albums from 1996–1999. Had this band sung in English and not German they would almost certainly have made significant impressions in both the U.K. and North America [Sleger "*Foppt*"].

All Music (review of Subway to Sally's *Bannkreis*): Like Jethro Tull, great attention is given to the complimentary effect that acoustic instruments create in an otherwise hard rock environment; acoustic guitar, lute, drehleier (hurdy-gurdy), involved vocal harmonies, and, of course, the violin all contribute throughout this recording to provide the rich seasonings that have become as much of a trademark of Subway to Sally as their overt heavy metal leanings [Sleger "*Bannkreis*"].

DeutschMusikLand.com (review of Subway to Sally's *Bastard*): Although it would be quite easy, in fact unavoidable, to compare the sound here to Rammstein, with their heavy guitars, or In Extremo, the comparison would not be quite fair. Subway to Sally definately (sic) has a sound all their own, a large, but not exclusive, part of that being the very distinctive vocals of Eric Fish [Landers].

Though Rammstein's presence as a Germanic band with metal connections lingers as a point of comparison for acts like In Extremo or Saltatio Mortis, distinctions based on instrumentation choices and song styles are also emphasized. Unlike the detractors of Gothminister or Hanzel und Gretyl, these reviewers perceive new stylistic paths and, as a result, allow notions of mittelalter rock to come to fruition (see for example, Winnick). This fruition is accentuated by Subway to Sally's tendencies to dress in medieval-esque clothing on stage and in publicity materials.

Interestingly, Subway to Sally, a band called "one of the most influential medieval German acts ever" (Sputnikmusic), presents a career arc which both reflects and resists the mittelalter trends. The band's debut, *Album 1994*, is the lone release in which both English and German lyrics are delivered atop what its liner notes describe as "folkedelic" tunes, some written by the band and some adapted from traditional folk origins. Releases from the mid- to late 1990s like *Foppt Den Dämon* and *Bannkreis* feature the acoustic instrumentation Sleger praises above, but releases like 2003's *Engelskrieger*, 2007's *Bastard* or the concert recording *Schrei* demonstrate more rock/metal elements.

Yet, as Landers' review suggests, the overall Subway to Sally presentation extends beyond distorted power chords and has garnered the band its reputation as a thriving German act equally capable of delivering a full spectacle rock show or an acoustic set (as documented on the 2006 *Nacht* and 2010 *Nacht II* CD/DVD releases). Innovation and performances with distinctive integrity mark the band as validly authentic.

Conclusion

Much like Kraftwerk or Einstürzende Neubauten reappear as staple references for music critics intent on displaying their knowledge of German popular musical history, Rammstein remains a common point of connection as well. Though Rammstein has become less visible on North American music charts (and in the States, given the gap between 2001's Pledge of Allegiance and 2012's Made in Germany concert tours), the legacy of their considerable commercial success assures their status as the leading German language band in hard rock. Inevitably though, rock criticism invokes the qualifier of being German as an implicit point of anomaly. The presumption that rock is a genre rooted in English language performance is covertly conveyed and those artists who breach this unspoken understanding are inherently othered. This othering often entails little more than the superficial stereotypical significations tied to the language itself. As Georgina Born and David Hesmonhalgh offer, this can become a form of "psychic tourism through music" which can "inscribe and reinscribe ... hierarchies and stratifications" (35) between self and other.

Rolling Stone (review of Rammstein's *Reise Reise*): Already a smash in Rammstein's native Germany, *Reise, Reise* pulls together sleek industrial stomp, raw kraut-rock power and Wagnerian choruses with iron precision. The only English chorus on the band's fifth album effuses a growing European sentiment: "We're all living in Amerika." Over here, the album should sound both scaryfunny (sic) and familiar to metal-attuned ears, though this sextet backs up its cartoonish clout with a decent-size bag of tricks [Hoard].

Rough Edge.com (review of In Extremo's *Sünder ohne Zügel*): What's perhaps most fascinating about these purveyors of "German folk metal" is how well they pull it off. You wouldn't think that bagpipes, glockenspiels and what sounds like a power saw (in track 6, "Vollmond") would play well next to a chunky electric guitar, but they do. In Extremo's arrangement and unique style of songwriting make every instrument not only fit, but seem necessary. It gives the band's sound a unique atmosphere and, again, majesty that makes everything bigger than life.... The lyrics, again, are all sang (sic) and printed on the CD cover in German. And, by the way, that German inflection enhances the music as well. I'm not so sure *"Sünder ohne Zügel"* would sound as good in English [Bolton "Sünder"].

In both instances above, the reviewers accentuate the importance of Germanness to the overall experience the record is presumed to have upon North American listeners. As applied to In Extremo, the exoticism of German lyric delivery accentuates the anachronistic historicization of amplified medieval musical adaptations. Something truly of the "old world" stands as being more "authentic" than an adaptation of an Anglo-accessible text (regardless of it being played, recorded, and consumed through modern technologies...). Hoard's review reveals the way in which the recurring ghosts of Germany's (militaristic) past slink between drawing reluctant praise and dismissive condescension. Unlike those responding to Hanzel und Gretyl's blatant performative exhibitions, Hoard writes his own prejudice onto the content regardless of actual applicability. What matters most, seemingly, is communicating that Rammstein reflects something non–American.

As the music industry undergoes a technologically-spurred metamorphosis and, as such, the means of publicity, distribution, and consumer contact alter as rapidly as technological innovation allows, the realm of music criticism somewhat surprisingly retains a formulaic predictability. The discursive tendencies of rock criticism developed in the early days of publications like *Rolling Stone, Creem*, and *Maximum Rock and Roll* have carried forth into successive generations of those writing about rock and its varied manifestations. When genre divides do occur, the process of developing a new discourse sensitized to particular aesthetic qualifiers understandably begins by drawing upon that from which it emerged. In the case of Rammstein, expectations of the Anglo-Americanization of rock could not be avoided and, oftentimes, were valorized by highlighting the exoticism of Rammstein's unexpected popularity.

It is from this juncture that the bands following Rammstein became contextualized. Subject to immediate comparison to Rammstein and the lingering hegemonies built within the Anglo-Americentric rock music industry, those following in the wake of Rammstein found themselves simultaneously aided and inhibited by rock praxis and the pre-existing discursive frames of rock criticism. Though the growth of localized European scenes and independent music labels provided outlets for bands like In Extremo and Gothminister, only once a body of new genre world comparatives had been established did rock journalists begin to overcome their tendencies toward lumping all the post–Rammstein acts into a singular, ill-fit collective.

The author extends his special thanks to Valerie Hauss-Smith for her assistance in translation of the Sylvia Martinez Garcia article and to Tonia Taherzadeh and Sean Kennedy for their collective editorial assistance.

Works Cited

Adelt, Ulrich. "Ich bin der Rock'n'Roll-Übermensch: Globalization and Localization in German Music Television." *Popular Music and Society* 28, no. 3 (July 2005): 279–295.

Anderson, Ryan. Review of *Über Alles* by Hanzel und Gretyl. AllMusic.com. http://www.al lmusic.com/album/uber-alles-mw0000596159 (accessed November 28, 2011).

Behr, Eric T. "Hanzel und Gretyl Show an Exhibition of an Unmissed Dying Genre." *Sound + Noise Presents* (24 October, 2011). http://thesoundandnoise.com/2011/10/24/ha nzel-und-gretyl-show-an-exhibition-of-an-unmissed-dying-genre/ (accessed November 28, 2011).

Bolton, R. Scott. Review of *Sünder ohne Zügel* by In Extremo. Rough Edge.com. http:// www.roughedge.com/cdreviews/i/inextremo.htm (accessed November 28, 2011).

_____. Review of *Verehrt und Angespien* by In Extremo. Rough Edge.com. http://www.r oughedge.com/cdreviews/i/inextremo.htm (accessed November 28, 2011).

Born, Georgina, and David Hesmondhalgh. "Introduction: On Difference, Representation, and Appropriation in Music." *Western Music and Its Others*, edited by Georgina Born and David Hesmondhalgh, 1–58. Berkeley: University of California Press, 2000.

Carlsson, Johan. Review of *Gothic Electronic Anthems* by Gothminister. *Release Magazine* (24 March 2003). http://www.releasemagazine.net/Onrecord/orgothministergea.htm (accessed January 30, 2012).

Clifford, Dave. Review of *Verehrt und Angespien* by In Extremo. *San Francisco Weekly* (1 March 2000). http://www.sfweekly.com/2000-03-01/music/in-extremo/ (accessed November 20, 2011).

Eddy, Chuck. "Recordings." *Rolling Stone* 779 (5 February 1998): 62.

Fenster, Mark. "Consumers' Guides: The Political Economy of the Music Press and the Democracy of Critical Discourse." *Pop Music in the Press*, edited by Steve Jones, 81–92. Philadelphia: Temple University Press, 2002.

Frith, Simon. "The Discourse of World Music." *Western Music and Its Others*, edited by Georgina Born and David Hesmondhalgh, 305–22. Berkeley: University of California Press, 2000.

_____. *Performing Rites: On the Value of Popular Music.* Cambridge: Harvard University Press, 1998.

Garcia, Sílvia Martínez. "La Production de genres: analyses depuis les périphéries du heavy metal." *Volume!* 5, no. 2 (2006): 91–113.

"Gothminister." Review of *Empire of Dark Salvation* by Gothminister. *Spike Magazine* (2006). http://www.spikemagazine.com/gothminister-empire-of-dark-salvation.php (accessed January 19, 2012).

Hoard, Christian. Review of *Reise Reise* by Rammstein. *Rolling Stone* 966 (27 January 2005): 61–62.

Jones, Steve. and Kevin Featherly. "Re-Viewing Rock-Writing: Narratives of Popular Music Criticism." *Pop Music in the Press*, edited by Steve Jones, 19–40. Philadelphia: Temple University Press, 2002.

Kenneally, Tim. Review of *Verehrt und Angespien* by In Extremo. *Spin Magazine* 16 (July 2000): 66.

Landers, Mikki. Review of *Bastard* by Subway to Sally. *DeutschMusikLand.com* (November 2007). http://www.deutschmusikland.com/reviews/bastard.php (accessed June 5, 2012).

Larkey, Edward. "Just for Fun? Language Choice in German Popular Music." *Popular Music and Society* 24, no. 3 (February 2000): 1–20.

Laurin, Hélène. "Triumph of the Maggots? Valorization of Metal in the Rock Press." *Popular Music History* 6, no. 1/2 (April 2012): 52–67.

Lechner, Ernesto. *Rock en Español: The Latin Alternative Rock Explosion.* Chicago: Chicago Review Press, 2006.

Malmstedt, Kalle. Review of *Empire of Dark Salvation* by Gothminister. *Release Magazine* (8 June 2008). http://www.releasemagazine.net/Onrecord/orgothministereods.htm (accessed January 30, 2012).

Moore, Allan. "Authenticity as Authentication." *Popular Music* 21, no. 2 (May 2002): 209–23.

Negus, Keith. *Popular Music in Theory: An Introduction.* Hanover, NH: University Press of New England, 1997.

Neilstein, Vince. "Hanzel und Gretyl: American Rammstein." Review of *Über Alles* by Hanzel und Gretyl. MetalSucks.net (16 December 2009). http://www.metalsucks.net/2009/12/16/hanzel-und-gretyl-american-rammstein/ (accessed November 28, 2011).

Perri, Dave. Review of *Sunder ohne Zugel* by In Extremo. *Brave Words and Bloody Knuckles.* http://www.bravewords.com/hardwares/1000378 (accessed November 28, 2011).

Popke, Michael. Review of *Scheißmessiah* by Hanzul und Gretyl. Sea of Tranquility.com (8 December 2004). http://www.seaoftranquility.org/reviews.php?op=showcontent&id=1942 (accessed November 28, 2011).

"Rammstein." *Rolling Stone* 802/803 (24 December 1998): 2.

Romanow, Rebecca. "But ... Can the Subaltern Sing?" *CLCWeb: Comparative Literature and Culture* 7, no. 2 (June 2005). http://docs.lib.purdue.edu/clcweb/vol7/iss2/6 (accessed June 10, 2012): 1–11.

Saeger, Eric. Review of *Zwanzig Zwölf* by Hanzel und Gretyl. *Spike Magazine* (11 March 2008). http://www.spikemagazine.com/hanzel-und-gretyl-zwanzig-zwolf.php (accessed November 28, 2011).

Side-line. Review of *Happiness in Darkness* by Gothminister. *Side-line Magazine* (20 November 2008). http://www.side-line.com/reviews_comments.php?id=37462_0_17_0_C (accessed June 5, 2012).

_____. Review of *Wer Wind Sät* by Saltatio Mortis. *Side-line Magazine* (29 September 2009). http://www.side-line.com/reviews_comments.php?id=43609_0_17_0_C (accessed June 1, 2012).

Slayer666. Review of *Anima Inferna* by Gothminister. Metal Storm.net (1 March 2011). http://www.metalstorm.net/pub/review.php?review_id=10145 (accessed November 25, 2012).

Smith, George. "Young and Reich." *Village Voice* (2 December 2003). http://www.villagevoice.com/2003-12-02/music/young-und-reich/ (accessed November 28, 2011).

Spahr, Wolfgang. "'Explosive' Rammstein ignites Europe." *Billboard* 109 (19 July 1997): 56.

Sputnikmusic.com. "Subway to Sally." Sputnikmusic.com. http://www.sputnikmusic.com/bands/Subway-To-Sally/3664/ (accessed June 5, 2012).

Vayo, Lloyd Isaac. "What's Old Is NEU! Benjamin Meets Rother and Dinger." *Popular Music and Society* 32, no. 5 (December 2009): 617–34.

Walser, Robert. *Running with the Devil: Power, Gender, and Madness in Heavy Metal Music.* Middletown, CT: Wesleyan University Press, 1993.

Williams, Alan. Review of *Anima Inferna* by Gothminister. AModelofControl.com (10 July 2011). http://www.amodelofcontrol.com/reviews/?pg=ehgothanima (accessed June 5, 2012).

Winick, Steve. "Ein Kleine Mittelalterliche Musik: German Folk-Rock Gets Medieval." *DirtyLinen* 123 (April/May 2006): 40–43.

Discography

Gothminister. *Anima Inferna.* Danse Macabre 6412983. CD. 2011.

_____. *Empire of Dark Salvation.* Dancing Ferret Discs #20625. CD. 2005.

_____. *Gothic Electronic Anthems.* Tatra 062. CD. 2003.

_____. *Happiness in Darkness.* Ewave 88697393562CD. CD. 2008.
Hanzel und Gretyl. *Scheissmessiah!.* Metropolis MET 349. CD. 2005.
_____. *Tranmissions from Uranus.* Energy Records 81127. CD. 1997.
_____. *2012: Zwanzig Zwölf.* Metropolis MET 519. CD. 2008.
_____. *Über Alles.* Metropolis MET 279. CD. 2003.
In Extremo. *Sängerkrieg.* Universal Distribution 1768062. CD. 2008.
_____. *Sterneneisen.* Universal/Vertigo 76135. CD. 2011.
_____. *Sünder ohne Zügel.* Metal Blade 14424. *CD.* 2002.
_____. *Verehrt und Angespien.* Metal Blade 14281. CD. 2000.
_____. *Weckt die Toten.* Metal Blade 142462. CD. 1999.
Rammstein. *Reise Reise.* Universal Distribution 9868149. CD. 2004.
_____. *Sehnsucht.* Motor 5396352. CD. 1997.
Saltatio Mortis. *Wer Wind Sæt.* Napalm Records NPR 305. CD. 2009.
Subway to Sally. *Album 1994.* Autogram 03102. CD. 1994.
_____. *Bannkreis.* Ariola 91712. CD. 1997.
_____. *Bastard.* Nuclear Blast NB 1934SP. CD. 2007.
_____. *Engelskrieger.* Universal Distribution 0771032. CD. 2003.
_____. *Foppt Den Dämon.* Red Rooster 59652. CD. 1996.
_____. *Nackt.* Nuclear Blast 273611753. CD. 2006.
_____. *Nackt II.* Universal Distribution UNI929014. CD. 2010.
_____. *Schrei!.* BMG Ariola 74321712282. CD. 2000.

Part II: Rammstein, Literature and Culture

5

Heimatsehnsucht: Rammstein and the Search for Cultural Identity

NICK HENRY AND JULIANE SCHICKER

Throughout their career, Rammstein has without doubt built an aesthetic program, which is often defined by an exploration of the grotesque, macabre, and the provocative. In some respects, Rammstein's artistic success lies in their willingness to explore the boundaries of Western society's taboos — and their eagerness to push, bend, cross, and break those boundaries as they see fit. To be sure, much of their creative packaging — from their songs, to their videos, to their albums' cover art, to their official merchandise — seems to be geared toward one thing: provocation. While this is by no means limited to their early works, many of their more recent songs show that this monochromatic view of Rammstein's aesthetic program is short-sighted. Indeed, many aspects of their aesthetics have been previously overlooked, including their exploration of national identity, which has been addressed repeatedly in their songs. In this essay we argue that Rammstein's songs reflect not only a sense of German heritage and *Ostalgie*,[1] but also a distinct rejection of both the former German Democratic Republic (GDR) and reunited Germany. Thus, their expressions of national identity display a longing for a new, non-existent *Heimat*.[2]

As one of the central themes present in Rammstein's music, identity has been important to the band since their inception. In fact, one of the motivating factors behind the group's formation was (co-founder, guitarist, and background vocalist) Richard Zven Kruspe's realization of "how important it is to look for one's own identity, to discover it, find it and hold on to it"[3] (Hof,

19). Musically, the band recognized that conforming to the sensibilities of American rock and punk bands would have been inauthentic because that music did not reflect their German heritage (Serba). Instead, in order to be true to themselves, they needed a project that was "concerned with German music"[4] (Hof, 19), and that fit with the German language (Serba). It is, then, unsurprising that one of the key characteristics in Rammstein's exploration of identity in their music is the exploration of "das Deutsche"—that which is German. Textually, this is evident in a wide variety of the band's songs, which borrow to varying degrees the stories, themes, and language from German literature.[5] For example, it is well known that the song "Dalai Lama" from the album *Reise, Reise* (Arise, Arise)[6] is a direct adaptation of Johann Wolfgang von Goethe's "Erlkönig" ("Erl-king")[7] following its narrative structure closely. Lüke ("Modern Classics," 17) notes, too, that the opening verse in the song "Rosenrot" ("Rose Red") on the album of the same name is very similar to the beginning of Goethe's poem "Heidenröslein" ("Rose on the Heath") and that the song also borrows narrative elements from Friederich Schiller's "Der Taucher" ("The Diver") and "Der Handschuh" ("The Glove").[8]

Rammstein also borrows heavily from Germany's folk and children's literature in several songs including "Hilf Mir" ("Help Me"), which retells the story "Die gar traurige Geschichte mit dem Feuerzeug" ("The Dreadful Story of Pauline and the Matches")—originally published in the now-classic children's book *Struwwelpeter*—from the perspective of the little girl Paulinchen, who plays with matches and burns herself alive (Lüke "Modern Classics," 18; Burns, 466). "Spieluhr" ("Music Box") and "Mein Herz brennt" ("My Heart Burns") also incorporate elements from children's classics: two of the three opening lines from "Mein Herz brennt" are borrowed directly from the introduction to the German TV show *Das Sandmännchen* (The Sandman), and the song "Spieluhr" incorporates into the chorus the phrase "Hoppe, Hoppe Reiter" ("Hop, Hop, Horseman") from a children's song of the same name (Lüke "Modern Classics," 18). Many of Rammstein's love songs, too, are consistent with, and in some cases, imply works from German authors such as Opitz, Gryphius, Hoffmannswaldau, Benn, and Heym, among others (Lüke "Modern Classics," 19).

Rammstein's exploration of "das Deutsche" is also evident in aspects of their musical style. Perhaps their most clearly "German" characteristic is the vocal performance of front-man Till Lindemann. To begin with, several qualities of Lindemann's voice embody the international stereotype of the powerful male German—his overly-trilled "Rs," his deep voice, and the force with which he sings (especially on the percussive one-word lines prevalent on the albums *Herzeleid* [Heartache] and *Sehnsucht* [Longing]). Less superficially, though, his performances make heavy use of a well-known vocal technique known as *Sprechstimme* ("speech-voice") (Burns, 163), which was made famous by Arnold Schoenberg, but also has origins in Wagner's operatic style. In this style of singing, vocalists engage in a sort of rhythmic talking, in which pitch is defined, not in absolute terms, but relative to a performer's starting note (which may or may not be specified in the score). In Rammstein's music, the technique can be heard to some degree in many of their songs, but is used to great effect in their more narrative works such as "Wiener Blut" ("Viennese Blood"), "Dalai Lama," "Mein Teil" ("My Thing"), "Heirate Mich" ("Marry Me"), "Spring" ("Jump"), and "Hilf Mir" ("Help Me").

Importantly, the use of *Sprechstimme* speaks to a larger element at work in their songs, namely, the tendency toward the dramatic and theatrical. In their musical performances, they achieve this by emphasizing key textual elements. One clear example of this technique is the song "Heirate Mich," in which Lindemann vocally captures the speaker's descent into madness during the final verse by slowing his delivery, taking deep audible breaths, and screaming the final word "abgehackt" ("chopped off"). The raw vocal performance is also heightened by two effects on the vocal track, which further capture the decent into madness—a flange effect throughout the final verse, giving the impression that there are two voices (and multiple personalities) speaking, and a slow fade-out on the final scream, which makes it sound as if Lindemann is falling off a cliff. Similar vocal work is also heard in the final verse of "Zerstören" ("Destroy"), which ends with a slower, less articulated delivery followed by several screams of release. Another example is the guitar solo in "Stein um Stein" ("Stone by Stone"), which emulates a power-drill, capturing the main action of the song—a man building a structure to entrap his beloved. An examination of Rammstein's catalog shows that these are not isolated examples, but rather part of their musical program; the band is deliberate in matching the form of the music to their lyrics. This not only heightens the imagery already present within the lyrical content, but it also provides context and adds to the narrative. Notably, it gives the audience the sense that the band members—and particularly Lindemann—are not simply onlookers, but rather characters that play integral parts in the stories they are telling.

Rammstein's role as storytellers is immediately apparent in their live shows, which are as much theatrical as they are musical. In "Heirate Mich," for example, Lindemann takes on the persona of lyrical subject who creeps around the church where his love was buried. For "Mein Teil," Lindemann dons a chef's costume—complete with bloody face-paint and a knife attached to his microphone—and plays the part of Armin Meiwes (the "Cannibal of Rotenburg").[9] Keyboardist Christian Lorenz plays the part of his victim, who is literally cooked (via flamethrower) inside a giant prop cauldron. Similarly, Lindemann becomes the victim of a crash at an air show, setting himself on fire during the song "Rammstein" (underscoring its first lyrics, "a person burns.")[10] In their most recent North American tour, the prelude to the song "Bück dich" ("Bend Down")—a song about submission and sado-masochism—features four members of the band crawling on leashes from the main stage to the stage at the back of the crowd. In less dramatic numbers, the staging for the song often performs the same role, adding to the imagery of the songs through careful choices of lighting, colored confetti, and fire. The positioning of the band members, too, adds symbolism to songs, such as "Los,"[11] a song about their formation as a band and rise in popularity. The drummer, who usually sits atop an enormous platform, joins the rest of the band members, who abandon their typical wide formation and come together in the middle of the stage.

In their live shows, the musical and visual elements work together to create an artistic expression unique to the concert experience. Rammstein elevates their music from a purely musical endeavor to a theatrical one, in which the work is incomplete if only heard. Notably, this effort approximates the Wagnerian ideal in that it seeks to synthesize all facets of art in the theatrical in order to reach a single expressive goal. Kruspe himself explains that their show is a combination of "humor, theater, and East German culture" (Serba), and he describes the combination of "costumes, pyrotechnics, light, etc." as part of a *Gesamtkunstwerk* (Hof, 3). In doing so, he connects Rammstein's live performances to heavy influences from the German theatrical and operatic tradition. In striving toward this *Gesamtkunstwerk*, Rammstein recalls the German roots of this fusion between music and theater. They also differentiate themselves from many of their American and British contemporaries, who see visuals as a mere addition to the music, and thus treat them as separate artistic expressions that do not necessarily work together toward one communicative goal.

As Burns (467–8) writes, Rammstein's textual incorporation of German classical and folk literature, their vocals, and their visual performance emphasize an expression of German national identity. While these elements can be readily connected to the rise of German nationalism in the 1930s (as Burns discusses at length), Rammstein's focus on "das Deutsche" seems to operate on a more personal—and less nationalistic—level. Recalling that the opportunity to find their identity was a major factor in the creation of Rammstein, one might question whether their focus on German culture is a true expression of German nationalism, or rather an outgrowth of their more personal search for an identity. By heightening the more Germanic elements of their music, the band ensures that their art is not a conglomeration of British and American influences, but rather is directly relevant to their experience as Germans.

However, Rammstein's exploration of identity as simply an exploration of "das Deutsche" is incomplete. Specifically, it ignores the fact that each of the six band members are former citizens of East Germany, and that the fall of the Berlin Wall brought with it the fall of a way of thinking, working, and living. As Littlejohn and Putnam (35–44) argue, Rammstein's East-German heritage — and the loss of their *Heimat*— is of central importance to understanding the themes in many of Rammstein's songs. Specifically, they argue that *Ostalgie*— a "nostalgic longing for aspects of the former Deutsche Demokratische Republik"—"represents a viable means of re-associating oneself with a lost core component of one's cultural identity" and that it plays a large and expanding role in Rammstein's music (35).

In his book *Neurose D*, Wolfgang Herles argues that many East Germans long for the socialist ideals of freedom, equality, and brotherhood. Although these ideals were expressed in the national anthem of the GDR (in the lines "If we unite in brotherhood"[12] and "free human generation will rise")[13] they were ideals which were largely not present in the GDR itself. The anthem of reunified Germany still upholds those ideals by articulating the desire to strive for "Unity, Justice, and Freedom."[14] East Germans do not consider the idea of socialism to have failed but only its execution. For them, reunified Germany presented itself as some kind of land of plenty that could have been able to provide them with a "more successful version of socialism"[15] (Herles, 214). At the same time, however, many East Germans believe that they are morally superior to the "Wessis," with a humanist attitude toward life that is actually opposed to the supposedly materialist and consumption-oriented life-style of the West (Herles, 216). Here, the inherent paradox becomes clear: the longing for both the new and the old, while rejecting both of them at the same time.

Rammstein picks up that very paradox by identifying themselves as a product of the East, while it becomes clear through their songs that they were never really at home in the GDR. The band members do not feel that they belong to the West either. Like many former citizens of East Germany today, Rammstein still searches for that place that is called *Heimat*, where they feel that they belong to a native land. While *Ostalgie* is a component of the group's identity, they are defined by a more general nostalgia,[16] which we term *Heimatsehnsucht*: a longing for a home that has not yet been found. For the band, both the former GDR and Germany today represent flawed versions of that *Heimat* to which they cannot return, or which they cannot call their "native land." Their *Heimatsehnsucht* could also be, as Kant suggested for *Heimweh* (homesickness), a yearning for their own youth (Boyer, 372), a time that has not yet been compromised by life's struggles. Through their provocative and sometimes self-reflective lyrics, Rammstein simultaneously embraces the freedom of the West and seeks to tear down its superficiality. The band members do not fantasize a return to the GDR but mourn the loss of that utopian dream of a *Heimat*. For now, they do not belong in either East or West and the search for this lost core component of their cultural identity is reflected heavily in their songs.

Rejection of the East

Members of the band clearly voice their criticism of the GDR in essays written for Gert Hof's 2001 book about Rammstein. Paul Landers, the band's rhythm guitar player and background vocalist, says that "nobody who'd ever lived there liked the GDR very much. That was true for me as well"[17] (Hof, 38). Lindemann notes that "pretty much everything was taboo"[18] (Hof, 31) there. He laments the GDR's censorship and the resulting silence, which fed back into a political agenda where flaws of the system were kept under wraps, such as controlled government elections, a malfunctioning planned economy, or the immense spy apparatus of the Ministry of State Security of the GDR (the East-German secret police). Kruspe reminds the interviewer that all of Rammstein's members grew up in a dictatorship where art was used as a weapon that helped "critically dissect the shortcomings of society"[19] (Hof, 20).

This critical attitude also projects in Rammstein's songs, especially "Stein um Stein" and "Moskau" ("Moscow"), which take a rather negative standpoint toward a socialist state. In "Stein um Stein," the lyrical subject is building a stone house around his beloved, literally walling her in. The song clearly alludes to the erecting of the Berlin Wall and the securing of the GDR-border with fences and guards in 1961, and many of the speaker's plans are parallel to the motivations of the *Sozialistische Einheitspartei Deutschlands* (SED, Socialist Unity Party of Germany). Ideologically, the SED desired to form a socialist state, peaceful and free of Fascism, achieved by building a "society from scratch"[20] (Ritter, 172). Examples for this *Planungseuphorie* (euphoria for plans) manifested in the country's *Planwirtschaft* (planned economy), new housing tenements where every square meter of each apartment had its distinct purpose, or the overall feeling of governmental control, among others. The lyrical subject of "Stein um Stein" aims at forcing his prisoner to obey his plans and to be content with the miserable situation of being walled in.

In the GDR, however, this feeling of control and the "acceleration of the transformation of economy and society and the stronger assimilation to the Soviet Model"[21] influenced more than 3.5 million people to leave the GDR before 1961 (Ritter, 176) because they saw that the above mentioned ideals were far removed from their reality. The newly built wall in Berlin and the fences all over the country were supposed to prevent the mass exodus, but they were also a public display of the state's failures. The house in the song stands for this state that turned its borders into highly-guarded walls and fences. Already in the third line of the song, the lyrical voice criticizes this wall by saying that its stones resemble the tears of the person who is forever trapped inside. Not only did the wall separate families, married couples, or friends; it also caused at least 136 people to lose their lives ("Die Todesopfer" 2012). Just as the song's house was constructed without windows or a door, the GDR became almost a prison for its inhabitants. Few citizens were allowed to (temporarily) leave the country and if they left for good, they usually had to leave loved ones behind. The wall also not only restricted the view to the other side; many high rise buildings near the West were even torn down so that the East Berliners literally could not see to the outside of their country.

In "Stein um Stein," the lyrical subject aims not simply to build a house for the beloved, he is literally cementing her into the foundation of the structure. Applied to the GDR, this refers to the idea that each citizen should serve as an integral part of the community; but it also is a biting criticism of the dictatorial pressure required to make the social structure of the GDR function. As a result of this pressure, people were left without a choice and were unable to flee; rather, they had to surrender to the will of the state, which used their presence as propaganda to "beautify the foundation."[22] As implied in the song, the physical isolation created by the wall — and the restrictions to freedom of speech — transformed the GDR into a prison, where nobody could hear its citizens scream. Thus, the socialist state could not ever be a suitable *Heimat* for its citizens because it also serves as their prison. "Stein um Stein" further heightens the imagery of the GDR as a prison by contrasting it with that of a garden that is opposed to the dreary and gray inside of the cement house. For many people from the former GDR, the West embodied the image of "blühende Landschaften" ("flourishing landscapes"), a term that quickly became a buzzword in the public debate about East and West (Peterson). In Rammstein's song "Stein um Stein," however, these flourishing landscapes are made inaccessible. The wall itself actually became such a normal part of the day-to-day life in East Berlin that the people "accepted [it] as an inevitable part of the landscape" (Barney, 138).

In their song "Moskau," Rammstein uses the GDR's "ideological model" as the song's subject.[23] Moscow, the capital of the former Soviet Union, is personified as a prostitute that is ugly but irresistible. This paradox emphasizes the torn relationship many people had with the idea of Communism in general and specifically GDR. They "came to lead a 'double-life' under totalitarianism, where the conformity and deference to the state co-existed alongside the 'authenticity' of their private lives" (Barney, 137). As Mary Fulbrook points out, the "passive conformity was an acceptable compromise if outright ideological commitment was unattainable" (qtd. in Barney, 137).

Through the imagery of the prostitute, "Moskau" describes several defects in the city. First and foremost are the city's "red spots,"[24] which symbolize the Communists' colors, and are also a blemish on its face. They could signify anger, exhaustion, or even illness, which would allude to the many defects the Soviet Union, and also the GDR, had. Furthermore, it is clear that the city is in poor health, but that this is masked and its appearance is whitewashed. First, its teeth have been replaced with luxurious gold fillings — but on the inside, they are rotten. Secondly, its skin is old and must be powdered to keep up the illusion that it is young and healthy. Similarly, the city required surgery to repair its sagging breasts — symbols for female fertility — further adding to the illusion of health, youth, and prosperity. Taken together, this imagery implies that much of the best parts of the GDR were artificially constructed, and it alludes to the fact that the government of the GDR consistently pretended that economic and social conditions were better than there were.

The lines that are repeated three times at the end of the song come from the title of a popular children's game, "I See Something That You Don't See,"[25] and refer to the societal conditions that are seen by the citizens (represented here by the lyrical subject), but that the state (represented here by the city) is not willing to acknowledge. In fact, the song ends with the speaker implying that the state will never become aware of its defects. Indeed, many of the state's internal problems were never addressed adequately, leading to its eventual failure.

Rejection of the West

From the previous discussion, it is clear that Rammstein portrays a very complicated relationship with the East. However, their clear — though not completely unambiguous — rejection of the East does not mean that they have fully embraced the West or reunited Germany. Like their attitude toward the East, which is filled with both nostalgia and criticism, Rammstein's attitude toward the West is defined by a simultaneous delight in its political and personal freedoms, and hostility toward its cultural materialism and superficiality. Paul Landers said that he didn't like the GDR too much. But in the same breath he says: "Then I saw the entire polished surface of the West and thought 'it needs to be destroyed'"[26] (Hof, 38).

Fittingly, Rammstein's disposition toward the shocking and provocative grows out of this conflicted view of the West. On the one hand, it comes from a desire to use newfound freedom to confront topics that were previously off limits. Lindemann writes:

> All of a sudden, the wall came down. Now the time had come, I thought, to let out all those repressed thoughts. So I tackled them all: violence in the family, loneliness, incest etc. I mean, topics that are very emotional, where a lot of anger had built up inside of me over the years. I wanted to communicate with people about these things and for that the song is a perfect medium[27] [Hof, 31].

On the other hand, the provocative is used as a means of searching out and breaking cultural boundaries. Landers writes: "[The reference and value system of the GDR] is always looking for boundaries. Not for the sake of provocation but confrontation"[28] (Hof, 38). Similarly, Kruspe emphasizes the role of art in East Germany in relation to provocation: "[Journalists] tend to forget about our biographies: we grew up in a dictatorship where art had a completely different function, art was seen as a weapon. RAMMSTEIN can only be understood in this context. That always has been and will remain to be our basis."[29] (Hof, 20). It is evident from these quotes that Rammstein's handling of taboo topics is not provocation for provocation's sake; rather, it is a way for the group to break down the cultural norms of society. By finding and crossing boundaries, they force the listener to confront the topics for themselves. In doing so, Rammstein seeks to tear down the West's cultural façades that hide violence, loneliness, incest, raw sexuality, and child molestation, and they destroy the superficiality that these façades create.

Rammstein also tackles the superficiality of the West through songs that deal with the failings of reunification and the American-driven politics of the West. This connection is most easily seen in songs that offer a criticism of the reunification and its failures. As Littlejohn and Putnam (38) discuss, the song "Mutter" ("Mother") portrays the former GDR as a clone of the West, which was only kept alive through the West's influx of capital, which acted like a "feeding tube"[30] for the East. Thus, Rammstein "relays a sense of abandonment" by the West and a feeling that the reunification has failed. This sentiment is not completely surprising or without basis: the infusion of capital was assumed to be enough to fix the problems of the East, but after a few years, the Eastern economy fell flat, and there was growing sense of disillusionment among many East Germans. For example, Arzheimer and Klein (2000) note that as many as 60 percent of East Germans were disappointed in the reunification, and Falter (1998) notes that 40 percent wanted an alternative to the capitalist system put in place. It is not surprising, then, that the song "Herzeleid" ("Heartache") seems to both command us to protect each other from loneliness and warn us to guard against togetherness. Here, Rammstein recognizes the central paradox of the reunification: that both separated Germany and united Germany lead to great heartache for the East German people.

"Moskau," too, hints at disappointment with the reunification.[31] In their representation of Moscow as a prostitute, Rammstein uses to great effect imagery of the old juxtaposed with that of the new: rotten teeth have golden caps, the prostitute's breasts have been augmented, and old skin has been made up. This juxtaposition conjures up images of not only the East's ugliness, but also the West's complete superficiality; the "new" in each case is more beautiful, but completely superficial. Importantly, it is also entirely transparent and obvious to the lyrical subject. If one accepts the premise that the East's appearance was less beautiful than that of the West — one could think of gray *Plattenbauten* (housing blocks) or ruins of buildings that were not restored due to the lack of money — then the analogy is clear: after the fall of the Soviet Union, the infusion of capital in the East bloc allowed the countries to cover up its ugliness; yet the transformation was entirely fake. The reunification was expected to "beautify" the East in a more profound way. This transformation should have been not just physical — one may think of the restoration of the Frauenkirche in Dresden — but also political and economic, correcting systemic flaws, such as the planned economy and political corruption. In this case, Moscow, as a pars pro toto for the Eastern bloc, has always been this ugly sex symbol, an ideal that never lived up to its promise. Capitalism in the West was supposed to actually make the East beautiful, but it only allowed for another fresh coat of paint: the former problems still remained, but were just hidden under more expensive make up. Everyone seems to be able to see it, but is not always willing to acknowledge the status quo.

However, this reading of the song is predicated on the inherent ugliness of the city, which Rammstein may not believe in. Prior to the main musical entrance, the guest vocalist shouts (in Russian) that Moscow is more beautiful than any other city in the world.[32] Taking this into account, the song becomes purely a commentary on Capitalism and the West: Moscow is actually a beautiful woman, but Capitalism has forced it to serve money instead of ideals, which has turned the city into an ugly whore. At the West's insistence, the city performs labors of love in order to create wealth and keep up with its expectations. Instead of real commitment, the city finds itself in an abusive relationship with the West, where the accumulation of wealth is the ultimate goal. The aforementioned "facelift" is not a result of the West's attempt to beautify the East but rather the result of the East's efforts to conform to a money-oriented superficiality of Western business and culture.

The ugliness of monetary greed is also on display in songs that deal less with the reunification than with shameless consumption and class warfare more generally. The most clear examples of this are "Mehr" ("More") and "Zerstören" ("Destroy") off of Rammstein's two most recent studio albums *Liebe ist für Alle Da* (Everyone Deserves to Be Loved)[33] and *Rosenrot*. It is difficult to state categorically whether these songs are intended to criticize the money-driven culture of "the West" per se. It is likely, however, that Rammstein's views on the reunification and the West's superficiality (which is inextricably linked to its wealth) did, at least in part, influence these songs. This is particularly true when one considers Rammstein's experience as East Germans and their ostalgic disposition.[34] Even if not a direct commentary on the West, these songs certainly represent commentary on current culture, which is dominated by a Western viewpoint.

In the song "Mehr," the lyrical subject is money-obsessed, and spends his time taking as much as he can, regardless of what it is. The most poignant commentary in the song comes in the bridge, when the speaker portrays himself not just as money-grubbing, but the direct and absolute opposite of philanthropic. His goal is to do nothing but accumulate never-ending wealth, even at the expense of others. He is never satisfied and strives to deprive even poor people from their possessions. He is directionless and does not know the concept of "enough." What is more, the speaker is completely unaware of any problems associated with his overpowering greed. Indeed, at one point in the song, he literally laughs off an apparent (though invisible) criticism on his lack of modesty, saying that it is just a matter of personal choice.

The song "Zerstören" can be seen as a further commentary on greed. In this regard, the song paints a much more destructive picture of the culture than does "Mehr." The lyrical subject in "Zerstören" proclaims that he wants to take care of his own things while reducing the rest "to ashes."[35] Repeated in the chorus is his claim that he would destroy anything that does not belong to him. The speaker, driven mad by his need for destruction, is still concerned about his own belongings. However, he shows no concern for others or for what they own. These lyrics, coupled with those of "Mehr," seem to suggest that current monetary culture has devolved into a mercantilist[36] class-struggle, whereby the wealthy seek to destroy the wealth of their neighbors in order to accumulate more for themselves.

"Zerstören" also has a distinctly political aspect to it that is easy to overlook, if not for comments given by guitarist Paul Landers in a promotional interview for the *Rosenrot* album release (Groß). In reference to the American invasion and subsequent occupation of Iraq, during which the song was written, he explains that "[the band] was interested in the parallels between a marauding horde of young people running through the streets and destroying everything, and states that invade other countries and destroy everything there." Similarly, "Amerika" likens world politics to a dance led by America. As the song's dictatorial dance-master, America proclaims itself to be the leader on matters, and tells the other nations (the dancers) that they should fall in line and do as America says. Moreover, the dance-master sees himself as the authority on the dance, telling the dancers that he will prevent them from making mistakes. The most damning part of the commentary comes from the transformation of this dance-master (who ultimately has influence, but no real control over the dance) into a puppet-master who states that all of them must take part in the dance in the end, even though they may not want to.

Interestingly, this representation of America as a sort of puppet-master is consistent with the cover art chosen for the *Amerika* single, which features a jester-like picture of Lindemann as Uncle Sam. This single contains an English version of the song with very different lyrics on the same theme. In this version of the song, Lindemann plays the part of America, asking if he is wanted, needed, and loved while he can lead those who dance with him. To each question, the answer comes from a voice in the background, calling out that it does not, will not, and cannot do these things. With these lines, Rammstein make reference to the lead up to the Iraq war. America is in a position where they are asking for assistance, and the other countries in the discussion — literally and figuratively voices in the background — are reluctant to commit to the war. But then America asserts its dominance, and the voices in the background realize that they have little choice: the wish for love and affection will only cause pain. The end result, according to the chorus (in both the German and the American version of the song), is a world in which we are all living in an essentially American world that has been commercialized and militarized.

On this point, Rammstein's rejection of American-driven politics is natural, given that the members have described themselves as belonging to the political left (Serba).[37] Yet, Rammstein's rejection of Western politics is ironic given that the fall of the Berlin Wall and, with it, their freedom of expression is due in part to America's involvement in European politics. It is equally ironic that Rammstein criticizes America's cultural expansion — again portrayed as superficial, materialistic, and "vacuous" — by mocking Wonderbra, Euro-Disney, and Santa Claus (Littlejohn and Putnam, 39). Rammstein has released seven songs featuring large amounts of English text,[38] and their unprecedented international success is due in large part to their ability to break into the American market and become part of its pop-culture.[39] Fortunately this irony is recognized in "Amerika," through the use of the English lyrics. Were the song meant purely as a protest song against American expansionism, singing in English would be antithetical to the cause. Instead, Lindemann proclaims that he is not singing a "love song" right before his own admission that he isn't singing in his native language. In this way Rammstein signals a simultaneous rejection of American politics and a reluctant acceptance of American culture. To be clear, the acceptance is half-hearted and comes without any "love" behind it, but the band's continued use of English on their albums suggests that Rammstein really has adopted portions of Western culture into their identity — even if unenthusiastically.

Heimatsehnsucht: Longing for Home

Rammstein's search for a *Heimat* is complicated given their paradoxical rejection and desire for both East and West. Similar to "Herzeleid," which recognized both the pain of unity and the pain of loneliness, "Ohne dich" ("Without You") articulates a paradox central in their search for *Heimat*[40] where the protagonist cannot exist without his counterpart, but is still utterly alone in his or her company. If we interpret the "you" as a country, then this text portrays the dialectic relationship between the speaker and his (home) country. He cannot be without a homeland, a place he can call his *Heimat*. A *Heimat*, therefore, is the foundation for his identity that would make him feel less alone. As soon as he is connected to such a country, however, he feels lonely despite (or because of) the presence of this land. For Rammstein, this would mean that their longing for a *Heimat* can never be satisfied, even though one of their primary goals was to create music through which they could stay connected to their native land. On the one hand, they feel alone or "heimatlos" ("without a home") because their original home country had ceased to exist (and may have never been their *Heimat*), but on the other hand, the West cannot offer them this *Heimat* either.

Values like freedom of speech, freedom of travel, or a democratic apparatus were corrupted in the GDR, which prevented a true feeling of *Heimat* in connection to the country. Yet, this feeling was lacking in a free and united Germany as well. "After the years behind walls in the GDR," Kruspe viewed America as "the embodiment of freedom"[41] (Hof, 19), but that did not mean that he (and the other band members) felt a strong personal connection to the country or its culture. Because Western society in America (and also reunited Germany) did not honestly address emotional topics that the band wanted to address, it was superficial and inauthentic, and thus it also failed to provoke true feelings of *Heimat*. Rammstein therefore incorporates elements of "das Deutsche" to emphasize a connection with the land and to reflect on the band members' background. Through this focus on their German identity, they hope to get closer to that feeling of belonging created by a *Heimat*.

Since their formation, Rammstein has portrayed this wish for such a place, which would have the capacity to form their identity. On their second album, *Sehnsucht*, they articulate this desire in a song of the same name. While utilizing imagery, which creates a melancholic atmosphere such as tears or unhappy clouds, the lyrical subject realizes that nothing is the same anymore and that the place he once called home and which is compared with the lap of a lioness is gone. He is looking "between [...] long legs"[42] for last year's snow and last year's sand, but laments the fact that it is gone. If this is linked with the band's past, then the dissolution of their home country, the GDR, in 1989 may have invoked this feeling of loss, understanding the sand as an earthly element that forms the soil of a country.[43] The lioness's lap and the long legs allude to a female being, just like the harlot Moscow, the mother in the song "Mutter," or the swimming woman in "Feuer & Wasser" ("Fire & Water"). Together with the sand, these females represent a Motherland — a protective and caring entity — which brings to mind a Freudian return to the mother's womb in order to feel at home. As Boyer (372) suggested, Rammstein are yearning for their own youth, a time that has not yet been compromised by life's struggles.

Within this sad moment in the song, the lyrical subject describes a feeling of longing that remains hidden, but which stings deeply when he sleeps; in this moment, he realizes that he will probably never reach a feeling of happiness anywhere he goes even though he is looking for a place to call home again: though he may move toward other places in search for that lost *Heimat*, he fails to reach it. The closing remarks condemn this longing as cruel but everlasting. His longing has dissolved into water, leaving the above-mentioned sand out of reach, and with it, the home country.

There does not seem to be an end to longing, which makes a homecoming impossible. The lyrical subject is primarily chasing after what could be a home, which is also articulated in the song "Feuer & Wasser." The image of the female returns, paired with erotic connotations, which reveals the lyrical subject's yearning for intimacy and appreciation. He loses all his hopes and confidence to ever be able to unite with her. The woman is compared to fire, which makes her incompatible with the lyrical subject, who represents water, having with wet, slippery, and cold hands. The same theme of a distant mother is taken up in the song "Du riechst so gut" ("You Smell So Good") from the album *Herzeleid* where a blind child crawls forward, following the scent of his mother, only reaching her to touch her skin. Yet as they are reunited, there is no closeness, no tender care.

As Freud suggests, there can be no final union with the mother, only a surrogate relationship with other adults that are mere substitutes for the original connection. Hence, every union can only be a flawed version of one original, but impossible, union with the mother. If we compare that to the connection with a homeland, then Rammstein suggests that, if the original union with one's home country is lost, a new union will never satisfy a person's need for closeness, belonging, and love. This song plays to the larger theme about longing for a homeland and the recognition that any union is a difficult venture, especially when both parties are opposed to each other like water and fire in the song, or Communism/Socialism and Capitalism in the case of the GDR and the Federal Republic of Germany. "Feuer & Wasser" may directly be linked to a man chasing a woman, but thematically, it is referring to any union of two contrasting partners.

Conclusion

Using sexual allusions in their texts as well as presenting provocative images in videos, Rammstein is acutely aware of the reaction to their art, but uses this shock-effect to point their audience to themes of great importance. The band also recognizes that they do not truly belong in their new world and address this question of identity in the autobiographical song "Los." In their comparison of their lives before and after their success (the first and third verses, respectively), Rammstein describes their transition from a collection of unknown individuals into an internationally recognized band, who through their artistic program has found a voice. Lindemann connects their development directly to the reunification when he describes the lack of freedom in the East and his personal explosion of expression after the wall came down. Kruspe connects it to his own search for identity, which began at the hands of the East-German police toward the end of the GDR (Hof, 16).

For Rammstein, finding a voice was not only about forming a successful band; it was about dissociating themselves from the personal and artistic boundaries of the East. What is interesting is that the song's second verse discusses the new boundaries in the West. Specifically, they talk about the reaction of their critics, who were shocked and did not know how to react to them. They lament their critics, who — they claim — have consistently misunderstood them, try to censor them, and who label them and their music as artistically deficient and morally corrupt. The contrast between their growth and the reaction to their art tells a story, wherein they find their voice only to be misunderstood and rejected. Perhaps the most telling line in the song comes just before its conclusion, when they say that they are "somewhat anchor-less."[44] This one line sums up the entirety of the discussion to this point: Rammstein's conflict of identity between East and West — their rejection of both and their rejection by both — makes them fundamentally incapable of belonging to either. Still, Rammstein does not shy away from this fact. The positioning of the verses in "Los," allows them a chance to claim their position on the outside of society in the final lines of the song, when they tell their critics that they will soon become silent and that they will never get rid of the band. With this, they defiantly make it known that they do not intend on changing for anyone. Thus, their version of Heimatsehnsucht is one not where they long to find acceptance in an existing place, but rather one which they create for themselves.

Rammstein's rejection of and by both the East and the West, and the band's search for *Heimat* becomes especially overt in their song "Mein Land" ("My Country"), which was released for the first time on their greatest hits album *Made in Germany* in December 2011. In addition to the textual elements, images from the corresponding video, in which the band is having fun on the beach, contribute to the symbolism.[45] In "Mein Land," there are three characters portrayed by Lindemann and defined by visual cues and voice effects: Person 1 yells to Person 2, asking him where he is going; Person 2 replies from offstage that he is going from East to South alone. The question is asked over and over again; Person 2 replies several times that he is moving from the South to the West and then to the North. Then Person 3 comes running, carrying a flag. He declares that this is his country and indicates with some hostility, that Person 2 is not welcome in his land.

The questioning goes on, but this time the one asking gives the reply himself: he had been moving from the North back to the East. Person 1 and 2 merge, revealing that he has been asking himself the question about his final destination the whole time. The search for a country went full-circle, but has not ended yet. Finally, the search goes directly to the West from what he considers East. But it is clear that he still travels completely alone. Notably, he never tries to go from West to East, which would be expected if *Ostalgie* were the defining characteristic of Rammstein's search for a *Heimat*. There is no possible "return" to the East, and indeed, there is no East to which he could return. The protagonist stays in the West, wandering from country to country, unsuccessful in his search for a place to settle. His search for *Heimat* is fruitless because other people seem to exclude him since nobody offers him a home.

For the video's dramatic finish, the heavens rip apart, and suddenly, the sky turns dark. The fun at the beach turns into an ocean-side concert scene, which includes characters from earlier in the video, and the sunny beach is transformed to one that is ghostly and uncanny. In contrast to the colorful shirts and shorts from the beginning, the band is now dressed in black clothes and face-paint reminiscent of the Joker from the movie *The Dark Knight.* They are standing among half-naked women, men with face-masks and leather clothing, fire-breathers, and other people who could belong in a circus or a grotesque show. This area stands in stark contrast to the earlier Hollywood-esque "feel-good," carefree atmosphere with beach girls, Baywatch-like life-guards that stand in front of the waving American flag, fake smiles, and cheerful dancing. But now, the dark, metal music and the images in the video seem to line up. A German flag is carried upside down through the camera's view, and the American flag is gone, indicating that this is no longer Germany or America. Through a sign over the entrance to this beach, we learn that it is Rammstein's country. It reads simply: "Rammstein. Mein Land." Finally, the character from the beginning seems to have found his country. It is not a sunny estate with smiling faces, but frightening and chaotic. The protagonist has arrived in a country that is far from the typical idyllic and utopian *Heimat,* but it is one which they have created, and one in which they belong.

Rammstein's search for a *Heimat* runs tangent to the search for identity through their art. This led them to consider multiple possibilities and oscillate between East and West. It is clear, however, that they cannot find an identity through (re)unification with any country, past or present. Any union can only be a flawed version of what could have been a *Heimat.* Especially the dark beach in "Mein Land" shows this through images and text. The protagonist of that song is considered an outcast and will always remain one because he is not allowed to stay anywhere. He is searching for a place to feel at home, but his country has been "forgotten."[46] Instead of tying themselves to an imperfect homeland, Rammstein has created their own *Heimat.* In doing so, they have positioned themselves on the outside of society — but through their art, they have created a unique identity and found a way to hold on to it.

Notes

1. The word *Ostalgie* is a blend of the German words *Ost* ("East") and *Nostalgie* ("Nostalgia") and refers to a nostalgia for East Germany. Often, it is expressed through the creation and consumption of goods that were popular during the GDR, or through art, which reminds one of (primarily the positive aspects of) life in the former East.

2. The concept of "Heimat" is difficult to translate because it includes notions of "feeling at home," "homeland," and a feeling of belonging. As pointed out by Smith (this volume), the word is only properly understood in its social and historical context. The reader

is referred to *Peter Blickle's Heimat: A Critical Theory of the German Idea of Homeland* (Rochester: Camden House, 2002).

3. Original text: "wie wichtig es ist, dass man seine eigene Identität sucht, findet, entdeckt und sie festhält für sich" (Hof, 19).

4. Original text: "ein Projekt zu schaffen, dass mit deutscher Musik zu tun hat" (Hof, 19).

5. As Lüke (this volume) explores in depth, Rammstein's aesthetic shares many elements with that of German Romanticism. As it is not the goal of this paper to explore Rammstein's connection to classic German literature, the reader is referred to that paper.

6. Translation by Williams. As Williams notes, *Reise, Reise* means "Journey, Journey" in today's standard language, but given the allusions to seamen in the song, it is likely that the phrase is being used as a wake-up call, as it was in the past.

7. Translations are by the authors of this essay if not otherwise noted.

8. Lüke also notes that the video for "Rosenrot" plays on the theme of the femme fatale, which is present in the narrative of the song and can be compared to classic German works such as Heinrich Heine's "Loreley" or Frank Wedekind's *Erdgeist* and *Büchse der Pandora* (17).

9. Meiwes gained notoriety in 2002, when he was arrested for killing and eating Bernd Jürgen Brandes, a man who responded to an internet post by Meiwes looking for a willing victim. See Adney (this volume).

10. In more recent versions of the live show, Lindemann is no longer set on fire, but wears a giant armor-like flamethrower. Original text: "ein Mensch brennt."

11. This title plays with several connotations. On the one hand, it means "to go" or "to start," on the other, it refers to something that is loose. *Los* is also a suffix that equates roughly to the English suffix -less, and is used in this manner in 26 of the song's 46 lines.

12. Original text: "Wenn wir brüderlich uns einen."

13. Original text: "Steigt ein frei Geschlecht empor."

14. Original text: "Einigkeit und Recht und Freiheit."

15. Original text: "gelungenere Variante von Sozialismus."

16. In his article "Ostalgie and the Politics of the Future in East Germany," Dominik Boyer gives a detailed analysis of the term Nostalgia and its origin (364).

17. Original text: "Die DDR hat man wahrscheinlich nicht so richtig gemocht, weil man darin gelebt hat. Mir ging es auch so" (Hof, 38). As Littlejohn & Putnam note, the translation provided by Hof "conveys an antipathy to the DDR as an entity that was not present in the original." Furthermore, they correctly point out that the original indicates that the public was bored with life in the GDR and wanted to experience something beyond it.

18. Original text: "Da war eigentlich alles tabuisiert" (Hof, 31).

19. Original text: "Sich mit den Missständen in der Gesellschaft kritisch auseinander zu setzen" (Hof, 20).

20. Original text: "Die Gesellschaft von Grund auf [...]."

21. Original text: "Forcierung der Transformation von Wirtschaft und Gesellschaft und die stärkere Angleichung an das sowjetische Modell [...]."

22. Original text: "Verschönerst [ ] das Fundament."

23. This song has several interpretations that relate to the East-West relationship. Two of them will be handled in this essay: one immediately and one in the section entitled "Rejection of the West."

24. Original text: "Roten Flecken."

25. In German, the game is called "Ich sehe was, was du nicht siehst."

26. Original text: "Ich habe dann die ganze glatte Oberfläche im Westen gesehen und ich dachte: 'Die muss man zerstören'" (Hof, 38).

27. Original text: "Und plötzlich fiel die Mauer. Jetzt war der Zeitpunkt gekommen,

dachte ich, wo man sich alles angestaute [sic] von der Seele reden kann. Also habe ich diese ganzen Themen angepackt: Gewalt in der Familie, Einsamkeit, Inzest etc. Also Themen, die sehr emotional sind, wo sich eine große Wut in mir angestaut hat. Ich wollte mit Leuten über diese Themen kommunizieren und da ist die Form eines Liedes optimal" (Hof, 31).

28. Original text: "[Das Bezugssytem der DDR] sucht die Grenzen. Nicht um der Provokation, sondern um der Auseinandersetzung willen" (Hof, 38).

29. Original text: "[Journalisten] vergessen die Biografien von RAMMSTEIN, wir sind alle in einer Diktatur groß geworden und da hatte Kunst eine ganz andere Funktion, Kunst war Waffe. Nur so kann man RAMMSTEIN verstehen. Und das war die Basis und wird sie auch bleiben" (Hof, 20).

30. Original text: "In meiner Kehle steckt ein Schlauch."

31. Note that the following are slightly different interpretations from what was presented earlier, though they are not completely incompatible with each other.

32. It is, however, not clear whether this statement is meant as an honest assessment of the city or if it is meant ironically. Furthermore, it is not clear whether the statement — which appears in Russian — is meant to reflect Rammstein's opinion or should be attributed to the Russian or soviet's point of view. The following interpretation reflects the reading that it is an honest statement attributable to Rammstein.

33. Literally translated: "Love is there for everyone."

34. Also given that the absence of greed was seen as a major advantage to the socialist system in the DDR — see, for example, the East German propaganda film *Roman einer jungen Ehe* (Story of a Young Couple), which portrays capitalists as greedy back-stabbers.

35. Original text: "in Schutt und Asche."

36. As an economic theory, mercantilism promotes the view that there is a fixed amount of wealth in the world, and thus the only way for a country to increase its trade is to take it from another country.

37. In fact, "Links 2-3-4" ("Left 2-3-4") was written in part to quell criticism that they were right-wing extremists (Serba), and it explicitly makes use of a quote by former SPD politician Oskar Lafontaine, who once said, "Mein Herz schlägt links" ("My heart beats on the left") ("Rammstein: Das Herz schlägt Links, oder?").

38. Included in this count are the songs "Amerika," "Stirb nicht vor mir (Don't Die Before I Do)," "Pussy," "Stripped" (a cover of Depeche Mode's song released as a single), "Pet Sematary" (a cover of the Ramones' song featured on the *Ich Will* ["I want to"] single), as well as the English versions of the songs "Engel" and "Du Hast" included as bonus tracks on American release of *Sehnsucht* (Longing).

39. This is not to mention that their founding member lived for a time in New York and is also the founding member of a group called Emigrate, which sings exclusively in English.

40. It should be noted that this central paradox seems to pervade much of Rammstein's work. Although this paper connects it directly to the band's search for *Heimat*, it may also apply to other facets of the band's identity, notably matters of religion and spirituality. The reader is referred to Putnam (this volume) for an extensive discussion of this issue.

41. Original text: "Der Inbegriff von Freiheit" (Hof, 19).

42. Original text: "Zwischen [...] langen Beinen."

43. The reader is referred to Littlejohn (this volume) for a comprehensive look at Rammstein's use of elemental imagery.

44. Original text: "Etwas haltlos."

45. The interpretation presented here includes the visual material to do justice to the set up of a *Gesamtkunstwerk*.

46. Original text: "Vergessen."

Works Cited

Adney, Karley K. "A Carnivalesque Cannibal: Armin, Meiwes, 'Mein Teil' and Representations of Homosexuality." This volume.

Arzheimer, Kai, and Markus Klein. "Gesellschaftspoltische Wertorientierung und Staatszielvorstellungen im Ost-West Vergleich." *Wirklich ein Volk? Die politischen Orientierungen von Ost und Westdeutschen im Vergleich*, ed. Jürgen Falter, Oscar W. Gabriel and Hans Rattinger. Opladen: Leske & Budrich, 2000, 363–402.

Barney, Timothy. "When We Was Red: Good Bye Lenin! and Nostalgia for the 'Everyday GDR.'" *Communication and Critical/Cultural Studies* 6 (2009): 132–51.

Blickle, Peter. *Heimat: A Critical Theory of the German Idea of Homeland*. Rochester: Camden House, 2002.

Boyer, Dominik. "Ostalgie and the Politics of the Future in East Germany." *Public Culture* 18 (2006): 361–81.

Burns, Robert. "German Symbolism in Rock Music: National Signification in the Imagery and Songs of Rammstein." *Popular Music* 27 (2008): 457–472.

Falter, Jürgen W. "Politischer Extremismus." in *Wirklich ein Volk? Die politischen Orientierungen von Ost und Westdeutschen im Vergleich*, ed. Jürgen Falter, Oscar W. Gabriel and Hans Rattinger. (Opladen: Leske & Budrich, 2000), 403–433.

Groß, Thorsten. "Rammstein. 'Wir sind linke Patrioten.'" *Motor.de*, 14 October 2005, accessed 20 May 2012, http://www.motor.de/motormeinung/motor.de/wir_sind_link e_patrioten.html.

Herles, Wolfgang. *Neurose D. Eine andere Geschichte Deutschlands*. München: Piper, 2008.

Hof, Gert. *Rammstein*. Berlin: dgv, 2001.

Littlejohn, John T. "Fire, Water, Earth and Air: The Elemental Rammstein." This volume.

_____, and Michael T. Putnam. "Rammstein and Ostalgie: Longing Yesteryear." *Popular Music and Society* 33 (2010): 35–44.

Lüke, Martina "Love as a Battlefield: Reading Rammstein as Dark Romantics." This volume.

_____. "Modern Classics: Reflections on Rammstein in the German Class." *Die Unterrichtspraxis* 41 (2008): 15–23.

Murray, Williamson, and Robert H. Scales. *The Iraq War: A Military History*. Cambridge: Bellknap Press, 2003.

Peterson, Thomas. "Blühende Landschaften." *Frankfurter Allgemeine Zeitung*, 22 Sept. 2010, accessed 23 Jan. 2012, http://www.faz.net/aktuell/politik/inland/allensbach-umf rage-zur-deutschen-einheit-bluehende-landschaften-11040029.html.

Putnam, Michael. "Discipleship in the Church of Rammstein: Religion, Spirituality, Ritual, and Afterlife in the Music of Rammstein." This volume.

"Rammstein: Das Herz schlägt Links, oder?" *Laut.de*, 14 December 2000, accessed 29 May 2012, http://www.laut.de/Rammstein/Das-Herz-schlaegt-links,-oder/14–12–2000# artikel.

Ritter, Gerhard A. "The GDR in German History." *Vierteljahreshefte für Zeitgeschichte* 50 (2002): 171–200.

Serba, John. "Operatic Vocals, Industrial Rhythms Mix for a Sound Distinctly ... German." *Grand Rapids Press*, 22 July 2001: B6. Print.

Smith, Erin Sweeney. "Fear, Desire, and the Fairy Tale Femme Fatale in Rammstein's *Rosenrot*." This volume.

"Die Todesopfer an der Berliner Mauer 1961–1989." Gedänkstätte Berliner Mauer. 2012, accessed 23 January 2012, http://www.berliner-mauer-gedenkstaette.de/de/todesopfer -240.html.

Williams, Jeremy. Herzeleid.com, 2009, accessed 27 May 2012, http://www.herzeleid.com.

Discography

Rammstein. "Amerika (English Version)." *Amerika* (Single). Universal Records. 2004.

_____. "Amerika." *Reise, Reise*. Motor Music and Republic Records. CD. 2004.

_____. "Bück dich." *Sehnsucht*. Motor Music and Slash Records. CD. 1997.

_____. "Dalai Lama." *Reise, Reise*. Motor Music and Republic Records. CD. 2004.

_____. "Du hast (English Version)." *Sehnsucht* (North American Release). Motor Music and Slash Records. CD. 1997.

_____. "Du riechst so gut." *Herzeleid*. Motor Music. CD. 1995.

_____. "Engel (English Version)." *Sehnsucht* (North American Release). Motor Music and Slash Records. CD. 1997.

_____. "Feuer und Wasser." *Rosenrot*. Universal Records. CD. 2005.

_____. "Heirate mich." *Herzeleid*. Motor Music. CD. 1995.

_____. "Herzeleid." *Herzeleid*. Motor Music. CD. 1995.

_____. "Hilf Mir." *Rosenrot*, Universal Records. CD. 2005.

_____. "Links 2-3-4." *Mutter*. Motor Music. CD. 2001.

_____. "Los." *Reise, Reise*. Motor Music and Republic Records. CD. 2004.

_____. "Mehr." *Liebe ist für Alle Da*. Universal Records and Vagrant Records. CD. 2009.

_____. "Mein Herz brennt." *Mutter*. Motor Music. CD. 2001.

_____. "Mein Land." *Made in Germany 1995–2011*. Universal. CD. 2011.

_____. "Mein Teil." *Reise, Reise*. Motor Music and Republic Records. CD. 2004.

_____. "Moskau." *Reise, Reise*. Motor Music and Republic Records. CD. 2004.

_____. "Mutter." *Mutter*. Motor Music. CD. 2001.

_____. "Ohne dich." *Reise, Reise*. Motor Music and Republic Records. CD. 2004.

_____. "Pet Sematary." *Ich will* (Maxi Single). Motor Music and Universal Records. 2001.

_____. "Pussy." *Liebe ist für Alle Da*. Universal Records and Vagrant Records. CD. 2009.

_____. "Rammstein." *Herzeleid*. Motor Music. CD. 1995.

_____. "Rosenrot." *Rosenrot*. Universal Records. CD. 2005.

_____. "Sehnsucht." *Sehnsucht*. Motor Music and Slash Records. CD. 1997.

_____. "Spieluhr." *Mutter*. Motor Music. CD. 2001.

_____. "Spring." *Rosenrot*. Universal Records. CD. 2005.

_____. "Stein um Stein." *Reise, Reise*. Motor Music and Republic Records. CD. 2004.

_____. "Stirb nicht vor mir." *Rosenrot*. Universal Records. CD. 2005.

_____. "Stripped." *Stripped* (Single). Motor Music. 1998.

_____. "Wiener Blut." *Liebe ist für Alle Da*. Universal Records and Vagrant Records. CD. 2009.

_____. "Zerstören." *Rosenrot*. Universal Records. CD. 2005.

6

Rammstein Rocking the Republic: A Cultural Reading of the Trans/National Shock 'n' Roll Circus

Corinna Kahnke

It is the year 2000, and I have just come to the U.S. to begin my graduate studies in German. I flip through the radio stations in search of a program that plays anything other than Top 40. As I find a rock station, I hear it with disbelief: "...Du hast Mich..." (You Have/Hate Me) Rammstein. I can't help but nod my head and sing along — of course I know the lyrics. I feel a little bit of home, as I keep driving through the flat Nebraska landscape. Wait a minute, what just happened? As a newly arrived German in the U.S., soon to represent the Berlin Republic to American undergraduate students, how can I associate Rammstein with home — what about the allegations of fascist imagery and right-wing sympathies? As a recovering Goth, how can I sing along to what is obviously a mainstream, sellout industrial band? But beyond anything: Why would Rammstein find a place on a Midwestern radio station?

Two weeks later, I find myself explaining to a dismayed German 101 student that the song "Heirate Mich" (Marry Me) (*Herzeleid* [Heartache] 1995) featured in David Lynch's *Lost Highway* (1997), which he and his football team mates employ to "get into the zone" is the first person account of a grave desecrator who begs his cold victim to marry him. I am given to understand that the coach has changed his music selection quite drastically since.

As one might well imagine, Rammstein has since accompanied me to every university and classroom I have since entered, and it is time now, to lay out a new perspective on Rammstein, going beyond the usual explanations of "No, they are not neo–Nazis" and "Yes, students really like them, so we can learn something by engaging with Rammstein's body of work."

Along with film, popular music is one of the most important cultural export products. In 1998, however, Simon Frith stated in the introduction to a special issue of *Popular Music*, that "German popular music has to be understood differently to popular music elsewhere: twentieth century history has posed German musicians and audiences particular problems of national identity." Revisiting this statement in the second decade of the 21st century, how does this statement pertain to popular music? Reading Rammstein's body of work, a band who delivers a nationally coded performance which is just as much embraced and well received by an international audience, uncovers a particular brand of German popular music that is functioning on both a national and trans-national scale.

Taking John Littlejohn and Michael Putnam's reading of Rammstein's ties to the *Ostalgie*[1] phenomenon as a starting point, this essay explores Rammstein as a band "made in Germany." Successfully walking the line between being accessible to an international audience and representing the "authentic" German, they have carved for themselves a special niche in the trans-national market. More a "spectacular subculture" as defined by Dick Hebdige than a one-to-one representation of Germany, Rammstein has to be viewed through the notion of "camp," allowing for an intrinsically ironic reading of their hyperbolic performance. This approach allows for a new layer in the reading of Rammstein that places the band's pastiche performances in a postmodern context of visual and textual quotations.

In his article on German symbolism in rock music, Robert Burns investigates the particular national qualities in Rammstein's work; my inquiry aims to extend the analysis to a trans-national scale, expanding on Edward Larkey's study of trans-cultural influences in popular music between Germany and the United States. What stands out in Rammstein's work is the particular interplay of respective national signifiers, which are employed to portray and speak critically about contemporary events in Germany while addressing and involving the larger global audience. Through this reading, Rammstein's performances can truly become an access point to the Berlin Republic, since their music illustrates the diverse influences and cultural confluences present in Germany today; a country that negotiates its identity within the parameters of the global village, the European Union and its own local idiosyncrasies. Simultaneously, though, their parodic performances also deliver encompassing statements about contemporary Western society, accessible to a trans-national audience.

Within a global context, statements about fascist aesthetics and right-wing leanings have surrounded Rammstein, allegations which were particularly prominent at the beginning of their career. While their audio and visual performance contains elements that at times are open to such mis-readings, such as rolling "r" or darkly militaristic costumes, their lyrics in and of themselves contradict such possibilities. The members of Rammstein make it very clear that they have no right-wing political leanings. "Seit ihren Anfängen provozieren und polarisieren Rammstein dadurch, dass sie sich selbst nicht provozieren lassen und weder ihren martialischen Stil noch ihre tabulosen Texte über Sex und Gewalt kommentieren" (Bauszus).[2] They position themselves as musicians, as critics of society, as people who hold up a mirror to society. Indeed, Till Lindemann and his merry men succeed in their endeavor, similar to Till Eulenspiegel, an impudent trickster figure originating in Middle Low German folklore.

Rammstein are securely drawing on a multitude of German narrative and visual traditions across the centuries in order to portray and communicate with the Berlin Republic. An additional facet of a more recent German-German phenomenon is revealed by John T. Littlejohn and Michael T. Putnam, when they analyze the songs as works of *Ostalgie*, claiming that "the works of Rammstein provide a concrete example of a lost society subsumed inside a larger whole" (36). Developing this angle further, one may claim that their personal background as citizens of the former East Germany lends them not only a certain credibility in the German-German portrayal, but also delivers a possible explanatory model for their employment of what some may read as fascist aesthetics. As Jana Hensel points out in *Zonenkinder* (*After the Wall: Confessions from an East German Childhood and the Life That Came Next*, 2002), the fascist past is one that the former East still had/has to accept as a shared German heritage; in the cultural product that Rammstein delivers, this critical engagement is apparent. The artists themselves become emblems of a unified Germany by working through past and contemporary issues of the Berlin Republic on stage just as much as through their own personal background and their identity as a Berlin-based band. Isabella van Elferen even goes so far as to claim that within the collectivity of the East German Goth culture, they might be able to offer "East Germans a sense of belonging that unified Germany fails to give" (93), as they are to be read as part of (East) German Goth culture. In the end "wurden die Rammstein-Jungs die ästhetische Rache Ostdeutschlands am Westen" (Rapp, 121).[3] What comes across as a tongue-in-cheek reading touches exactly on the approach that the band delivers: In over-performing an assumed German image, expected by, produced and located within a trans-national arena, they take a critical stance toward Western traits such as consumerism, overstimulation, and decadence, ever aware and not sparing their own position within the process.

Located within the music industry, they benefit from its machinations just as much as they protest capitalist tendencies, having long since left the status of musical subcultures behind and entered the arena of mainstream popular culture. For a detailed musicological analysis of Rammstein's music, I would like to point once again to Robert Burns' detailed article. Here, as in most other articles discussing Rammstein's work in the context of musical subcultures, the genres mentioned for categorizing Rammstein are usually Heavy Metal, Industrial or *Neue Deutsche Härte* (New German Hardness). Within this context, they deliver a sound that shares commonalities with such bands as Nine Inch Nails, Laibach, KMFDM, Wumpscut, Front 242, and Marilyn Manson. Once again, trans-nationally recognized musical markers allow easy access and identification for an international audience. At the same time, Rammstein puts its own spin on the material, thereby claiming a nationally inspired niche in the trans-national setting.

One musical subculture that at this point has been largely neglected in the reading of Rammstein, though, is the Goth scene, upon which the band draws musically, visually and thematically. This in turn resonates with Larkey's observation that the "darkly insistent music" of such albums as *Herzeleid* and *Sehnsucht* (Longing) "share[s] some qualities of musical and aesthetic Romanticism," in which, as Schlegel writes, "a fantastically formed and generically ambiguous artwork turns concerts into quasi-mystical events" (Quoted in Larkey "Just for Fun?" 14). This additional placement of both Rammstein's aesthetic and their musical roots illuminates the national-trans-national tension that is so typical for the band. The Goth subculture is very much alive and popular in contemporary Germany, especially the former East, and in that it alludes to a specific German trait, which is in turn one that is an often utilized element in a stereotypical depiction of German musical (sub)cultures. Nonetheless, it is a trans-national musical genre, which can be decoded musically and visually by a global audience, confirming Rammstein as an "authentic" German but also international accessible phenomenon. Such an approach enables Rammstein to address in their performance multiple levels of codes and audiences. Visually, they reach out in a confirmation of parody-cum-social-criticism in their imagery employed on stage, as well as within their video productions. Drawing on elements from many different aspects of both nationally-coded German imagery as well as trans-nationally acceptable generic conventions, they succeed in creating a postmodern pastiche uniquely suited to portray and upset the Berlin Republic. On example is the band's utilization of industrial and BDSM versions of Bavarian *Lederhosen* (leather pants). In combining what are internationally understood to be "German" traits, they succeed in ridiculing Germans and their international audience at the same time when delivering a combined parody of traditional clothing items and allegedly preferred sexual practices. The artists succeed in making fun of German culture as well as those who believe that these elements represent German culture, employing specific nationally coded signifiers, which ultimately have been globally commodified. Another example of the re-appropriation of traditional or folkloristic material can be found in the music video for "Sonne" (Sun) (*Mutter* [Mother] 2001), where the band draws on the universally known fairy tale *Schneewittchen* (Snow White), giving a new dark spin to the traditional plot: The seven dwarfs labor for their dominatrix Snow White, the gold they mine serves her as a drug, an overdose of which sends her into a glass coffin. This is obviously a Rammsteinian twist, but the fact is that it lies in the appropriation of American iconography, namely Walt Disney's Snow White, which has become the trans-nationally recognizable image preferred to the more traditional Germanic depictions.

Next to the expected reviews in music blogs and journals, Rammstein has been discussed in the feuilletons both on a national and international level with varying degrees of understanding towards their parodic performances. Their songs have received attention from a rather unexpected side, namely foreign-language teaching. Until just recently, it would have been unthinkable to employ Rammstein in the German language classroom, which usually favors less aggressive and controversial musicians, such as Die Prinzen. In an effort, though, to appeal to the student body and to cater to their interests, Rammstein has become quite popular among educators, at least at the college level. Their materials are employed to explore children's classics such as *Struwwelpeter* und *das Sandmännchen*, German love poetry from Gryphius to Goethe, classic fairy tales, and grammar, as several articles in pedagogy journals such as *Die Unterrichtspraxis/Teaching German* indicate.

Gruesome topics in popular culture are nothing new per se, as we can see from Marilyn Manson to Nick Cave's *Murder Ballads*. Within the metal genre as well as in the Goth subculture, death, sexual violations, and dismemberment; all those are part of the show, and German bands such as Das Ich or Wumpscut (mildly successful in the U.S.) deliver similar scenarios. Once again, though, Rammstein succeeds in delivering both; the national within a trans-national context when they present their fans in "Ich Tu dir weh" (I Hurt You) (*Liebe ist für Alle Da* [Love Is There for Everyone] 2009) with a song located within the S&M scene, thereby drawing upon an international subculture with border-crossing signifiers, while playing with the stereotype that Germans in particular display a strong affinity for such power play. This song called the *Bundesprüfstelle für jugendgefährdende Schriften* (governmental censoring organ aiming to protect German youth from inappropriate and dangerous materials) into action, and, just as Falco's "Jeanny" and "Geschwisterliebe" (Sibling Love) by Die Ärzte in their day, the song was censored, which, of course, only added to the discourse, as well as to national and international PR; a few months later the censoring ban was lifted. What Rammstein provides are images of Germany that German officials do not want to have represented in the country, nor represent the country itself. "Wenn viele tausend junge Menschen in aller Welt diese deutsche Lyrik mitsingen, so liegt das an einem vom Staat nicht subventionierten, dafür aber immer wieder mal zensierten Kunstprojekt" (Gorkow, 4).[4] By doing this in a self-conscious and ironic way, Rammstein both subverts mainstream culture and undermines their very own subversive efforts in depicting the Berlin Republic and its issues on a large scale.

Fitting right into this discourse of representation, their most recent album, a retrospective work, has been entitled *Made in Germany 1995–2011*, a name, which points at a self-understanding by the band that supports the reading this article plans to deliver. The title references and evokes several factors simultaneously. First, it calls upon a trade mark introduced at the end of the 19th century, denoting the place of production, which during the time of industrialization had become of stronger importance. Soon enough, due to high quality products originating from Germany, the phrase becomes a seal of quality and, in the 1960s, a symbol of the West German Economic Miracle Years with Germany as a strong exporting nation. By utilizing this phrase, Rammstein represent their work as high quality performance while emphasizing Germany as their point of origin. With this, they embed themselves linguistically and semiotically into a trans-national context, utilizing English as an internationally recognized trade language and presenting their work as an export product. This affords them an authenticity at the same time as it denotes a distance, which combined affords them two seemingly contradictory yet complementary vantage points from which to talk about and represent the Berlin Republic.[5]

Upon its release on December 2, 2011, the best-of compilation immediately went to the top position of the German album charts; the album and title were furthermore utilized to kick off a highly successful world tour. After 16 years of performing in the public eye, causing numerous international and national controversies, there is a selection of key terms, which most people familiar with popular culture will connect to Rammstein's body of work, such as metal, sex, censorship, fire and fascist imagery. It may seem strange therefore, to claim this band as a representative for, and segue-way into, contemporary German culture and society. Utilizing music production as a reflection of political goings-on, though, is a well-established practice, and reading pop-cultural artifacts for their representation of society delivers meaningful insight, as can be seen in projects ranging from *Sangspruchdichtung* (a specific type of medieval political song and poetry) to the Love Parade. Despite the fact that Rammstein claims to be a non-political group, their body of work tells a different story and provides colorful socio-political commentary.

Taking the song selection of the retrospective album as a road map through Rammstein's materials, one can easily decode the selected works for their relevance and sociopolitical reference. The goal is to investigate and highlight the national vis-a-vis the trans-national elements, thereby drawing upon the tension in the accessibility of Rammstein materials as specific to their body of work and in turn illustrative for the Berlin Republic in a national and trans-national context. Though this essay cannot provide a detailed interpretation of every single song, a brief exemplary reading of selected songs highlights their approach.

The standard edition of *Made in Germany* begins with "Engel" (Angel) (*Sehnsucht* 1997), the first Rammstein song to be played on radio, garnering commercial success for the band. At the same time, it takes on the Christian faith, when depicting angels contrary to well-known lore as frightened and lonely creatures. More so, the declarations of fear and loneliness sung in the small voices of children may very well refer to the numerous scandals that Catholic priests have been involved with, which became a focus of both, the German and national press especially in the mid-nineties.

"Links 2-3-4" (Left 2-3-4, *Mutter*, 2001) served as the only work immanent response that Rammstein ever delivered against the right-wing and nazism allegations after utilizing footage from Leni Riefenstahls propaganda movie *Olympia* (1938) for the video accompanying a cover of Depeche Mode's "Stripped." Verse and chorus are reminiscent of Bertolt Brecht's "Einheitsfrontlied" (United Front Song, 1934), which has also been employed by left wing bands such as Ton, Steine, Scherben and Slime. As with many of their pieces though, Rammstein does not take one clear position, as they represent left-wing inspired fights by marching sounds in the beginning and call upon militant movements on the political left. With this, they do not idealize the political left over the right, but rather portray both sides of a political struggle that led not only to lethal street fights in Berlin of the 1930s but also bloody encounters between militant representatives of both groups particularly in Hamburg and Berlin of the 1980s. Taking on the issue of gene manipulation and artificially created life, "Mutter" (*Mutter* 2001) represents the voice of such a being, calling out for its non-existent mother, bemoaning its fate but also promising vengeance by creating an illness, which can be read as an allusion to viral warfare. One of the images employed, the birthmark on the forehead, is of biblical nature, linking this latest foil of humankind with the story of Cain's murder of his brother Abel. The phrase stating that an eel resides in her (the mother's) lungs in turn calls upon a well-known sexualized incident in Günther Grass' *Die Blechtrommel* (The Tin Drum, 1959), involving an eel and the protagonist's mother.

Following in line with their provocative behavior, Rammstein premiered the video for "Pussy" (*Liebe ist für Alle Da* 2009) on an internet pornography site. The main focus of the song, however, is the sex tourism and trade that German society engages in. Once again touching on Western decadence and simultaneous impotence, the lyrics also employ English language excerpts to underline the trans-national character of the criticized issue.

The special edition of *Made in Germany* contains remixes of the original songs and additional ones. They were composed by German and international artists, bringing together electronic and hard rock music through artists such as Westbam, Scooter, Laibach, Faith No More, and the Pet Shop Boys, confirming Rammstein's international stardom and musical cross-over capabilities.

The prime example of this is the single excerpt from the album, the only song not previously released. "Mein Land" first aired on November 14, 2011, reaching position 5 of the German Single Charts. The seemingly nation-related title is contradicted by the video airing together with the song. It portrays Rammstein as a surfer group from the 1960s, similar to the Beach Boys; indeed, the video was shot at a California beach. In typical Rammstein fashion, the band succeeds in utilizing stereotypes to simultaneously mock Germans, Americans, and trans-national trends.

The lyrics present a first-person narrator, who wanders alone across the land. In doing so, he is repeatedly asked by an unknown speaker about where he is going, to which he replies with different geographic directions, none of which welcomes him or invites him to stay. In each chorus, a second first person narrator takes over, declaring the first speaker is walking in his land, insinuating there is no room for the wanderer, which is confirmed by a third voice, seemingly emanating from the heavens, declaring that there is no room anymore. The deceptively simple question-response structure of the lyrics calls upon a wealth of connotations ranging from Biblical imagery and Christian tradition over historical to contemporary cultural and political events. The wanderer being told that there is "no more room" evokes the search of Mary and Joseph seeking space on the night that Jesus was born; an image that is often called upon in the context of immigration and asylum issues.

When presenting a voice from above that denies access to the land, Rammstein changes the original plot, turning what might be a helpful being from above into a supporter of the negative second narrator. This clearly calls to mind the Old Testament Exodus, especially as the 40 years in the desert fits in with the 40 years of the GDR existence between 1949 and 1989. The celestial voice represents in this context a power that delivers rejection and might very well stand in for the German government. In this phrase, xenophobia and asylum policies of the German people and its government are criticized.

Visually this is juxtaposed with the video that depicts a 1960s surfer movie scenario, including the type face, outfits and style of a Beach Boys music video—what could be further from Rammstein's dark music and oppressive lyrics? "Dabei ist das neue Video, wie schon frühere Songs wie 'Amerika' ziemlich klar politisch lesbar als Kritik an der kulturellen Hegemonie der USA, an einer Kalifornisierung der Welt. Gegen das Leichte und Sonnige stellen Rammstein das Schwere, Harte und Düstere, eben das Deutsche" (Hoffmann).[6] Germany's love-hate relationship with America is clearly thematized and the song serves as a criticism of both American culture imperialism and the absurd discrepancy of Germans' desire for other faraway places, California prominently standing in for a desirable paradise,[7] while they display rampant xenophobia in their own country.

Hoffman makes a crucial point when she asks, "Warum singen Rammstein am Ende von 'Mein Land' Worte wie 'Vertrieben — Vergessen'? Damit sind wohl kaum die amerikanischen Ureinwohner gemeint. Es gibt in unserem Land eine Subkultur, die sich auf solche Texte ihren eigenen Reim macht."[8] To answer this question, a further analysis of the accompanying video can be employed. It is important to understand Rammstein's body of work as a *Gesamtkunstwerk*, in which lyrics, music, visuals, and performance conflate.

Towards the song's end, as the chorus goes into repetition, the video's scenario changes: the viewer is transported into a contemporary setting, where Rammstein in their usual dark leather garb, faces painted in the style of *The Crow* (1994), preside over a dark shock-n-roll circus. They are performing as their musical selves, luring the audience into a place reminiscent of a freaky side show. This breach of illusion de-masks the idealized California beach scenario as a delusion, supporting a reading of anti–American, anti–capitalist, and anti-imperialist politics, while drawing attention to those that have been driven out and forgotten. The subculture Hoffman is referring to would clearly be located within the right-wing political German arena, and their reading of these terms refer to the *Kriegsvertriebene* (people displaced from their home areas after war) after World War II. Drawing on the ever-present association of Rammstein and right wing groups, this is a reading that cannot be completely disregarded. The much more prominent analysis though, leads to a critical stance toward, and comparison with, immigration policies in both Germany and the U.S. Not only is California a place that was home to numerous tribes of the First Nation, people who indeed were killed, driven away and are now largely forgotten by the general populace, it is also a state that is at the center of the Mexican guest worker and immigration laws debate. At the same time, German issues of immigration, asylum policies and Germans with a migration background are evoked, all of which are placed into a critical trans-national context. Who can make such a claim that a space is their land and theirs alone? Not one group. It is in the hyperbole of Rammstein's performance that we find the critical element, where they are visually and contextually linked with political cabaret and socio-political agendas. In his very last glance, Lindemann challenges the audience to look behind the obvious, invites them to partake in his criticism, but also ties the onlooker into his accusations, not allowing for a neutral stance of observation.

Rammstein might be a few years past their heyday, but their retrospective album, as well as the accompanying world tour, has been highly successful. Taking the circus around the world has brought them to major cities in Germany, Europe, and the Americas. Here, they have already made their name and confirm their status as a high quality performance act and ambassadors of the Berlin Republic. Like it or not, they are currently Germany's most successful and recognizable pop-cultural export. Their attraction lies in both their exotic character and their accessibility on the trans-national market. The shock value of their live stage performance might be somewhat diminished by the fact that by now one expects fire displays and has seen artists like Marilyn Manson push similar and related visual boundaries; nonetheless, the sheer force and energy of a Rammstein spectacle draws in the audience.

It is the year 2012, 12 years, several Rammstein lectures, and one article after my arrival in the U.S., I stand in Atlanta's Philips Arena, waiting for Rammstein to appear on stage. I cannot help but feel intrigued to finally come face-to-face with the band that has been both the bane of my existence and my inspiration for the last 12 years. Of course I will maintain an academic and analytical mindset during the soon-to-start performance; this is research after all....

In the audience, one can see several Bavarian costumes, worn in pride by their owners. While this indicates a misunderstanding of German culture and regionalisms (*Lederhosen* are after all still a specific trait of Bavarian culture), it also confirms Rammstein's position as cultural ambassadors for all of Germany. The ironic play with national imagery and stereotypes succeeds in the end.

As the six members of the band march into the stadium, they carry large torches, from which they light large flat cauldrons, reminiscent of the traditional opening ceremonies for the Olympic Games, which will occur later in the year in London. Both Leni Riefenstahl's *Olympia* and Susan Sontag's deliberations on the imagery of *Fascinating Fascism* (1975) come to mind, as the flames rise, and fire balls ascend to the sounds of the opening song, "Sonne." The song was originally commissioned as a title song for Ukrainian born boxer Wladimir Klitschko, and in the end deemed too hard by his management. The lyrics are structured around the counting preceding the proclamation of a knock-out, as is customary for the boxing ring. And the count-down begins. The over-the-top stage show and pastiche character of the performance that follows during the next two hours, however, lead the audience through a highly engaging spectacle, while providing a critical swipe at cultural and socio-political notions worthy of any cabaret satire.

When Rammstein launches for their encore into "Amerika" (*Reise, Reise* [Journey, Journey / Rise, Rise] 2004), the crowd goes wild. Similar to "Pussy," this song employs partial English language elements. In a highly ironicized way, the song depicts and ridicules American cultural imperialism and the cultures across the globe that fall prey to it. Nonetheless, the video, supporting the song's imagery with vivid illustrations does include the band's and ultimately Germany's fascination with the U.S. It succeeds in simultaneously representing stereotypes about and accomplishments of the nation in calling upon iconic images such as Coca-Cola, Santa Clause, Mickey Mouse and the first team of astronauts landing on the moon, where they discover that Rammstein has arrived before them. Breaking the illusion in a Brechtian manner, the audience is let in on the "making-of" the video at the very end.

This is directly followed by a rendition of "Ich will" (I Want) (*Mutter*, 2001), which presents itself as warning call for blindly following charismatic figures, when it lays out the strategies of exactly one such person in numerous "ich will" declarations. All too well aware of being part of the machinery, Rammstein's text switches from first person singular to plural, including the band in the media criticism and directly speaking from the stage to the audience, transposing the exchange into the here and now.

"Pussy" concludes the second encore, and having doused the audience one last time with fake pink ejaculate from the famous penis-canon, the six members of the band sink down into a Tebowing[9] position. They deliver an unexpected pop culture and satirical reference, once more utilizing a cross-cultural reference to illustrate their trans-national ability to engage in humorous and critical discourse.

Conclusion

As Jens Bauszus writes on the occasion of the Munich show on November 23, 2011, "Kritiker, die sich mit den Berlinern nicht befassen wollen, werfen ihnen faschistisches Gedankengut vor. Dabei enttarnen sie gerade dessen Inszenierung — sowie [sic] beim Einmarsch in die Olympiahalle. Im Ausland werden sie dafür geliebt. In Deutschland gefürchtet. Auch in Bayern."[10]

What is it then that Rammstein can reveal to us about the Berlin Republic? In the end, they are not as provocative as some might want to make them out, just as fears that a re-united Germany might start a third world war have not come true. Rammstein succeeds in walking the line with its postmodern pastiche, drawing on the past, present, and future, tying together national and trans-national elements. In this then, they also effectively portray the Berlin Republic, albeit in a somewhat darker mode than some might have it. What we find is a Germany which is, despite such cultural markers as Walser's *Gedanken beim Verfassen einer Sonntagsrede* (Thoughts While Writing a Sunday Sermon) still heavily influenced by its recent past and pasts, be that the Nazi era or unification. A Germany, though, that also claims a certain voice when (re)discovering German traits and carefully testing out the waters for modes of national understanding with and beyond the trade mark "Made in Germany." In his title story of the July 6, 2012 *Süddeutsche Zeitung Magazin* Alexander Gorkow, having traveled the last leg of the U.S. tour with Rammstein, writes: "Man wird Rammstein nicht verstehen, wenn man sich mit Widersprüchen nicht abfinden mag."[11] Rammstein, like the Berlin Republic, is positioned simultaneously in a German and trans-national context, communicating with and pointing at the issues of its audiences: Made in Germany — and at home on the globe.

Notes

1. The term "Ostalgie," a combination of the words *Ost* (east) and *Nostalgie* (nostalgia), refers to a nostalgic longing for the culture of pre-unification East Germany.

2. Since their early days, Rammstein have provoked and polarized through the fact that they themselves cannot be provoked and do not comment on their menacing style nor their taboo-free texts about sex and violence.

3. In the end, the Rammstein guys became East Germany's aesthetic revenge towards the West.

4. If several thousand young people sing along to this German poetry, then this is not due to an art project financially supported by the state, but one that gets frequently censored.

5. German singer Nena, internationally known through her 1980s hit "99 Luftballons," released an album of same title in 2009.

6. In contrast, the new video, similar to earlier songs like "Amerika," is an easily accessible political critique of the U.S.'s cultural hegemony, a Californization of the world.

Against the light and sunny character, Rammstein positions the hard, heavy and dark; the German disposition.

7. Another German "paradise," Thailand, had already been critically referenced two years earlier in "Pussy."

8. Why do Rammstein sing at the end of "Mein Land" words like "cast out" and "forgotten?" Surely they cannot mean America's original inhabitants. There is a subculture in our country, which will arrive at its very own conclusions.

9. Tebowing, a pop-cultural phenomenon, denotes to get down on a knee and start praying, even if everyone else around you is doing something completely different. It is inspired by and performed in satirical reference to American football player Tim Tebow.

10. Critics who are not willing to engage with the Berliners accuse them of fascistic ideas. But they specifically expose its orchestration — as for example during their entry march into the *Olympiahalle*. Abroad, they are loved for it. In Germany, they are feared. In Bavaria, also.

11. One will not be able to understand Rammstein, if one cannot accept contradictions.

Works Cited

Bauszus, Jens. "Auf der Peniskanone durch den Totendienstag." *Focus Online* (2011). http://focus.de/kultur/musik/rammstein-auf-made-in-germany-tour-auf-der-peniskanone-durch-den-totendienstag_aid_686956.html (accessed September 9, 2012).

Burns, Robert G.H. "German Symbolism in Rock Music: National Signification in the Imagery and Songs of Rammstein." *Popular Music* 27, no. 3 (October 2008): 457–472.

Elferen, Isabella van. "East German Goth and the Spectres of Marx." *Popular Music* 30, no. 1 (January 2011): 89–103.

Gorkow, Alexander. "Wer zur Lebzeit gut auf Erden. Rammstein — Mit Deutschlands größtem Kulturexport auf Tour in Amerika." *Süddeutsche Zeitung Magazin* (July 6, 2012): 4–31.

Hebdige, Dick. *Subculture. The Meaning of Style.* New York: Routledge, 1979.

Hensel, Jana. *Zonenkinder.* Reinbek: Rowohlt Verlag, 2002.

Hoffmann, Christina. "Das ist mein Land." *Die Welt Online* (2011). http://www.welt.de/print/die_welt/kultur/article13717634/Das-ist-mein-Land.html (accessed September 10, 2012).

Larkey, Edward. "Just for fun? Language choice in German popular music." *Popular Music and Society* 24, no. 3 (February 2000): 1–20.

_____. "Transcultural Influences in Popular Music between Germany and the United States." *Jahrbuch für Internationale Germanistik* 94 (2008): 219–237.

Littlejohn, John T., and Michael T. Putnam. "Rammstein and *Ostalgie*: Longing for Yesteryear." *Popular Music and Society* 33, no. 1 (February 2010): 35–44.

Rapp, Tobias. "Aus der Sicht des Täters." *Der Spiegel* (November 16, 2009): 120–121.

Sontag, Susan. "Fascinating Fascism." *The New York Review of Books* (6 February 1975). http://www.nybooks.com/articles/archives/1975/feb/06/fascinating-fascism/?page=1 (accessed December 6, 2012).

Discography

Rammstein. *Herzeleid.* Slash. CD. 1995.

_____. *Liebe ist für Alle Da.* Vagrant. CD. 2009.

_____. *Made in Germany 1995–2011.* Universal. CD. 2011.

_____. *Mutter.* Republic. CD. 2001.

_____. *Reise, Reise.* Republic. CD. 2004.

_____. *Rosenrot.* Republic. CD. 2006.

_____. *Sehnsucht.* Slash. CD. 1997.

7

A Carnivalesque Cannibal:
Armin Meiwes, "Mein Teil"
and Representations
of Homosexuality[1]

KARLEY K. ADNEY

"There's absolutely no way back for me, only forwards, through your teeth" (Jones, 4). So said Bernd Jurgen Brandes, the man Armin Meiwes, the infamous Maneater of Rotenburg, slaughtered. Meiwes relished in butchering and eating his victim while Brandes celebrated the destruction of his genitalia, which he demanded Meiwes remove first. Most reports simply capitalize on the demented sexual fantasies these men had and avoid discussion of the catalysts for their fantasies, the most prevalent being their lives as gay men, excluded and often ashamed of their sexuality. Rammstein's notorious single "Mein Teil" sensationalizes Meiwes and Brandes' story, but, through the use of carnival, emphasizes the complexity of the lives of gay men, thus creating awareness in their viewers about the struggles the gay community faces. Banned for its content, "Mein Teil" instead deserves thorough analysis as a carnivalesque episode that ultimately creates awareness about problems faced by gay men in heterocentric society.

Discussions of cannibalism undeniably call forth images and stories about Hannibal Lecter, portrayed by Anthony Hopkins in the popular film *The Silence of the Lambs*. Lecter's tales of killing and consuming his victims echo in the public consciousness. In the novel *Hannibal Rising*, readers witness Lecter's transformation into a cannibal. An orphaned Lecter sees his sister devoured by a group of Nazi soldiers. His desire to avenge his sister's death fuels him to finally hunt down her killers. He enters medical school and eventually uses his intimate knowledge of the human body and mind to become a master criminal.

133

The popular character of Hannibal Lecter exhibits one of the most prevalent characteristics of a cannibal: intelligence. He does not however, demonstrate all of the traits typically shared by cannibals. According to Lois Jones, "A cannibal was usually under thirty-five, unmarried and of high intelligence. He tended to be sexually dysfunctional, with little or no experience of normal sexual intercourse. A cannibal killer often had a strong, ambivalent relationship with his mother, both loving her and hating her. He was often seen as a 'mama's boy' as an adult" (174). Meiwes' relationship with his mother Waltraud echoes the description Jones provides. Meiwes admits to interviewer Günter Stampf that "My relationship with my mother [...] could have been described as love-hate" (42). Later, in another interview, Meiwes agrees when Stampf asks him if his mother was controlling, dominant, decisive, and wounding; he also admits to thinking of killing her once when he was a teenager while he was helping her down a flight of stairs. "I thought to myself, one good shove to my mother and it's finally over" (Stampf, 43–44). The use of the word "finally" here is quite telling, especially since Meiwes was merely fifteen years old at the time. His first fifteen years were fraught with painful situations for the young boy, created by his overbearing, old-fashioned mother. The point at which Meiwes had the urge to kill his mother and "finally" be rid of her was not even half-way through her reign of tyranny. When Waltraud did die (she had been bed-ridden after a terrible car accident and then, several years later, suffered a heart attack), Meiwes explains he felt "shocked and relieved at the same time. Somehow, I was glad it was all over" (Stampf, 116).

What had Waltraud done to make Meiwes feel so relieved by her passing? A woman left by every man she had ever been with, Waltraud suffered from severe abandonment issues. These abandonment issues transformed her into a woman who did not trust men except for the one over which she had complete control: Armin. A document produced by the District Court of Kassel during Meiwes' trial included the following information: "Waltraud Meiwes could not accept men as individuals with their own interests and needs, and tried to shape them according to her own views, infantilized them, directed them or — after she had been abandoned by them — tried to annihilate them socially" (Stampf, 8). The document also expressed that Armin, "The defendant, who felt abandoned by the departure of his father and his half-brother [...], indentified himself with his mother Waltraud Meiwes in her abandonment and bent to her wishes and needs, seeking thus to avoid falling out of her favor. The defendant had no close emotional connection with his mother" (Stampf, 10). Left with no one but Armin to share her life with, Waltraud fiercely claimed him for herself alone. Indeed, "[Waltraud's] youngest son was the last man in her life, and she would chain him to her side" (Jones, 6).[2]

Examples of how Waltraud manipulated and dominated her son abound. One key example includes her creating a sign reading "Kinderzimmer" (child's room) to hang on his bedroom door; Meiwes could not remove the sign and it remained on his door well into his teen years (Jones, 13). Waltraud wanted her son for herself and she had high standards for men: she expected this last man in her life to have impeccable manners and style. Regardless of the way she knew he would be teased, Waltraud "exposed him to unrelenting mockery from his classmates by forcing him to wear a traditional white shirt with Bavarian-style lederhosen to school" (Jones, 7).[3] This outdated clothing made Meiwes a ready target in groups of school children, but he appeared the perfect little man to his mother. Jones also chronicles how, as an adult, Meiwes dressed flawlessly, always presenting himself as a perfect gentleman in pressed shirts, suits, and ties, undoubtedly selected by his mother.

Unsurprisingly, Waltraud determined with whom Meiwes was allowed to associate in the neighborhood, relegating his list of acquaintances to a few acceptable people. One such neighbor included a man who slaughtered animals: "Isolated, Armin's only example of a happy family life were stolen minutes he spent with his neighbors, watching animals being slaughtered on the local farm. Pigs, ducks, hens, geese, a deer, a wild hog — all were killed to be eaten. Slaughter became an everyday event for him, one he associated with love" (Jones, 8).[4] She was likely unaware of the consequences, but Waltraud's rigorous control of whom Meiwes could see, in this case, helped cultivate his longing to mutilate and consume flesh, even though the neighbor was a kind man.

The other neighbor who had a transformative effect on Meiwes was, conversely, a woman who glorified death and the dark arts. Ulla von Bernus, a self-proclaimed witch who could have people killed simply by uttering spells, moved into the neighborhood next door to Waltraud and soon became her best friend. Following Waltraud's lead, Armin came to identify with and even glorify the witch. Without a doubt, Waltraud was aware of what von Bernus believed, yet she trusted the witch to spend time alone with her son. Jones mentions that "Whenever Armin popped next door for a coffee and a chat, he was instructed in the religion of a world ruled by Satan, of the flesh, the carnal, and of death" (18). Meiwes began stealing marzipan from his mother's kitchen; he used the substance to mold body parts that he would douse in ketchup and then photograph. Spending a wealth of time with the witch influenced the young boy's actions further:

> Since meeting her, his dreams had been dipped in tinges of black magic. The occult exercised its influence over his weak personality and encouraged him to pursue his dark desires. He started to act out his savage fantasies. He dismembered Barbie dolls as if they were real victims. He cooked their severed limbs on

the barbecue in the garden. The dolls' smiling faces disintegrated between the metal bars; their bright, cheerful colors melted into a black charcoal mess. Legs and arms dissolved under the heat of the barbecue and dripped through to the grill pan below [Jones, 18].

Meiwes' yearning to play with, control, destroy, and eventually eat human flesh flourished.[5] His mother assisted in implicitly cultivating this desire.

Meiwes attempted to strike out on his own as an adult, but was unsuccessful.[6] He joined the military and looked forward to serving as a soldier. He received several promotions but his career quickly stalled since fellow soldiers did not respect him or follow his commands; they viewed him as someone dominated easily and had no fear of retribution for ignoring his orders. A fellow soldier recounts a story in which Armin asked the men to sweep; the men responded by telling Armin to do the sweeping himself ("The Man"). When the annual military Christmas party occurred, Meiwes arrived with a date: his mother. On a few rare occasions, Meiwes did go on dates with women, but not without his mother serving in the role of chaperone (Jones, 22). "The Man Who Ate His Lover" (an episode in the *Bodyshock* series) includes interviews from some of Meiwes' acquaintances, including school friends and neighbors. One of Meiwes' neighbors, when asked about his relationship with his mother, says: "It is always said that when Armin brought women to the house, she drove all of them away. I think she always only wanted the best for her son. She had a certain idea of a daughter-in-law. Only she overlooked that this type of daughter-in-law, who she wanted, was in a different league from the one Armin played in."[7]

Meiwes may have been happy with the women he dated (happy in the sense that he always wanted to marry and start a family since he never had one himself; this marriage would not provide Meiwes, a closeted gay man for most of his life, with sexual satisfaction), but Waltraud helped destroy any possible relationships Armin might have fostered with other women. As Jones mentions, Waltraud "taught him the correct way to lay the table and hold his china cup — but she didn't show him how to function socially. [...] The rigorous parameters she set denied her son the world of girls, dating and stolen kisses. Armin's sexuality had, instead, been deformed during its nascent years" (78). Similarly, scholars argue that "[c]onfusing little boys by dressing them in female clothing or repressing their heterosexual desires is prevalent among parents of mass murderers and serial killers" (Havill, 4). Though Meiwes qualifies as neither a mass murderer nor serial killer, most critics agree that had Armin not been caught bragging about murdering Brandes, he would have continued to butcher any willing participants and, thus, would rank as a serial killer.

Though Meiwes admits to feeling some relief at his mother's passing, her death failed to destroy the connection between himself and Waltraud. Her death had even more adverse effects on Meiwes' psyche. Try as he might, he could not break free of Waltraud's grasp, and she remained present with him in their home, and even at the butchering ceremony. He was, without question, lost without Waltraud's strict direction, so he devised ways of keeping her present. Shortly after her death, Meiwes "reportedly constructed a shrine to her in the house, complete with a plastic mannequin that he would lay on a pillow each night" ("Biography"). One of Meiwes' friends visited the house after Waltraud's death and detailed the experience as follows: "Her dressing gown was laid out neatly on the bed, beautifully pressed, as if he's expecting her back at any moment. His world's frozen in the time when she was still alive. It's spooky. Armin has become his mother" (Jones, 28). Perhaps these descriptions remind readers of Norman Bates in Alfred Hitchcock's critically-acclaimed film *Psycho*; Jones also makes this comparison and explains that Meiwes "started imagining he *was* his mother, wearing her dresses and impersonating her voice" (Jones, 28). Once, in fact, Meiwes answered the door wearing his mother's clothes, makeup, and even a wig (Jones, 28). When Meiwes butchered Brandes eighteen months after finding his mother dead in her bed (her corpse was already stiff), Waltraud was also present: he used one of her pristine bed sheets as his apron (Jones, 113).

Ultimately, Meiwes, like Waltraud, feared being alone. They both needed someone to depend on and desperately wanted someone with whom they could always be connected. This desire, instilled in him by his mother, claims Meiwes, remains the catalyst for his cannibalistic desires. If he ate someone, he reasoned, he would never be alone. Stampf asked Meiwes about how his mother would have reacted to him butchering and eating a man. The conversation follows:

MEIWES: Well, my mother tried to have me with her always at home. When I was older, she even scared off my girlfriends. She never wanted me to leave her.

STAMPF: Can it be that your mother had cannibalistic fantasies also?

MEIWES: There could have been a similarity in some aspects.

STAMPF: In what way?

MEIWES: In that one wants to always have someone with him [...].

STAMPF: [H]ow would your mother have reacted to your deed if she were still alive?

MEIWES: My mother, if she had known of it [...] she might have assented to the whole thing, but I don't know, I can't say.

STAMPF: Would she have tasted human flesh?

MEIWES: Perhaps she might have tasted it, it's possible. As I said, my mother's and my imaginings had a commonality. She often read me gruesome bedtime stories like *Grimm's Fairy Tales* and such. They were interesting.

STAMPF: What was interesting about the stories?
MEIWES: "Hänsel and Gretel," for example. Hänsel is supposed to have been eaten
    by the witch. Decades later I exchanged e-mails with people on the inter-
    net. You wouldn't believe how many people named 'Hänsel' are buzzing
    around out there in cyber land [22].[8]

Meiwes admits that he always felt intrigued by the two lost children who were
to be eaten — by a witch, no less, like the very woman who lived next door: "As
a child he used to act out the scene time and again, playing the role of the witch
and delighting in the idea of roasting and devouring Hansel" (Jones, 2).[9]

Waltraud reading her son fairytales beloved by children around the world
cannot alone be held responsible for her son morphing into a "maneater."
When coupled with her refusal to allow Meiwes to grow as an individual,
making him associate with troubled individuals like von Bernus, and denying
him a support network of friends and lovers, can Waltraud be held partly
responsible for the creation of the monster her son became? In the preface to
his in-depth study of serial killer Hadden Clark, Adrian Hall also discusses
the roles mothers play in the formation of sons who transform into twisted
cannibal criminals: "Are the mothers sometimes to blame for these outrageous
deeds? Charles Manson's prostitute mom refused to give him a name when
he was born and was said to have once traded him away for a pitcher of beer"
(4). While ultimately each person must be held responsible for their own
choices, the way in which Waltraud manipulated and shaped her son cannot
be dismissed. But the media, judges, and jury found something else to blame
for the butchering of Bernd Jurgen Brandes: the internet, the vehicle that
brought butcher and victim together.[10]

It was in a cannibal chat room where Meiwes posted the following advertisements: "Hi, I am Franky from Germany, I seek young men between 18
and 30 years old, to slaughter" and "Do you have a normally-built body, then
come to me, I slaughter you and eat your delicious meat" (Jones, 42).[11] Bernd
Jurgen Brandes, delighted by these posting, responded immediately. He told
Meiwes, shortly after they began communicating, "There's absolutely no way
back for me, only forwards, through your teeth" (Jones, 4). Brandes wanted
to destroy himself since he was a child. He wanted to be completely annihi-
lated, a desire he housed since the death of his mother when he was only five
years old. His mother worked in a hospital and held herself responsible for
the death of a patient. The Brandes family went on vacation, the purpose of
which was primarily to restore Mrs. Brandes' confidence in herself. The vacation would hopefully provide her with an opportunity to rest and forgive herself for the accident at the hospital. Instead, she intentionally drove herself
into a tree and died.

Her young son was confused by his mother's departure: "It was his fault, he decided, that his Mummy had gone away. He was responsible for her death. His father never contradicted this childish belief; in fact, he never spoke to his son about his mother's death. [...] Bernd learned not to discuss his inner turmoil, or his deeper emotions" (Jones, 53). Completely confused and with no one to talk to about his feelings, the young Brandes boy made unfounded links between his mother's death and his own body: "As a young boy, he started to connect his sexuality and his genitalia with the death of his mother. The only way he could see of atoning for her fatal accident was through his own annihilation and endless suffering. Bernd started to dream about being slaughtered and eaten. This childhood preoccupation would develop into an overwhelming desire for self-destruction" (Jones, 53).

Brandes was a man of secrets. He kept his despair from nearly everyone, save a choice group of prostitutes he visited regularly. These prostitutes could infer the depths of Brandes' despair simply from the requests he made of them: he begged each of them to bite, mutilate, and even remove his penis. Several of the prostitutes entertained Brandes' pleas, but none of them would actually do as Brandes requested.[12] He also kept his homosexuality a secret from most people, ashamed of himself and his feelings. Brandes' lover René testified that they rarely were in the "gay scene" (Stampf, 174). Some people were obviously aware of their relationship, but those closest to Brandes remained uninformed. Several days after Brandes disappeared, René called Siemens (the company for which Brandes worked), looking for him; when Brandes failed to answer, René left an impassioned voicemail message. Brandes' colleagues listened to the message and felt shocked. The raw emotion in René's voice sounded like the worry a lover would experience, but not a platonic roommate, which is how Brandes always spoke of René.

None of Brandes' colleagues could fathom what their coworker was doing in lieu of coming to work on Friday, March 9, 2001. Before taking a day's leave (the reason for which Brandes did not identify), Brandes sold his car, wrote a will in which he left everything to his partner, and wiped his computers clean of any evidence about what he had been doing or where he was going. Meiwes picked Brandes up from the train station. They went back to Meiwes' house and Brandes delighted in the "slaughter room" Meiwes had fashioned on the second floor.[13] They had sex and then Brandes begged Meiwes to bite off his penis. Meiwes could not. Disappointed and frustrated, Brandes asked Meiwes to take him to the train station so he could return home. At the train station, Brandes changed his mind. They returned to Meiwes' home and soon thereafter, Meiwes used a knife to remove Brandes' penis. While Brandes bled to death in a bathtub, Meiwes read one of his favorite *Star Trek* novels, waiting impatiently for Brandes to finally die. Meiwes carried a semi-conscious Brandes back to the butchering table, made sure his video camera was recording, and then fulfilled Brandes' request to die by stabbing him in the throat. Meiwes then bled Brandes like an animal and proceeded to butcher him expertly, based on knowledge he had amassed via numerous cannibal websites. Meiwes then dined on his friend's flesh while he preserved the rest in a freezer that also stored a pizza and a dead mouse.

Since no law explicitly stated cannibalism was illegal in Germany, Meiwes was convicted of manslaughter, even though his defense team emphasized that Brandes wanted to die (as evidenced in various communications with Meiwes and on the videotapes of the slaughter itself). Critics argue that Meiwes and Brandes, during a "twisted whirlwind romance" ("The Man"), made a "mutual pact rooted in sado-masochistic homosexual fantasy" ("Profile"). Both men, Jones argues, "harbored violent sexual fantasies. [...] Pain was their pleasure" (3).[14] The public was fascinated with the case and stood divided on the ruling. Brandes clearly wanted to die and Meiwes had assisted in the suicide, some argued; these people felt satisfied with the verdict of manslaughter that yielded Meiwes eight years, six months in jail. Many others, though, were disgusted by the verdict. The case was quickly appealed and the German high court repealed the manslaughter charge and instead dealt a verdict of murder, the minimum sentence for which is fifteen years.

Regardless of Meiwes' sentence, what remained most troubling was the verdict regarding Meiwes' mental state.[15] One reviewer asserted Meiwes exhibited "no indication of mental illness" ("Profile"); another explained that Meiwes was "not insane but has a 'severely disturbed soul'" ("First TV Interview"); still others claimed that Meiwes was "extremely smug and self-assured" and had a possible "schizoid personality" but with "no indication of mental illness" (Jones, 190). After the sentence of manslaughter was overturned for murder, Meiwes said he looked forward to composing his memoirs because he "want[ed] to show people with similar fantasies 'that it can never bring them fulfillment'" ("Retrial Delivers Tougher Sentence"). Strangely enough, Meiwes now serves as the leader of the Green Party group in the prison where he currently carries out his sentence: "Bavaria Radio reported that another inmate said Meiwes has sworn off meat in his new role as an [environmentalist...]. 'He finds the idea of factory farming as distasteful as his crime was,' said the convict. 'He now sticks to vegetarian dishes'" (Hall).

Jon Wiederhorn, in his 2004 article "German Cannibal Helps Rammstein Write New Single," states that Meiwes' case "captivated the European media, and provided East German industrial metal band Rammstein with some ripe new material with which to return from a three-year self-imposed exile." The band's lead singer, Till Lindemann, was intrigued by the case and demonstrated his perverse sense of humor with the following comment: "It's so sick that it becomes fascinating and there just has to be a song about it" ("German Rock"); similarly, Meiwes' story was "manna from hell for singer Till Lindemann" ("German Rock"). Lindemann was not the only band member fascinated with the story. Lead guitarist Richard Kruspe said:

> I was really interested to find out about why he would want to kill a man and eat [him...]. What I figured out from some research was that Meiwes' mother totally destroyed all kinds of relationships he had in his childhood. So, he felt that if he did this, his victim would stay with him forever. It was just a really interesting story, so we decided to make a song about it [Wiederhorn].

"Mein Teil" ensued. The title literally translates to "My Part," which is slang for "my penis."

Rammstein's song opens with the sound of knife blades being sharpened, followed shortly thereafter by a haunting voice repeating excerpts from advertisements Meiwes posted in various cannibal chat rooms (including details like "looking for well-built men between the ages of eighteen and thirty to slaughter, the Master Butcher").[16] While guitars pump heavily, a chorus of what sounds like a perverted church choir sings. The first verse describes a butcher who has met a man who looks tasty to him. The butcher explains that the man's parts — both hard and soft ones, will be listed on the menu for consumption. The second verse shares details about the victim, who is bleeding and feeling sickly. The lyrics discuss the best way to prepare and serve the flesh. The chorus, using trite conventional wisdom, reminds listeners that "you are what you eat." The song rocketed to second on the German charts the week it was released ("German Rock").

The video for "Mein Teil" tellingly appears on horrornews.net. After its release, it was banned from airing during the day on nearly every channel and was only broadcast after 11:00 p.m. on MTV because of its content ("German Rock"). Rammstein was aware that Meiwes had recorded Brandes' slaughter, and the band "initially wanted to use some of the footage for the song's video. But the tape was in police custody" (Wiederhorn). Kruspe revealed the creative process for constructing the official video: "The director had everyone in the band come into the room for two hours and do anything he wanted. And nobody knew what the other guys were doing. It came out even darker than I thought it would. But I'd still like to see the police video" (Wiederhorn).

The band members remained unaware of what each did during their performance time for the video, but they unwittingly complemented each other and commented directly on Meiwes and Brandes' situation. Rammstein employs the spirit of carnival discussed, at length, by Mikhail Bakhtin. Bakhtin claims that "[the carnival spirit] frees human consciousness, thought, and imagination for new potentialities" (49). The outrageous elements of the "Mein Teil" video allow viewers to, as Bakhtin says, "imagine new potentialities" for, specifically, the gay men upon which the song's story is based. Meiwes himself embodies the spirit of carnival. Jones asserts that Meiwes' "very ordinariness, the shocking discrepancy between the person Armin *seemed* to be and what he had *done*, disturbed people greatly" (Jones, 183). No one expected that the impeccably dressed computer wizard could butcher a man and then dine on him regularly, using recipes from various cannibal websites. Spectators waited outside the courthouse to catch a glimpse of the "Maneater of Rotenburg;" many were disappointed when Meiwes arrived looking well-groomed and normal. Meiwes himself provides a striking example of carnival. Brandes also embodied the spirit of the grotesque, of carnival. Wolfgang Kayser, in his seminal piece *The Grotesque in Art and Literature*, claims that "The grotesque expresses not the fear of death but the fear of life" (qtd. in Bakhtin, 49–50). Brandes undoubtedly feared life and embraced his annihilation. Meiwes and Brandes together created a carnival of blood and butchery, all of which would eventually turn critical attention to cannibalism and the lives of gay men.

Through use of the carnivalesque, Rammstein's "Mein Teil" implicitly forces listeners and viewers to question their assumptions about gay men. Bakhtin asserts that in the carnivalesque, prevailing ideologies are challenged by representations of chaos and absurdity. In their video, Rammstein showcases men in drag rubbing their genitalia, gorging and then spitting out a thick and bloody substance, and walking other men like dogs on leashes. The video also incorporates many scenes in which the lead band member, Till Lindemann, receives oral sex from "Federfleisch" (literally "feather flesh") in the form of an angel. This twisting of the profane with the glorious coupled with the repeated and prevalent imagery of men in drag masturbating and using bondage to control one another creates a powerful instance of carnival in which negative stereotypes of gay men are examined. Similarly, Rammstein's video offers insight to Meiwes and Brandes' complicated histories as men persecuted for their sexuality.

The "Mein Teil" video shows each band member performing alone combined with some group scenes.[17] Though Rammstein did not intend to make a video about cannibalism or the plight of Meiwes and Brandes, careful analysis shows that their video does, in fact, comment on these important issues and, through the use of carnival, asks viewers to consider the issues thoughtfully.

The video opens with Christoph "Doom" Schneider, dressed as a woman. He wears a blonde wig with hair in tight curls, a suit coat, a blouse, a scarf, a skirt, and a smart pair of heels. He avoids direct eye contact with the camera and turns his head coyly away until the lyric "Der Metzgermeister," when he looks directly at the camera. His next major scene occurs at 1:44, in which he sits primly on a chair, holding a box in his lap. He looks at the box disdainfully, removes the lid, and puts some of the contents in his mouth. The box resembles that of a fancy candy box, but Schneider clearly is not eating candy. At 2:37, the video shows a brief clip of Schneider lying on the floor, his skirt hiked up above his hips, while he rubs his crotch. The video then alternates between various images and Schneider stuffing his mouth with the contents of the box. Two minutes and 48 seconds into the video, Schneider begins to choke on what he has been chewing. Seconds later, he turns to the side and lets a thick, red, concoction flow from his mouth.[18] In "Rammstein — Making of 'Mein Teil,'" Schneider explains that the character he plays is "the mother [...]. I am the perpetrator's mother."

While those completely unaware of the back story for the video of "Mein Teil" will not appreciate Schneider's performance, those familiar with Meiwes and Brandes' story will make an association between Schneider's character and Meiwes. Schneider's performance provides the first example of carnival in the video, in which stereotypes of gay men are stretched to hyperbole. Do all gay men regularly dress in women's clothing and then touch themselves? No. Schneider's performance, however, can be viewed as a statement about how living a closeted life, like Armin, can have disastrous mental effects. Armin did not dress himself in women's clothing simply because he was gay; he dressed in women's clothing to cope with the loss of his domineering mother who would not have approved of her son being gay. Taking on her personality after her death allowed Armin to be himself, make his mother aware of who he really was, and allowed him to keep Waltraud with him.

The video introduces Paul Landers' character next. He screams and his open mouth shows rotting, blackened teeth. He wears shredded clothing and flings his body around destructively for the first forty seconds of the video.[19] Landers' performance shares similarities with Kruspe's. During Kruspe's performance, he meets and wrestles with his own double. At 0:59, he even licks tongues with his double, looking at him longingly; conversely, at 2:25, he collides with his double and begins a fierce wrestling match, one Kruspe trying to dominate the other. The performances by both Landers and Kruspe capitalize on the mental torment of anyone wrestling with their identity.

These performances also apply even more specifically to Meiwes and Brandes, both of whom were at war with themselves because of painful experiences in their pasts that they would and could not reveal to anyone. Consider, for instance, how Brandes wanted to annihilate himself due to his psychomachia: "I want to destroy myself. To disappear from the face of the planet. I hate myself so much. I despise my sexuality and the way I want sex all the time. I'm just a worthless piece of meat and bones. There's no place left for me in this world. I've had it" (Jones, 74). Similarly, Meiwes experienced a great deal of emotional and mental pain from hiding who he was — both as a gay man and a cannibal. For instance, "Armin Meiwes led an outwardly quiet life, described by one woman he befriended as a friendly and sensitive person" ("Profile"). Yet another acquaintance shared that "he has a charisma like you would imagine from a homosexual" ("The Man").[20] Regardless of his charisma, Armin never revealed who he truly was to the people who knew him. He, like many members of the gay community, carried the secret of whom he was and who he loved. This secret serves as an enormous pressure that can have devastating mental implications, as demonstrated by the battles both Landers and Kruspe engage in with themselves.

The focus of the video, however, remains Lindemann, who also enacts the most shocking example of carnival. Lindemann appears roughly forty second into the video, stating the first lines of the first verse. He wears a tattered suit coat from which the sleeves have been removed; he also wears a thick black belt around his neck. Some of his teeth, like Landers,' are also black and rotting. Starting at 1:05, the video begins to incorporate scenes in which Lindemann chews on and pulls feathers from a creature between his knees. At 2:03, the video shows Lindemann receiving oral sex from a female angel. His eyes are closed as he leans back in his chair with the angel moving back and forth as she performs fellatio on him. This scene reappears frequently until Lindemann attacks and kills her. He drags her lifeless, naked body across a feather-covered floor at 3:18.

No other example in the video does a more expert job of entwining the godly and profane, as expected with carnival theory. Knowing the impetus for the song and video allows viewers to truly appreciate this performance. The scene emphasizes that Lindemann, a man with rotting teeth and rags for clothing, has the ability to capture, control, and kill the divine. The pure outrageousness of this scene, combined with the other images in the video, gives viewers pause; the absurdity of Lindemann's situation reminds viewers of the ridiculousness of the other extreme scenes in the video, namely Schneider dressed as a woman, eating what is presumed to be flesh, while masturbating.[21]

Christian "Flake" Lorenz appears at 1:39; the video then intersperses scenes of him dancing in dirty pointe shoes and black tights. His movements are both awkward and sexual, like when the camera focuses on the bulge of his genitalia as he directs his hand toward the bulge in his tights. His long greasy hair and thin frame makes him the most stereotypically feminine of the bunch, a role he typically serves in within the group (recall that he played the role of "Heeshie" in the video for "Pussy"). Lorenz's role as a feminized ballet dancer draws attention, again, to men who exhibit feminine traits. His performance in this video is meant to unnerve viewers, but considering the element of carnival and hyperbole in this video, his role as a ballet dancer actually reminds viewers that men who do ballet are not at all unusual.

Oliver "Ollie" Riedel appears at 1:03. Covered in some type of powder, he wears nothing more than a diaper. He resembles a ghostly corpse, and at 1:17, he falls to the ground, looking as if rigor mortis has already set in. The grimace on his face coupled with his stiff limbs haunt viewers as he partially crawls and thrashes around the floor. Those familiar with the back story of "Mein Teil" cannot help but connect Riedel's performance with Brandes' situation shortly before his death. Meiwes, having already amputated Brandes' penis, helped fashion a diaper for the man so he could join Meiwes downstairs to eat his own genitalia for dinner. Riedel continues to scream as his corpse of a body thrashes about, a situation that mirrors closely what Brandes experienced himself.

The video also incorporates group scenes. One includes all band members, save Schneider, standing together in filth. The video comes back to this scene time and again, finally culminating at 3:20 when the men fight each other, water and mud flying. These men all strive for dominance in this group because, as viewers learn soon enough, they have all been dominated by Schneider. Shortly after this penultimate battle, the video switches to a scene in which all of the men wear leashes as Schneider, still dressed as a woman, walks them up the stairs of the Deutsche Oper U-bahn, a famous subway stop in Berlin.[22] Schneider looks disengaged and bored as he makes his way up the subway steps, the five other men still yearning for dominance (Kruspe bears his teeth and nearly bites Riedel). At 4:04, Schneider asserts his dominance again by pulling on the leashes to stop the men from crawling into oncoming traffic. The video ends with Schneider walking the men lazily down the street.

These group scenes also employ the technique of carnival, which allows for challenging of the dominant social structures. Traditional power dynamics assigned to men and women are turned completely on their head as Schneider, the woman, dominates five strong and forceful men. The scene undeniably hearkens back to Meiwes' relationship with his mother Waltraud, who dominated his entire existence. The scene also causes viewers to question the association between the gay men who served as the catalyst for the song (Meiwes and Brandes) and forms of sado-masochism like the leashes the men wear.

While Meiwes and Brandes got pleasure from pain, the hyperbole created by this video causes viewers to question the stereotype that gay men in general enjoy sado-masochistic acts like wearing leashes or using whips to punish one another.

"Mein Teil" brought critical attention to the issues Meiwes and Brandes faced, but Meiwes did not appreciate Rammstein using his story without his permission; he sued the band and won 5.5 million dollars in damages ("Rammstein"). What matters most to the band, though, is not that they lost their case against Meiwes, but that people appreciate and study their music: as Lorenz states, "The controversy is fun, like stealing forbidden fruit. But it serves a purpose. We like audiences to grapple with our music, and people have become more receptive" ("Rammstein"). Rammstein remains known for its shock performances, ranging from Lindemann being sexually serviced by an angel in "Mein Teil" to him riding a canon that spews white foam during live performances of "Pussy." These scandalous images seem tame considering Rammstein's plagued history of being associated with neo–Nazism or the Columbine massacre. But Rammstein's sole goal is not simply to shock. They must be acknowledged for their masterful use of the carnivalesque, as in "Mein Teil," and the way in which their carnival encourages viewers to think critically about issues like the creation and perpetuation of the maneater of Rotenburg.

Notes

1. Translations of German text are original.

2. Rammstein capitalizes on Waltraud's dominating nature in their depiction of her in the video of "Mein Teil."

3. This outfit remains the stereotypical attire associated with German men in general. Paul Landers exploits this stereotype himself when he wears lederhosen and a variation of the traditional sepplhut.

4. Many thanks to Michael Putnam for making the connection between Meiwes's story and Jeffrey Dahmer, as represented in the Slayer song "213" (Jeffrey Dahmer's apartment number), in which the band also intertwines the concepts of slaughter and love.

5. Jones states that "by the time he reached puberty at twelve, the idea of eating another boy had started to arouse Armin sexually" (10).

6. Meiwes joined a sailing group which afforded him some reprieve from his mother, though she required him to call her at least every other day for a visit. During these trips, Meiwes tended to the sails. In "The Man Who Ate His Lover," video footage shows Meiwes sailing with the group, looking up at a damaged sail.

This image calls forth Till Lindemann's untitled poem in which he writes "Dein Fleisch ist ein zerrissenes Segel" (Lindemann 22). The tearing of flesh here serves as an interesting, albeit coincidental, connection between Meiwes and the band who chronicle his butchery in detail.

7. This passage appears in German in the documentary: "Es wird immer gesagt, dass sie, wenn Armin Frauen nach Hause gebracht hat, die alle rausgeekelt hätte. Ich denke mir, sie wollte für [...] ihren Sohn immer nur das Beste. Sie hatte eine bestimmte Vorstellung von [einer] Schwiegertochter. Nur hat sie wahrscheinlich übersehen, dass diese Art

von Schwiegertochter, die sie gern wollte, eine andere Liga war [...] als die in der Armin gespielt hat."

8. Meiwes' fondness for this German fairytale is obvious. He made a similar comment in his first television interview after his conviction: "The bit where Hansel is to be eaten was interesting. You wouldn't believe how many Hansels are whizzing around the internet" ("First TV Interview").

9. The film based on Meiwes' story, *Cannibal*, begins with a mother reading her son "Hansel and Gretel." The film was banned in Germany and the few used copies currently available on Amazon.com sell for a minimum of $48 as of September 12, 2012.

10. The focus remained on how the internet helped Armin explore and indulge his cannibalistic fantasies, but attention was also afforded to the gruesome movies Meiwes also enjoyed: "The court heard how horror movies had fuelled [sic] Armin Meiwes' childhood fantasies of eating school friends" ("German Cannibal Tells").

11. The advertisements appeared originally in German as "Hi, ich bin Franky aus Deutschland, ich suche nach jungen Maennern zwischen 18 und 30 Jahren, zum schlachten" and "Hast du einen normal gebauten Koerper, dann komme zu mir, ich schlachte dich und esse dein koestliches Fleisch."

12. Brandes told Meiwes, via an online chat, "I am Cator. [...] Yes, I really do want it. I want you to cut off my cock, tear the flesh off my bones while I'm still alive, and eat me up" (Stampf, 175), and Meiwes was the only one willing to fulfill Brandes' wishes.

13. Jones' and Stampf's works provide photos of the Meiwes house; Jones' book includes various photos of the "slaughter room." This "slaughter room" included a cage, a pulley system for stringing victims up so they could be properly bled, meat hooks, a bed frame with heaters beneath it so victims could be barbecued, and, most importantly, the butchering table, accompanied by a set of tools used to skin, rip, and divide flesh into meal-sized portions.

14. The case sparked worldwide interest and has been studied time and again in psychology and law review journals around the world. Scholars like Roberto Gutierrez and Roger Giner-Sorolla discuss Meiwes' case while investigating taboo and taboo-breaking in the article "Anger, Disgust, and Presumption of Harm as Reactions to Taboo-Breaking Behaviors."

The case also served as rich fodder for lawyers and analysts of the law. Meiwes' case remains a point of study in articles likes Katherine Biber's "Cannibals and Colonialism," and Lawrence Friedman's articles "Front Page: Notes on the Nature and Significance of Headline Trials" and "Cannibal Rights: A Note of the Modern law of Privacy."

15. Another troubling aspect of this case were the statistics it helped to publicize about cannibalism and people eager to also slaughter or be slaughtered. Due to the research conducted because of Meiwes' actions, "police estimate there are 8,000 to 10,000 people in Germany alone who are using Internet chat rooms to share fantasies about eating a person or being eaten" ("Retrial Delivers Tougher Sentence").

16. Due to copyright restrictions, a line-by-line translation of "Mein Teil" cannot be provided. Hence, a summary of each verse and the chorus is provided instead.

17. "Mein Teil" remains a fan favorite at Rammstein concerts. It was first performed during the *Reise, Reise* tour in 2004. The band did not perform "Mein Teil" during the *Liebe ist für Alle Da* tour, which I was fortunate enough to see on May 10, 2011, in Rosemont, Illinois. The song returned to the set list, however, for the *Made in Germany* tour, which I attended on May 6, 2012, in Auburn Hills, Michigan.

For "Mein Teil," Lindemann enters the stage with an enormous cooking pot. Much like Meiwes during the butchering, Lindemann is doused in blood (though the apron he wears surely is not one of his mother's bed sheets). Christian Lorenz, also known as "Flake," appears in the pot while playing the keyboard. Midway through the song, Lindemann aims a flamethrower at the pot and begins cooking Flake. Flake eventually escapes the pot and runs around the stage in flames, with Lindemann chasing him with his massive flamethrower. A special touch for this performance includes the microphone Lindemann uses, which in this case has a large butcher's knife attached to the end.

Though the number was not performed during the *Liebe ist für Alle Da* tour, I argue that Rammstein still paid their respect to Meiwes and one of their most famous numbers via the artwork for the CD of the same name. One cover for the *Liebe ist für Alle Da* album showcases the men, grouped around a table on which a naked woman rests. Lindemann holds a massive meat cleaver over the woman and looks as though he is about to dissect her. The other band members watch longingly as Lindemann prepares the meal.

18. This substance must be a direct reference to the blood Meiwes would have ingested while removing and eating Brandes' penis and other flesh.

19. Images on the screen alternate quickly between Landers and Doom, emphasizing the torment Meiwes felt because of his controlling mother.

20. The original German statement is: "Er [Armin] hat doch so eine Ausstrahlung wie man sich einen Homosexuellen vorstellt."

21. Please see Michael Putnam's "Discipleship in the Church of Rammstein" (this volume) for a more detailed exploration of angelic figures in the Rammstein canon. Specifically, the section "Being an Angel Ain't Everything It's Cracked Up to Be" discusses how Rammstein's angels typically appear "less-than-glorious" and beings that "engage in sexual acts."

22. This location is especially significant since Brandes came from Berlin.

Works Cited

Bakhtin, Mikhail. *Rabelais and His World*. Bloomington, Indiana: Indiana University Press, 1984.

Biber, Katherine. "Cannibals and Colonialism." *Sydney Law Review* 27 (2005): 623–637.

"Biography: Armin Meiwes." *Crime and Investigation Network* (2011). http://www.crimea ndinvestigation.co.uk/crime-files/armin-meiwes-german-cannibal/biography.html (accessed January 20, 2012).

Cannibal. Marian Dora, director. Carsten Frank and Tobias Sickert. Unearthed Films, 2008.

"First TV Interview With German Cannibal: 'Human Flesh Tastes Like Pork.'" *Spiegel Online* (October 16, 2007). http://www.spiegel.de/international/zeitgeist/first-tv-interview-with-german-cannibal-human-flesh-tastes-like-pork-a-511775.html (accessed May 16, 2012).

Friedman, Lawrence M. "Front Page: Notes on the Nature and Significance of Headline Trials." *Saint Louis University Law Journal* 55 (2011): 1243–1284.

_____, and Nina-Louisa Arold. "Cannibal Rights: A Note on the Modern Law of Privacy." *Northwestern Interdisciplinary Law Review* 4, no. 1 (2011): 235–246.

"German Cannibal Tells of Fantasy." *BBC News* (December 3, 2003). http://news.bbc.co.uk/2/hi/3286721.stm (accessed March 11, 2012).

"German Rock Band's 'Part' Song Tells of Cannibals' Repast." *Tapei Times* (August 29 2004). http://www.taipeitimes.com/News/world/archives/2004/08/29/2003200719 (accessed September 2, 2011).

Gutierrez, Roberto and Roger Giner-Sorolla. "Anger, Disgust, and Presumption of Harm as Reactions to Taboo-Breaking Behaviors." *Emotion* 7, no. 4 (2007): 853–868.

Hall, Allan. "World's Most Infamous Cannibal Becomes a Vegetarian." *Daily Mail Online* (November 20, 2007). http://www.dailymail.co.uk/news/article-495132/Worlds-infamous-cannibal-vegetarian.html (accessed May 28, 2012).

Havill, Adrian. *Born Evil: A True Story of Cannibalism and Serial Murder*. New York: St. Martin's Press, 2001.

Jones, Lois. *Cannibal: The True Story Behind the Maneater of Rotenburg*. New York: Berkley Books, 2005.

Lindemann, Till. *Messer.* Frankfurt: Eichborn, 2010.

"The Man Who Ate His Lover." *Bodyshock.* 2012. http://www.channel4.com/programmes/bodyshock/episode-guide/series-4 (accessed May 25, 2012).

"Mein Teil." *Reise Reise.* Motor Records. CD. 2004.

"Mein Teil." YouTube. http://www.youtube.com/watch?v=sJ3kVtd2CCA (accessed June 11, 2012).

"Profile: Armin Meiwes." *BBC News* (May 9, 2006). http://news.bbc.co.uk/2/hi/europe/3443803.stm (accessed May 16, 2012).

"Rammstein." *The Guardian* (2012). http://www.guardian.co.uk/music/rammstein (accessed July 15, 2012).

"Rammstein — Making of Mein Teil (English Subtitles) Part 2/3 HD." Youtube. http://www.youtube.com/watch?v=hfREQp9jI_o (accessed September 10, 2012).

"Retrial Delivers Tougher Sentence: German Cannibal Gets Life for Eating Willing Victim." *Spiegel Online* (May 9, 2006). http://www.spiegel.de/international/retrial-delivers-tougher-sentence-german-cannibal-gets-life-for-eating-willing-victim-a-415313.html (accessed May 11, 2012).

Stampf, Günter. *Interview with a Cannibal: The Secret Life of the Monster of Rotenburg.* Beverly Hills: Phoenix Books, 2008.

Wiederhorn, Jon. "German Cannibal Helps Rammstein Write New Single." *MTV* (December 30, 2004). http://www.mtv.com/news/articles/1495200/rammstein-inspired-by-german-cannibal.jhtml (accessed August 1, 2012).

8

Fear, Desire and the Fairy Tale *Femme Fatale* in Rammstein's "Rosenrot"

Erin Sweeney Smith

Awash in murder, torture, and the machinations of a diabolical seductress, Rammstein's "Rosenrot" unfolds with all the gleeful excess of an eighteenth-century Gothic novel. Existing discussion of the band has tended to focus on the group's shock-rock aesthetic, and analyses of individual songs and music videos have been few and far between. A close reading of the cultural influences on this title track from the band's 2005 fifth studio album opens a window into the ideological and social implications of Rammstein's work. Scrutinizing its violence and sexual imagery foregrounds symbols that glorify the band as a homosocial collective and generate a particularly gendered and nationalist discourse. Erupting into a catharsis of fire and distortion, its hyper-masculine scenario rejects the emergence of female power and sexual influence by purging Rammstein's communal body of her contaminations.

Sources and Musical Facets

"Rosenrot" incorporates an array of German Romantic tropes, primarily through the appropriation of Goethe's "Heidenröslein" (Rose on the Heath) and references to fairy tale and folk genres. Goethe's poem becomes a template for Rammstein's lyrics, which follow the poem's narrative trajectory and emulate divisions of verse and refrain. Seeking to emphasize connections between the two works, singer and lyricist Till Lindemann retains the principal characters of the rose and the young man who desires to pluck and possess the little flower. In Goethe's scenario, the anthropomorphized rose resists the "fierce" boy's advances. Though its thorns stab the youth's fingers in self-

150

defense, the flower is powerless to prevent the boy from violently ripping its body from a hedge. This image of deflowering, and possibly symbolic rape, is particularly disturbing within the text's lighthearted tone and in the cheerful art song settings that followed the poem's publication. Writing on Goethe's thematic mixture of love and death, Ellis Dye disparages a passive reception of the poem as if it were "a benign little skit of bucolic playfulness," noting that, "To read it adequately is to shudder at its invitation to enjoy a voyeuristic pleasure in the destruction of a girl by a red-blooded, therefore violent young man."[1]

Rammstein retains the sexual connotations surrounding the rose, as well as the poem's themes of violence and obsession. Their brooding adaptation redirects the plot into an unambiguously heterosexual tale by replacing Goethe's flower with the figure of the "Mädchen" (girl or maiden). Rammstein's rose remains tied to a female identity as an object of desire and conquest despite this shift in characterization. Lindemann continues to modify Goethe's character traits and power structures, and it is the masculine youth of "Rosenrot" who finds himself helpless to resist the will of his female lover. Retrieving the Mädchen's blossom requires this "Jüngling" (young man) to risk life and limb scaling a high cliff-side. He struggles against nature's defenses as he races to fulfill her command, but on plucking the flower he is plunged to his death as the treacherous ground gives way beneath his feet.

"Rosenrot" was originally intended to be a track on the band's previous release, *Reise, Reise* (Arise Arise, 2004), and would have appeared alongside a second Goethe adaptation, "Dalai Lama."[2] Though its ties to the German art tradition are obscured by the title, the plot and formal structure of "Dalai Lama" mirror that of Goethe's "Erlkönig" (Erl-King). Rammstein relocates the Elf King in this scenario from the forest to the sky, while the father and son's horseback ride becomes a journey by airplane. These changes both update the work and create a localized time frame for its events.[3] "Rosenrot," however, allows for a wider range of characterization and interpretation by maintaining its setting in the ambiguous time and space of folk narrative genres. Neither *Reise, Reise* nor *Rosenrot* mention the connection to Goethe in their respective liner notes, though the lyrics clearly refer to the poet's work. This silence might be seen as a missed opportunity for Rammstein to advertise these songs as homage to an icon of German literature, particularly for international audiences who would not recognize the references. However, the fans themselves are well aware of the connection, identifying and validating the band's choice of source material on the popular culture hub of Wikipedia and on the loose networks of internet fan sites, message boards, and online video comment sections.

The title of "Rosenrot" likewise emphasizes Rammstein's investment in their German heritage by conjuring associations with the Brothers Grimm fairy tale "Schneeweißchen und Rosenrot" (Snow-White and Rose-Red). The Grimms' tale describes the adventures of Snow White and her sister Rose Red, or "Rosenrot." In this lesser-known tale, the girls encounter an enchanted bear who returns to his true form as a handsome prince and marries Snow White. This prince's brother in turn marries Rose Red. Rammstein's title encourages those familiar with the Brothers Grimm collection to compare the works and to consider whether "Rosenrot" serves as a Gothic rewrite of the character. Such a revision would stand alongside two music videos that already featured fairy tale adaptations of "Snow White and the Seven Dwarfs" (or "Schneewittchen") as the subject of "Sonne" (Sun, Dir. Jörn Heitmann, 2001) and "Little Red Riding Hood and the Big Bad Wolf" (or "Rotkäppchen") in "Du riechst so gut" (You Smell So Good, Dir. Philipp Stölzl, 1998).[4] Within "Rosenrot," the band limits its carryovers from the Grimms' work to only the name and the presence of a female figure associated with roses. Rammstein thus conflates two representations of Germanic heritage by using the fairy tale title to distort and destabilize their appropriation of "Heidenröslein." Both sources meld together through a shared focus on rose imagery and youthful characters, allowing Rammstein to position "Rosenrot" as a locus of art and folk genres. Its lyrics form a strong statement about idealized German legacies by enfolding the adaptation of Goethe's plot into the settings and storytelling aesthetic of the Grimms' tale, two sources that speak primarily to German listeners or those fluent in German culture.

Throughout the verses, Till Lindemann takes on the role of third-person storyteller. His reserved and fairly unemotional descriptive tone emulates the brevity, lack of background information, and dispassionate relation of events characteristic of folk narratives.[5] Following the narrative episode of each verse, Lindemann intones the recurring phrase "she wants it"—a kind of motto in this song—to describe the dominating will of the Mädchen. Defining the Mädchen's power in terms of fear and desire, Rammstein equates her female agency with the Jüngling's subjugation and death.[6] An undercurrent of menace slips into the lines during the second and third verses through the addition of whispered and growled backing vocals that heighten a sense of masculine anxiety. The words instigate the chorus's furious response to a female-centric power structure, and it is here that Rammstein at last unleashes the crushing sounds and aggressive musical gestures relished by their listeners. Lindemann's chorus twists the adage "still waters run deep" into a contradictory version of the saying, emphasizing that beneath the surface all is *not* still. Delivered in an ominous tone, the phrase suggests a reference to both female duplicity and a masculine resentment towards the Mädchen's authority. The emotional, verbal, and musical participation in the chorus amounts to a forceful rejection of the submission described in the verses. The title word of "Rosenrot" at last enters the lyrics within this heightened confrontation, although the destabilizing references to the Goethe and Grimm sources render the word's identity unclear. A layered effect built up by the song's overlapping quotations creates instability as to whether "Rosenrot" refers to the Mädchen, the anthropomorphized rose from Goethe's poem, or to the Rosenrot of the Grimms' tale. In this regard, the incarnations of female villain, victim, and protagonist are collapsed into the single word of "Rosenrot" to signify female treachery and warn against the dangers that follow a loss of masculine social and sexual control. Such themes draw on the homosocial imperative that arises in much of the band's work, whether through their emphasis on strength and the masculine body, mixtures of misogyny and irony as discussed in Edward Larkey's examination of "Wollt ihr das Bett in Flammen sehen?" (Do you want to see the bed in flames?), the use of militaristic themes as described in Valerie Weinstein's study of "Links 2-3-4" (Left 2-3-4), or in lyrics that resist a heteronormative subjectivity as in Matthias Weiß' analysis of "Du riechst so gut."[7]

The only vocalization in "Rosenrot" apart from Lindemann's vocal track is a sound effect that resembles the echoing cry of a child. Placed within the instrumental interludes, the identity of this figure is as ambiguous as that of Rosenrot, and it is again unclear what figure should be associated with this wail. The insecurity regarding age and gender only adds to the uncannily human, yet inhuman effect. In the context of the lyrics, the sound could be intended merely to enhance the macabre atmosphere, or could represent anything from the young boy falling from the cliff side to the cry of the plucked rose as a reference to "Heidenröslein." The heavily layered echo effect blanketing this cry suggests that "Rosenrot" takes place in a distant moment outside of time and space. This musical choice revisits the band's earlier Goethe adaptation, as "Dalai Lama" used the technological manipulation of reverb to place its elfin choir in a supernatural realm separated from the modern world.

Rammstein's bass, guitar, drums, and keyboard all contribute to a larger message regarding gender and power. Together, the instruments create three sonic environments for the verse, chorus, and instrumental interlude that function as a musical stage to support and augment Lindemann's text. The sparse instrumentation in the verses and opening material enhances the power of the chorus's dynamics and thick textures. The distorted buzz of Oliver Riedel's bass line opens the track as it rocks back and forth on a dour minor third. Leaving its monotonous litany, his melody stabs upwards in harsh gestures soon to be joined by countless striking and falling motions. Christoph

Schneider's drums acquire their own layer of distortion in postproduction, and the crack of his snare drum bleeds across the aural spectrum. Riedel's drone and the anarchic distortion coating the two lines conjure a gothic haze that once more reinforces the impression that the narrator's tale emerges from a distant space. Subtle touches of color surface during the second verse in the form of synth interjections. These emulate the chorus's description of wells and water, and likewise counterpoint Lindemann's description of the youth's struggle against nature. The short surges mimic a bubbling spring, its gurgling ebb and flow linking verse to chorus through imagery that continues to present the natural world as a subversive and threatening force. Nature itself becomes an adversarial female body that the Jüngling means to scale and conquer, a theme that returns for greater play throughout the band's music video.

The long delay of Richard Kruspe and Paul Landers' guitar entrances builds the anticipation for the sonic assault of the chorus. Power chords and jagged, unison riffs in the guitar and bass lines form walls of sound that express an ideal of phallocentric strength through unison motion and sheer decibels. Warning against the title figure of Rosenrot, Rammstein's group response chastises her incursion into the band's masculine domain of violence and destruction. Following each of the two final choruses, the instruments break off into interludes that function as the most virtuosic moments of the song. The economy of their group motion becomes even more focused as unison intervals of octaves, ninths, and sevenths stab downward in a series of lightning strikes. The band's response is wordless here in its intensity, implying that for Rammstein a zenith of masculine emotion can only be communicated through a textless explosion of guitars and drums. The effect is one of brutal strength, appealing to listeners through a devastating unity of purpose intended to musically and metaphorically overthrow the gender inversions established in the verses.

Visualizing "Rosenrot"

If "Rosenrot" as an album track forms its meaning in relation to the legacy of Goethe and the Brothers Grimm, its music video adds a visual narrative that frames the discussion in a new cultural context. Music video occupies its own unique space as a visual medium and can present perplexing difficulties for the analyst. Serving a commercial function as much it does an artistic one, the purpose of the form is to advertise or supplement a preexisting music track. The crux of music video as an art form lies in the images' dependence upon self-contained audio tracks that function perfectly well on their own. The form and narrational patterns in the video rely almost completely on said track and revolve around the discrete moment of hearing the song.[8] Ideally, from a perspective of album advertisement, the visuals are meant to enhance the listening experience without distracting the viewer from a proper focus on the song. Tensions within the form arise based on whether or not these visual and audio elements have a balanced dialogue. Shots that feature lip-syncing or other simulations of live performance help to create a tempered relationship between the audio track and its accompanying images, however "Rosenrot" provides few examples of this kind. Instead, the video constructs a separate but related narrative framework for the song's lyrics. A dialogue between the video's visual and audio realms comprises what Nicholas Cook has aptly described as "a collision between two competing hierarchies ... the result is to destabilize the meaning of the words and, through them, the closure of the song as a whole." Shots, and the particular arrangement of these shots, work to "open the song up to the emergence of new meaning."[9] A study of "Rosenrot" relies then on investigating what director Zoran Bihać's visual and audio pastiche brings to the table, with its mixture of resonances formed through overlapping constructions of music and image.

Bihać directed two controversial videos for Rammstein prior to filming "Rosenrot," the first being the militaristic video for "Links 2-3-4" and the second for the cannibal-related subject of "Mein Teil" (My Part), where the band members portray crazed victims of mental illness. The plot of this third collaboration was no exception to the shock-rock aesthetic. The storyline features the conquest of a Catholic priest by an underage female supplicant, a subject that would find immediate topical resonance in the Catholic Church's pedophilia scandals. The band members portray monks dressed in both Catholic and Greek Orthodox vestments acting out a plot that includes group flagellation, murder, and an Inquisition-style burning at the stake. Most of the members remain in character throughout the video, with Lindemann being the only one to mime musical performance by lip-syncing during two of the video's visual threads. The majority of the lip-syncing shots take place throughout the chorus and blur the line between Lindemann's fictional role as monk and his real-life role as the singer of Rammstein. Here, his eye-contact with the camera engages the audience in a more direct fashion by creating a visual and aural link between hearing Lindemann's voice and seeing a corresponding motion of his mouth as if he speaks to the individual viewer. The second lip-syncing thread emerges during the second verse and contrasts the chorus' appeals to the audience by having Lindemann avoid eye-contact with the camera. The shots instead emphasize the verses' narrative mode of third-person storytelling to create a stronger visual link between "Rosenrot" and the fairy tale genre.

Opening shots quickly suggest a bare-bones narrative and feature the band as a group of traveling monks who stumble across a village where they are treated to feasting and dancing. By focusing primarily on Lindemann's character, the video suggests that the motivation for the action springs from his obsession with a young girl whose dance charms the monk and places him in her power. Following dream-like scenes of desire and a nightmarish tryst, the singer murders a couple who are visually established as having some relationship to the girl. Bihać's arrangement of shots implies that it is this Mädchen who inspires the monks' flagellation sequences and who instigates the murder through her seductive wiles. Following the killings, she turns on her lover with cries that alert the villagers and Lindemann's fellow monks to his blood-spattered presence. The video concludes with his bandmates and the angry villagers burning the singer at the stake, the young girl throwing the first torch.

The undercurrent of panic that permeates Bihać's video is the result of filming and editing techniques that create a whirlwind of fractured images meant to assault and overwhelm the viewer. As acclimated as audiences have become to a quick editing pace in film and television, the kaleidoscope of shots making up "Rosenrot" disorients the brain and eye. The viewer is forced to coordinate a staggering flow of information from shots that often change at a rate of one or more per second. Rammstein's song acts as a musical spine, and Bihać drapes his visual threads over its stable structure. The track's verse/chorus form and regular alternation of instrumentation creates an organized audio framework to balance the chaos of the director's images. Images within the chorus and interlude sections move at a particularly frantic pace, assaulting the audience's eyes and ears in tandem. Paralleling the violence of Rammstein's musical gestures, the temporal and spatial locations of the shots shift and twist as the audience attempts to track a coherent path through the visual information.

The hundreds of shots within "Rosenrot" spring from at least seven different threads, a technique fairly common to the music video medium.[10] Bihać references and differentiates between these image groupings with visual motifs created via sets, lighting, props, and color palette. His ordering of the various shots creates the appearance of a linear storyline broken into a pile of scattered pieces. Although the verse/chorus form of the song discourages a truly linear narrative path through the work, the viewer is given the impression that if these images could only be rearranged and reconstructed much like a jigsaw puzzle, then the various visual threads would form a coherent story. Carol Vernallis underscores the range of functions that can be found in effective editing choices, where: "Not only does the editing in a music video direct the flow of narrative.... Like film editing, it can color our understanding of characters ... it can elucidate aspects of the song, such as rhythmic and timbral features, particular phrases in the lyrics, and especially the song's rhythmic structures."[11] Bihać's own editing creates interactions between the music and images of "Rosenrot" that often take the form of rhythmic matching. Here, physical motions are mapped onto musical beats through the deliberate slowing or speeding of the film. As the editing cuts snap abruptly from one shot to the next, the director aligns the sharp edges of a cut with a particular musical beat. These cuts combine with the actors' silent gestures and collisions to generate a visual percussion that augments the song's musical percussion. The range of film speeds mixed and matched within the video and its constant temporal frenzy emphasize the violence of Rammstein's lyrics and musical gestures.

In contrast to the frantic action that will dominate the body of the video, Bihać chooses to open with the slow-motion entrance of the band members. The rhythmic flow in their gliding gestures imparts a sense of grandeur to augment the otherworldly quality of the setting. This quality is further intensified through the choices of costumes, sets, and color palette, which quickly confirm that the video operates within the timeless space of fairytale. Establishing shots present images of a pastoral community whose picturesque buildings and landscape are depicted through saturated, hyper-real colors dominated by vivid reds and greens. The trappings used to create this idyllic setting draw on what Cristina Bacchilega calls "stereotyped and industrialized fragments" that locate a work within folk narratives or as a parody of an established narrative with only a few words or images.[12] Brightly patterned folk dress dominates the costuming, although it may be lost on Rammstein's international audience that the designs and patterns are not those of a specifically German folk past. The people represented in the video may be "Volk" (People or Nation), but the strangers greeting the heroes are the *wrong* Volk. Bihać's visual cues steadily reveal this space to be filled with a mysterious and threatening female essence. Through stereotyped tropes of a sensual and irrational Eastern Other — in this case an Eastern European Other — the video emphasizes for its viewers that the band has left the safety of a masculine-oriented "Heimat" (homeland).[13]

Where the identity of Rosenrot remains ambiguous throughout the original audio track, the video frequently overlaps Lindemann's lyrics with images suggesting that the young seductress is synonymous with the title character of the song. Aspects of the visual layout use fairy tale cues to strengthen this interpretation and form a strong parallel to the Grimms' "Schneeweißchen und Rosenrot." Fourteen-year-old Romanian model Catalina Lavric portrays the video's enigmatic, rose-obsessed figure, whose face and form frequently coincide with the chorus tag "Rosenrot, oh Rosenrot." Her dark hair, tan skin, and rose-adorned costuming emphasize her charms through a characterization that draws heavily on the Western fantasy of a licentious and exotic East. Lavric becomes the focal point for the lyrics' description of the Mädchen whose demands end in masculine destruction. In the context of the visuals, the maiden not only ensures the death of the male protagonist, but her motivation appears to be a violent rejection of the traditional female roles of wife and mother. In this regard, the Mädchen's characterization as *femme fatale* aligns with Jess Sully's analysis of the "exotic, sexually promiscuous 'otherness' of the *femme fatale* [who] threatens to destabilize the established cultural order."[14] By manipulating the monk, her spiritual Father, the girl pits her desires against social mores and the patriarchal structure of the Church, whose historical position stressed women's second-class status as submissive wife, daughter, and mother. There are no details within the video as to why the girl seeks to murder the couple and to further cause the death of her accomplice. Her role as *femme fatale* requires only the video's brief character sketch that relies on the audience's evaluation of Lavric's facial expressions and body language. As Joy Ramirez notes in her study of the *femme fatale* in Italian silent film, "Theirs is a purely physical, plastic and transcendent reality, which does not require language and is all the more effective because of its absence. The diva's gestures and repertory of symbolic language, her eyes, her makeup, and the tropes of the theater tell her story better than a verbal performance could."[15] Indeed, Lavric's mouth only moves in speech twice, with both instances framed as acts of treachery; the first as she orders the monk into the house where he murders the couple, and the second when she betrays him by crying out for the villagers and his fellow monks. Relying on these visual cues, the viewer quickly understands her role as *femme fatale* and fills in any gaps in characterization through familiarity with the ancient "treacherous woman" figure, whose subversive power poses a larger threat to the institutionalized control of masculinity itself.

The video was shot on location in Romania, and its opening scene features cliff walls that overwhelm and diminish the bodies of the band members. This introduction parallels the landscape described in Lindemann's opening lyrics as the men enter what is subtly delineated as a threatening female space. Bihać's establishing shot positions the monks next to the primal image of a gaping cave mouth. Rife with psychosexual connotations, its blackness looms over the men before the band descends into the lush valley sheltering the pastoral community. Female figures both young and old dominate shots of this village as the monks wander into the midst of a folk celebration. Though smiles and laughter fill the scene, this environment is quickly posed as one hostile to men. A burned goat's head swings onscreen, startling the viewer and doubling not only as a reference to sacrilege but also as the exaggerated foreshadowing of Lindemann death as the scapegoat. A second shot lingers on a long loaf of bread. Sawed in half by a woman's hand, the castration imagery is nearly comical in its heavy-handedness. Such shots fly by so quickly, however, that they may only provoke sensations of uncertainty or foreboding in the viewer. Lindemann's facial expression anchors the viewer's attention as the Mädchen enters into the carnivalesque whirl. Paired with the first iteration of the "Rosenrot" "she wants it" motto, editing leans on the powerful continuity tool of close-up shots that alternate between the face and eyes of Lindemann and young Lavric. The camera frame moves closer and closer until this focus on the actors' eyes completely dominates the frame. This visual exchange strengthens the impression that the girl has bewitched and subjugated the man of the cloth by catching and holding his gaze. Clad in a dress distinguished from the other dancers by its red flower design, the siren of Lindemann's lyrics has been transformed into an underage Salome whose plaited hair bounces and sways suggestively around her as she performs her dance of temptation. Her indefinable and all-encompassing nature, from forbidden Lolita to exotic Carmen, underscores her function as the *femme fatale*, a role Helen Hanson and Catherine O'Rawe describe as "both unknowable and an index of unknowability, always representing more than can be articulated ... a locus of mystery ... culturally resonant and ideologically challenging."[16] Although Bihać creates a visual persona for Rosenrot that moves beyond the lyrics of the audio track, it quickly becomes clear that she is drawn straight from the same virgin/whore archetype as the Mädchen described in the song.

Transitioning into the second verse, the narrative leaps from the village celebration to a communal religious ceremony that resembles a wedding scene. Lavric stands between an older man and a motherly figure as she suggestively accepts the communion host from Lindemann's fingers. This action overlies the lyrics' description of the Jüngling's struggle and torment, transforming the words into a metaphorical struggle that aligns the priest's spiritual fall from grace with the Jüngling's physical fall as detailed in the third verse. Once more framing the village as female, the daytime action shifts to a forest riverbank and continues to emphasize a connection between women and nature. The singer now stands completely separated from his bandmates, who remain on the opposite bank and express their frustration at the abduction of their comrade. The body language between the singer and the girl as they walk and talk suggests that she has further subjugated the singer to her will. His gestures of denial are quickly overcome by her physical presence, and the couple's smiles and body language suggest his capitulation to her desires as they walk arm in arm.

The temporality of the scenes is particularly vague, and the viewer is unclear whether the events occur over a single day or a greater period of time. Daylight shots center on Lavric and the village community, where a realist style of filming provides a greater level of narrative coherency. In contrast, the nighttime settings become a fractured, topsy-turvy site of conflict and opposition. Dark backdrops and vibrant color saturation dominate the dream-like images overlaying the third verse's climax of treachery and death. The video fulfills Bihać's foreshadowing of the scapegoat, as a blood-spattered Lindemann leaves what we assume to be Lavric's house after dispatching its occupants. Lavric herself appears in the grandest of *femme fatale* poses, her body superimposed over darkness as thick as that of the gaping cave maw from the video's opening shots. The vibrant greens and reds of the grass, set pieces, and the costuming return to the exaggerated ambience of a fairy tale aesthetic, particularly in Lavric's costuming reminiscent of Disney's Snow White. As the girl's mouth opens in a scream, her pointing finger activates the slow-motion entrance of a mob of bandmates and villagers who spew out of the Stygian blackness behind her. The Mädchen of "Rosenrot" ultimately reveals herself to be an incarnation of Lilith, the mother of monsters. Describing this figure as a forebear of the *femme fatale*, Hanson and O'Rawe open their volume *Femme Fatale: Images, Histories, Contexts* with the common phrase that the figure of the treacherous woman is "'as old as Eve,'" before qualifying "or indeed as old as Lilith, Adam's first wife, turned demon and succubus."[17] An ancient mythological archetype, whose temptations inspired men to "frenzy and perverse sexuality," Lilith's mythology, centers on her revolt against male rule.[18] Her act of defiance resulted in an expulsion from the Garden of Eden as punishment for her presumptions to either equality or dominance. Set apart from humanity as a nightmarish symbol of female uprising, this malevolent temptress emerges in the body of Rosenrot to incite chaos, rebellion, and the destruction of mankind.

The strong contrasts between the unison chorus activity and the verses' stripped-down instrumentation likewise appears in visual terms throughout the video. The chorus and interlude sections are not only the site for the band to reunite musically, but to reunite visually as well. Rammstein's projections of homosocial strength are then glorified simultaneously in both sound and image. Containing the most visual fragmentation, the filming and editing style of the chorus and interlude sections respond to the audience's desire to see Rammstein operate as a unit. Bihać's judicious use of overhead shots emphasizes power and ferocity in the band's collective body through the group activities of flagellation and the band members' reclaiming of Lindemann's body during the pyre scene. A hectic pace creates an aggressive display on both visual and audio fronts, and the stabbing and whipping parallel the leaps and strikes of the instrumental gestures. These flagellation shots occupy the greatest amount of screen time, making up almost a quarter of the combined shots. The bandmates' frenzied motions augment the slashing riffs throughout the chorus and interlude. When layered over the chorus lyrics, these shots generate a new meaning for the digging of "deep wells." Close-ups focus on the rivulets carved into the band members' skin, recreating historical depictions of flagellants and the accompanying religious act of being washed in blood. Beyond an opportunity to match the lyrics to resonant visual symbols, these moments operate primarily to portray Rammstein's members as erotic visual objects placed in highly sexualized positions. The shots form a homo-erotic, yet intensely hyper-masculine scene as the men kneel together on the ground in a circle. Shirtless and each wielding the highly phallic object of a whip, the visual composition suggests an image of masochist group masturbation.[19] The sequences are the centerpiece of a video that revolves around physical pain, its exaggerated and fetishized displays posed as a site of pleasurable contemplation for both male and female viewers. In his analysis of pain and pleasure in Gothic literature, Stephen Bruhn contends that "the history of pain, then, is in many ways a history of looking; it is a narrative of watching a pained object while occupying a contradictory space both *within* and *outside* that object."[20] As an album track alone, the morbid plot and screams of "Rosenrot" describe a situation that can only be enacted in the listener's imagination. Bihać's video, however, delivers a finite arrangement of images where the viewer has been defined as equally outside the subject through overhead shots and inside the subject through the internal subjectivity established in its point-of-view shots. Threads positioned as dream images within the singer's subconscious likewise invite the audience to enjoy the experience of entering and sharing Lindemann's fictional body through the intimacy of the point-of-view experience. Although the pain of its onscreen characters has been distanced and cauterized through the actors' silence, "Rosenrot" encourages Rammstein's fans to feel a lascivious shiver in response to the band members' suffering.

Redefining the Sacred as Salacious

Rammstein's depiction of flagellation has a long historical precedent. Though generally considered to be an abandoned relic of religious fanaticism, woodcuts, illustrations, and the artwork of Goya all depict a practice that can still be observed in areas of Europe during Holy Week.[21] In Rammstein's hands, such whipping invokes the sexual practices of sadomasochism as much as it does religious fervor.[22] "Rosenrot" is not concerned with historical fidelity, but rather uses its elements as ironic props in a depiction of the Catholic Church as an institution whose ascetic exterior masks corruption and perversion. Such imagery draws on historical fascination with the Church and the conflicting relationships amongst its structures and symbols. Ellis Hanson details the contradictions found in an organization that is "at once modern and yet medieval, ascetic and yet sumptuous, spiritual and yet sensual, chaste and yet erotic, homophobic and yet homoerotic, suspicious of aestheticism and yet an elaborate work of art."[23] Here, Rammstein exploits histories of stake burning and contemporary sex scandals for their mockery of Catholicism and its rituals. Defining the priesthood as a homoerotic brotherhood, their images depict a group subject to immorality through unnatural codes of chastity and a masochist obsession with Christ's death.

Indeed, the video's storyline bears a marked resemblance to Matthew Lewis's *The Monk*, a 1796 novel that became the pinnacle of grotesque spectacle in 18th century Gothic literature. Lewis's tale abounds with similar plot devices, including themes of temptation, corruption, and the death of a fallen monk guilty of sexual depravity. Drawing on the underlying horror and instability felt throughout Europe during the period of the French Revolution, Lewis's salacious tale details the seduction of the pure monk, Ambrosio, who succumbs to the advances of a demonic, gender-bending *femme fatale*. This succubus, Matilda, inspires the clergyman to commit acts of rape and murder before his capture by the Inquisition and sentencing to death by burning. Like "Rosenrot," the book almost certainly promoted its negative view of female power and gender inversion as part of its reaction to political and cultural upheaval.[24] Enraged with homicidal lust, desire, and perverted pleasures, Lindemann's Mad Monk springs not only from Bihać's imagination, but also from historic constructions carrying a wealth of cultural baggage.

Defending Hardness and the Heimat

For "Rosenrot," fears and contemporary tensions have been arranged into images that show a fierce concern with dictating cultural and spatial boundaries. By establishing an imaginary East, its narrative inevitably establishes expectations of a corresponding West. An explicit Western identity is never depicted onscreen, but the group's role implies a Western Heimat shown in opposition to a land of Eastern strangers. Onscreen relationships in "Rosenrot" are shot through with tropes derived from colonial narratives, and Rammstein finds itself in the role of white, Western European adventurer. As monks, their expedition into the wilderness brings the Church's patriarchal authority to villagers of a distant community who have been separated by geographical barriers. This West has been further stereotyped as masculine through the focus on the band's bodies in relation to the female-dominated village. The video further aligns itself with colonialist conventions by associating the stranger with the characteristics of nature, darkness, and irrationality, all in the guise of Rosenrot's over-sexualized body. The monks' status as travelers establishes primary points of difference between the two groups. As E. Ann Kaplan points out, "Paradoxically, while travel may destabilize a fixed notion of culture, it heightens a sense of national belonging. People's identities when they are traveling are often more self-consciously *national* than when they stay home. In addition, travel provokes conscious attention to gender and racial difference."[25] Attributes assigned to the characters of "Rosenrot" not only mark boundaries of gender behavior, but also build a conception of what should or should not be characteristic of the Heimat. One of the primary functions of fable and fairy tale is to likewise mark such boundaries, often through their ability to discuss taboo subjects. Both song and video lean on German texts in such a fashion, looking back on folk references and mythologies as the voice of cultural authority. Rammstein's cautionary tale of "us versus them" allows the fears and tensions surrounding foreign bodies and immigrant relations to bubble to the surface. Its narrative both promotes and normalizes an elevated position for white German masculinity, and allows Rammstein to revisit its paranoia regarding cultural diffusion and Americanization.

In the previously mentioned video for "Sonne," the band had already used a parody of Disney's Snow White to censure the appropriation and commodification of European folk culture. Towering over the band members as an imperialist behemoth, she claims for herself the money and native folk culture of a European audience all too willing to offer up its national treasure, as symbolized by the band in its role as subservient dwarves. This preoccupation with material goods resonates with Mary Wood's explorations into the rise of the transgressive female in Italian cinema, a figure who becomes synonymous with "excessive materialism" in the 1990s and even more so throughout the 2000s. A variation on the *femme fatale* character, her appropriation of power, dominance over men, and sexual rebelliousness embodies "a multitude of social ills" for its audience and reflects "anxieties about female power, corruption, immigration, the mafia, and materialism."[26] Rammstein's use of Disney imagery appeared again in their explicitly negative depiction of Western materialism in the 2004 single "Amerika" (America), where Lindemann's lyrics reference the company's mascot, Mickey Mouse, amongst a range of corporate brand names. Both the song and its video (Dir. Jörn Heitmann) indicted the United States for a pollution of European culture through rampant commercialism and worldwide capitalist influence. The flipside of this criticism is that the song likewise chastises Germany for its embrace of these foreign products, suggesting an idealization of an unsullied Germany free from such culturally polluting foreign influences.

The specific targeting of the Church in "Rosenrot" was timely, given the intense media coverage in 2005 of the death of Pope John Paul II and his replacement by conservative German theologian, Cardinal Joseph Ratzinger. The focus on a corrupt priest and Rammstein's portrayal as monks communicates disdain and mistrust for an institution that maintains significant international influence. However, Bihać's shirtless flagellation sequences stand less as an enactment of violence against the body of the Church or even a wish to see physical harm done to pedophilic priests, so much as a reflection of Rammstein's relationship to the body and the ideal of hardness. The desire to communicate physical strength has been a crucial component of Rammstein's visual appearance, and indicates a corresponding concern for the body as a source of potential weakness. Controversy has surrounded the band's advertisement of this aesthetic since their earliest releases. Outcries in the German press brought attention to the popularity of "Stripped" (Dir. Philipp Stölzl, 1998), whose footage was inspired by Leni Riefenstahl's film "Olympia" (1938). The cover of Rammstein's debut album *Herzeleid* (Heartache, 1995) also drew accusations of promoting fascist ideals, with the shirtless band members posing as muscular exemplars of German manhood. When studying such iconography in album covers, publicity materials, or videos, it is important to remember that this imagery has been approved and promoted by record companies as advertising materials representative of the band. Videos like "Rosenrot" are a means to communicate a band's philosophy and aesthetic, and these are able to reach a wider audience than those attending live shows or reading interviews. The level of Rammstein's control over their video scenarios is difficult to determine, but the characterizations in album covers and videos nevertheless generate concepts of who and what Rammstein "is" and what ideologies the band supports.

Within "Rosenrot," flagellation concentrates on destroying or subjugating the weakness of the body and the body's desires, not to the glory of God, as would a religious flagellant, but to the glory of Rammstein's brotherhood and their homosocial ideal. Two of the four music videos released to promote the band's previous release, *Reise, Reise,* revolve around this concern for bodily weakness. Jörn Heitmann directed both videos alongside that of "Amerika."

The scenario of the first, "Ohne Dich" (Without You), once again pits Rammstein against nature. Dressed as mountain climbers, the band struggles against the elements until Lindemann falls from a cliff side, a scenario reminiscent of "Rosenrot." The band joins together to compensate for his weakness by carrying the singer up the mountain in a gesture of solidarity, unlike "Rosenrot," where weakness for sex and the *femme fatale* leads to Lindemann's amputation from the collective body of the band. Heitmann's second video, "Keine Lust" (I Do Not Feel Like It), pushes the dialectic of hard and soft to extremes. The scenario takes place in a future world where Rammstein's success has led to decadence and an excess of fleshly pleasures. Dressed in fat suits to indicate a horror of literal softness, the unified body of Rammstein has been disbanded. The group members are unable even to walk without the assistance of women, making a transparent correlation between weakness, femininity, and indulgence in sensual pleasures. "Rosenrot" continues to play on these themes, and the monk's capitulations to nature and the indulgent body act as harbingers of weakness in a scenario wherein feasting and sex correlates to a painful death.

The video's proscription against the Western adventurer's sexual relationship with an Eastern female resurrects colonialist fears of miscegenation. Recurring motifs in the imagery tie the Mädchen to the valley's landscape and correlate daylight scenes with the innocent exterior of the green valley, as opposed to the violence, sexuality, and murderous impulses that fill the nighttime shots. This connection between an idyllic landscape and its dark and dangerous inverse echoes Ella Shohat and Robert Stam's observations on the intersection in colonial discourse between the female Other and the foreign land where

> interlinked with the coy virgin metaphor is the opposite pole of libidinous wild femininity. This 'no man's land' or wilderness may be characterized as resistant, harsh, and violent, a country of savage landscapes to be tamed.... The split discourse of virginal and libidinous nature, homologous to the Madonna/whore dichotomy, operates even in the same text.... Colonialist discourse oscillates between these two master tropes, alternately positing the colonized as blissfully ignorant, pure, and welcoming on the one hand, and on the other as uncontrollably wild, hysterical, and chaotic, requiring the disciplinary tutelage of the law.[27]

Implying that Lindemann's body has been polluted by his interaction with the Mädchen, a red filter effect covers and distorts the singer's face during the murder scene. His crazed behavior and the weakness brought on by his lovesickness draws on historic categorizations that defined the feminine as "a spiritual, non-rational principle close to the processes of nature in contrast to the notions of progress, culture, and rationality typically associated with males."[28]

In the case of "Rosenrot," the spiritual moves into the realm of the supernatural when her contaminating presence is expressed through the mythological role of succubus during the chorus and instrumental interludes. Two such threads revolve around nighttime bedroom settings, the first emphasizing a sense of realism through washed out lighting and colors that feature symbolic and literal images of roses. Lavric appears clad in a nightgown covered in rose-like blotches that resemble and foreshadow the wounds inflicted only moments later on the older man and woman. She sits atop the singer in the traditional pose of the succubus, springing from Lilith's refusal to lie below Adam in the Garden of Eden. The vixen places her seduction prop, a red rose, into Lindemann's hands before violently thrusting his hands against its thorns. Coinciding with the second verse's return to the "Rosenrot" motto, these actions emphasize the castrating effect of her domination over the monk.

As the track returns to the chorus and its description of digging, the camera executes a point-of-view shot that allows viewers to see Lindemann's bloody palms as if through the singer's own eyes. This perspective presents a rare view of the protagonist by transporting the viewer into the singer's body to focus attention on his wounds. The torn palms not only respond to the digging imagery by aligning wounds with wells and blood with water, but these gouges also provide a reference to "Heidenröslein," where pricking stands as a symbol of virginal wounding. Bihać's choice of lens manipulates Lavric's body by transforming the girl into a menacing blur who lurks behind Lindemann's foregrounded hands. In this topsy-turvy world, it is she who has assaulted the monk, and the Christ-like stigmata of his bloody palms reference the monk's loss of innocence or virginity as much as it would the girl's. In this moment, Lindemann takes on symbols of female sexuality and biology to stress the reversal from the hardness found amongst the safety of the band.

The emasculating woman of "Rosenrot" has made several appearances in Rammstein's video repertoire. Armed with her bewitching body, the band and its video directors seem fascinated with this figure who subjects the members to acts of sexual degradation. Besides the Snow White of "Sonne," the ultimate expression of the Lilith figure in "Rosenrot" appears in the body of the snake-covered stripper from director Hannes Rossacher's "Engel" (Angel, 1997). Filmed on a set dressed to resemble an underground fetish club, this video reenacts Salma Hayek's snake dance from Robert Rodriguez's *From Dusk Till Dawn* (1996). Rossacher's dancer, a dark-skinned woman with wild hair and glowing eyes enters as a latter-day Josephine Baker clad in only a python and a chainmail bikini. This woman is sex and nature personified, exploiting the jungle-woman tropes that rocketed Baker to stardom in European clubs of the 1920s. Baker, and in extension the *femmes fatales* of "Engel" and "Rosenrot," draw on what Wendy Martin has described as the "fascinated, often admiring gaze of the white audience on the primitive Other, who represents erotic energy repressed by European civilization."[29] Both the snake woman and Bihać's embodiment of Rosenrot stand as threatening, and not entirely human, intermediaries between man and the forces of nature. In her analysis of recent *femme fatale* roles, J. Kate Stables considers such a figure to be part of a larger context whose role "combines sadistic and masochistic male fantasies [as] a potent lightning rod for male anxieties."[30] In this sense, Rosenrot and her myriad incarnations have been constructed as flashpoints for the fears and instabilities drawn into her capacious body.

Sympathy for the Devil

Placed within its contemporary political climate, perhaps the most troubling quality of "Rosenrot" is that although the narrative defines Lavric as the victim of the priest's sexual attentions, she clearly does not portray a sympathetic character. Her abuser may have become a victim himself with a death that reverses the role of women as the primary victims of Inquisitional burnings, but his punishment is consistently framed as injustice. This phenomenon of encouraging the audience to take a sympathetic stance towards abusers occurs in several examples of Gothic literature. Kate Ellis explains that "by emphasizing the absence of 'kind' in the protagonist's life," — in this case "kind" being the monk's estrangement from his bandmates and the Heimat — "the author elicits the sympathy of the reader in the presence of manifestly horrendous crimes.... Yet in their isolation those outsiders appear to be more sinned against than sinning, and the burden of blame is shifted toward social institutions and away from the villains themselves."[31] Unlike "Heidenröslein," the sympathy generated from the Jüngling's violent assault will not transfer onto "Rosenrot." As Ella Shohat and Robert Stam point out, white men in such travel narratives as that depicted in the video are never described as raping the dark-skinned Eastern woman, whose body has been defined as over-heated and desirous of a white master.[32] For "Rosenrot," then, the focus on the "she wants it" motto within each verse has the insidious potential to frame victims of sexual assault as responsible for their own abuse when this phrase is applied to Lavric's blatant sexuality.

The major stumbling block to reading Bihać's video solely as an antireligious statement is that music video makes it extremely difficult to separate the band members' public personas from the characters they portray onscreen. Unlike film actors, who take part in an implied contract dictating that for the duration of the film they become a different person, viewers likely cannot make such a distinction between the band's acting roles in "Rosenrot" and their roles as members of the band. The very purpose of the video, to promote Rammstein through calling attention to "Rosenrot" as a work by Rammstein, makes it nearly impossible to accept anything other than the barest veneer of character portrayal in its short, four-minute form. Bihać built a further sense of reflexivity into the video's form through Lindemann's lip-syncing and the comic effect of seeing Rammstein clothed as monks who smoke and bow their heads in postures of prayer. The audience's default response to identify with Rammstein provokes a strong reaction from many fans on online video forums, where those who self-identify as males convert their approval of Lindemann into sympathy for this pedophilic priest.[33] Interestingly, receptions by those who self-identified as female, or implied an identity as such, did not limit themselves solely to empathy for the singer. These viewers often reveled in a subversive reading of the video through the fantasy of having Lavric's power to subjugate the singer or the band to the viewer's own wishes. These reactions, and their detour away from political interpretations, demonstrate the difficulty of overcoming what Andrew Goodwin terms the "popular *auteurism*" of star power.[34] Focusing on the band as the protagonist is the primary purpose of music video, particularly when Rammstein have been portrayed as scopophilic objects of desire for the audience's pleasure.

In both its song and video forms, "Rosenrot" could be dismissed as simply another example in a surge of adult fairy tales produced by the various entertainment industries.[35] However, its provocative themes and the band's masculine hysterics regarding female sexuality in their video and recording repertoire beg for a deeper reading of source materials and a wider cultural context for their representations. At its core, "Rosenrot" reveals insecurities regarding a traumatic loss of authority and a further loss of physical, emotional, and mental control. The band delivers a response of crushing strength that appeals to its audience through a unification of voice, body, and instrument. Much like the fairy tales and fables emulated in both song and video, "Rosenrot" serves a didactic purpose as much as it does an entertaining one by consistently equating female power with death. Both song and video invoke the sexual predator of the *femme fatale* and assert the need for maintaining a united front against her emasculating presence. Lost in his weakness throughout Bihać's video, Lindemann and his contamination must be purged from the body of Rammstein. The singer becomes a martyr to this cause, offering himself as a sacrifice in a fiery salvation that restores freedom from the *femme fatale*. Playing to its ambiguity, the array of images and symbols within "Rosenrot" shift and twist, and their gestures to the past reinscribe boundaries of masculine behavior in the present. Rammstein's cautionary tale warns that there can be no happily ever after until this female threat has been expelled from its homosocial body. Allied to its construction of a folk past, the Gothic narrative of "Rosenrot" speaks to the danger of seductive charms ever ready to enmesh the male body in a dark dream of fear and desire.

Notes

1. Ellis Dye, *Love and Death in Goethe: "One and Double"* (Rochester: Camden House, 2004), 50. A further parallel emerges between "Rosenrot" and "Dalai Lama" as, in Dye's estimation, "Erlkönig" and "Heidenröslein" are linked by mutual rape imagery that "seeks beauty in violence," an ideal that finds constant play within Rammstein's works and performances.

2. Footage of drummer Christoph Schneider recording the drum track was featured on a "Making of the album *Reise, Reise*" featurette released as part of a bonus DVD for the special edition of *Völkerball* (2006). Interviews and publicity materials accompanying the release of *Rosenrot* frequently mention the album as an outlet for material that did not make the track list of *Reise, Reise*.

3. Martina Lüke, "Modern Classics: Reflections on Rammstein in the German Class," *Unterrichtspraxis/Teaching German* 41/1 (2008): 17. Both songs would also ally Rammstein to the world of art song and Franz Schubert's high-profile settings of both texts. It would not be surprising if "Rosenrot" and "Dalai Lama" were released separately due in part to a sense that two Goethe adaptations on a single album would appear to be overly derivative rather than a gesture of cultural fluency.

4. All three tales were adapted into successful motion pictures by East Germany's state-supported film studio DEFA, or *Deutsche Film Aktiengesellschaft*, between the 1960s and early 1970s. Details are available from the University of Massachusetts Amherst's archive of East German films and filmmaking found at www.umass.edu/defa.

5. D.L. Ashliman details the form and style of the many genres of folk narrative that typically fall under the umbrella term of fairy tale in his *Folk and Fairy Tales: A Handbook* (Westport, CT: Greenwood Press, 2004), 44.

6. In his classic study of heavy metal, Robert Walser details metal's concern with "the danger of pleasure — loss of control," wherein "the greater the seductiveness of the female image, the greater its threat to masculine control." *Running with the Devil: Power, Gender, and Madness in Heavy Metal Music* (Middletown, CT: Wesleyan University Press, 1993), 116.

7. Edward Larkey, "Just for Fun? Language Choice in German Popular Music," in *Global Pop, Local Language*, edited by Harris M. Berger and Michael Thomas Carroll (Jackson: University Press of Mississippi, 2003); Valerie Weinstein, "Reading Rammstein, Remembering Riefenstahl: 'Fascist Aesthetics' and German Popular Culture," in *Riefenstahl Screened: An Anthology of New Criticism*, edited by Neil Christian Pages, Mary Rhiel, and Ingeborg Majer-O'Sickey (New York: Continuum, 2008), 130–148; Matthias Weiß, "'Sense and Sensibility': Two Versions of Rammstein's *Du riechst so gut*," in *Rewind, Play, Fast Forward: The Past, Present and Future of the Music Video*, edited by Henry Keazor and Thorsten Wübbena (Bielefeld: Transcript, 2010).

8. Carol Vernallis' indispensible guide to music video analysis addresses such aspects as temporality and narrative or lack of narrative in *Experiencing Music Video: Aesthetics and Cultural Context* (New York: Columbia University Press, 2004), 17.

9. Nicholas Cook, *Analysing Musical Multimedia* (Oxford: Clarendon Press, 1998), 159.

10. Vernallis, 15.

11. Ibid., 27.

12. Cristina Bacchilega, *Postmodern Fairy Tales: Gender and Narrative Strategies* (Philadelphia: University of Pennsylvania Press, 1997), 2.

13. Succinct translations of terms as loaded as "Volk" and "Heimat" cannot convey

their historical and social significance as explored in texts such as Peter Blickle's *Heimat: A Critical Theory of the German Idea of Homeland* (Rochester: Camden House, 2002).

14. Jess Sully, "Challenging the Stereotype: The *Femme Fatale* in *Fin-de-Siècle* Art and Early Cinema," in *The Femme Fatale: Images, Histories, Contexts*, edited by Helen Hanson and Catherine O'Rawe (New York: Palgrave Macmillan, 2010), 47.

15. Joy Ramirez, "Silent Divas: The *Femmes Fatales* of the Italian *Cinema Muto*," in *The Femme Fatale: Images, Histories, Contexts*, edited by Helen Hanson and Catherine O'Rawe (New York: Palgrave Macmillan, 2010), 63.

16. Helen Hanson and Catherine O'Rawe, "Introduction: 'Cherchez la *femme*,'" in *The Femme Fatale: Images, Histories, Contexts*, edited by Helen Hanson and Catherine O'Rawe (New York: Palgrave Macmillan, 2010), 2.

17. Ibid., 3.

18. Barbara Fass Leavy, *In Search of the Swan Maiden: A Narrative on Folklore and Gender* (New York: New York University Press, 1994), 162, 185.

19. Walser points to one of the primary functions of the *femme fatale* in metal recordings and music video, where "the presence of women as sex objects stabilizes the potentially troubling homoeroticism suggested by the male display." This function is particularly pertinent in relation to Bihać's flagellation shots, which blur the homosocial and the homoerotic. Walser, 116.

20. Steven Bruhm, *Gothic Bodies: The Politics of Pain in Romantic Fiction* (Philadelphia: University of Pennsylvania Press, 1994), xx.

21. Niklaus Largier, *In Praise of the Whip: A Cultural History of Arousal*, trans. Graham Harman (Brooklyn: Zone Books, 2007), 52,164.

22. A further cultural disconnect results from the traditional flagellant dress of white robes and conical white hoods, or pirotta, that clothe Lindemann during the stake-burning scene. This may be a recreation of historical flagellant dress, but an international audience could experience a jarring interpretation of the robe, fire, and pointed hood in the context of the Ku Klux Klan.

23. Ellis Hanson, *Decadence and Catholicism* (Cambridge: Harvard University Press, 1997), 7.

24. Maria Beville, *Gothic-Postmodernism: Voicing the Terrors of Postmodernity* (Amsterdam: Rodopi, 2009), 23, 33. I am not at all suggesting that Bihać was attempting to adapt an 18th century Gothic novel with "Rosenrot," and based on the ambiguous narratives and visual relations in music video plots, it seems best to open up a video for the broader interpretation of its symbols rather than focus too closely on directorial intent.

25. E. Ann Kaplan, *Looking for the Other: Feminism, Film, and the Imperial Gaze* (New York: Routledge, 1997), 5–6.

26. Mary Wood, "*Chiaroscuro*: The Half-Glimpsed *Femme Fatale* of Italian *Film Noir*," in *The Femme Fatale: Images, Histories, Contexts*, edited by Helen Hanson and Catherine O'Rawe (Basingstoke: Palgrave Macmillan, 2010), 166.

27. Ella Shohat and Robert Stam, *Unthinking Eurocentrism: Multiculturalism and the Media* (London: Routledge, 1994), 143.

28. Sara Friedrichsmeyer, "Romantic Nationalism: Achim von Arnim's Gypsy Princess Isabella," in *Gender and Germanness: Cultural Productions of Nation*, edited by Patricia Herminghouse and Magda Mueller (Providence, RI: Berghahn Books, 1997), 57.

29. Wendy Martin, "'Remembering the Jungle': Josephine Baker and Modernist Parody," in *Prehistories of the Future: The Primitivist Project and the Culture of Modernism*, edited by Elazar Barkan and Ronald Bush (Stanford: Stanford University Press, 1995), 311.

30. Kate Stables, "The Postmodern Always Rings Twice: Constructing the *Femme Fatale* in 90s Cinema," in *Women in Film Noir* (London: BFI, 1998), 166.

31. Kate Ferguson Ellis, *The Contested Castle: Gothic Novels and the Subversion of Domestic Ideology* (Urbana: University of Illinois Press, 1989), 132.

32. Shohat and Stam, 157.

33. The vast majority of uploads, hits, and comments on Rammstein materials are found on YouTube. Here, various fans take part in discussing interpretation of the band's works, often panning negative reactions to the group and frequently educating new listeners through opinions on Rammstein's ideological intent.

34. Andrew Goodwin, *Dancing in the Distraction Factory: Music Television and Popular Culture* (Minneapolis: University of Minnesota Press, 1992), 98.

35. Such recent adaptations have appeared in films, television series, literary anthologies, and graphic novels amongst others.

Works Cited

Ashliman, D.L. *Folk and Fairy Tales: A Handbook.* Westport, CT: Greenwood Press, 2004.

Bacchilega, Cristina. *Postmodern Fairy Tales: Gender and Narrative Strategies.* Philadelphia: University of Pennsylvania Press, 1997.

Berdahl, Daphne. *On the Social Life of Postsocialism: Memory, Consumption, Germany.* Bloomington: Indiana University Press, 2010.

Beville, Maria. *Gothic-Postmodernism: Voicing the Terrors of Postmodernity.* Amsterdam: Rodopi, 2009.

Blickle, Peter. *Heimat: A Critical Theory of the German Idea of Homeland.* Rochester: Camden House, 2002.

Bruhm, Steven. *Gothic Bodies: The Politics of Pain in Romantic Fiction.* Philadelphia: University of Pennsylvania Press, 1994.

Burns, Robert G.H. "German Symbolism in Rock Music: National Signification in the Imagery and Songs of Rammstein." *Popular Music* 27, no. 3 (2008): 457–472.

Cook, Nicholas. *Analysing Musical Multimedia.* Oxford: Clarendon Press, 1998.

Dye, Ellis. *Love and Death in Goethe: "One and Double."* Rochester: Camden House, 2004.

Elferen, Isabella von. "East German Goth and the Spectres of Marx." *Popular Music* 30, no. 1 (2011): 89–103.

Ellis, Kate Ferguson. *The Contested Castle: Gothic Novels and the Subversion of Domestic Ideology.* Urbana: University of Illinois Press, 1989.

Friedrichsmeyer, Sara. "Romantic Nationalism: Achim von Arnim's Gypsy Princess Isabella." *Gender and Germanness: Cultural Productions of Nation,* edited by Patricia Herminghouse and Magda Mueller, 51–65. Providence, RI: Berghahn Books, 1997.

Goodwin, Andrew. *Dancing in the Distraction Factory: Music Television and Popular Culture.* Minneapolis: University of Minnesota Press, 1992.

Hanson, Ellis. *Decadence and Catholicism.* Cambridge: Harvard University Press, 1997.

Hanson, Helen, and Catherine O'Rawe. "Introduction: 'Cherchez la *femme.'*" *The Femme Fatale: Images, Histories, Contexts,* edited by Helen Hanson and Catherine O'Rawe, 1–8. Basingstoke: Palgrave Macmillan, 2010.

Kaplan, E. Ann. *Looking for the Other: Feminism, Film, and the Imperial Gaze.* New York: Routledge, 1997.

Largier, Niklaus. *In Praise of the Whip: A Cultural History of Arousal.* Translated by Graham Harman. Brooklyn: Zone Books, 2007.

Larkey, Edward. "Just for Fun? Language Choice in German Popular Music." *Global Pop, Local Language,* edited by Harris M. Berger and Michael Thomas Carroll, 131–151. Jackson: University Press of Mississippi, 2003.

Leavy, Barbara Fass. *In Search of the Swan Maiden: A Narrative on Folklore and Gender.* New York: New York University Press, 1994.

Littlejohn, John T., and Michael T. Putnam. "Rammstein and *Ostalgie*: Longing for Yesteryear." *Popular Music and Society* 33, no. 1 (2010): 35–44.

Lüke, Martina. "Modern Classics: Reflections on Rammstein in the German Class." *Unterrichtspraxis/Teaching German* 41, no. 1 (2008): 15–23.

Martin, Wendy. "'Remembering the Jungle': Josephine Baker and Modernist Parody." *Prehistories of the Future: The Primitivist Project and the Culture of Modernism*, edited by Elazar Barkan and Ronald Bush, 310–325. Stanford: Stanford University Press, 1995.

Ramirez, Joy. "Silent Divas: The *Femmes Fatales* of the Italian *Cinema Muto*." *The Femme Fatale: Images, Histories, Contexts*, edited by Helen Hanson and Catherine O'Rawe, 60–71. Basingstoke: Palgrave Macmillan, 2010.

Shohat, Ella, and Robert Stam. *Unthinking Eurocentrism: Multiculturalism and the Media*. London: Routledge, 1994.

Stables, Kate. "The Postmodern Always Rings Twice: Constructing the *Femme Fatale* in 90s Cinema." In *Women in Film Noir*, edited by E. Ann Kaplan, 164–182. London: BFI, 1998.

Sully, Jess. "Challenging the Stereotype: The *Femme Fatale* in *Fin-de-Siècle* Art and Early Cinema." *The Femme Fatale: Images, Histories, Contexts*, edited by Helen Hansen and Catherine O'Rawe, 46–59. Basingstoke: Palgrave Macmillan, 2010.

Vernallis, Carol. *Experiencing Music Video: Aesthetics and Cultural Context*. New York: Columbia University Press, 2004.

Walser, Robert. *Running with the Devil: Power, Gender, and Madness in Heavy Metal Music*. Middletown, CT: Wesleyan University Press, 1993. Waters, Melanie, ed. *Women on Screen: Feminism and Femininity in Visual Culture*. New York: Palgrave Macmillan, 2011.

Weinstein, Valerie. "Reading Rammstein, Remembering Riefenstahl: 'Fascist Aesthetics' and German Popular Culture." *Riefenstahl Screened: An Anthology of New Criticism*, edited by Neil Christian Pages, Mary Rhiel, and Ingeborg Majer-O'Sickey, 130–148. New York: Continuum, 2008.

Weiß, Matthias. "'Sense and Sensibility': Two Versions of Rammstein's *Du riechst so gut*." *Rewind, Play, Fast Forward: The Past, Present and Future of the Music Video*, edited by Henry Keazor and Thorsten Wübbena, 111–134. Bielefeld: Transcript, 2010.

Wood, Mary. "*Chiaroscuro*: The Half-Glimpsed *Femme Fatale* of Italian *Film Noir*." In *The Femme Fatale: Images, Histories, Contexts*, edited by Helen Hanson and Catherine O'Rawe, 157–169. Basingstoke: Palgrave Macmillan, 2010.

Discography

Rammstein. "Amerika," *Reise, Reise*. Motor. 2004.
_____. "Dalai Lama," *Reise, Reise*. Motor. 2004.
_____. "Rosenrot," *Rosenrot*. Universal. 2005.

Filmography

Rammstein. "Du riechst so gut '98." *Lichtspielhaus*, Motor. 2003.
_____. "Engel." *Lichtspielhaus*, Motor. 2003.
_____. "Keine Lust." Accessed September 15, 2012. 2005. http://vimeo.com/heitmann/videos.
_____. "Links 2-3-4." *Lichtspielhaus*, Motor. 2003.
_____. "Mein Teil." Accessed September 15, 2012. 2004. http://vimeo.com/zoranbihac/videos.
_____. "Ohne Dich." Accessed September 15, 2012. 2004. http://vimeo.com/heitmann/videos.
_____. "Rosenrot." Accessed September 15, 2012. 2005. http://vimeo.com/zoranbihac/videos.
_____. "Sonne." *Lichtspielhaus*, Motor. 2003.
_____. "Stripped." *Lichtspielhaus*, Motor. 2003.
_____. *Völkerball*, special ed. DVD. Universal Music Germany. 2006.

9

Rammstein, Johann Gottfried Herder and the Origin of Rock and Roll

Simon Richter

How old is rock and roll? Are its origins to be found among the "singing neanderthals" of Stephen Mithen's speculative research?[1] Almost certainly, on one level, but not in ways that are interpretively traceable to the music of Rammstein. If we follow Rammstein's lead, we can locate an origin of rock and roll — and certainly of their music — in the musico-anthropological work of the eighteenth-century German *Sturm und Drang* philosopher and collector and theorist of folk songs, Johann Gottfried Herder. We find in Herder's early aesthetic thought a deep affinity with the corporeal thrust of rock and roll, a dimension that is cognate with what I take to be its primal scene. And we find in Rammstein's "Rosenrot," the title song of their fifth album (2005), a startlingly perceptive, allusive and self-ironic engagement with Herder.

Who first and officially invoked the name rock and roll is difficult to specify, precisely because the component parts of the name seem to crop up independently and to seek each other's company. The same might be said of *Sturm und Drang*, the literary and musical style of the 1770s, the name of which derived belatedly from the title of a play by Max Klinger, but whose complementary parts already figured in the radical thought of the *Sturm-und-Drang* authors' favored philosopher, no other than Herder. "Rocking and rolling" preexisted its official use on Alan Freed's radio broadcast[2] in the early 1950s by several decades "as secular black slang for dancing or sex," for instance, in 1922 on Trixie Smith's "My Man Rocks Me with One Steady Roll."[3] Before that the term had a place in the music of religious revivalist culture. By all accounts, Rock and Roll designates a scene of intense corporeal engagement, sexually inflected. From sex to dance to music to religious enthusiasm — these contexts readily elide in a manner that defies systems of abstract signification. The corporeal aspect in all of them is key.

Now for Herder, it was not the name rock and roll, of course, which captured the notion of his restless and corporeally oriented thought, nor, incidentally, was it *Sturm und Drang*, even if a youthful Finnish metal band has adopted the latter to name its sound. As Herder wrote his essay "Auszug aus einem Briefwechsel über Ossian und die Lieder alter Völker" (Excerpt from a Correspondence about Ossian and the Songs of Ancient Peoples) in 1771, he fixed on two moments, *Sprung* and *Wurf*— leap and throw — and saturated them with a density of meanings ranging from formal issues of syntax and style to primal scenes of sexuality and the hunt. My purpose in this paper is to evoke in the strongest manner possible the "shake, rattle, and roll"— the *Sprung und Wurf*— that constitute the corporeal intensity of Herder's early take on folk music. By immersing ourselves in Herder's thought, we will be all the more able to detail the remarkable extent to which that same corporeal intensity is purposefully instantiated in Rammstein's "Rosenrot," both as song and music video. "Rosenrot" is more than a clever cover of Johan Wolfgang von Goethe's iconic poem "Heidenröslein," first introduced anonymously as a folk song by Herder in "Briefwechsel über Ossian." As I will show, Till Lindemann's song and Rammstein's video amount to a musical, literary, and visual homage to Herder as a father of rock and roll. That it concludes with an *auto de fé*, a masochistic fantasy of punitive self-immolation, is a matter reserved for later.

Ossian and Primitivism

Among the frauds of literary history, the story of Ossian stands out. In the 1760s the Scotsman James MacPherson published a series of epic poems that purported to be his translations from original sources of the ancient Celtic epic poet Ossian. The poems were the focus of enthusiastic and critical attention across Europe. In Germany, translations began to appear in 1764 and by 1768 the Viennese poet Michael Denis's translation of the complete poems along with MacPherson's accompanying notes was well under way. That same year, Herder wrote a critical review of the translation, principally objecting to Denis's use of Klopstockian hexameter.[4] Denis would also serve him as straw man in his Ossian essay of 1771.

Quite apart from the question of their literary authenticity, which was more hotly debated in England than on the continent, Ossian became the occasion for imagining and valorizing a primal, northern European sensibility uniquely different from that of the ancient Greeks. The art historian Johann

Joachim Winckelmann had argued for the fundamental harmony between nature and Greek culture in antiquity in 1755. And only slightly more than a decade later, Herder identified an authenticity of life in Ossian and the *Volkslieder* of other northern peoples that consisted precisely in its rawness and artlessness. It would not be amiss to credit Herder, as Erhard Bahr has done, with first introducing a notion of primitivism to German aesthetic discourse.[5] To the fictional recipient of his letters on Ossian, Herder writes:

> Wißen Sie also, daß je wilder, d. i. je lebendiger, je freiwürkender ein Volk ist, [...] desto wilder, d. i. desto lebendiger, freier, sinnlicher, lyrisch handelnder müßen auch, wenn es Lieder hat, seine Lieder seyn![6] [Herder, "Auszug," 452].
> [Did you know that songs of a people, if they have songs, will be livelier, freer, more sensuous, more lyrically active, the wilder, that is, the livelier, the freer the people themselves are.]

By rendering Ossian's songs in an imitation of Klopstock's imitation of Greek hexameter, Herder argued, Denis formally distanced and displaced the language from its point of origin, perpetrating a kind of fraud more egregious, frankly, than that of MacPherson. For Herder, Ossian is "[ein] wild[er] Apollo" (a wild Apollo) whose distinctive poetic practices anchored in human life are "die Pfeile [...], womit er die Herzen durchbohrt, und woran er Seelen und Gedächtnisse heftet" (the arrows with which he penetrates hearts and rivets souls and memories; Herder, "Briefwechsel über Ossian," 452). At this point, let me merely call attention to the fact that Herder's wild Apollo, a kind of hybrid Marysas/Apollo figure, doesn't play the lyre *or* the flute — he shoots arrows.

The Psychology of Ossian

At three points in the "Briefwechsel über Ossian," Herder promises to continue his argument in a second publication that would take the form of "eine *Psychologie aus den Gedichten Ossians*" (a psychology based on the poems of Ossian; Herder, "Briefwechsel über Ossian," 453, 456, 494). We know of other projects Herder pursued concurrently that also point in the direction of psychology. As he writes to his fiancé Karoline Flachsland in 1771 from far-off Bückeburg, he is simultaneously working on essays about Ossian, Shakespeare, the book of Genesis, the origin of language, and cognitive processes (11 September 1771). In his mind, all of these are related. With respect to the latter he means his essay "Vom Erkennen und Empfinden" (On Cognition and Feeling) in which he plans to work out a psychology based on the famed medical scholar Albrecht von Haller's empirical physiology. He describes this project as "Hallers physiologisches Werk zur Psychologie erhoben und wie

Pygmalions Statue mit Geist belebt" (Haller's physiological work elevated to psychology and, like Pygmalion's statue, brought to life with spirit; Herder, "Erkennen," 340). My suspicion is that Herder's planned psychology of Ossian and his Hallerian psychology were to be cut from the same cloth: emphatically *not* a rational psychology of the faculties of the soul in the manner of Christian Wolff,[7] but rather a unitary account of cognition and sensation grounded in the empirical human body. What Haller had described as a fundamental property of organic tissue, the phenomenon of irritability, that is, an automatic non-cognitive reaction to painful stimuli, was understood by Herder as the signature process of all human life from the minute contraction of a fiber to the experience of love.[8] In an expansive metonymical sense, pain rivets body and soul together along the whole line, such that neither is conceivable apart from the other. When the copy-editor prepared the 1771 edition of Herder's *Letters*, he struck Herder's promised *psychology* of Ossian and replaced it with the word *philology*. In the afterword to the 1773 edition published as the opening essay of *Von deutscher Art und Kunst* (Of German Manner and Art). Herder understood this misprision as a signal indicator of the incapacity of modernity to comprehend the unity of human life as experienced by Ossian and his primitive forebears (Herder, "Briefwechsel über Ossian," 494).

Sprung und Wurf

No one should expect Herder to be systematic about the introduction of terms. They seem to arise of their own necessity. If certain words start to cluster and form patterns of meaning and dense connotation there is a good chance they are in the process of coalescing into conceptual terms, not imposed from without, but rather generated from within. Such is the case with *Sprung und Wurf*, the key terms of Herder's "Briefwechsel über Ossian." The notion of the *Sprung* has received a great deal of philosophical and literary attention in other contexts, whether we are talking about the *Ur-Sprung* of language or another cultural phenomenon or the leap of the *salto mortale* at the point where rationalist philosophy meets its limit.[9] But Herder's use of *Wurf* and other grammatical and lexical variations of *werfen* is so anomalous as to have earned him a definitional entry all his own in Grimms' *Deutsches Wörterbuch*, the O.E.D. of the German language:

> Seit *HERDER*s Ossian-aufsatz (1773 in den blättern 'von deutscher art u. kunst') gilt wurf (namentlich in der fügung erster wurf) als bezeichnung für den dichterischen schaffensvorgang, den die poetische theorie des sturm und drang im gegensatz zur rationalistischen kunstauffassung der aufklärung als genialen, schöpferischen gestaltungsakt verstehen lehrte.

[since HERDER's Ossian essay (1773 in the pages 'of german manner and art') wurf (namely in the construction 'first throw') counts as a designation for the poetic creative process, which the poetic theory of the sturm und drang, in contract to the rationalistic conception of art of the enlightenment, taught us to understand as an ingenious, creative act of formation.]

Inevitably, the dictionary definition seeks to fix a term whose efficacy for Herder consists precisely in its resistance to such operations. While the editors of the dictionary specify the original context as that of "erster Wurf"—nothing more than a glorified first draft, so to speak—Herder actually repudiates that meaning, and most often combines *Wurf* with the adjective *kühn* (meaning bold in an extreme sense). Thus we read: "Nichts in der Welt [hat] mehr Sprünge und kühne Würfe als Lieder des Volks" (nothing in the world has more leaps and bold tosses than the songs of the people; Herder, "Auszug," 477). Ulrich Gaier's attempt to grasp the meaning of *Wurf* is suppler than that of the lexicographers of Grimms' dictionary. In his commentary to the "Briefwechsel über Ossian" and other material relating to Herder's *Volkslied* project, he writes: "'Wurf'" bezeichnet die Spontaneität, die sich in abrupten Kehren und Wendungen der Fabel äußert, in abbrechender und anderswo neu ansetzender Argumentation—Herder spricht mehrfach von den 'Würfen und Sprüngen' einer nicht logisch strukturierten Rede" ('Wurf' designates the spontaneity, which expresses itself in the abrupt turns and pivots of the fable, in the truncations and new beginnings of argments—Herder speaks frequently of the 'throws and leaps' of non-logically structured speech; "Briefwechsel über Ossian," 1122). The *Wurf* engages the auditor or reader in an almost physiological response. The song's abrupt and impulsive movement amounts to a sequence of thrusts (of painful stimuli to use Haller's term) aimed at auditors that rivet their attention, affect them viscerally, and propel them relentlessly forward. Herder's prime example—and I should probably recall here that Herder's discourse depends on a series of exemplary folk-songs—is "ein Jägerlied" (a hunting song) in which "kein Vers ohne Sprung und Wurf des Dialogs [ist]" (no verse is without the leap and throw of dialogue; Herder, "Briefwechsel über Ossian," 477). Should a modern poem contain this "thrust and jump," writes Herder, it would certainly cause astonishment and outrage among lame critics for its incomprehensible, bold dithyrambs.

The dialogue in Herder's *Jägerlied* consists in the thrust and parry of a hunter and his prey:

Ich bin ein Jäger, und fang dich schier,
    Alleweil bei der Nacht!
"Bist du ein Jäger, du fängst mich nicht"

Alleweil bei der Nacht! [Herder, "Briefwechsel über Ossian," 477].

[I am a hunter and I'll catch you clean, every single night!
"You are a hunter and you'll catch me not," every single night!]

The prey insists that her "hohe Sprünge" (high leaps) will help her elude the hunter, but the hunter is confident that he's her match. What Herder particularly likes is the abrupt unfolding of the drama:

> "Sehen Sie, plötzlich, ohne alle weitere Vorbereitung erhebt sich die Frage: 'Was hat sie an ihrem rechten Arm?' und plötzlich, ohne weitere Vorbereitung die Antwort: 'Nun bin ich gefangen, u. s. w. / Was hat sie an ihrem linken Fuß? / 'Nun weiß ich, daß ich sterben muß!' und so gehen die Würfe fort, und doch in einem so gemeinen, populären Jägerliede! Und wer ists, ders nicht verstünde, der nicht eben daher auf eine dunkle Weise, das lebendige Poetische empfände?" [Herder, "Briefwechsel über Ossian," 478].
>
> [Look, suddenly, without any further preparation, the question arises: "What's that on her right arm?" and suddenly, without further preparation, the answer: "Now I am caught, etc. / What's that on her left foot? / Now I know that I must die!" and in this manner the thrusts continue, and even in such a common, popular hunting song! And who is not able to understand, who is therefore not able to sense viscerally the lively poetic quality?]

Indeed. It is more than clear that this hunting song is in fact an erotic song and that the original semantic domain of the *Wurf* is that of the primitive hunt (i.e., spears and arrows) elided with sexual conquest and transposed to a corporeally grounded poetics with an implied and equally corporeally grounded theory of reception. And from this perspective it becomes clear that many of Herder's exemplary folk songs come from precisely this domain, that they imply a fantasy scenario of nothing more and nothing less than the corporeal intensity of erotic encounter between an uncomplicated youth and an uncomplicated maiden, what I will later refer to as a primal scene of rock and roll in connection with Rammstein's "Rosenrot." No wonder Herder writes that the modern reader of folk song is bound to run into tropes and language "vor der gleichsam die Gedanken erröthen" (that cause the thoughts themselves to blush, so to speak).[10]

Herder's *Volkslied* project is clearly over by 1778 when he submits a *Preisschrift* (an essay entry) to the *Baierische Akademie ueber Gegenstände der schönen Wissenschaften* (the Bavarian Academy for Objects of the Aesthetic Sciences) with the title "Ueber die Wurkung der Dichtkunst auf die Sitten der Völker in alten und neuen Zeiten" (On the Effect of Poetry on the Morals of Peoples in Ancient and Modern Times). Gone are the *Sprung und Wurf* of the *Briefwechsel* and the prefaces to his anthologies of *Volkslieder*.[11] Although his concept of poetry remains consistent with a corporeally oriented approach to cultural expression, it's been cleansed of erotic valence. Instead of the *Wurf*, he gives us *Würkung* (effect) confined to considerations of moral good or ill. In his final word on Roman moral and poetic decadence, he upbraids Wilhelm Heinse, a younger contemporary who pursued the agenda of the young Herder, for his translation of Petronius's *Satyricon*: "Die deutsche Ueberset-zung Petrons wird also Stellen, Noten und dem Geiste des Buchs nach, trotz ihrer Kunst, ein Flecken unserer Sprache bleiben" (The German translation of Petronius will, on account of passages, tones and the spirit of the book, and despite its artfulness, remain a stain on our language).[12]

Karoline Flachsland

I turn now briefly to Karoline Flachsland, the fiancée and later wife of Herder, not in a biographical gesture — as if biography could provide answers to interpretive questions — but because Herder's engagement with Flachsland is mediated by his engagement with *Volkslieder*. In a word, Herder wants to understand himself as the uncomplicated youth and wants her to understand herself as the uncomplicated maiden. Now it is a fact that Herder's collecting and translating of folk songs in Strasburg and Bückeburg in the early 1770s coincides with a period of his epistolary courtship with Flachsland back in Darmstadt. His letters frequently include folk songs from his hand, translations or songs by others.[13] While he lauds her for being moved by Klopstock's sen-timentality — "Daß Sie Klopstock und Geßner nachempfinden können, ist hold und schön" (that you can feel with Klopstock and Geßner is sweet and beautiful) — he urges her repeatedly to be open to the rawness of the primitive folk song.[14]

The passage I want to consider is in a letter dated 2 October 1771. It is a rhetorical performance of the *Sprung und Wurf*, the corporeal intensity he hopes to savor in a shared fantasy with Karoline.

> Daß Ihnen meine Schottische Lieder aber beßer gefallen, freut mich ungemein. Ein kühner Empfindungsschauer den sie mir abjagen — ach, liebstes Mädchen könnte ich sie Dir vorlesend abjagen! u. Dich denn eben so kühn umarmen. "Du bist doch mein Mädchen! Du fühlst wie ich!"[15]
>
> [That you like my Scottish songs more pleases me enormously. A bold shiver of sensation which they 'hunt down' in me — oh, dearest girl, if only I could hunt them down while reading them to you! And then just as boldly embrace you. "You are my girl! You feel as I do!"]

First, we will take notice of the fragmentary quality of the syntax, what Herder would call its *Wurf*. By the same token, the short passage is animated by a series of major leaps, Herder's *Sprünge*: From his own reading context and the physiological effect of the songs on his body (the *Empfindungsschauer*), to *her* reading context where he hopes to achieve an analogous effect on *her* body, followed by a bold embrace (notice the *kühn,* almost in the sense of impertinence) and a concluding quotation, as if from a folk song, that emblematizes their relationship in the common primitive feeling of erotic tension shared by a youth and a maiden. Notice too the transition from the formal *Sie* and *Ihnen* to *Du, Dich,* and *Dir.* Nor is it by accident, of course, that the verb that is used in both reading contexts is constructed on the word *jagen,* implying the hunt. The fantasy scenario of the folk song is also the framework for the epistolary space in which Herder seeks to encounter his beloved. "Mein Eden," writes Herder, "ist mehr eine alte Celtische Hütte auf einem rauhen Gebürge, zwischen Frost und Sturm und Nebel; als mir Geßner und Klopstock ihr süßestes Eden in Orient, ihren Himmel und ihr Paradies mahlen können" (My Eden is more in the way of an old Celtic hut on a rough mountain between frost and storm and fog; much more than the heaven and paradise of the sweetest oriental Eden Geßner and Klopstock can paint; 28 October 1770). That she will make him withdraw these forward thrusts with parries of her own is merely part of the game, even if it gives the lie to Herder's confidence in the recoverability of primitive modes of feeling.

Heidenröslein

One of Herder's corollary accomplishments in "Briefwechsel über Ossian" is that he is the first to publish a poem best known as "Heidenröslein," easily one of the most famous poems in the German language, the iconic *Volkslied,* typically attributed to Goethe, masterfully set by Schubert, but also more recently by Rammstein. Engaging in a diminutive fraud reminiscent of MacPherson's much larger one, Herder suppresses any authorship and represents the poem as "ein älteres Deutsches [Lied]" (an older German song)." In 1789, more than fifteen years after its first and until then only appearance in print, Goethe published the poem with slight though significant revision as his own. It is speculated that the origin of Goethe's poem is to be sought in the Strasburg period around 1770 when he first met Herder and that Herder reproduced Goethe's poem from memory — hence the variations — and included it anonymously in the *Briefwechsel über Ossian.* However, there are two additional points of origin for the poem — regardless of whether it is to be ascribed to Goethe or Herder.[16] Indeed, it may have been Herder who acquainted Goethe with early modern songs that establish or perpetuate the tradition of the broken rose motif, such as Paul van der Aelst's song collection of 1602.[17] In addition to adducing the "Heidenrößlein" poem in *Letters on Ossian,* Herder crafted another variation, "Die Blüthe. Ein Kinderlied" (Blossom. A Children's Song), which he sent to Karoline around 1771 and which was eventually taken up into what is called *Das silberne Buch* (The Silver Book), a collection of poems Herder sent to her. Alternatively or additionally, Herder was aware of a passage in Samuel Richardson's *Clarissa*, which both he and Karoline were reading and discussing in 1771, in which Lovelace calls a seventeen-year-old woman whom he subsequently ravages his "Rosebud." Herder elaborates a poem on the basis of the passage and sends it to Karoline under the title "Das Rosenknöspgen. Lovelace an Belford" (Rosebud. Lovelace to Belford). It concludes with the telling line: "Nur, Bube, brich das Knöspgen nicht" (But, boy, do not break the rosebud). I should add that the "Jägerlied" (hunting song) which Herder used to introduce the concepts of *Sprung und Wurf* concludes with a line in which the violated virgin asks to be buried underneath the "Rößlein roth" (red rose). In *Schubert's Goethe Settings*, Lorraine Byrne baldly attributes "Heidenrößlein" to Goethe without reference to philological complexities and speculates that Goethe "transmits his experience ... into a reflection of his early love for Friederike Brion, the daughter of the pastor at Sesenheim."[18] The evidence indicates that an equally strong case could be made for the relevance of Herder's experience with Karoline. Regardless, what is clear on any reading is that this cluster of poetic activity around the motif of the broken rose in the mode of the folk song is premised on a fantasy of erotic encounter inflected with violence.

It is therefore not surprising that "Heidenröslein" is typically read as a none-too-subtle allegory of defloration and/or rape.[19] Obviously the "Jägerlied" would lend itself to such a reading also. The crucial question in relation to this cluster, indeed, to Herder's entire *Volkslied* project as I am conceiving it here, concerns the moment of suffering, the imagined pain that figures corporeal intensity. If we look at the third stanza of Herder's version, we see that the "wilde Knabe" (wild boy, recalling Herder's wild Apollo) makes good on his threat and breaks the "Rößlein," who in turn defends herself and pricks him. "Aber er vergaß darnach / Beim Genuß das Leiden!" (But he forgot in the aftermath / pain in the midst of pleasure). Pain belongs to the boy, even as it is recuperated and overwhelmed by the feeling of pleasure. The reader is left to conjecture the death of "Rößlein roth," perhaps in the unspoken rhyme on her name, her *Tod* (death). Her counter threat, namely that because of the pain she inflicts on him he will be reminded of her for eternity, is left unrealized. Thomas Althaus discerns a typical Anacreontic gesture in Herder's take. My own sense is that *Genuß* layered over *Leiden* is the best Herder can do for his fantasized moment of corporeal intensity. What Herder is trying to articulate is the corporeally intense counterpart to what Moses Mendelssohn theorized as "gemischte Empfindungen" (mixed feelings) i.e., pain *and* pleasure.[20]

Goethe handles the moment of pain differently in his version of 1789: "Röslein wehrte sich und stach, / Half ihr/ihm doch kein Weh und Ach, / Mußt' es eben leiden" (Röslein defended herself and pricked / No woe and ouch could help her/him, / Had no choice but to suffer). The pain clearly belongs to "Röslein"—ihr—at least until the *Ausgabe letzter Hand*, i.e., the last edition published under Goethe's authority, at which point Goethe or a copyeditor corrected the grammar and replaced *ihr* with *ihm*. In other words, in all previous editions, Goethe violated grammatical propriety (using a feminine pronoun in place of the appropriate neuter) in order to preserve gender propriety—her suffering, her pain—as though it were a law: "Mußt' es eben leiden." David Wellbery, however, has recently advanced an interpretation that discerns complementary moments of rape and castration (the violence that reciprocates "ich steche dich) and resists what he calls a gesture of hermeneutic stabilization in favor of the one or the other, preferring to acknowledge an "essential ambivalence of sexuality."[21] The grammatically accurate *ihm* allows for both the youth and the girl to inhabit the space of pain. On this reading Röslein's threat *is* realized and the poem itself becomes the abiding memory of reciprocal, if assymetrical violence—a *Doppelwurf*, so to speak—underlying erotic encounter.

"*Rosenrot*"[22]

The young Herder was convinced that corporeal intensity was the necessary condition for any song to outlive its historical context and retain currency despite historical change. "Je länger ein Lied dauern soll, desto stärker, desto sinnlicher müssen diese Seelenerwecker sein, daß sie der Macht der Zeit und den Veränderungen der Jahrhunderte trotzen" (The longer a song is supposed to last, the stronger and more sensual must these psychic stimuli be, so that they are able to defy the power of time and the changes of the centuries; "Briefwechsel über Ossian," 452–453). If you do not share the young Herder's convictions, the leap we are about to make from the "Briefwechsel über Ossian" and "Heidenröslein" to Rammstein may seem just a little too bold, especially nowadays when historicist orthodoxies prevail. According to Herder's understanding, folk song is a transcultural genre, which combines cultural specificity and anthropological universality, both of them grounded in corporeal intensity. On that account I feel completely justified in turning my attention to a version of "Heidenröslein" created by the German industrial metal band Rammstein. It would certainly be possible to present an argument designed to bridge the gap over which I propose to leap—a genealogy of the *Volkslied*, perhaps, that constructs a connection between 1770 and 2005, or, more likely, a cultural history of "corporeal intensity" which takes in *Lebensphilosophie*, Nietzsche, Artaud's theater of cruelty, Whitehead's process philosophy, and other attempts to think through and enable "authentic modes of life"— but I am not inclined to pursue them, even though the concept of intensity (without the emphasis on corporeality) is receiving considerable attention presently— I am thinking of Erich Kleinschmidt's *Die Entdeckung der Intensität* (2004) in which Herder plays a crucial role. In the final analysis, the strongest reason for turning to Rammstein is the fact that their song "Rosenrot" and the accompanying video offer a profound revisionist interpretation of "Heidenröslein" and Herder's concept of corporeal intensity.

Rammstein is one of the foremost bands in the German metal scene also known as the *Neue Deutsche Härte* (NDH). The band combines a *Stahlsturm* metal sound with literate, allusive and punning German-language lyrics and has achieved worldwide success selling more than 15 million albums. Although the band was founded in 1994, the individual members share cultural roots in the music scene of pre–*Wende* Schwerin and the surrounding countryside. The band's tendency to become enmeshed in controversies over sexual display, fascist aesthetics, and hot-button political and cultural topics may distract from the serious playfulness of their musical and theatrical ambitions.[23] One measure of their aesthetic aspirations is the fact that they frequently collaborate with Berlin-based artist and theater director Gert Hof, also a citizen of the former GDR, to produce inventive and provocative videos and pyrotechnical stage shows. I will leave aside the band's notoriety and the various scandals they have provoked, and proceed immediately to a discussion of "Rosenrot" and the accompanying video.

"Rosenrot" is written by Till Lindemann, band lyricist, lead vocalist and main actor in the video. We should note that Lindemann is an accomplished poet in his own right and the son of Werner Lindemann, a GDR-era poet and children's poet with numerous titles to his credit. *Mike Oldfield im Schaukelstuhl. Notizen eines Vaters* by the elder Lindemann renders a lightly veiled account of life together with his son in a Mecklenburg village in the year before the *Wende.* The only evidence I wish to derive from these biographical facts is that Lindemann has always and necessarily operated in a literate and poetic milieu that included knowledge of the *Lied* tradition inaugurated by Herder. In other words, I am going to assume, and believe that my reading bears out, that Lindemann's "Rosenrot" is aware of itself as a complex intervention with the "Heidenröslein" material, in particular with respect to gender. If Herder evoked the fantasy of primitive erotic encounter and Goethe problematized it with gender ambiguity, Rammstein takes the implied masculinity seriously to task.

From the first verse we are aware that this is another version of "Hei-denröslein," but with a difference.[24] Instead of the *Knabe* (boy), we're presented with a desiring *Mädchen* (girl)—a girl sees a little rose. The horizontal expanse of the heath in Herder's and Goethe's versions has been flipped 90 degrees, so that it stretches vertically from the heights to the depths, deep water, and the ground. Complying with *Mädchen's* wish, *Jüngling* (youth) scales the heights to claim the rose. Whereas both Herder and Goethe insist on scopophilic pleasure ("Und blieb stehn, es anzusehen" [and remained standing to see it; Herder] and "Lief er schnell, es nah zu sehn" [went quickly to see it up close; Goethe]), *Jüngling* is indifferent to the view provided by the heights. In an odd conferral of subjectivity and volition, a stone seizes the occasion of contact with the boy's shoe to plunge both of them into the abyss. *Mädchen* remains unharmed.

Lindemann has expanded the three strophes of Herder's and Goethe's versions of "Heidenröslein" to nine such that the narrative sketched in the paragraph above is limited to strophes one, four and seven. To be more precise, the refrain Herder and Goethe share at the end of each of their strophes, "Röslein, Röslein, Röslein rot, / Röslein auf der Heiden," has given way to two independent refrains, one which enunciates a law to counter the law of Goethe's version: *not* "Mußt' es eben leiden," but rather, it's perfectly fine that she gets what she desires. That's the way it always was and will always be—essentially a version of whatever she wants, she gets, expressed as law. The other refrain takes up the repetition of the name and negates a folk expression about the stillness of deep waters.

"Rosenrot" also engages in pronominal play in the manner of Goethe with his equivocation about the *ihr* and *ihm*. (*Mädchen* is technically a neuter noun and would therefore take the neuter pronoun *ihm*, in this case, not the feminine pronoun *ihr*.) The awkward array of pronouns involving *er, es,* and *ihr* in the fourth line of the first strophe lays out the gender positions: he, it, she. What draws our attention through repetition and syntax, however, is the "es." Obviously *es* refers to *Röslein*, but *Röslein* is now distinct from *Mädchen*—it is the flower and not the girl. We notice too that the *es* is crucially repeated in the first refrain, so insistently, in fact, that we might imagine it, that is, *es,* as the equally legitimate subject of the modifications articulated in the verses describing the law of female desire. Following Herder's lead we may surmise that *Röslein* and *Rosenrot*, too, for that matter, signify fantasies of erotic encounter. At the same time, we can associate the *es* with the deep water of the second refrain. In the final analysis, as I am sure you have guessed, *es* names nothing less than *das Es* (the id), the vast unconscious region of Freud's model of the psyche, and thus names an aspect of the corporeal ground from which song proceeds.

The *Sprung und Wurf* of Herder's concept of folk song is certainly present in Lindemann's poem "Rosenrot," but where it really comes into its own is in the music video, co-produced with Gert Hof, to which we now turn. The stream of images and the musical intensity (characteristic for metal) are overwhelming. The video interprets the narrative of the poem by suggesting an alternative narrative that corresponds to the primal scene of Herder's folk song concept and the basic scenario of "Heidenröslein"—*Jüngling* meets *Mädchen*. Six mendicant monks chance upon a small village in a valley—the setting aspires to timelessness and invokes numerous romantic tropes. One of the monks (the lead singer Till Lindemann) is erotically affected by a village girl, played by Romanian model Catalina Lavric, who was fourteen at the time, when she dances and later takes communion. He takes a stroll with her, and, apparently at her bidding, kills her parents. Pleased with the result, she nonetheless turns on him and with an accusing gesture sets a process in motion that ends with his being burned at the stake. In the final scene we see the five remaining monks leaving the village, the site of execution still smoldering in the background. This narrative roughly corresponds to a reversal of the narrative limned in Herder's and Goethe's versions of "Heidenröslein."

However, the narrative is continually intercut with scenes from two other narratives or, perhaps more accurately, two other positions, from which the main narrative as fantasy proceeds.[25] On the one hand, we see shots in which Lindemann lies beneath the girl's bed, or asleep in it, or responds to her as she brushes a rose across his face or presses its thorns into his hands. On the other hand, we see shots where the monks, played by all the band members including Lindemann, ritually and vigorously flagellate themselves in a circle. On my reading these two scenes are the visual counterparts of the two refrains and stand in complementary relation to the fantasy narrative.

From a feminist perspective, the best one can say is that the girl does not get raped. Instead she becomes the instigator of multiple murders and easily falls into the category of femme fatale or vamp. We have not come far or anywhere at all in that respect. However, the video makes it clear that the narrative is a male fantasy—as is the fantasy of "Heidenröslein"—and a self-punitive one at that. In other words, "Rosenrot" may be enacting vengeance against the genre of the *Volkslied* itself as Herder conceived it. We see that the fantasy narrative elaborated in strophes one, four and seven emerges from the figurative position Lindemann assumes under her bed, whence dreamlike sequences of erotic encounter proceed. In one of them, the *Mädchen* wakes him by stroking his face with a rose. She places it into his hands and then presses them together over the thorns. This is definitely his "Weh und Ach." The flagellation scene, by contrast, represents a penitential, not to say self-punitive position vis-à-vis the fantasy. If the position underneath the bed lines up with the id, the self-castigation can readily be assimilated to the position of a severe *Überich* (the superego).

The real accomplishment of Rammstein's song and video, however, seems to me to lie in the extreme realization of Herder's concept of corporeal intensity as the key moment in folk song. The video was shot in a Transylvanian valley in Romania in freezing temperatures — hence the crystalline light quality.[26] What the physiologist Albrecht von Haller would call the "irritability" of bodies was assured. When it came to shooting the self-flagellation scene, the band members stripped to the waist in the bitter cold, grasped whips and proceeded to strike themselves to the rhythm of the frantic instrumental bridge of "Rosenrot." I take this to be an ironic gesture in keeping with Rammstein's generally self-ironic stance. Here the violence often associated with metal is self-critically redirected to the music itself— the scene of self-flagellation stands in for the more typical climaxing scene of musicians flailing at their instruments. In the context of "Heidenröslein" and *Letters on Ossian* that I have tried to develop in this essay, however, there is something more going on. By capturing the essence of Herder's investment in *Volkslied* and its corporeally intense primal scene, Rammstein pays homage to Herder as a father of rock and roll. By putting the song writer and lead singer Till Lindemann to death in an *auto de fé*, on the one hand, and assimilating the instrumental frenzy of the band members to fevered self-flagellation on the other — taking the folk song and its enabling fantasy severely to task, in other words, and its originator, Johann Gottfried Herder, with it — Rammstein stages what we might call, with all due hyperbole and in conclusion, the death of rock and roll. Long live rock and roll.

Notes

1. Stephen Mithen, *The Singing Neanderthals: The Origins of Music, Language, Mind and Body* (Cambridge: Harvard University Press, 2007).

2. For more on Alan Freed, see John A. Jackson, *Big Beat Heat: Alan Freed and the Early Years of Rock & Roll* (New York: Schirmer Books, 1991).

3. "History of Rock," http://www.acesandeighths.com/rock.html, accessed 19/7/2011.

4. The review is in J. G. Herder, *Werke in zehn Bänden*, vol. 2, *Schriften zur Ästhetik und Literatur 1767–1781*, ed. Gunter E. Grimm (Frankfurt/Main: Deutscher Klassiker Verlag, 1993). Klopstock was an eighteenth-century lyric poet whose experiments in prosody opened the way for freer poetic expression in German literature.

5. Erhard Bahr, "Ossian-Rezeption von Michael Denis bis Goethe: Ein Beitrag zur Geschichte des Primitivismus in Deutschland," *Goethe Yearbook* 12 (2004): 1–15. Of course, Rousseau should be credited with the introduction of primitivism in general, while Herder works out the aesthetic dimension. See Eugene E. Reed, "Herder, Primitivism and the Age of Poetry," *The Modern Language Review* 60 (1965): 553–67.

6. J. G. Herder, "Auszug aus einem Briefwechsel über Ossian und die Lieder alter Völker," in *Werke in zehn Bänden*, vol. 2, *Schriften zur Ästhetik und Literatur 1767–1781*,

ed. Gunter E. Grimm (Frankfurt/Main: Deutscher Klassiker Verlag, 1993), 452. Subsequent references to this work will be indicated by page numbers in parentheses.

7. For Wolff's psychology, see Frederick C. Beiser, *Diotima's Children: German Aesthetic Rationalism from Leibnitz to Lessing* (Oxford: Oxford University Press, 2009), 56–60.

8. I discuss this background in detail in a chapter called "Herder: Laocoon in Pain" in *Laocoon's Body and the Aesthetics of Pain* (Detroit: Wayne State University Press, 1992), 90–130.

9. Frederick C. Beiser, *The Fate of Reason: German Philosophy from Kant to Fichte* (Cambridge: Harvard University Press, 1987), 109–129.

10. Johann Gottfried Herder, "Alte Volkslieder," in *Herders Sämmtliche Werke*, vol. 25, ed. Bernhard Suphan (Berlin: Weidemann, 1877–1913), 70.

11. Cf. Ulrich Gaier in Herder, *Werke in zehn Bänden*, vol. 3, 885.

12. Herder, *Werke in zehn Bänden*, vol. 8, 338.

13. Flachsland collected the poems in the hope of eventually publishing them.

14. Brief vom 28. Oktober 1771 (DA 1, Nr. 110, S. 270).

15. Johann Gottfried Herder, *Briefe: Gesamtausgabe 1763–1803*, 14 vols., ed. Karl-Heinz Hahn (Weimar: Böhlau, 1977), vol. 2, 77.

16. For an excellent discussion of the complex intertextual history of the poem, see Thomas Althaus, "Ursprung in später Zeit: Goethes 'Heidenrößlein' und der Volksliedentwurf," *Zeitschrift für deutsche Philologie* (1999): 161–88.

17. Paul van der Aelst, *Blüm und außbund Allerhandt Außerlesener Weltlicher, Züchtiger Lieder und Rheymen* (Deventer, n. p.: 1602).

18. Lorraine Byrne, *Schubert's Goethe Settings* (Burlington, VT: Ashgate, 2003), 211.

19. For a heavy-handed reading of the poem along these lines, see Christine Kuenzel, "Knabe trifft Röslein auf der Heide: Goethes 'Heidenröslein' im Kontext einer Poetik sexueller Gewalt," *Ariadne* 39 (2001).

20. See Moses Mendelssohn, "Rhapsodie oder Zusätze zu den Briefen über die Empfindungen" (1761), in Mendelssohn, *Ästhetische Schriften in Auswahl*, ed. Otto F. Best (Darmstadt: Wissenschaftliche Buchgesellschaft, 1774), 127–165.

21. David Wellbery writes about "Heidenröslein" in *The Specular Moment: Goethe's Early Lyric and the Beginnings of Romanticism* (Stanford: Stanford University Press, 1996), 223–233; here 231.

22. My reading of "Rosenrot" is similar to Martina Lüke's reading of Rammstein as dark romantics in two respects. First, we both (justifiably) posit considerable literary erudition on the part of Til Lindemann. And second, the early Herder can be seen as a forerunner of the dark romantics. See Lüke, "Love as a Battlefield: Reading Rammstein as Dark Romantics," in this volume.

23. See, for example, Valerie Weinstein, "Reading Rammstein, Remembering Riefenstahl: 'Fascist Aesthetics' and German Popular Culture," in *Riefenstahl Screened: An Anthology of New Criticism*, ed. Neil Christian Pages, Mary Rhiel, and Ingeborg Majer-O'Sickey (New York: Continuum, 2008), 130–148.

24. Because copyright laws make citation of songs difficult, I will paraphrase relevant lyrics and trust that readers will obtain a copy of the song's text.

25. Hof calls them "Traumebene." "Making of Rosenrot," http://www.youtube.com/watch?v=fBDnUquFMb4&NR=1 (accessed 19 July 2011).

26. "The Making of 'Rosenrot'" video on YouTube includes details about the sub-zero temperature as the shoot proceeds through the day and into the night.

Works Cited

Aelst, Paul van der. *Blüm und außbund Allerhandt Außerlesener Weltlicher, Züchtiger Lieder und Rheymen*. Deventer, n. p.: 1602.

Althaus, Thomas. "Ursprung in später Zeit: Goethes 'Heidenrößlein' und der Volksliedentwurf." *Zeitschrift für deutsche Philologie* (1999): 161–88.

Bahr, Erhard. "Ossian-Rezeption von Michael Denis bis Goethe: Ein Beitrag zur Geschichte des Primitivismus in Deutschland." *Goethe Yearbook* 12 (2004): 1–15.

Beiser, Frederick C. *Diotima's Children: German Aesthetic Rationalism from Leibnitz to Lessing.* Oxford: Oxford University Press, 2009.

_____. *The Fate of Reason: German Philosophy from Kant to Fichte.* Cambridge: Harvard University Press, 1987.

Byrne, Lorraine. *Schubert's Goethe Settings.* Burlington, VT: Ashgate, 2003.

Herder, Johann Gottfried. *Briefe: Gesamtausgabe 1763–1803.* 14 vols. Ed. Karl-Heinz Hahn. Weimar: Böhlau, 1977.

_____. *Sämmtliche Werke.* Ed. Bernhard Suphan. Berlin: Weidemann, 1877–1913.

_____. *Werke in zehn Bänden.* Ed. Gunter E. Grimm, Frankfurt/Main: Deutscher Klassiker Verlag, 1993.

Jackson, John A. *Big Beat Heat: Alan Freed and the Early Years of Rock & Roll.* New York: Schirmer Books, 1991.

Kuenzel, Christine. "Knabe trifft Röslein auf der Heide: Goethes 'Heidenröslein' im Kontext einer Poetik sexueller Gewalt." *Ariadne* 39 (2001).

Lüke, Martina. "Love as a Battlefield: Reading Rammstein as Dark Romantics." This volume.

Mendelssohn, Moses. "Rhapsodie oder Zusätze zu den Briefen über die Empfindungen" (1761). Mendelssohn, *Ästhetische Schriften in Auswahl.* Ed. Otto F. Best. Darmstadt: Wissenschaftliche Buchgesellschaft, 1774. 127–165.

Mithen, Stephen. *The Singing Neanderthals: The Origins of Music, Language, Mind and Body.* Cambridge: Harvard University Press, 2007.

Richter, Simon. *Laocoon's Body and the Aesthetics of Pain.* Detroit: Wayne State University Press, 1992.

Weinstein, Valerie. "Reading Rammstein, Remembering Riefenstahl: 'Fascist Aesthetics' and German Popular Culture." *Riefenstahl Screened: An Anthology of New Criticism.* Ed. Neil Christian Pages, Mary Rhiel, and Ingeborg Majer-O'Sickey. New York: Continuum, 2008. 130–148.

Wellbery, David. *The Specular Moment: Goethe's Early Lyric and the Beginnings of Romanticism.* Stanford: Stanford University Press, 1996.

10

Love as a Battlefield: Reading Rammstein as Dark Romantics

Martina Lüke

> The human being is this night, this empty nothing, which contains everything in its simplicity.... A bloody head shoots up suddenly, there another white ghastly apparition suddenly emerges, only to disappear again. One catches sight of this night when one looks another human being in the eye — and there gazes upon a night that becomes awful.
> — Georg Friedrich Hegel (1770–1831), "Die Nacht der Welt" (The Night of the World, 1805).[1]

The Berlin band Rammstein is time and again referred to as "Horror Romantics" and the controversial and dark romantic contents of their songs undoubtedly contribute as much to their unparalleled success as their captivating rhythms and melodies. A metal band and Romanticism[2] in general appear, at a first glimpse, as natural opponents. There are however many aspects which Rammstein shares with Romanticism as theorized by Friedrich von Hardenberg/Novalis (1772–1801), Clemens Brentano (1778–1842), Achim von Arnim (1781–1831), August Wilhelm (1767–1845) and Friedrich Schlegel (1772–1829), Johann Gottlieb Fichte (1762–1814), et al. Both suggest (poetic) imagination and feelings as important and consider lyric poetry and music as powerful facilitators for an aesthetic experience.[3] Both explore the borders between reality, dreams and fantasy and prefer an unfinished or fragmentary aesthetic system over closure and symmetry. Thus, even the prominence of irony, wordplay and double meaning as well as the fascination with extremes is similar. I would also like to point out, that the band uses many visuals (which unfortunately, cannot be discussed in depth in this essay) that contain (dark) romantic elements.[4] In addition to Rammstein's lyrics, the Romantic's fascination with antagonistic extremes such as darkness/irrationality/fear and broad daylight/rationality/enjoyment of life, is also reflected in the covers of Rammstein's albums *Sehnsucht* (Longing)[5] *Herzeleid* (Heartache),[6] and *Liebe ist für Alle Da* (Love Is There for Everyone, standard version).[7] The cover of the album *Rosenro*t also presents a ship frozen in an icy sea, which is very much reminiscent of the famous painting *Die gescheiterte Hoffnung/Das Eismeer* (The Wreck of Hope/Sea of Ice, 1823–24) by the German romantic painter *par excellence*, Caspar David Friedrich (1774–1840).[8] The inside of the album furthermore bears an image of King Ludwig II of Bavaria's (1864–1886) castle *Neuschwanstein* (constructed 1869–1892; unfinished), which might possibly be the most famous and kitschy adaptation of a romantic castle. Due to the destructive and mystical character of Rammstein's lyrics, I claim, that the texts of the band can be read in the tradition of Dark Romanticism. Like "Romanticism" the term "Dark Romanticism" is often used in a very expansive context, so that I, before providing an analysis of the lyrics, would prefer to briefly recall major aspects that are relevant for this analysis of Rammstein's lyrics.

Reading Rammstein as Dark Romantics

Dark Romanticism, in this essay, refers to the literary genre that was initiated at the end of the eighteenth century by British Gothic fiction, most specifically by novels such as Edward Young's (1683–1765) *Night Thoughts on Life, Death or Immortality* (1742–1745), Horace (Horatio) Walpole's (1717–1797) *The Castle of Otranto* (1765) and Matthew Gregory Lewis's (1775–1818) *The Monk* (1796), as well as by the shock about the horrors of the French Revolution.[9] In the German context prominent scientific and philosophical publications such as Gotthilf Heinrich Schubert's (1789–1860) *Ansichten von der Nachtseite der Naturwissenschaft* (Views of the Dark Side of Natural Science, 1808) and *Symbolik des Traums* (Symbolism of the Dream, 1814) suggested that rational science cannot present the full range of the phenomenal world, where irrational and rational elements collide.

These ideas had a profound influence on contemporary authors. Carl Friedrich August Grosse's (1768–1847) *Der Genius. Aus den Papieren des Marquis C* von G** (The Genius. From the Papers of Marquis C* from G*, 1790–1795), Friedrich (von) Schiller's (1759–1805) fragment "Der Geisterseher" (The Visionary, 1789), Johann Wolfgang von Goethe's (1749–1832) poem "Die Braut von Korinth" (The Bride of Corinth, 1797) as well as the novels by E.T.A. Hoffmann (1776–1822) can be considered as exemplary works of this literature. Accordingly, many works by Hoffmann, who influenced other writers on dark romantic topics, such as Edgar Allan Poe (1809–1849), Herman

Melville (1819–1891), and Nathaniel Hawthorne (1804–1864), deal with these topics of death, beauty, and desire.[10] Death as a romantic principle of life is also most notably depicted in Novalis's *Hymnen an die Nacht* (Hymns to the Night, 1800).[11] There is, however, no fixed scholarly definition of Dark Romanticism in established reference works on Romanticism.[12] Detlef Kremer, for example, refers briefly to the Gothic tradition and defines the *Schauerroman*[13] as a "more or less trivial novel, in which the *Schauerliche* takes the center place. Insofar as crime is very often a topic, the *Schauerromane* as robber novels establish themselves in the realm of crime novels."[14] This *Schauerliche* is described in Gerhard R. Thompson's standard collection of essays on Gothic Literature, *The Gothic Imagination. Essays in Dark Romanticism,* as the emphasis of "dread — whether physical, psychological, or metaphysical, whether of body, mind, or spirit ... by combining terror with horror and mystery" as the essential element of Gothic romance.[15] Even Mario Praz, in his groundbreaking analysis of Dark Romanticism, *La Carne, e Morte e il Diavolo nella Letteratura Romantica,*[16] provides many examples from British, German, Italian, and French literature and fine arts to illustrate the genre but does not present a precise definition. Praz however summarizes the fascination with destructive and cruel yet sublime and aesthetic elements, as the romantics' interest in the "beauty of a medusa," a beauty which contains at the same time "pain, depravity, and death."[17] These generally associative descriptions of Dark Romanticism are also given in the German context, where the terminus is described as the "irrational tendency of Romanticism towards the uncanny-ghostly, fantastic-absurd and demonic-grotesque as composition of fear, dreams, hallucinations and the dark side of the human, particularly in the *Schauerroman*, ghost stories and in Satanism."[18] From this perspective Gerhard Schulze summarizes: "Thus, Dark Romanticism remains as gloomy as the subjects and topics which it intends to enlighten."[19] An excellent overview of essential Gothic elements in literature and arts can however be found in the first volume of David Punter's standard work *The Literature of Terror. A History of Gothic Fiction from 1765 to the Present Day* and in Linda Bayer-Berenbaum' s chapter "Literary Gothicism."[20] In this essay, these descriptions, which span from a discussion of the term to the analysis of archetypes, imagery, settings, themes, and narratives, provide important thoughts for my analysis of dark romantic elements in the lyrics of Rammstein.

Even though Dark Romanticism originates in the eighteenth century, there is a continuation of these elements, particularly in Neo-Romanticism and the Décadence. Furthermore, as a result of the traumatic historical experiences of the twentieth and twenty-first century (e.g. the two world wars) as well as a result of a general fascination with irrationality/fantasy as reaction to modern scientific rationalism/technology,[21] there is an ongoing contemporary interest in works that deal with a transcendental evil and an imaginary expression of terror and fear.[22] In 1922, Friedrich Wilhelm Murnau (1888–1931), for example, with *Nosferatu* established the genre of Dracula movies which were soon followed by other cinematic horror genres. Music groups and solo artists such as The Cure, Wolfsheim, Schiller, Nick Cave, Joachim Witt, and Peter Heppner as well as writings by authors such as Anne Rice, Stephen King and H. P. Lovecraft also reflect this contemporary fascination with morbid and at the same time aesthetically pleasing artistic representations of uncanny topics. Elisabeth Bronfen, in her groundbreaking work *Over Her Dead Body*, describes this ongoing interest, which she furthermore links to the conjunction of beautiful women and death, as a cultural expression to "experience death by proxy."[23] Allegorical articulations of current unconscious desires and fear thus find their articulation in aesthetic representations. And indeed, as stated in an interview with *New York Rock*, Rammstein seem also to be captivated by, and to play with this (dark) mysticism.[24]

Based on these thoughts and definitions I claim that lyrics by Rammstein can be interpreted in the tradition of Dark Romanticism. Since many of Rammstein's songs are based on classic works of German literature and music,[25] this, as discussed in this essay, includes dark romantic compositions. Due to the expansive nature of the topic, I focus my analysis on one central motif of Dark Romanticism: the representation of love and desire, which is also an essential topic of the majority of Rammstein's songs and is furthermore reflected in the choice of title for their albums *Sehnsucht*, *Herzeleid* and *Liebe ist für Alle Da*. Accordingly, Mario Praz most notably states in the opening line that "the main purpose of this book is to analyze literature of Romanticism (the decadence of the *fin de siècle* is simply another one of its forms of appearance) in regards to a particularly distinctive aspect: its erotic perception."[26] And he resumes "In my opinion in no other literary period the sexus has been as obviously been the center of literature."[27] Praz's observation is reflected in Novalis' comment in his *Fragmente und Studien* (Fragments and Studies, 1799/1800) on the inseparable association of "lust, religion, and cruelty."[28] Similarly Rammstein employs themes of love and sexuality in a dark romantic approach. Based on Rammstein's provoking exploitation of concepts of love and gender,[29] in this essay "love" is used in a very broad and even contradictory sense. It spans from romantic love to extreme sadism and perversion and often culminates in the total destruction of the object of desire. The acceptance and the pursuit of ambiguities are essential for Romanticism. Different from Classicism in the pursuit of balance and proportion, Romanticism focuses on the partial and extreme, and none other than Johann Wolfgang von Goethe, in number 863 of his *Maximen und Reflexionen* (Maxims and Reflections, published posthumously in 1833) thus famously emphasized the dichotomy of a "healthy" Classicism and a "sick" Romanticism.[30] Most importantly for this analysis, the band's fascination with the intensity of human extremes such as mental illness, insanity and violence,[31] as essential topics in German Dark Romanticism,[32] results in lyrics that repeatedly resist traditional interpretation.

Due to the often demonstratively cryptic and bewildering nature of Rammstein's lyrics I would like to point out that the interpretations given in this essay thus represent but shall not be limited to my specific readings alone. The song "Weißes Fleisch" (White Flesh) from the album *Herzeleid*, for example, simply addresses someone on the schoolyard as love interest and gives no identification of age or gender[33] and thus could refer to a child (implying pedophilia — if the unknown narrator would be an adult) or to another adult such as a teacher (implying hetero- or homosexuality). Rammstein leaves the interpretation to the listener or reader of these texts, which has the result that in "Weißes Fleisch," for example, the idea of the degradation and of the punishment of the desired person becomes even more evident and challenging. Due to the fact that all six members of the band are male and the texts are composed by them, in this analysis, if not stated otherwise, the unknown narrator in the lyrics is assumed to be male. Since this essay focuses on an analysis of Rammstein's texts, I would like to give into consideration that many of Rammstein's videos furthermore play with the provoking nature of the graphic display of love and sexuality.[34]

In the tradition of Dark Romanticism, in songs such as "Du riechst so gut" (You Smell So Good), "Heirate mich," "Sehnsucht," "Spiel mit mir" (Play with Me), "Morgenstern," "Stein um Stein" (Stone By Stone), "Ohne Dich" (Without You), "Stirb nicht vor mir (Don't Die Before I Do)," "Feuer und Wasser" (Fire and Water), "Wiener Blut" (Vienna Blood), the darkness, mostly of the night, explicitly functions as an uncanny and sinister place or even as a hiding ground for evil forces. It is, moreover, a general counterpoint to innocence and the naïve as well as to a lighthearted lust for life, represented in bright colors.[35] This contrast is particularly obvious in "Du riechst so gut" and "Weißes Fleisch," where, in a reverse play on standard perceptions of good and evil, brightness is portrayed as a dangerous counterpart of malevolence and as an uncanny force that confuses the (evil) senses. In "Weißes Fleisch" a brightness is specifically mentioned as the reason for strong destructive feelings of the unknown narrator since he[36] hopes to be enlightened and thereby redeemed by the victim.[37]

The distinction between darkness and lightness is also a central topic of

"Wilder Wein" (Wild Vine). In this song, however, Rammstein provides erotic dimensions: darkness is linked to the night, a strong (sexual) longing for the lover as well as a woman's lap, while the brightness refers to the daylight and peaceful relaxation after the intercourse, which the lyrics even present as a kind of healing process from desire. Similarly, "Frühling in Paris" presents a seductress as a figure of light who helps a young man to discover his body. Since this happens also in daylight, brightness, according to these lyrics, also metaphorically refers to a physical and psychological enlightenment.

In many songs by Rammstein, the intensity of feelings is reflected in the choice of colors within the lyrics. In "Weißes Fleisch," for example, white, which is commonly associated with innocence and purity, is the color of the skin of the love interest and (potential)[38] victim. This is contrasted with both black, the color of the blood of the perpetrator, which furthermore intensifies connotations of something unnatural and evil, and red, the welts inflicted by him. Red as the color of blood and therefore as a symbol for life or for the destruction of life is also mentioned in songs such as "Du riechst so gut," "Tier," "Frühling in Paris," "Roter Sand," "Liese," and "Führe mich."[39] In the song "Moskau" (Moscow), red spots on the face of an aged prostitute might indicate a sexual disease.[40]

Violent activities driven by feelings of love or lust have, in many songs, religious undertones: the battle of the sexes in "Wollt ihr das Bett in Flammen sehen" (Do You Want to See the Bed in Flames) is accompanied by the vision of crosses on the bed, "Bestrafe Mich" (Punish Me) uses the structure and the context of a prayer and "Wiener Blut" refers to Psalm 23. In "Wilder Wein" the sexual union between man and woman also has religious undertones.[41] Fire in the sense of a (religious) catharsis is also mentioned in "Feuer und Wasser"[42] and finally the longing for (physical) redemption[43] is the center of violence in "Weißes Fleisch." Rammstein's songs on love often contain highly sensual lyrics, since they deal with smell (e.g. "Du riechst so gut"), taste ("Küss mich Fellfrosch," Kiss Me Furfrog), skin (e.g. "Weißes Fleisch," "Wollt ihr das Bett in Flammen sehen," "Heirate mich," "Sehnsucht," "Liese," "Frühling in Paris") or wet skin/wet lips (e.g. "Du riechst so gut," "Küss mich Fellfrosch," "Wilder Wein"). Rammstein's lyrical settings, such as an abandoned church and the cemetery at night ("Heirate mich") as well as the infinite sea and fog ("Nebel," Fog; "Seemann," Seaman; "Laichzeit," Spawning Time),[44] can be interpreted as a dark continuation of the Romantic's fascination with the Middle Ages, the unspeakable/indefinable,[45] and their often quoted "taste for ruins."[46] After making these general observations about dark romantic elements in Rammstein, in the following part of this essay, I will provide a more close reading of the band's lyrics from this perspective.

Sublime Darkness

"Frühling in Paris," "Sehnsucht,"[47] "Ohne Dich," "Nebel," "Herzeleid" and "Wilder Wein" are some of the few songs by Rammstein that deal with romance and desire in a less or even non violent way. In poetic words, which in their erotic dimension are reminiscent of Paul Zech's (1881–1846) illustrious poem collection *Die lasterhaften Lieder und Balladen des François Villon* (The Vicious Songs and Ballads of François Villon, 1931,[48] itself based on Villons (c. 1431-c. 1463) works,[49] "Wilder Wein" describes the feelings of a man who is in the process of sexually uniting with his lover. Her lap is compared to a castle,[50] covered by wild vine referred to in the song's title,[51] which will open the gates just for the king (himself). While he feels a kind of peace after their union, he is also already aware that his longing for her will not stop and that he will wait for her again. The wild vine thus can also be interpreted as a metaphor for a never completely satisfied longing for the woman and her body: as the plant grows fast and covers everything, his desire appears as a threat which has already taken control over his actions, and in the future, might even become more obsessive.[52] In Rammstein's portrayal, an almost spiritually beautiful union of lovers thus contains simultaneously sad and tragic elements.

As depicted in literary works such as Franz Wedekind's (1864–1918) play *Frühlingserwachen* (Spring Awakening, 1891), "Frühling in Paris," in a literal turn on the city's common image as the city of love,[53] deals with the seduction of a young man by a sexually experienced woman. The woman, who might be a prostitute,[54] as the active partner in the relationship, initiates the young man's sexual discovery of his and her body. She furthermore introduces him to sexual variations.[55] According to the lyrics, the intensity of this understanding, which is compared to bleeding,[56] is still a delightful memory of the grown-up man.[57]

"Sehnsucht" also describes in poetic words a sexual discovery but includes the pain of losing the intimate closeness between lovers. A finger follows the course of a teardrop on the naked skin and thereby leads to the sensual discovery of the female body. This exploration is compared to a familiar landscape; here, the landscape and the animals of Africa, which reaches from desert sands to the snow on a mountain like Mount Kilimanjaro. The vision of a hot tropical night continues with the song's mention of a stinging insect. As excruciating as desire and longing in the dreams of lonely nights, the insect torments a helpless sleeper. In the end, the finger, which is exploring the body, seems to lose the course, ends up, as it is described, on the Mexican peninsula and finally sinks in a, not specified, sea. The shed teardrops that are referred to in the beginning and the center of the song seem thus to end in an ocean of tears and the song closes with the remark that longing is something cruel.

"Ohne Dich" similarly poetically portrays a seemingly unbearable loneliness caused by the absence and most likely the loss of a loved one.[58] According to the song, the beauty of nature and life as a whole seems to have come to a total end.[59] The impression of darkness and a lifeless scenery is given by birds that have stopped singing and by dark and empty woods. The reference to ditches which are without life reminds one of gravesides. Most notably, in the beginning of the song, a "Tuch" (cloth) which is thrown over a country is mentioned, which is very much reminiscent of the expression "ein Leichentuch über das Land legen" (literally "to cover land with a shroud") which refers to death and despair as a result of war, a plague or famine.[60] The repeated reference to being without the other person further intensifies the perception of a tragic love story and it expresses a complete desperation of the surviving lover. He also claims to be lonely with and without the other and that life has lost all meaning again bringing death and a graveside into mind.

Given these skeptical perspectives on love, the lyrics of "Herzeleid," the title song from the first album, demands an end of all form of togetherness. According to the logic of this song, even when many years are spent (happily) together, in the end separation is unavoidable. "Herzeleid," however, does not indicate whether this is a result of people becoming emotionally estranged from each other over the course of time or if the song might even hint at the fact that at one point in time death must finally separate all lovers, which would be a central topic of Dark Romanticism.

"Nebel" also deals with this topic by portraying an elderly couple standing at the seaside. While the woman is fully aware that she must die soon, she hesitates to let her husband (or lover) know about this. Overall, their relationship is depicted as very tender and sweet; she, for example, kisses him gently on his forehead and holds his hand with a shivering[61] hand. The woman then rests her head in the old man's lap in order to die[62] and asks him for a last kiss. This brings him to tears and makes him think about the last time he kissed her. Sadly, he cannot remember anymore, how long ago this was.[63] Thus, even this non-violent song focuses on heartrending and tragic aspects of love.

The loss of love is also the central topic in "Wo bist Du" (Where Are You) and "Roter Sand." "Roter Sand" tells the story of a young man who dies in a duel.[64] Challenged by the former partner[65] of his loved one, his bullet has missed the target and the other man could draw faster and hit the unknown narrator. The song describes his final moments lying in red sand and his regret at not being able to keep his promise to his loved one, to come back to her.

He furthermore dies with the knowledge that she will now belong to the other man forever.[66] Lyrical and mystical elements add a romantic transformation of the man's otherwise rational narration of the events. He for example refers to two white doves which refresh themselves on his blood[67] or when he compares his failed shot to a kiss of powder. With "Roter Sand" Rammstein exploits the motive of lovers that are separated or threatened by a duel which, in the German context, brings particularly classic works such as Theodor Fontane's (1819–1898) novels *Cécile* (1886) and *Effi Briest* (1895) and Arthur Schnitzler's (1862–1931) play *Liebelei* (Flirtation/The Reckoning, 1895) to mind. Tragic love, violence, and death are thus once again Rammstein's central and inseparable topics.

As in "Nebel," "Ohne Dich," and "Sehnsucht," the lyrics of "Wo bist Du" provide insight into the suffering after the experience of being left by the other: everything seems to be without meaning and the world, overall, appears to have come to a standstill. In "Wo bist Du," however, this feeling of being left behind[68] has obviously caused massive aggression towards the former partner[69] since the song concludes with the description of a knife taken into the bed. While it is not clear whether it is his own bed or the bed of the lover, overall, in my opinion, the lyrics indicate the wish by the unknown narrator to take (fatal?) revenge. Reading the lyrics in this bitter way, the title of the song, which is repeated six times, particularly at the end of the song, by this means, expresses a rising obsession with finding the other one. Thus, the song as a whole can also be read as a massive threat by a maniac to kill the object of desire that has left him.[70] Hence romantic feelings such as longing and admiration are once again transformed into hostile thoughts of destruction.

The search for a lover is also the topic in "Stirb nicht vor mir." From a female perspective, this song articulates a severe longing which is based on the belief that at some point in the future someone will love her. Meanwhile, the woman experiences nightly visits by a mysterious stranger, who attempts to suffocate her in her bed until the unknown narrator passes out. These nightly visits might be a play by Rammstein with nightly visits by a demon lover as well as the incubus-succubus myth, as presented in works such as Samuel Taylor Coleridge's (1772–1834) poems "Kubla Khan" (1797) and "Christabel" (1797/1800), the previously mentioned poem "Die Braut von Korinth" by Goethe and, most notably in the tradition of Dark Romanticism, in Bram Stoker's (1847–1912) novel *Dracula* (1897).[71] In the reading of a classical *Schauerroman*, the portrayal of the strange nightly visits would then remind one of the motif of the innocent maiden who finally falls victim to evil forces.[72] The dark figure can also be read as a metaphor for an overwhelming desperation at night.[73] In either case, the song "Stirb nicht vor mir" also provides a linkage of violence, death, and sexuality in a mystical setting.

Even less drastic songs such as "Morgenstern," "Nebel" or "Liese" present love on the borderline of something sublime and at the same time uncanny and sad. In "Morgenstern" a man declares his strong attraction to his seemingly horrible looking beloved one. In a fairy tale-like narrative a girl or woman is hiding in the dark[74] in order not to scare the broad daylight. She pleads with the Morningstar, which she is able to see in the twilight, to make her beautiful. Her lover is also heartbroken about her appearance although it is not clear whether he is sorrowful because she suffers, since he loves her and, on several occasions, refers to her as his dearest, or if he is simply disgusted by her appearance, which would contradict any feelings of love for her.[75] In either case he also pleads to the Morningstar to bring loveliness to the ugliness of her face. The last verse provides a kind of conclusion: the star seems to shine on the beloved one[76] and her lover suddenly feels warmth in his breast and considers her to be extremely beautiful. Either her outside appearance really changed, which would support the fairy tale-like plot, or his perception of her has changed in that she appears to him as gorgeous.[77] Despite this openness of the song, love is overall presented as something simultaneously wonderful and painful.

As in "Frühling in Paris" a sexual awakening is the topic in "Liese." In a bucolic setting, the (virtuous) goose girl Liese herds the geese on a green meadow when she is seduced and most likely impregnated[78] by a young man named Jacob. Rammstein once again provides dark romantic undertones to their approach to that classic topic of the seduction of an innocent maiden. In an eerie choice of words, the lyrics describe him approaching her with a scythe-like instrument, which, after their sexual encounter, is described as being bloody. Reading the scythe as a metaphor for an erect penis, the blood clearly is an allusion to a defloration which would be in accordance with the overall topic of seduction.[79] A similar ambiguity of naïve romance, desire and brutality involving a goose girl is at least also depicted in the popular fairy tale "Die Gänsehirtin" (The Goose Girl) collected in the 1813 edition by Jacob and Wilhelm Grimm.[80] Taking an even darker approach to the lyrics of Liese, one could also argue that the scythe implies sexual violence, particularly since, in the last two lines of the song, the young man seems to threaten her if she does not give in to his sexual advances. In this reading of the text, the description of a scythe that will be rusty from blood, if she will not be his sexual partner willingly, might then refer to his plan to take her by force and rape her. On the contrary, however, the mention of rust, which often has the color of dried blood, and is commonly associated with slow decay or ruin, might also imply neglect. Thus Jacob's notion that he will become rusty could refer to the plain fact that he will remain sexually dissatisfied if she does not want him anymore. In either case, the song "Liese" combines exceedingly violent elements with longing and sexuality.

Wicked attraction as portrayed in "Morgenstern" is also a topic in the song "Moskau" which compares the Russian capital to a prematurely aged but irresistible prostitute. In an ironic play with the common perception of female beauty as something young and healthy, this woman is portrayed as being old, sick[81] and fat; she furthermore had rotten teeth that had to be replaced with gold crowns, her breasts had to be replaced by new ones and even her skin has to be covered with powder. Her lover, however, is sexually completely aroused by her appearance and suffers if he cannot be with her.[82] Her dominance is so strong that he is more than willing to pay any price to be with her. Thus, in contrast with most other songs by Rammstein, in "Moskau" the female is in total control of her sexual power and controls the man. Rammstein's portrayal of wicked attraction and female sexuality as an inter-action of vulnerability and empowerment, danger and pleasure is also a topic in novels that encompass romantic and gothic elements such as Samuel Richardson's (1689–1761) *Clarissa, or The History of a Young Lady* (1748), Mary Shelley's (1797–1851) *Frankenstein, or The Modern Prometheus* (1818), Charlotte Brontë's (1816–1855) *Jane Eyre* (1847), and Hoffmann's *Sandmann* and *Die Elixiere des Teufels*.

This lack of control as a result of love and sexual desire is in the central topic of *"Amour Amour."* Love is compared to a wild animal which is untamable and, in a reversion of the traditional notion of an animal and the human hunter, hunts down the human and captures him in a trap.[83] Moments of hot desire and lust thus finally result in broken hearts and pain. Thus, the desperation about the uncanny feeling of being at someone's mercy, in the last line of the song, results in the dramatic demand by the narrator to be given poison in order to end this otherwise unstoppable cycle.

Similarly, relentless aspects of a woman's lust are described in "Küss mich Fellfrosch," where a blind[84] female longs to be orally satisfied by men. Due to the lack of punctuation, the title refers either to the woman, who longs to be kissed by a man, who is then the Fellfrosch, the hairy frog, ("Küss mich, Fellfrosch") or, which might be more plausible, in an allusion of the Grimm fairy tale,[85] she herself is the Fellfrosch[86] that longs to be kissed and then is released in a sexual way (Küss-mich-Fellfrosch). In either way, according to the lyrics the woman and her men share violence: she, out of lust, bites into the tongue of the men in order to force them to stay with her and satisfy her sexually. Caused by her bitterness[87] men seem to reject her most of the time and even appear to turn violent. The woman is said to be hit vigorously by one tongue[88] and to start to bleed terribly from the nose. The final repetition of her longing to be kissed despite this bitterness might thus also allude to her having such a strong sexual drive that she would even willingly accept pain as a kind of price for carnal pleasure.

Homosexual love linked with aspects of violence is the topic of "Mann gegen Mann." The title stems from an expression used in combat and thereby accentuates right from the beginning the intersection of violence and sexuality. According to the play with words and fixed German idioms in the lyrics of this song, the narrator feels like a traitor to either his family or his gender (which might refer to heterosexual men), and feels threatened by it. A constant defense against the surrounding world and social perceptions thus appears to be one central motif of "Mann gegen Mann."

The motif of a *femme fatale,* in the form of an idealized woman, in Dark Romanticism is often associated with demonic powers that lead to the moral and physical destruction of men.[89] This inter-connection is used by Rammstein for the song "Rosenrot,"[90] a reversed version of Goethe's depiction of painful desire in the classic poem "Das Heidenröslein" (Little Rose on the Heath, 1770),[91] one of the most popular German poems. In Rammstein's adaption a maiden indirectly lures an innocent young man onto the road to ruin.[92] She demands that he brings her a flower which is on the top of a mountain. He suffers during his attempt to ascend the mountain and in the end falls to death.[93]

As provocatively as the controversial songs "Mein Teil" (My Part)[94] and "Eifersucht" (Jealousy) [95] deal with cannibalism,[96] "Heirate mich" has necrophilia as a central topic.[97] As portrayed in "Heirate mich," a man has lost all senses after the death of his lover. Over a year he spends the nights on the cemetery and sleeps on her grave in order to be close to her, when he finally decides to dig her up and fulfill the marriage. He tries to hold her but she literally falls into pieces. In the end, he kills a rooster, which reminds him of her and their time together.[98] The animal announces the beginning of a new day and thereby indicates that everything passes, which the man cannot or will not accept.[99] In this context, the title and his remark that she escapes him a second time, when he cannot hold her decayed body, might imply that both have been previously promised to each other in marriage. This topic of lovers who were tragically separated by the fate or death is a theme in Dark Romantic novels such as E.T.A. Hoffmann's "Der Sandmann." It is also conceivable that the fictional woman in the song died because she did not want to marry him, maybe because she was afraid of the uncontrollable nature of his feeling for her,[100] which would be a topic in dark romantic novels such as *Clarissa* or Emily Brontë's (1818–1848) *Wuthering Heights* (1847). In either way the depiction of death and the attraction to a dead woman in "Heirate mich" brings Edgar Allan Poe's famous comment in his "Poetry of Composition" (1846) into mind: "The death, then, of a beautiful woman is unquestionably the most poetic topic."[101] Thus, his dark romantic works such as "The Oval Portrait" (1842), "Ligeia" (1838), and "Leonore" (1843) deal with similar topics of love, desire, decay and death of a (beautiful) woman as Rammstein's "Heirate mich."

Dark Romantic Destruction

The first song on Rammstein's debut album sets the tone for many other songs by the band that deal more directly and explicitly with love and violence. "Wollt ihr das Bett in Flammen sehen" literally equates sex and combat as well as, on a larger scale, love and warfare. Describing a bed in flames and the complete downfall of a lover, Rammstein provides a modern version of the motif of essential gender wars. Impressions of violence are furthermore enhanced by mentioning weapons, people who have been killed, and the shedding of blood. This fascination with "pain and torture, with sadism and masochism described in bloody gruesome detail" is one essential aspect of literature in the Gothic and dark romantic literature.[102]

Violence and obliteration are also central topics of the song "Zerstören," which describes the unknown narrator's inevitable urge for complete destruction. In the final lines, a formerly blind woman leaves a man, as soon as she is able to see the dimensions of his demolishing path.[103] The title thus refers both to his general behavior but also to his incapability to love and be loved. Following the setting of songs such as "Wo bist Du," a similarly disturbing conclusion remains in "Zerstören:" since the narrator takes good care of his own possessions, but has to destroy everything that is not his, might he not also feel the urge to harm or kill his former lover, now that she is not his anymore?[104] In this case, Rammstein plays once again with fatal lust and desire.

While "Moskau" was already given as an example for the reduction of sexuality to a financial act, songs like "Bück dich" (Bend Over), "Rein Raus" (In Out), "Te quiero, Puta" (I Love You, Whore) and "Pussy," the sexual partner is literally transformed into a sexual object and thereby overall resembles a violent conquest.[105] In "Rein Raus" the choice of words accordingly implies a contrast of superiority and (penetrative) activity on the one hand (the rider, the key) and inferiority and passivity on the other hand (the horse, the lock) so that, once again, Rammstein plays with the concept of submission and dominance in a sexual perspective. Even more drastically, the refrain of "Bück Dich," commands the partner to bend down and to look away which cruelly designates the body and not the face[106] as the important factor for any desire. The dehumanization[107] of the other in "Bück dich" is also indicated through the portrayal of the sexual partner walking on a leash on all fours.[108] Similarly, "Bestrafe Mich" can be read as a masochistic desire. Rammstein's provocative play with sado-masochism is expressed most bluntly in the song "Ich tu Dir weh." The lyrics describe a variety of SM practices and emphasize the willingness of the masochist to endure and the sadist to inflict pain and disfigurement. As in Gothic and dark romantic literature, sexual variations and perversions, as presented in Rammstein's lyrics, are "important for their intensity born of repression and for the expansion they provide in the range of sexual practice. Homosexuality, sodomy, incest, rape, or group copulations are inserted into ordinary experience in order to destroy the boundary between the normal and the perverse, infecting the normal with the germ of the perverse so that all behavior becomes susceptible to possible perversion."[109]

A burning desire that has violent undertones and is also concentrated solely on a woman's genitals is the essential topic of "Feuer und Wasser." According to the lyrics, a man experiences a strong sexual attraction to a woman who swims the breaststroke and, by watching her, is tormented by his intense feelings. His secret fantasy centers on the view of her genital area and the idea of grabbing her with wet hands while she is swimming by. As signified by the fire and water in the title, a reference to his burning desire and her cool unawareness of this, he is fully aware that they will never be together. Aside from the fantasy of holding her and the uncanny observation of the swimmer, the violent connotations in the song are not directed to a potential victim but to a voyeur himself, who feels like standing in flames and to be burning alive.

In a similar way "Liebe ist für Alle Da," as a provocatively disturbing interpretation of the common expression in the song's title,[110] portrays the sexual fantasies of a man. As does the man in "Feuer and Wasser" the narrator in this song appears to be a voyeur, who in "Liebe ist für Alle Da" gets sexually aroused as soon as he sees beautiful women sunbathing. The unknown narrator seems to be portrayed as a kind of outcast, who has to sneak around and pretend friendliness towards others.[111] Whenever he closes his eyes and uses his imagination, he is able to take control over and to lock up those women he desires. Rammstein thereby exposes once again a world of fantasy and latent violence. Unlike the narrator in "Feuer und Wasser," however, the narrator of "Liebe ist für Alle Da" does not seem to suffer as a result of his unfulfilled desire but seems to be happy about the alleged power he experiences in his fantasy. In a more sinister reading, the song can be also interpreted as the description of preliminary feelings of a sexual perpetrator, whose violent fantasies finally become reality. In the beginning of the song, he is portrayed as creeping around unaware women and is claiming that he has to be friendly in order to achieve his lust. The last stanza then describes a woman having the eyes closed (she might be blindfolded or dead), who cannot defend herself anymore nor can the others hear her crying and come to her aid. It is at this stage of total (sexual) control and violence that the unknown narrator expresses his content that he could finally find love.

The willing and total destruction of a love interest, in the horrible version of an immurement, is portrayed in "Stein um Stein."[112] Using a cynical approach, the narrator informs the victim that he will build a home and promises the victim to be a part of the whole process. The fact that the house is built on the tears of the unknown narrator and that he or she threatens to ram nails into the body of the immured one, might be a reference to former acquaintance with each other, maybe, as in other songs by Rammstein, an act of revenge due to a rejection of an expression of love?[113] The use of the old-fashioned substantive "Leib" for body, rather than the more neutral substantive "Körper," also indicates, at least to some extent, intimacy or something desirable. According to this interpretation, the immurement would also ensure in a macabre way both to "never lose the other" and to "never move out" (something similar to what the narrator repeatedly promises within the lyrics).[114]

A fatal immurement, based on similar reasons, is also the central topic in "Klavier." A man, the narrator, loves the piano playing[115] of a woman or girl[116] so much, that he does not want to let her go. He constantly asks her to play for him alone and stops his breath whenever he is listening to her playing. She even promises to never leave him, which could be a real (or forced) statement by her or, given his obsessive nature, it could also be that this potential promise only exists in his mind.[117] In either case he feels that she has broken the promise and therefore betrayed him, so that he, full of fury and rage, has locked her in. Now in a completely reversed situation, she is forced to listen to him, until she does not breathe anymore. After a long while, people begin to ask for the woman or girl and finally discover her,[118] locked to the piano which is already covered by dust. The uncanny effect, as in "Stein um Stein," lies in the fact that this planned disappearance of a (formerly) loved one refers "not only to the absent thing but also to an endless dialectic of absence as presence,"[119] as Elisabeth Bronfen writes in her analysis of Edgar Allan Poe's metapoetic story "The Oval Portrait." The horrible discovery in "Klavier" leads to violent outbursts by those who found her[120] as well as by parents,[121] while the man himself declares that he has a deadly illness and that nobody would believe him, thereby implying that his illness caused him to commit the atrocities.[122] Rammstein's narratives thus deal once more with the dualisms of love and hate, death and life as well as creation and destruction.

Incest is also a topic in many songs by Rammstein. The shocking Fritzl case provided the background for Rammstein's song "Wiener Blut," which deals with the perspective of the sexual perpetrator who held his daughter captive for over twenty-four years and during this imprisonment physically assaulted and sexually abused and raped her. In "Wiener Blut," in his sickness he promises his daughter a castle as well as a paradise in the basement. He even praises her life in darkness, desperation and loneliness as a safe way to discover life together. The uncanny effect of the song is furthermore based on the contrast with the 1873 "Wiener Blut" Waltz (op. 354) by Johann Strauss the Son (1825–1899). Similarly, "Tier" (Animal) describes the animal-like stage of a man who has gone beyond all cultural and moral boundaries that separate animals from human beings and who decides to sexually abuse his young and beautiful daughter.[123] Rhetorical questions about his actions in the refrain point out his complete lack of feelings for this child and his cruel selfishness. Unusually for Rammstein's songs, "Tier" also emphasizes the suffering of the victim of this sexual violence. The grown-up daughter is described as a broken human being who is no longer able to differentiate between men and animals herself. Her father, as the lyrics state, has given her a childhood without a soul. Furthermore, the description of the woman writing a letter to herself— the father's blood is the ink —[124] also points to her broken personality.

Incest between brother and sister is a topic in the song "Spiel mit mir."[125] The child play of "Father-Mother-Child"[126] is turned into a perverse sexual imitation of the parents, when a younger brother[127] is forced to use his hands to sexually stimulate the sibling[128] at night. Brutality, incest and sodomy are also topics in the deeply disturbing song "Laichzeit." The song portrays a man or boy having intercourse with his mother and sister as well as a dog. Sexual connotations and the man's obsession with sexuality are reflected in the constant repetition of the title (which can be translated as "spawning time") and a fish, which could be references to his ejaculation and his genitalia. In the end, the man is completely left alone, which might indicate that he was abandoned by his family or that he is now held in isolation, e.g. in a mental asylum.

Accordingly, "Hallelujah" and "Pussy," which were undoubtedly inspired by recent discussions on cases of sexual abuse in religious institutions and of sex tourism, present sexual fantasies with an emphasis on violence and criminality and thereby challenge existing cultural perceptions. This brings Rammstein furthermore into the realm of the libertine writings by de Sade,[129] who also described the dark side of human nature. "Hallelujah" deals with pedophilia committed by a priest and "Pussy" describes the sexual ravenousness of men travelling abroad in order to buy sexual satisfaction. In addition to the already repulsive content, the eerie effect of "Hallelujah" is based on the appalling double meaning of seemingly harmless events, e.g. the statement that he loves the innocent boys of the church choir. Alternatively, the song "Pussy" uses and derides a series of German words which, through commercials, public culture or historical events, etc., have become more or less popular internationally (e.g. *Fahrvergnügen, Schnaps, Sauerkraut, Blitzkrieg*). Here, in tradition of the Romantic's fascination with ambiguity and irony, the disturbing result of "Pussy" is based on a mixture of ridiculousness and shocking directness.

Conclusion

The representation of the inter-relations of love and violence in Rammstein's songs can be analyzed in the literary tradition of Dark Romanticism. As in works by prominent authors of the genre such as E.T.A. Hoffmann, Edgar Allan Poe, Emily Brontë, or Samuel Taylor Coleridge but also as with references to cruel topics from classic German fairy tales, the songs by the Berlin group focus on uncanny and destructive elements of relationships. In this tradition, love is often closely linked to cruel thoughts and actions as well as to questions of death and mourning. The classic duality of *eros* and *thanatos* in Rammstein's lyrics ranges from sensitive erotic poetry with violent undertones to latent aggressive and even fatal sexual fantasies. Sensuality, desire, and longing in those lyrics are thus inter-connected with brutality and destruction. In accordance with the Dark Romantic's fascination with these binary conceptualizations as well as with uncanny extremes, fear, and the dark side of humans, Rammstein's lyrics deal with deeply confrontational topics such as sado-masochism, incest, necrophilia, and the immurement of a loved one. The band's choice of intensive colors and an uncanny setting intensify strong emotions in the tradition of the Gothic novel or the *Schauerroman*. And finally, Rammstein's masterly use of wordplay and fragmentary perceptions in their lyrics provide general challenging and even distressing feelings within the audience. Based on Dark Romantic perceptions of a constant presence of exigent thematic and emotional juxtapositions, Rammstein's lyrics reflect the post-modern skepticism of an absolute truth and precise classifications. Thus, from the setting to the provoking and ambiguous nature of the lyrics, in tradition of the so called "dark side" of Romanticism, Rammstein provide insight into modern approaches towards the Hegelian "human night" and an overall perception of "love as a battlefield."

Notes

1. Georg Friedrich Hegel, *Jenaer Systementwürfe III* (Hamburg: Felix Meiner, 1987), 172. Emphasis by Hegel. I would like to thank the editors of this collection as well as the anonymous reviewers of this essay for their very insightful comments and suggestions on the initial version. I am also most grateful for Kevin Kearney's, Peter Dorn's and Reinhild Lüke's excellent comments and help with the first draft of and their assistance in obtaining important secondary literature for this essay. Finally, I would like to thank my students in my lectures and classes on "Contemporary Germany," "German Culture and Civilization," and "German History since 1815" at the University of Connecticut for excellent discussions concerning Rammstein and (Dark) Romanticism.

2. Since Rammstein is a German band, "Romanticism," if not indicated otherwise, refers to German Romanticism.

3. Johann Gottfried Herder's (1744–1803) and Ludwig Tieck's (1773–1853) plea for the renewal of folk literature led to the collections of folk-songs, anecdotal tales, fairy-tales and sagas by von Arnim, Brentano, Jacob (1785–1863) and Wilhelm Grimm (1786–1859), and Johann Peter Hebel (1760–1826). Many texts by Rammstein also deal with elements of folk literature, e.g. "Rosenrot" (Rose-Red), "Mein Herz brennt" (My Heart Burns), or are based on the *Volksliedstrophe* (folk-song-stanza), e.g. "Alter Mann" (Old Man), "Links 234" (Left 234), "Morgenstern" (Morning Star), "Roter Sand" (Red Sand). The ballad, which can combine lyric and dramatic elements, was as attractive for the Romantics as it is now for Rammstein, e.g., "Rosenrot," "Heirate Mich" (Marry Me), "Dalai Lama," "Roter Sand," "Liese."

4. Video clips such as "Rosenrot," for example, resemble visualizations of narratives in the meaning of a tragic love drama.

5. *Sehnsucht* contrasts the brightness and color intensity of a tropical beach on the inside of the cover with a dark background and pictures of the dead-like faces of the individual band members on the outside of the cover. The contrast with the idyll of the seaside is furthermore enhanced by the band being portrayed as being decapitated and wearing torture-like instruments on their faces.

6. The cover of the album *Herzeleid*, contrasts a fragile flower with the muscular nude torsos of the band. The inside of the album shows dark flowers/visually alienated flowers in contrast to the overexposed faces of the band members, who thereby have the appearance of aethereal and uncanny figures. The *Blaue Blume* (blue flower), as depicted in Novalis' novel fragment *Heinrich von Ofterdingen* (published posthumously in 1802), which stands for love, desire, and a (metaphysical) longing, is generally considered to be *the* symbol of German Romanticism (see also note 47).

7. The cover of *Liebe ist für Alle Da* depicts the different stages of a cannibalistic meal and sadistic brutality committed by members of the band. Pale nude bodies of women stand out against a dark background and the group dressed mostly in black or grey colors (see also notes 9 and 107). The draping of the shrouds and the stark contrast between background and female nudity as portrayed in the booklet is also reminiscent of the famous painting *Der Anatom* (The Anatomist, 1869) by Gabriel Cornelius Ritter von Max (1840–1915), who was similarly fascinated by dark romantic and mystical traditions.

8. On references to Caspar David Friedrich see also note 44.

9. On this aspect of the impact of the French Revolution and contemporary social-political life and cultural production see most famously Donatien Alphonse François Marquis de Sade's (1740–1814) critique in *Idee sur les Romans* (Reflections on the Novel, 1800), Edmund Burke's (1729–1797) *Reflections on the Revolution in France* (1790) and Adam Müller's (1779–1829) *Die Elemente der Staatskunst* (1803). The cover of *Liebe ist für Alle Da*, with the contrast of bright flesh and surrounding darkness and the placement of rugs, furthermore resembles paintings reminiscent of this time such as Jacques-Louis David's (1748–1825) *Marat Assassiné* (The Death of Marat, 1793, see also note 7).

10. Hoffmann's novel *Der Sandmann* (The Sandman, 1817), for example, which was most famously interpreted by Sigmund Freud in his essay "Das Unheimliche" (The Uncanny, 1919), centers around the traumatized protagonist Nathanael who is torn between feelings of estrangement and love towards the attractive Clara but is also fascinated by the beautiful Olimpia, who is later revealed to be a lifeless automata, which leaves Nathanael in a state of insanity and finally leads to his suicide. Similarly, Hoffmann's *Die Elixiere des Teufels* (The Devil's Elixirs, 1815/1816) deals with the destructive (sexual) desires of Franz/monk Medardus and deals with uncanny topics such as the *Doppelgänger*, deadly nightly encounters, rape, incest, and poisoning.

11. Published in the *Athenäum*, the most influential literary journal of German Romanticism, in 1800, the six parts deal with Novalis' deep grief at the death of his fiancée Sophie von Kühn (1782–1797) and the arousal of strong religious feelings.

12. See for example publications such as Ricarda Huch, *Die Blütezeit. Ausbreitung und Verfall* (Tübingen: Reiner Wunderlich Verlag Hermann Leins, 1951); Gerhard Hoffmeister, *Deutsche und europäische Romantik* (Stuttgart: J.B. Metzler, 1990); Detlef Kremer, *Romantik* (Stuttgart: J.B. Metzler, 2003); Helmut Schanze, *Romantik-Handbuch* (Tübingen: Alfred Kröner, 2003); and Gerhard Schulz, *Romantik. Geschichte und Begriff* (München: Verlag C.H. Beck, 1996).

13. In this context this word literally means "shudder novel" but the adjective "schauerlich" also implies something "uncanny" and "eerie" therefore my decision to leave this term in the original form. Similarly "das Schauerliche" refers to something "eerie" and (subconsciously) "nightmarish."

14. Kremer, *Romantik*, 143.

15. G. R. Thompson, ed., *The Gothic Imagination: Essays in Dark Romanticism* (Pullman: Washington State University Press, 1974).

16. All citations are from the German edition *Liebe, Tod und Teufel. Die schwarze Romantik* (München: Deutscher Taschenbuchverlag, 1988). Remarkably, even that this *oeuvre* is considered a basic text for the study of Dark Romanticism and, in this German edition has Dark Romanticism as a subtitle, Praz himself never uses this term in his editions from 1930 and 1948, see also André Vieregge, *Nachtseiten. Die Literatur der Schwarzen Romantik* (Frankfurt am Main: Peter Lang, 2008), 15.

17. Praz, *Liebe, Tod und Teufel*, 65, 104–112 and 119 (see also the previous comment).

18. von Wilpert, Gero, *Sachwörterbuch der Literatur* (Stuttgart: Alfred Kröner, 2001), 743. On this debate see also Jürgen Klein, *Schwarze Romantik. Studien zur englischen Literatur im europäischen Kontext* (Frankfurt am Main: Peter Lang, 2005), 10–15, and Vieregge, *Nachtseiten*, 12–16 and 301–304.

19. Schulz, *Romantik*, 125.

20. See David Punter, *The Literature of Terror. A History of Gothic Fiction from 1765 to the Present Day. Volume I. The Gothic Tradition* (London: Longman, 1996); Linda Bayer-Berenbaum, *The Gothic Imagination. Expansion in Gothic Literature and Art* (Rutherford: Fairleigh Dickinson University Press; London: Associated University Press, 1982), 19–46. See also Vieregge, *Nachtseiten*, 14; 29–39, 87–88; 271–276. For a variety of theoretical approaches as well as contemporary examples for Gothicism, see Mark M. Hennelly Jr., "Framing the Gothic," *From Pillar to Post-Structuralism. College Literature* 28:3 (Fall 2001): 68–87.

21. The pictures in the booklet for the album *Rosenrot* furthermore reflect this uncanny perception of technology since they portray the band in scary facial make-up surrounded by an industrial-like, sterile setting (potentially a reference to a fictional interior of the submarine *Rosenrot* on the cover).

22. See, for example, Bayer-Berenbaum, *The Gothic Imagination*, 11–16; Hennelly; David Punter, *The Literature of Terror: A History of Gothic Fictions from 1765 to the Present Day. Vol. II. The Modern Gothic* (London: Longman, 1996); Vieregge, *Nachtseiten*, 11–12, 25–

85, and 303–304. A similar contemporary fascination with this genre is also expressed in Diane Long Hoeverler and Tamar Heller, *Approaches to Teaching Gothic Fiction. The British and American Traditions* (New York: Modern Language Association of America, 2003).

23. Elisabeth Bronfen, *Over Her Dead Body. Death, Femininity and the Aesthetic* (New York: Routledge, 1992), x.

24. NY Rock, "Interview with Rammstein (November 1998)," http://www.nyrock.com/interviews/rammstein_int.htm.

25. On this topic see Martina Lüke, "Modern Classics. Reflections on Rammstein in the German Class." *Die Unterrichtspraxis/Teaching German* 41:1 (Spring 2008): 15–32.

26. Praz, *Liebe, Tod und Teufel*, 16.

27. Ibid.

28. Novalis, *Werke, Tagebücher und Briefe Friedrich von Hardenbergs. Drei Bände. Band II*, ed. Hans Joachim Mähl and Richard Samuel (Darmstadt: Wissenschaftliche Buchgesellschaft, 1999), 765.

29. Rammstein's songs deal for example with hermaphroditism ("Zwitter," Hermaphrodite) or conjoined twins ("Führe mich," Lead Me). Due to the ambiguous nature of Rammstein's lyrics, *Zwitter* might possibly also be interpreted as the representation of a total unity between lovers. The reference to semen and a "Zwailaib" (which could be translated as "twinbody") in my opinion more convincingly implies the description of conjoined twins, thus my decision not to include this song into my analysis.

30. Johann Wolfgang von Goethe, *Werke. Hamburger Ausgabe in vierzehn Bänden. Band XII. Kunst und Literatur*, ed. Erich Trunz (München: Deutscher Taschenbuch Verlag, 1998), 487.

31. The song "Zerstören" (Destroy), for example, clearly describes the urge to destroy everything that does not belong to the lyrical self.

32. Vieregge, *Nachtseiten*, 249.

33. Even the use of the word "Kleid" might either specifically refer to a woman's/a girl's skirt or might also be a colloquial or old fashioned version of "Kleidung" (clothes in general) which gives no identification at all.

34. The provoking, and therefore highly discussed video of *Pussy*, for example, shows the members of the band in different stages and variations of intercourse.

35. See for example "Morgenstern," "Frühling in Paris" (Springtime in Paris) or "Mann gegen Mann" (Man Against Man). The song "Sonne" (Sun), however, illustrates particularly the painful and destructive capacities of intense sunlight.

36. Since the unknown narrator refers to himself as a "Gigolo" the perpetrator appears to be male.

37. In order to intensify the portrayal of the horrible events of the Ramstein air base air show disaster on August 28, 1988, in the song "Rammstein" bright sunshine, reminiscent of a beautiful day, is mentioned in the refrain.

38. It is not clear whether the brutal act is a fantasy by the narrator or if indeed a perpetrator describes his actions.

39. The most popular tale in a dark romantic context that plays with the perceptions of colors might be Edgar Allan Poe's "The Masque of the Red Death" (1842).

40. She is described as having a red spot in her face which might, according to her profession, imply a sexual disease such as syphilis. Sickness is therefore once more linked to desire and sexual attraction (see note 81).

41. Overcome by emotion and lust the man in the song sends a prayer to God to be at his side. The lyrical descriptions of the sexual relief furthermore contain resemblance to feelings as associated with spiritual redemption.

42. In "Du riechst so gut," however, the burning of a bridge symbolizes the end of the last feelings of sanity.

43. The perpetrator longs for purification and redemption through the innocence of

the victim, which implies a human sacrifice and therefore a religious act, even given that the narrator states that he has no god in his heaven.

44. In "Nebel" the elderly couple standing at the sea and possibly surrounded by fog or nightfall could be seen as the description of actual weather, which brings again portrays by romantic painter Caspar David Friedrich into mind (see the comment on Rammstein's album covers in the beginning of this essay and note 8). I am speaking of paintings such as *Kreuz am Meer, Der Mönch am Meer* (The Monk by the Sea, 1808–1810) or *Wanderer über dem Nebelmeer* (Wanderer above the Sea of Fog, 1818). One could also interpret "Nebel" as a reference to their age, possible dementia, the fear of losing each other, or death (see note 63).

45. See also the comments on the fascination of the Romantics for the fragmentary.

46. Charles Rosen, *The Romantic Generation* (Cambridge: Harvard University Press, 1995), 4. See also Bayer-Berenbaum, *The Gothic Imagination*, 24–28.

47. *Sehnsucht* as an unspecified (metaphysical) longing can be read as one of *the* essential motive of German Romanticism (see note 6).

48. Particularly the poem "Ich bin so wild nach deinem Erdbeermund /Eine verliebte Ballade für ein Mädchen namens Yssebeau" (I Am So Crazy for Your Strawberry Mouth/A Ballad Written in Love for a Girl Named Yssebeau) from this collection, deals with the comparison of a woman's genitals and a strawberry. After the notorious readings by actor Klaus Kinski (1926–1991) this association became part of the pop culture. The poem is also the title of the actor's 1975 autobiography with which he reinforced his image as (sexually) driven and as a ferocious and obsessive character.

49. Similar to Rammstein's provocative choice of contents, the French poet often chose to write against and to revise the existing medieval courtly ideal.

50. The choice of the word "Schloss" (castle) to describe the woman's pubic area encloses, in addition to the general romantic fascination with medieval times and ruins, as described above, wordplay with "Schoß" (lap).

51. This is most likely a reference to her pubic hair.

52. One line of the song even states that one cannot find a defense against these overpowering feelings.

53. Édith Piaf's (1915–1963) famous song "Je ne regrette rien" (I Regret Nothing, 1960) is the basis for the refrain and intensifies overall impressions of (romantic) love in the French capital. In Rammstein's turn of *omnia vincit amor*, the sexual attraction between the lovers/the prostitute and her client tears down all language barriers as well as all age and potential social differences.

54. The lyrics state that the woman's lips where sold a couple of times, which might either refer to her mouth or her genitals.

55. The three stanzas refer to different body parts: her mouth and her lap are mentioned and she is furthermore described as bending down really low.

56. See the comments on color in the beginning of this essay.

57. In a very sinister interpretation of the song, one could also read the encounter as the murder of the prostitute by the man, since in the refrain blood is mentioned as soon as he left her skin. Read in a less sinister way however, this blood could also be understood as a metaphor for the loss of his virginity or his sexual innocence. In a more romantic reading, the blood might refer to "Herzblut" (blood of the heart) as a result of the "Herzeleid" (heartache) as a result of the (unavoidable) final separation of her. *Herzeleid* is at least both the name of Rammstein's 1995 album and song.

58. The claim that he or she saw her last time in the fir trees could point at a (secret) meeting place of the lovers or, in a twisted way, to the spot where he or she might even have buried the other one (which could imply a tragic death as well as a *Lustmord*, see also note 83).

59. The description of a general difficulty to breath also can be read as something life threatening.

60. In the German context this is most often associated with the Thirty Years' War (1618–1648) which was the most devastating war on German soil. The most famous literary text using this expression is Heinrich Heine's (1797–1856) political poem "Die schlesischen Weber" (The Silesian Weavers, 1844), which, based on the uprising of weavers in Peterswaldau in the same year, contains the repeated curse "Deutschland, wir weben Dein Leichentuch" ("Germany, we weave your shrout").

61. It is not fully obvious if the lyrics refer here to her age, her anxiety, her sickness or a combination of all three.

62. Her lips are hereafter described as being pale and weak.

63. Here, the text implies either a result of the shock about her (near) death or maybe even dementia (see note 44).

64. The whistling in the beginning of the song thus reminiscent on the whistling in classic Western soundtracks such as Sergio Leone's *The Good, the Bad and the Ugly* (1966) or *Once Upon a Time in the West* (1968).

65. It is not stated whether it is a husband, a fiancé or a lover. The concept that he dies in a duel, however, might hint at a time of strict moral codices so that the opponent in this song might be a husband or fiancé.

66. This might even more indicate that the challenger is the husband (see the previous note).

67. The doves might be a reference to something spiritual or maybe a metaphor for love or the loss of love.

68. According to the lyrics the other one does not love him (or her) any more.

69. Since the narrator states that all other women seem to have lost any attractiveness, it seems obvious that the object of desire is a woman.

70. Focusing on this disturbing reaction towards a split and the knowledge about Rammstein's fascination with extremes and (mental) sickness, one feels also tempted to question his/her motive at all. Maybe, the relationship and/or the potential's victim's love existed just in fantasy?

71. A still excellent overview of this topic in regards to British literature is provided by Nicolas K. Kiessling, "Demonic Dread. The Incubus Figure in British Literature," in *The Gothic Imagination: Essays in Dark Romanticism,* ed. G.R. Thompson, 22–41 (Pullman: Washington State University Press, 1974).

72. On this topic in a dark romantic setting see Praz, *Liebe, Tod und Teufel,* 97–111.

73. This reminds also on the famous images by Johann Heinrich Füssli (1741–1825), most notably the versions of his painting *Der Nachtmahr/Der Alp* (Nightmare, around 1781).

74. In this case of word-play of "grauen," Rammstein either indicates that it gets dark outside as soon as she shows her face or that the face is so ugly that one experiences plain horror when one catches sight of her. Darkness is once more portrayed as something evil and uncanny.

75. See also note 82. Rammstein's teasing transformation of classical love concepts becomes also obvious in the song "Du hast" (You Have). The lyrics play with the perception of "Du hast" (in German this can be either understood as "you have" (Du hast) or "you hate"(Du hasst), see Lüke, pp. 20–21) and with the German wedding vow, which is repeated throughout the song. While the unknown narrator in the beginning of the song says he won't answer the question of marriage at all, later in the song the answer to the directly posed question of marriage is twice an aggressively yelled "no." In the song, the pronunciation of separation ("scheiden" in German) can furthermore be read as a provocative word play with "Scheide" (German for vagina).

76. Rammstein's lyrics again leave a final interpretation with the recipient of the song, since it is just indicated literally in the text that the Morningstar *tries* to shine.

77. The sudden warmth in his heart at least indicates new and tender feelings.

78. The fifth verse describes him, after he made love to Liese for a whole day, singing to a child which might be a metaphor for him giving life.

79. "Liese" describes the young woman as getting infected by Jacob which might imply that she embraced her sexuality. During their first sexual encounter, which they continue all day and which is another indication for her enjoyment and consensual intercourse, he is explicitly allowed to lick her. Her hair is described as getting erected which furthermore might imply a sexual arousal. In this context the choice of describing the taste of her genitals as a pear puts Rammstein once more in the tradition of poems by Zech (see also note 48).

80. "Die Gänsehirtin" deals with a princess, who, while traveling to her future husband, gets deprived of the magic protection of her mother and is forced to change places with her cruel and ambitious maid. She lives as a goose maid at the new destination and, with her beauty, arouses the desire of her fellow goose herd Konrad, who tries to steal locks from her golden hair, and the prince. The cruel undertones of the fairy tale are culminated in the slaughter of the Princess' beloved talking horse Falada by the maid, who fears discovery. Bribed by the princess, the butcher does not bury the horse's head but hangs it on the wall of the gate, where it is greeted every morning by the princess.

81. As described in the beginning of this section, the red mark in her face might imply a sexual disease (see note 40).

82. This topic brings other stories by Dark Romantics with a dark approach towards the concept of "love is in the eye of the beholder" into mind, most notably, the previously mentioned story *Der Sandmann* by E.T.A. Hoffmann. One feels also reminded on Edgar Allan Poe's comic turn on (dark) romantic elements in the short story "The Spectacles" (1844), where a young man develops a passion for his grandmother.

83. In this context of "manhunt" I would like to point out that Rammstein's song "Waidmanns Heil" (Good Hunting, the title stems from the traditional greeting of hunters in Germany), which describes the excitement of the hunt for female deer, on a more sinister level, can be read as an hunt for and the potential murder of a woman. The clever use of German hunting terminology in the lyrics, transforms the text thus in a provocative portrayal of sexual desire and brutality which bears resemblance to a *Lustmord* (see also note 58).

84. This might be, as in "Zerstören," a metaphor (see note 103).

85. In the popular fairy tale "Froschkönig oder der eiserne Heinrich" (The Frog King or Iron Henry, collected 1812) by Jacob and Wilhelm Grimm, the frog demands to sleep during the night in the princess' chamber. The spell of the ugly frog is broken, as soon as the princess throws him in disgust against a wall. Rammstein clearly plays with this interconnection of violence, redemption, and sexuality.

86. In "Küss mich Fellfrosch," the woman is also described to lay in the grass and to puff herself up. The mentioning of "fur" in addition to "frog" in the title–in opposition to the hairless skin of an amphibian–might refer to her (pubic) hair and therefore emphasize her human status.

87. Rammstein's play with double meaning does not indicate clearly whether this is meant figuratively or literally.

88. In the meaning of *pars pro toto*, this might be her perspective and refer to a man.

89. Vieregge, *Nachtseiten*, 114.

90. The title stems from the German fairy tale "Schneeweißchen und Rosenrot" (Snow-White and Rose-Red), collected by Jacob and Wilhelm Grimm in their 1813 edition of fairy tales. The tale is about two virtuous sisters that rescue a bear (an enchanted prince) and, on several occasions, rescue an ungrateful dwarf. The dwarf is later killed by the bear, which breaks the curse of the prince. In a kind of reversion or play with the content of this classic tale, according to Rammstein's lyrics a seemingly ungrateful woman leads a young man into his death.

91. "Das Heidenröslein" tells the story of a young man who falls deeply in love with a beautiful rose (a maiden) and, against her rejection, picks her up by force while she stings him with her thorn. Franz Schubert's (1797–1828) musical adoption (D 257) from 1815 is the most popular of many musical versions. In reading the breaking of a resistant flower by the boy in Goethe's poem as a symbol of a more or less forced defloration, even the original version would allow to note a connection of sexual undertones and violence. On the other hand, in a less violent reading, one could assume that the young women, touched by the young man's desire, fell in love for the first time and thereby experienced, similar to the man, a painful desire or a painful loss of a childlike innocence.

92. This topic is furthermore explicitly portrayed in songs by Rammstein such as "Frühling in Paris" and "Liese."

93. This topic of a man who tries to win the love of or prove his love for a woman is also a topic in classic German poems such as "Der Taucher" (The Diver) and "Der Handschuh" (The Clove), both written in 1797 by Friedrich Schiller. In "Der Taucher" the lover tragically dies during this attempt.

94. The song is based on the gruesome 2001 Armin Meiwes cannibalism case and is also an ominous parody of the German expression "Du bist was Du isst" (literally: "you are what you eat"), which originally implies either that one should live healthy or that a successful life is reflected in the choice of (expensive or good) food.

95. "Eifersucht" also deals with cannibalism and portrays it as a consequence of jealous feelings over another one's possessions. The song is thereby a sinister satirical transformation of the German expression "Eifersucht kocht" (literally: "jealousy cooks") by Rammstein, which compares the intense emotions caused by jealousy with different stages of heating or someone or something in heat. Accordingly, the song links a rising jealousy with rising forms of cannibalism and summarizes these by naming the expression in the last line. The group's play and fascination with madness is also expressed in a psychotic laughter at the end of "Eifersucht."

96. Cannibalism with strong sexual undertones is also the topic of the cover of Rammstein's *Liebe ist für Alle Da* (see also notes 7 and 9).

97. The Dark Romantic's fascination with gravesides is also expressed in "Der Vampir" (The Vampire, 1828) by E.T.A. Hoffmann, which describes nightly visits on a cemetery by vampires that dig up corpses for food (see also Vieregge, *Nachtseiten*, 159–160). On necromancy in literary texts and visuals in a dark romantic tradition see also Bronfen, *Over her dead Body*, 291–323 and Carol Christ, "Painting the Dead: Portraiture and Necrophilia," in *Victorian Art and Poetry. Death and Representation,* ed. Sarah Webster Goodwin and Elisabeth Bronfen (Baltimore: Johns Hopkins University Press), 133–151.

98. In the text, he previously referred to the red animal as a symbol for her heart.

99. This could also be an indicator for an unusually violent and obsessive temper of the man.

100. See the previous comment.

101. Edgar Allan Poe, "The Poetry of Composition," in *Essays and Reviews*, ed. G. R. Thompsen. 13–25 (New York: Library of America, 1984), 19.

102. Bayer-Berenbaum, *The Gothic Imagination*, 29–30 (see also 31 and 36, 40–42).

103. Her "blindness" might therefore be a metaphor (see note 84).

104. At least, as described in this essay, this is the central topic in "Klavier" (Piano) and might be also a topic in "Stein um Stein." Furthermore, he considers it a supreme task to pull the head of a doll, which might be a foreshadowing of violence against or the murder of a woman.

105. The lyrics of "Pussy" and "Te quiero Puta" reduce women to the use of their genitals. "Pussy" overall deals with sex tourism and plainly names the quick satisfaction of sexual desire as the reason to travel abroad. In "Te quiero, Puta" "the fruit" of a woman stands in the center of a man's desire, which is once again reminiscent of the poetry by

François Villon/Paul Zech. The narrator's declaration of love for the woman, as stated in the title, can thus be read as a cynical exclamation or simply as another emphasizing of the potential intercourse. Within the lyrics the focus on the mechanical aspect in this song is furthermore implied by the counting to three. On similar aspects of desire and mechanization in fantastic literature as a result of the new consumer society in the nineteenth century, see Jutta Fortin, "Brides of the Fantastic: Gautier's *Le pied de momie* and Hoffmann's *Der Sandmann*," in *Comparative Literature Studies* 41:2 (2004): 257–275.

106. This can be interpreted as *pars pro toto* for the person as a whole.

107. Rammstein's description of a loss and dissolution of identity as well as feeling of a robot like existence can thus be read in the tradition of other prominent *Krautrock* albums such as Kraftwerk's *Radio-Activity* (1975) and *Man-Machine* (1978). On this topic see John T. Littlejohn, "Kraftwerk: Language, Lucre, and Loss of Identity," *Popular Music and Society* 32:5 (December 2009): 635–653.

108. In "Bück Dich" the band is also once more playing with expectations, since, in contradiction to physical law, the tears of the dominated one run upwards.

109. Bayer-Berenbaum, *The Gothic Imagination*, 40. See also Praz, *Liebe, Tod und Teufel*, 112–113 and 119.

110. The meaning of the expression "Liebe ist für Alle Da" is that everybody, at one point in his or her life, will find love. In a sarcastic play with this expression in the song's title, indeed, according to the lyrics, everybody seems to be able to find love, even if it is in a (weird) fantasy or the result of a most violent control of the *objet du désir*.

111. He states in the text that the beautiful bodies he sees in the sunlight are not for him.

112. One could also read this song as a political statement, e.g. as a reference to the (Berlin) Wall and the atrocities committed against those who wanted to leave the GDR. On the thematic prominence of *Ostalgie* (nostalgia for aspects of life in East Germany) in the works of Rammstein, however, see John T. Littlejohn and Michael T. Putnam, "Rammstein and Ostalgie: Longing for Yesteryear," *Popular Music and Society* 33:1 (February 2010): 35–44. The lyrics in "Stein um Stein" also mention a home with garden which might rather indicate the idea of a family house. In another reading the song could be also interpreted figuratively as the attempt to entrap the other one emotionally. Based on the dark romantic tradition by Rammstein, this essay, however, prefers the more sinister, literal approach.

113. See, for example, the comments on the lyrics of the songs "Klavier" und "Zerstören" in this essay.

114. This is also a topic in famous tales by Edgar Allan Poe, e.g. "The Cask of Amontillado" (1846) or "The Fall of the House of Usher" (1839).

115. The piano playing might just be a metaphor for her being as a whole or her sexuality. In the latter case, is could be then implied that the woman was, in reality or his fantasy, unfaithful and therefore was murdered by the man.

116. This person could be his girlfriend, his wife or even his daughter.

117. See similar interpretations in the "Heirate mich" analysis.

118. The text also refers to a horrible smell which might be a reference to a rotten body, which might be one reason, why people got suspicious.

119. Bronfen, p. 117.

120. This is maybe a reference to the police who started searching for her. One is also reminded of similar uncanny discoveries as represented in Poe's tales "The Black Cat" or "The Tell-Tale Heart" (both 1843).

121. It is not clear whether these are his or her parents.

122. In the full texts he complains that nobody believes him "here," which could be an indication that he holds his monologue from a police station during interrogation, a prison, or even a mental asylum.

123. The choice of words in the description of the young girl and the action of the man bear reference to the ancient language of a fairy tale. Incest, for example, is a topic in the fairy tale "Allerleirauh" (All-Kind-of-Fur/Thousandfurs, collected 1812) by Jacob and Wilhelm Grimm, in which a young princess, who resembles in her beauty her dead mother, is desired by her widowed father. She flees the royal court in order to live an animal like life in the forest of a neighboring country.

124. See the comments on the use of intense colors at the beginning of this essay.

125. The lyrics are also based on the popular German child song "Brüderlein, komm tanz' mit mir" (Little Brother, Come and Dance with Me) and thereby exaggerate the overall impressions of the perversion of an innocent childhood. In 1986 the song "Geschwisterliebe" by the popular Berlin punk rock band *Die Ärzte* had stirred a huge controversy in Germany by dealing with the same topic.

126. This might be translatable as "playing house."

127. In "Spiel mit mir," the choice of diminutive forms for the brother highlights the young age of the boy. This is also intensified through the statement that his (little) hands hurt from the sexual act.

128. It is not clear whether this refers to a boy or a girl.

129. See note 9. De Sade is undoubtedly influenced by Gothic literature or the *Schauerroman* and employs gothic topics. Since his novels lack mythical elements he is not considered a Dark Romanticist. Similarly, Rammstein's "Hallelujah" and "Pussy" deal with extreme situations without being dark romantic. They are however included in this analysis since they present the culmination of a provocative and perverted approach toward the romantic topics of love and desire.

Works Cited

Bayer-Berenbaum, Linda. *The Gothic Imagination. Expansion in Gothic Literature and Art.* Rutherford, NJ: Fairleigh Dickinson University Press; London: Associated University Press, 1982.

Bronfen, Elisabeth. *Over Her Dead Body. Death, Femininity and the Aesthetic.* New York: Routledge, 1992.

Christ, Carol. "Painting the Dead: Portraiture and Necrophilia." *Victorian Art and Poetry, Death and Representation.* Ed. Sarah Webster Goodwin and Elisabeth Bronfen. 133–151. Baltimore: Johns Hopkins University Press, 1993.

Fortin, Jutta. "Brides of the Fantastic: Gautier's *Le Pied de Momie* and Hoffmann's *Der Sandmann.*" *Comparative Literature Studies* 41, no. 2 (2004): 257–275.

Goethe, Johann Wolfgang von. *Werke. Hamburger Ausgabe in vierzehn Bänden. Band XII. Kunst und Literatur*, ed. Erich Trunz. München: Deutscher Taschenbuch Verlag, 1998.

Hegel, Georg Friedrich. *Jenaer Systementwürfe III.* Hamburg: Felix Meiner, 1987.

Hennelly, Jr., Mark M. "Framing the Gothic." *From Pillar to Post-Structuralism. College Literature* 28, no. 3 (Fall 2001): 68–87.

Huch, Ricarda. *Die Blütezeit: Ausbreitung und Verfall.* Tübingen: Reiner Wunderlich Verlag Hermann Leins, 1951.

Hoffmeister, Gerhard. *Deutsche und europäische Romantik.* Stuttgart: J.B. Metzler, 1990.

Kiessling, Nicolas K. "Demonic Dread. The Incubus Figure in British Literature." *The Gothic Imagination: Essays in Dark Romanticism.* Ed. G.R. Thompson. Pullman: Washington State University Press, 1974. 22–41.

Klein, Jürgen. *Schwarze Romantik. Studien zur englischen Literatur im europäischen Kontext.* Frankfurt am Main: Peter Lang, 2005.

Kremer, Detlef. *Romantik.* Stuttgart: J.B. Metzler, 2003.

Littlejohn, John T. "Kraftwerk: Language, Lucre, and Loss of Identity." *Popular Music and Society* 32, no. 5 (December 2009): 635–653.

_____, and Michael T. Putnam. "Rammstein and Ostalgie: Longing for Yesteryear." *Popular Music and Society* 33, no. 1 (February 2010): 35–44.

Long Hoeverler, Diane and Tamar Heller. *Approaches to Teaching Gothic Fiction: The British and American Traditions.* New York: Modern Language Association of America, 2003.

Lüke, Martina. "Modern Classics: Reflections on Rammstein in the German Class." *Die Unterrichtspraxis/Teaching German* 41, no. 1 (Spring 2008): 15–32.

Novalis. *Werke, Tagebücher und Briefe Friedrich von Hardenbergs. Drei Bände. Zweiter Band,* ed. Hans Joachim Mähl and Richard Samuel. Darmstadt: Wissenschaftliche Buchgesellschaft, 1999.

NY Rock. "Interview with Rammstein (November 1998)." Accessed October 05, 2012. http://www.nyrock.com/interviews/rammstein_int.htm.

Poe, Edgar Allan. "The Poetry of Composition." *Edgar Allan Poe. Essays and Reviews,* ed. G. R. Thompson. 13–25. New York: Library of America. 1984.

Praz, Mario. *Liebe, Tod und Teufel. Die schwarze Romantik.* München: Deutscher Taschenbuchverlag, 1988

Punter, David. *The Literature of Terror: A History of Gothic Fiction from 1765 to the Present Day. Volume I. The Gothic Tradition. Volume II. The Modern Gothic.* London: Longman, 1996.

Rosen, Charles. *The Romantic Generation.* Cambridge: Harvard University Press, 1995.

Schanze, Helmut. *Romantik-Handbuch.* Tübingen: Alfred Kröner, 2003.

Schulz, Gerhard. *Romantik. Geschichte und Begriff.* München: Verlag C.H. Beck, 1996.

Thompson, G. R., ed. *The Gothic Imagination: Essays in Dark Romanticism.* Pullman: Washington State University Press, 1974.

Vieregge, André. *Nachtseiten. Die Literatur der Schwarzen Romantik.* Frankfurt am Main: Peter Lang, 2008.

von Wilpert, Gero. *Sachwörterbuch der Literatur.* Stuttgart: Alfred Kröner, 2001.

Discography

Rammstein. *Herzeleid.* Universal, 1995.

_____. *Liebe ist für Alle Da,* extended version. Universal, 2009.

_____. *Liebe ist für Alle Da,* extended version. Universal, 2009.

_____. *Mutter.* Universal, 2001.

_____. *Reise, Reise.* Universal, 2004.

_____. *Rosenrot.* Universal, 2005.

_____. *Sehnsucht.* Universal, 1997.

11

Liebe ist für Alle Da: A Visual Analysis of Rammstein's 2009 Album Artwork

Robert G. H. Burns

The German rock band Rammstein has often been identified within the industrial metal and *Neue Deutsche Härte* categories, although closer inspection of their visual, sonic and lyrical aesthetics reveals a collage of performance styles that are woven around their German nationality. They create a stylistic bricolage that borrows from different periods of German text, German (and wider European and American) imagery, and Berlin cabaret–influenced vocal performance. In this respect, consideration of their album cover artwork reveals several themes that relate to their song texts. This essay firstly provides an overview of Rammstein's cover art prior to 2009 before discussing the influences of the artwork on the cover of their album *Liebe ist für Alle Da* (Love Is There for All) (2009). Any discussion of the themes portrayed on this cover cannot be divorced from the themes of violence, sadism, incest and human cannibalism that are part of the texts of several songs on this album, as well as songs on several of those albums that preceded it. This album, however, also features allusions to nineteenth century gothic, a well–documented influence in most heavy metal music, in its album cover art (and, as usual with Rammstein compositions, in its song texts).

In my 2008 *Popular Music* journal article examining Rammstein's use of German symbolism, which includes constructivist and mechanical kinetic imagery, Romantic literature and early twentieth century cabaret performance styles, I discussed ways in which the band successfully takes signification patterns from earlier periods of German history as a means of providing an individual identity in a medium saturated by the formulaic nature of modern rock music.[1] The use of monumental imagery, period clothing, German

Romantic texts and guttural chants, which include nasal *gestic* speaking, all combine to make up what I regard as the Rammstein "formula." This formula has been apparent on all of Rammstein's recordings since *Sehnsucht* (1998) and in their stage performances, such as those in the DVDs *Live aus Berlin* (1999) and *Völkerball* (2006).[2]

Prior to this study, my research into Rammstein's aesthetics in performance had not extended to the band's use of album cover artwork, and it is also worth noting that the band's texts follow the darkly humorous and gothic themes that are used in their cover artwork and stage performances. For this reason, I will refer to lyrics, (in English rather than in the sung German) as well as artwork during this essay.[3] While I will mainly focus on the band's album recording, *Liebe ist für Alle Da*, it is useful to firstly discuss earlier covers in order to contextualize the developments and changes in the most recent ones. There is a consistent thematic lineage between all Rammstein cover artwork that is "on point" and linked to song texts, the combination of which is designed to shock.[4] Unfortunately, due to copyright issues, I have not received permission to reproduce Rammstein cover art at the time of publication.[5]

The cover of the first Rammstein album, *Herzeleid* (Heartache) (1995), is a photograph of the band superimposed over an enlarged photograph of a blooming flower (with the overt sexual connotations that this combination of images implies). The six members of the band appear naked above the waist, and those in the front row of the photograph display sculpted, oiled, muscular physiques that accentuate the band members' masculinity similar to the monumental sculptures of the perfect Aryan form, as discussed by Peter Adam.[6] The cover of *Herzeleid* attracted criticism from the band's record company in the United States prior to its later release in 1996 due to what the company regarded as the cover's Aryan imagery and its suggestion of concepts of "master race," issues that Rammstein have always denied. The band's second album, *Sehnsucht* (Longing) (1997) portrays images of the band members' heads either restricted from sight and speech by a metal frames and opaque spectacles or in stages of biological experimentation, torture or enforced examination. Alluding to Stanley Kubrick's *A Clockwork Orange* (1971) imagery, these elements often make up a significant part of the band's textual and visual identities in cover art as well as in videos and live performance. I also suggest that this imagery is inspired by German expressionist poets, such as Gottfried Benn (1886–1956), and Georg Heym (1887–1912) who both wrote poetry concerning human death, dissection and decay.[7] The cover of *Live aus Berlin* (Live from Berlin) features Rammstein band members in sombre dark suits, perhaps projecting an East German image of austerity and reflecting some members' place of origin. They are standing in front of stone columns reminiscent of older architecture in Berlin, such as the Brandenburg Gate, which is a significant example of the architecture of pre- and post-war Berlin. This image can therefore be linked to German notions of nostalgia, or *Ostalgie*.[8] The picture creates an arguably nostalgic image of what might have been some members' introduction to rock and pop music in East Germany, with a contrast between the gothic columns of an earlier German identity and the almost surreptitious use of the transistor radio and its connotations with an illegal cultural modernity. The East German authorities frowned upon rock and pop music in the 1950s and 1960s while jazz was regarded as worthy of state support. East German jazz became distinctly different from its western counterpart during the 1960s and 1970s, a period when the German Democratic Republic widely promoted jazz, despite the continuing influence of the propaganda of Nazi years during which jazz had been regarded as "degenerate art."[9]

Later Rammstein albums continued the trend of taking cover imagery from the nature of the album's textual content. *Mutter* (Mother) (2001) has a facial and torso image of a human fetus on its cover, while inside sleeve artwork features photographs of band members inside what appears to be an isobaric floatation tank, suggesting to the onlooker a womb–like experience. The band's following album, *Reise, Reise* (a German naval form of a Reveille, or more literally Journey, Journey) (2004), features a song called "Dalai Lama" and its lyrics, a contemporized version of Goethe's "Der Erlkonig" (The Elf King), describe a father and son travelling in an aircraft at night while being pursued by the god of the winds. The song has a sense of impending disaster throughout its often spiritual and hymn–like choruses. The album's cover features pictures of aircraft parts, including a flight data recorder, indicating the possible demise of one of the song's protagonists. Many Rammstein songs allude to the bleakness of Baltic sea imagery, sea travel and the heroism of sailors — for example the songs "Reise, Reise" and "Seemann" (seaman) — and the cover of the band's album *Rosenrot* (2005) is a photograph of a modern naval ship frozen in ice in a bleak, Antarctic scene. The band's video for "Seemann" drew on earlier Baltic maritime imagery with band members performing in a deserted dockyard, as well as hauling on ropes that tow a wooden ship through sculpted unmoving waves in the style of a Renaissance theater production. The lyrical content of *Rosenrot* (the title song's text using a storyline taken from Goethe's "Heidenröslein") provides a contemporary take on lyrical themes explored comprehensively by Martina Lüke in her essay in this volume, *Love as a Battlefield: Reading Rammstein as Dark Romanticists*, as well as a thematic lineage between music and other visual album cover art themes, given the inclusion on the inner cover of the gatefold sleeve of a German gothic castle.[10]

In consideration of any album cover art with historic or national over-tones, it is worth examining visual clues with which the work in question is imbued.[11] Mireia Ferrer Álvarez does not think that a work of art can be analyzed without taking into account the diachronic nature of art history and that analysis cannot be reduced to mere formal study. She also maintains that one cannot make an exclusive correspondence between a work's meaning and the society in which it was produced and understood.[12] These are critical points in the consideration of the Rammstein's most recent album, *Liebe ist für Alle Da*, given that its imagery is firmly rooted in overt references to Renaissance and contemporary artworks that have previous and current meanings. The inner and outer covers of the album are a collage of photographs that draw upon works by Renaissance and Realist painters and photographers. Each photographic portrait of the band is in the style of artists such as Michelangelo Merisi da Caravaggio (1571–1610), Rembrandt van Rijn (1606–1669), and Thomas Eakins (1844–1916), as well as photographer Jan Saudek (b.1935). The cover art photographs are dimly lit, gothic in style, and they are in keeping with the macabre nature of influential works by the above artists, as well as the dark sense of theatrical parody espoused by Rammstein. The front cover of *Liebe ist für Alle Da* is a photographic image drawing from three works dealing with the dissection of corpses — Rembrandt's *The Anatomy Lesson of Dr. Nicolaes Tulp* (1632) and Eakins' *The Clinic of Dr. Gross* (1875) and *The Agnew Clinic* (1889).

The primary influence is arguably *The Anatomy Lesson of Dr. Nicolaes Tulp*, although the subject of the autopsy is female and is facing right to left, rather than the original left to right.[13] With regard to this painting, Lorretta Kopelman and Kenneth De Ville state that dissection in the sixteenth century was still carried out by theater technicians while surgeons looked on and taught students from texts by the Roman anatomist, Galen.[14] By the time of Rembrandt's painting, the instructing professor is still giving instruction from an open book while the students themselves are inspecting the cadaver. This change, for Kopelman and De Ville, is Rembrandt's "tour de force" and "a metaphor for the enlightenment's rejection of traditional explanations that lack confirmation by human experience and thought."[15] They also argue that there exists in the painting an inherent notion that student onlookers would learn from direct observation rather than being provided with a "correct" view that already existed, and did not explain the current medical situation.[16] The Rammstein front cover is similar in this respect, having one band member dissecting the corpse with the other band members as onlookers. As Malcolm

Salcman points out, the Rembrandt painting is only one in the tradition of the numerous commissioned portraits of guild members that Rembrandt, Rubens, and other Dutch artists produced for the middle class of the period.[17]

Meanings are not, however, inferred without debate. Sarah Burns, for example, ponders whether Thomas Eakins had a "dark" side, and asks whether there are grounds for reconsidering other "oddballs and eccentrics so far from the center."[18] She suggests that Eakins should be considered a gothic artist in the same way that Edgar Allan Poe and Herman Melville are considered to be gothic writers.[19] While Burns has it that Eakins was "a mainstream artist if ever there was one," there exists in *The Agnew Clinic* a bleakly gothic image of human suffering combined with the stark modernity of sanitized surgery of the period.[20] This imagery is supported by the combination of somber and bright colors — the onlookers at the rear and the surgeons in their white theater garments. Eakins has Dr. Agnew standing away from the surgical procedure and the participating students, scalpel in his left hand and contemplating the next point in his lecture. Unlike *The Anatomy Lesson of Dr. Nicolaes Tulp*, the foreground of *The Agnew Clinic* therefore seems illuminated with the background onlookers in the shade. In this respect, the Rammstein front cover bears more similarity to the Rembrandt painting, although Eakins' painting does portray a slight air of detachment that is reflected by Rammstein band members being detached from the surgery/autopsy being performed. Unlike Rembrandt, Eakins studied medical dictionaries and also studied anatomy. Speaking from his own viewpoint as a surgeon, Michael Frumovitz has it that, by making himself an observer, Eakins demonstrated that he could portray surgical scenes with great accuracy.[21] In his painting *The Gross Clinic*, Eakins portrays Dr. Gross as calmly performing surgery despite the recoiling nature of the onlookers, who are portrayed in semi–darkness in the background.[22] A further detail separating both of Eakins' paintings by fifteen years is that Dr. Gross and his colleagues are wearing dark suits (like the black clothing of the Rammstein personnel) whereas Dr. Agnew and his colleagues are wearing sanitized surgical garments, given that Lister's treatise on antisepsis had by then become established in medical science.[23]

From a musical perspective, gothic horror has always been a guiding force in heavy metal music.[24] Robert Walser bases the origins of the gothic with Edmund Burke's theorization of the aesthetic category of the Sublime in 1756, a theory that included horror as well as astonishment, pain and terror.[25] For Walser, this theory has more recently legitimized popular music's relationship with the gothic, particularly with bands whose stage presentations are of a theatrical nature. The images on the cover of *Liebe ist für Alle Da* have a similar visual perspective to early gothic horror films such as *Nosferatu*

(1922), *Dracula* (1931) and *Frankenstein* (1931), despite these films' monochromatic imagery. Walser also suggests that heavy metal, and in particular, dark metal, is intimately related to an emotional response to war, external control and fantasies of empowerment.[26] As with composers of the Enlightenment (such as J. S. Bach), "heavy metal musicians explore images of horror and madness in order to comprehend and critique the world as they see it."[27] Furthermore, Bach was a master of the fugue, a very orderly art form. Similarly, Celan's "Todesfuge" partially serves as an attempt to make order out of the Holocaust and World War II. Rammstein's imagery and lyrical content therefore follows a heavy metal tradition that started with theatrical heavy metal, such as that performed by Kiss, Alice Cooper and Ozzy Osbourne, and in Germany by Udo Lindenberg and Nina Hagen, in which spectacle and audience reaction to it become as important as the music played.

While the Rammstein outer cover image of *Liebe ist für Alle Da* (a photograph taken by Eugenio Recuenco) may be influenced by all three of the above paintings, it suggests the dissection or sacrifice of a female rather than the Rembrandt and Eakins illustrations of surgical procedures. There is, however, a commonality in that the prone figure in Rammstein's image is female and bare–breasted, and therefore reminiscent of Eakins' *The Agnew Clinic* in that Eakins' portrayed a female mastectomy for which he was criticized by Philadelphia society and by his artistic peers in New York. Margaret Stuplee-Smith points out that, while the amputation of a woman's breast might be medical fact, it violated notions of decorum in painting at the time, and she suggests that it was "not cheerful for ladies, or anyone else for that matter."[28] For Stuplee–Smith, the painting is a complex program that both "explicates and obscures the complicated, and changing, values in the nineteenth-century worlds of art and medicine as they confronted modern life, and today it continues to challenge ours."[29] Rammstein band members are, on close inspection, eating body parts as they are perhaps removed from the subject. This action is one of the principal aspects that caused controversy so much so that when I purchased the album in New Zealand in 2009, I had to ask for it at the shop–counter as it was not displayed with other Rammstein albums in the Rammstein album section.[30] This was because the album artwork was regarded as distasteful by the New Zealand censor. It is useful at this point therefore, to refer to the notion of human cannibalism in Rammstein's music.

The nature of this topic is in common with other dark themes that the band portray with humor in their stage performances that represent comical theatricality, while also seeking to perhaps shock the audience. The topic is reflective of an earlier song by Rammstein, "Mein Teil" ("My Part," although the "Part" is actually a reference to the victim's penis), which is recorded on the album *Reise, Reise.* The song deals with the killing in Germany in 2001 of a victim who agreed to be slaughtered and eaten.[31] Rammstein have often expressed that their stage act and lyrical content are located within an overt sense of theatricality and dark humor, and Rammstein continue a historically constituted theme of insanity, cruelty and criminality in a song on *Liebe ist für Alle Da* entitled "Wiener Blut" (Vienna Blood). The song title is taken from a nineteenth century Johann Strauss operetta of the same name and starts with a 3/4 meter waltz–style string arrangement before switching to a 4/4 rock pattern in the formulaic style of most Rammstein songs. It is significant that Til Lindemann, the Rammstein vocalist, uses his familiar *gestic* speaking technique to accentuate the horrific theme of the song's text. The song's text again represents part of what I have referred to as the Rammstein "formula." The lyrics are a reference to the case in 2008 of Josef Fritzl, an Austrian (hence the title and the opening section in waltz meter) who imprisoned his daughter in a cellar underneath his house for twenty–four years, and had an incestuous relationship with her that led to the birth of seven children. This song is one of several on the album whose texts portray an overwhelmingly dark thematic nature, and which may explain the dark backgrounds in the cover artwork. Another example of darkly sadistic thematic textual matter is the song "Ich Tu Dir Weh (I'm Hurting You)," which, after almost a minute of a solo arpeggiated synthesizer, uses extremely over–driven guitars, bass and drums played in 12/8 meter, providing a heartbeat–like pulse to support the painful and violent nature of the lyrics.

The inner sleeve and insert photographs (also taken by photographer Eugenio Recuenco) are in a similar gothic vein to the above lyrics, and they use similar sadistic sexual and homo–erotic imagery. Inner cover pictures feature still life fruit compositions, with one including a limp female figure being carried to a table that bears fruit as well as an amputated human limb. The fruit aspects are, to an extent, reminiscent of the works of Caravaggio. For example, the variety of fruit (excluding amputated limbs and lifeless body) in *Boy with a Basket of Fruit* (c. 1592), as well as Rembrandt's still life paintings and those by other northern European Renaissance artists.[32] Caravaggio established his reputation during the Italian Renaissance and he often painted still life images, such as vases or baskets containing flowers or fruit, that are presented in highly detailed accuracy in inanimate displays. As Hanns Swarzenski suggests, his still life paintings create "an illusory *trompe l'oeil* effect of special reality."[33] Swarzenski also notes that Caravaggio was referred to as a "naturalist" painter whose works display a "seemingly casual but rhythmically calculated order, in closets, niches, or on ledges, behind half opened doors or windows through which are seen vistas of unpopulated cities and landscapes."[34] This description could be aptly applied to Rammstein's inner cover photographs on *Liebe ist für Alle Da*. The band's combination of still life imagery amid violent and sexual themes that take place in a basement–like structure is consistent with the band's use of sadomasochism and black humor.

The inside pictures featuring males and females in transgressive sexual and bondage formations may also be compared to the photographs of Jan Saudek and further reinforce the shock value of the album cover art.[35] Saudek's erotic photographs often feature highly posed, sexually staged male and female figures that are in combinations of being dressed, partially dressed or nude. His work has a well–established reputation in the Czech republic, perhaps raising further indications of the origins of Rammstein's artistic aesthetic given that several members came from the former East Germany and would have experienced growing up in Eastern Europe during the Cold War. Saudek's work was initially criticized by the Czech authorities, particularly after his return from a visit to the United States in the 1960s. By the 1980s, he had, however, become established as a prominent and innovative photographer not only in what was then Czechoslovakia, but also in Western Europe. Fittingly, in light of Rammstein's philosophy of audience shock, it is therefore significant that many public art galleries outside northern Europe have refused to exhibit Saudek's photographs. This supposed impropriety could be an influence on the lurid nature of Rammstein's cover art on this album. Similarly, Eakins' reputation in the late nineteenth century suffered due to the parochial nature of society in Philadelphia, his home city, in which his work was regarded as scurrilous, although this view has changed in more recent times.

Saudek's work is often sepia toned with subdued colors and focuses on death and what Martyna Markowska refers to as heterotopia, or a juxtaposition of ugliness and "doubtful" beauty.[36] In describing heterotopia, she provides an apt statement that can be applied in a description of other photographs used in the inner covers of *Liebe ist für Alle Da*, "The manner of posing, con-stellation [assemblage] in which they are shown and [interpersonal] relations among the bodies create stories."[37] For Markowska, it is this assemblage that makes Rammstein's imagery different from standard portraits in that they "tell, provoke and hide stories" that are often ordinary and banal.

In Rammstein's inner cover album art (when one first opens the gatefold cover), the fruit can be said to represent the "beauty" of life while the later images of death, sexual debauchery and amputation contradict this vision for the onlooker. The image of the Rammstein bassist using an old treadle sewing machine may seem at odds with the other pictures of amputated limbs, sado-masochism and seemingly lifeless bodies, but it does invoke a storyline that is in keeping with the dark themes presented in the other pictures. The rear inner cover imagery is also influenced by the photographs of Jan Saudek. Potentially a coulrophobic concept (thus fitting with the band's theatrical performance philosophy), the band are wearing clown make up. Several members are laughing at the posed state of sexual debauchery of one member who appears to have almost passed out after his revelries. The remaining band members, as clowns or cabaret artists in the style of Karl Valentin or Frank Wedekind, are watching a television set seemingly oblivious to the naked females on the floor. Again, as with the front cover image, the band members portrayed are posing with a sense of detachment to the gravity of what they are witnessing. I suggest that this is a further attempt by Rammstein to provide the audience/onlooker with an image intended to shock, perhaps also to amuse, and certainly to provoke closer inspection.

As stated earlier, I maintain that Rammstein's stage performance philosophy of audience shock and theatrical parody mostly draws on 1920s German cabaret styles and mechanical constructivist imagery, as I noted in my 2008 article. In conclusion, however, I put it that the concepts of shock and theatrical parody have more recently influenced an artistic decision to combine a similar pictorial bleakness with that of Rembrandt's Renaissance autopsy room. It also reflects that of Eakins' somber, sanitized (yet slightly brighter) nineteenth century surgical room. The recent Rammstein images also provoke the onlooker to examine them more closely and to ponder the dark nature and possible storyline in much the same way as one would view a horror film, despite the possibility that there will be disturbing scenes. The album artwork of *Liebe ist für Alle Da* may be disturbing at times but its combination of, or juxtaposition with, the components that would normally appear with a certain familiarity in still life settings offsets the horrific nature of the cannibalism, debauchery, sadism and amputation, thus creating a sense of disbelief for the onlooker. While the impact of Rembrandt's and Eakins' surgical studies would have been greater in their respective time periods, their contemporary impact may be somewhat lessened by the passage of time in a similar way to audience desensitization to the content of suspense and horror films that has gradually occurred since the early history of the cinema.

This album's visual content follows a clear trajectory of themes established in earlier Rammstein cover art. The covers of *Herzeleid*, *Sehnsucht* and *Mutter* draw upon images that portray sexuality, nudity, torture and bondage at a primal level, issues that the band further reinforce in live performance. As stated earlier, this is part of an overall performance policy that aims to both shock audiences and parody issues that many other bands would be wary of addressing. It is therefore unsurprising that the artwork of the band's most recent album should be as I have described above. Rammstein's performance philosophy and cover art are as much about spectacle as they are about shocking audiences and theatrical parody. In being spectacular in both album artwork and live performance, the band transcends the formulaic nature of most American and European rock music by the use of visual effect in presentation media. It is worth noting that this particular album cover carries high artistic production values due in part to the success of the band's previous albums, as well as their concert schedules. This ongoing success enables Rammstein's record company, Sony/Universal/BMG to confidently market the band's recorded output at a time when other bands rely on single digital downloads, despite some of the dark themes alluded to by Rammstein in recorded and live performance. It is therefore significant that, at a time when record companies are finding themselves negotiating the notion of music becoming a computerized digital commodity, a band such as Rammstein is able to invest in such an elaborate cover for *Liebe ist für Alle Da*, in keeping with the artistic nature of their earlier albums. Moreover, the band's reinterpretations of art from the Renaissance, the nineteenth and twentieth centuries, are further means by which the band presents, and parodies, historic spectacle and art and thus continues to be successful in an extremely crowded musical arena.

Notes

1. Robert G. H. Burns, "German Symbolism in Rock Music: National signification in the imagery and songs of Rammstein." *Popular Music* Volume 27, Issue 3 (2008): 457–472.

2. The band's formula is also similar to that used by the art and rock influenced band Laibach, whose origins pre–date those of Rammstein. Laibach are the musical component of what is referred to as "Neue Slovenische Kunst" (NSK), an art movement based of the concept of a virtual artistic society in which, as Laibach put it, there are no concepts of originality and consequently, no concepts of artistic theft. Rammstein have acknowledged Laibach's influence on their artistic output, one particular example being the Rammstein logo, a cruciform similar to that used by the NSK. The NSK movement has been accused of both right and left wing leanings and of extreme nationalism. The movement, however, denies any political extremism stating that they are merely an artistic group.

3. I must acknowledge the assistance of Associate Professor Mark Stocker and Professor Terence Dennis at the University of Otago. Both gave me the benefit of their expertise in this discussion.

4. The Rammstein formula, or bricolage, is thus an interlinked and interwoven package.

5. "Rammstein Shop," Rammstein. 2012. http://www.rammstein.com/. All Rammstein album cover art discussed in this essay can be found at the band's website at this URL.

6. Peter Adam, *The Arts of the Third Reich* (London: Thames and Hudson, 1992), 15–16.

7. The Expressionist poets of the Neue Sachlickeit are also worthy of consideration in this respect (cf. Martina Lüke "Modern Classics: Reflections on Rammstein in the German Class," *Die Unterrichtspraxis / Teaching German* Volume 41, Issue 1 (2008): 15–23. Lüke advocates using Rammstein texts in the teaching of German, despite their often sexual, sadistic and violent nature. Her theory is based on the existence of classical German literature in some songs, which, on the other hand, I support).

8. The concept of nostalgia for the German Democratic Republic by the former East German population, and its functions in Rammstein's music, has been comprehensively discussed by John T. Littlejohn and Michael T. Putnam, "Rammstein and *Ostalgie*: Longing for Yesteryear," *Popular Music and Society* Volume 33, Issue 1 (2010): 35–44.

9. Gunther Huesmann, "Jazz in Germany after 1945," Goethe Institut (2009), accessed February 27 2012, /kue/mus/jaz/rue/bis/en4932331.htm.

10. For a further discussion on Rammstein's album cover artwork, see the essay "Fire, Water, Earth and Air: The Elemental Rammstein" by John T. Littlejohn in this volume.

11. For example, see Robert G. H. Burns, "'Depicting The Merrie': Historical Imagery in English Folk–Rock," *Music and Art: The International Journal of Music Iconography* Volume 35 (2010): 105–118.

12. Mireia Ferre Álvarez, "The Dramatisation of Death in the Second Half of the 19th Century: The Paris Morgue and Anatomy Painting," in *Faces of Death: Visualising History* (Pisa: Pisa University Press, 2009),178.

13. "The Anatomy Lesson of Dr. Nicolaes Tulp," Rembrandt van Rijn, *Encyclopædia Britannica Online*, 2011, http://www.britannica.com/EBchecked/media/76038/The-Anatomy-Lesson-of-Dr.

14. Loretta M. Kopelman and Kenneth A. De Ville, "Rembrandt's Anatomy Lesson as a Metaphor for Education," *Current Surgery* Volume 60, Issue 2 (2003): 150–151.

15. Ibid., 150.

16. Ibid., 150.

17. Michael Salcman, "The Anatomy Lesson of Dr. Deyman, Rembrandt van Rijn," *Neurosurgery* Volume 36, Issue 4 (1995): 865.

18. Sarah Burns, *Painting the Dark Side: Art and the Gothic Imagination in Nineteenth-Century America* (Berkeley: University of California Press, 2004), xv.

19. Ibid.

20. Ibid. See "The Agnew Clinic." Thomas Eakins, University of Pennsylvania Art Collection, 2012, http://sceti.library.upenn.edu/PennArt/SlideShow/index_slide.cfm?showStart=11.

21. Michael M. Frumovitz, "Thomas Eakins' Agnew Clinic: A Study of Medicine Through Art," *Obstetrics & Gynecology* Volume 100, Issue 6 (2002): 1297.

22. Frumovitz, 1299. See "The Gross Clinic." Thomas Eakins, *Encyclopædia Britannica Online*, 2011, http://www.britannica.com/EBchecked/topic/592888/Thomas-Jefferson-University?anchor=ref17611.

23. Frumovitz, 1299.

24. Robert Walser, *Running with the Devil: Power, Gender, and Madness in Heavy Metal Music* (Middletown: Wesleyan University Press, 1993), 160–161.

25. Ibid., 163.

26. Ibid., 163.

27. Ibid., 170.

28. Margaret Stupplee-Smith, "*The Agnew Clinic*: Not Cheerful for Ladies to Look At," *Prospects* Volume 11 (1987): 178.

29. Ibid., 178.

30. It is worth noting that the album cover was also banned in Germany for a while after its release.

31. The text of "Mein Teil" concerns masochistic sexual fantasy and cannibalism and is based on a manslaughter case that took place in 2001 in which Armin Meiwes killed Bernd Jürgen Brandes during the process of dismembering, cooking and eating him. Brandes had answered a classified advertisement published by Meiwes asking for a male volunteer who wished to be slaughtered and eaten.

32. "Boy with a Basket of Fruit," Michelangelo Merisi da Caravaggio, Fine Art America, 2006, http://fineartamerica.com/featured/caravaggio-fruit-granger.html.

33. Hanns Swarzenski, "Caravaggio and Still Life Painting: Notes on a Recent Acquisition," *Bulletin of the Museum of Fine Arts* Volume 52, Issue 288 (1954): 26.

34. Ibid.

35. For examples of Jan Saudek's photographs, see http://www.photography.ca/fine-art-photographers/saudek/ (accessed September 30, 2012).

36. Martyna Markowska, "Corpus Turpis — Body Aesthetics in Jan Saudek's Photography Art," (2009) 9, accessed February 14, 2012. www.formazione.unimib.it/DATA/hot/677/markowska.pdf.

37. Markowska, 10.

Works Cited

Adam, Peter. *The Arts of the Third Reich*, London: Thames and Hudson, 1992.

Álvarez, Mireia Ferre. "The Dramatization of Death in the Second Half of the 19th Century: The Paris Morgue and Anatomy Painting." In *Faces of Death: Visualising History*, 163–187. Pisa: Pisa University Press, 2009.

Burns, Robert G. H. "Depicting the Merrie: Historical Imagery in English Folk–Rock" in *Music and Art: The International Journal of Music Iconography* 35 (Spring-Fall 2010): 105–118.

_____. "German Symbolism in Rock Music: National Signification in the Imagery and Songs of Rammstein." *Popular Music* 27, no. 3 (2008): 457–472.

Burns, Sarah. *Painting the Dark Side: Art and the Gothic Imagination in Nineteenth-Century America*. Berkeley: University of California Press, 2004.

Frumovitz, Michael M. "Thomas Eakins' *Agnew Clinic*: A Study of Medicine Through Art." *Obstetrics & Gynecology* 100, no. 6 (2002): 1296–1300.

Huesmann, Gunther, "Jazz in Germany after 1945." Goethe Institut. kue/mus/jaz/rue/bis/en4932331.htm (accessed February 27, 2012).

Kopelman, Loretta M., and Kenneth A. De Ville. "Rembrandt's Anatomy Lesson as a Metaphor for Education." *Current Surgery* 60, no. 2 (2003): 150–151.

Littlejohn, John T. "Fire, Water, Earth and Air: The Elemental Rammstein." This volume.

_____, and Michael T. Putnam. "Rammstein and *Ostalgie*: Longing for Yesteryear." *Popular Music and Society* 33, no. 1 (2010): 35–44.

Lüke, Martina. "Love as a Battlefield: Reading Rammstein as Dark Romanticists." This volume.

_____. "Modern Classics: Reflections on Rammstein in the German Class." *Die Unterrichtspraxis / Teaching German* Volume 41, no. 1 (2008): 15–23.

Markowska, Martyna. "Corpus Turpis — Body Aesthetics in Jan Saudek's Photography Art." 2009. www.formazione.unimib.it/DATA/hot/677/markowska.pdf (accessed February 14, 2012).

Salcman, Michael. "The Anatomy Lesson of Dr. Deyman, Rembrandt van Rijn." *Neurosurgery* 36, no. 4 (1995): 865–866.

Stupplee-Smith, Margaret. "*The Agnew Clinic*: Not Cheerful for Ladies to Look At." *Prospects* 11 (1987): 161–183.

Swarzenski, Hanns, "Caravaggio and Still Life Painting: Notes on a Recent Acquisition." *Bulletin of the Museum of Fine Arts* 52, no. 288 (1954): 22–38.

Walser, Robert. *Running with the Devil: Power, Gender, and Madness in Heavy Metal Music*. Middletown: Wesleyan University Press, 1993.

Websites

"The Agnew Clinic." Thomas Eakins, University of Pennsylvania Art Collection, 2012, http://sceti.library.upenn.edu/PennArt/SlideShow/index_slide.cfm?showStart=11.

"Anatomy Lesson of Dr. Nicolaes Tulp, The." Rembrandt van Rijn, *Encyclopædia Britannica Online*, 2011, http://www.britannica.com/EBchecked/media/76038/The-Anatomy-Lesson-of-Dr.

"Boy with a Basket of Fruit." Michelangelo Merisi da Caravaggio, Fine Art America, 2006, http://fineartamerica.com/featured/caravaggio-fruit-granger.html.

"Gross Clinic, The." Thomas Eakins, *Encyclopædia Britannica Online*, 2011, http://www.britannica.com/EBchecked/topic/592888/Thomas-Jefferson-University?anchor=ref17611.

"Rammstein Shop." Rammstein. 2012. http://www.rammstein.com/.

Discography

Rammstein. *Du Riechst So Gut*. Motor Music 044–033–2. Compact disc. 1998.

_____. *Herzeleid*. Motor Music 529160–2. Compact disc. 1995.

_____. *Lichtspielhaus*. Universal 986604. DVD. 2003.

_____. *Liebe ist für Alle Da*. Universal 2719515. Compact disc. 2009.

_____. *Live aus Berlin*. Universal PY685. DVD. 1999.

_____. *Mutter*. Universal 5496392. Compact disc. 2001.

_____. *Reise, Reise*. Universal 9688150. Compact disc. 2004.

_____. *Rosenrot*. Universal 987458–9. Compact disc and DVD. 2005.

_____. *Sehnsucht*. Universal 537304–2. Compact disc. 1997.

_____. *Stripped*. Motor Music CD 044–141–2. Compact disc. 1998.

_____. *Völkerball*. Universal 06025 170506–7. Compact disc and DVD. 2006.

Part III: The Elemental and the Metaphysical

12

Fire, Water, Earth and Air: The Elemental Rammstein

JOHN T. LITTLEJOHN

On their debut album, *Herzeleid* [Heartache, 1995], Rammstein immediately accosts its audience with fire. The opening song's title, and this song's first line, is "Wollt ihr das Bett in Flammen sehen?" [Do you want to see the bed in flames?]. This is by no means the only time that one of Empedocles' four elements appears in Rammstein's works. Now, nearly two decades after Rammstein released *Herzeleid*, one can see that the band continually uses elemental imagery. Fire, water, earth, and air course through Rammstein's oeuvre.

Even a glance at the name Rammstein reveals a connection to the elements. While many know that the group (in)famously named itself after the disaster at the U.S. Air Force base in the German city Ramstein, relatively few native English speakers realize that the second syllable of this name represents an earth symbol: *Stein* = stone. In fact, by adding the second "m," the band emphasizes this aspect of their name, changing a city into a "ramming stone." A look back at the incident reveals a still deeper link to the elements beyond that simple earth image present in the band's name. Inspired by a fiery disaster at an air show,[1] the name Rammstein recalls three of the four elements: earth from the name of the city/air force base, fire and air from the event which took place there. Whether this heavy dose of the elements prompted the band to choose the name "Rammstein," or whether they took a cue from the imagery associated with it when crafting their lyrics remains unclear.

Rammstein has gained renown through their use of one particular element: fire. A great number of journalists and scholars have noted the pyrotechnics on display in their live shows; "Beware of Flaming Germans," "Ramm-stein: Vorsprung durch Pyrotechnik...,"[2] and "Having a Blast with Ramm-stein..." are just three of the innumerable headlines which allude to the band's fiery live show (Ratliff, E24; Cole, 5; "Having" E2). Fire has been a key — perhaps the key — component in their live shows since the very beginning. In the early days, the band poured gasoline on the dance floor and set it alight, much to the dismay and delight of the audience. Singer and lyricist Till Lin-demann continues to set himself alight onstage, while guitarists Paul Landers and Richard Z. Kruspe spit fire from gas masks. In the words of Ross Raihala, "Imagine a Kiss concert where Gene Simmons doesn't just breathe fire for a few seconds during 'Firehouse,' but he also shoots it from his hands, from his angel wings and from numerous other orifices — during nearly every song, for two straight hours. That, in a nutshell, is Rammstein..." (Raihala). For both safety and liability reasons, Lindemann has become a licensed pyrotechnician (Pearson, 6).

The question arises: does the emphasis on Rammstein's fiery stage per-formances correspond to the thematic dominance of fire in other aspects of its work? To answer this question, one must analyze all four elements in Rammstein's oeuvre. There exists the possibility that the band's everyday — that is, everynight — experience has seeped into its work, or, more cynically, that the band has crafted song texts which support their infamous and lucrative live show. An examination of the four elements in Rammstein's work will reveal whether fire does indeed feature as the dominant element in their corpus as a whole.

This analysis will look at Rammstein's six studio albums, as well as the three singles released independently of those albums. While focusing primarily on lyrics, this paper will also look at videos for those songs whose lyrics are particularly rife with elemental imagery. Other aspects of Rammstein's works, e.g., CD packaging, which betray clear elemental imagery will not be over-looked. In this examination of Rammstein's works, one must answer many basic questions. Do the four elements appear with the same regularity across the band's work, or does their frequency increase or decrease throughout the course of the band's career? Does the band use all four elements relatively equally, or does it focus on one element? If the latter, does the thematically dominant element change over time? Upon answering these questions, one can examine the prominence of fire imagery compared to imagery for water, earth and air in order to determine whether the band's lyrics and imagery merely serve as a calculated front for their stage show, or whether Rammstein's connection to the elements proves more profound.

This paper will restrict itself to the most basic vocabulary, that which is indubitably related to one of the four elements.[3] Such words are plentiful in Rammstein's song texts. Substances made up of each element fall in this category: e.g., flames and sparks for fire; sand, stone and mountains for earth; sea, waves and tears for water; and wind, sky, and breath for air. Animals, people or things commonly related to a particular element, such as sailors, fish or boats for water, would also fall into this category. Verbs such as burning, flowing, blowing and digging belong here as well. The words for the four elements themselves—"Feuer," "Wasser," "Erde(n)," and "Luft" [fire, water, earth, air]—which each make multiple appearances in the Rammstein song texts, will naturally be a part of this examination.

Herzeleid, the band's first album release, appeared in Germany in late 1995. As mentioned above, the first song asks the question: "Wollt ihr das Bett in Flammen sehen?" Fire imagery appears repeatedly throughout this album, up to and including the final track, "Rammstein." The song begins with the utterance of the title, quickly followed by the line: "Ein Mensch brennt" [a person is burning]. Fire is by no means the only element to turn up in *Herzeleid*, as one can ascertain from a simple glance at the song listing: a title like "Seemann" [sailor] clearly points to the presence of water as a key component to the language of *Herzeleid*.

Rammstein's use of the elemental imagery on this album proves quite complex. For instance, though "Rammstein" starts out with the above strong fire image, the song eventually includes all the other elements. That is quite a feat in light of the song's minimalist lyrics. Multiple air and earth images appear in the song, the latter including the name "Rammstein" itself which is repeated continually. The image of the "Flammenmeer" [sea of flames] joins the two contrary elements fire and water together even more elegantly than they had done in the earlier track "Asche zu Asche" [Ashes to Ashes], with its image of a fire which washes the soul. As a result, the song the band names after itself contains the most complex use of the elements on their debut album.

The fire which begins both the opening and closing tracks might initially lead one to believe that fire easily dominates the elemental imagery on *Herzeleid*. And though fire appears in some form in over half the songs, the dominant element is water. Water turns up in even more songs than does fire, while the two tracks which most prominently feature one of the elements focus on water. "Laichzeit" [Spawning Time] concentrates extensively and almost solely on water, while "Seemann" mentions water in its various forms even more often. Although one might expect elemental language in "Seemann" to consist entirely of the water and the sea, both fire and air present themselves among that water language. Adding these images subverts the purity of elemental usage in a track whose title would most likely raise expectations for an uncomplicated use of a single element. Here the surfeit of one element calls upon the other elements for support and contrast, with air and fire serving here to temper any overabundance of water imagery. The video for "Seemann," which appeared as a single in 1996, further undercuts the water language and the song title. The video depicts the members of Rammstein attempting to propel the boat, not by rowing it across the water as in a Roman galley, but by towing it across sand. The band thereby presents a visual image akin to the "Flammenmeer" in the album's final track, here a sea of sand instead of a sea of flame. Water itself appears rarely in the video, and then only showing reflections of fleeting images. Even in these brief moments they are double exposures laid upon or laid under other images. Already at this early point in their career, Rammstein's use of the elements proves both expansive and complex.

Sehnsucht [Longing], Rammstein's 1997 second album, propelled them to prominence on the national (German) and international level. Rammstein continued to draw upon the elements on this second album, though not to the same extent as they had done on the first. Three of the eleven titles on *Sehnsucht* lack any depiction of the elemental whatsoever. While that still leaves eight tracks which contain at least modest elemental imagery, that number is still lower than on *Herzeleid*, where all but one song uses the elements to some degree. "Du hast," one of the two big singles off *Sehnsucht*, contains no such images at all.

Nonetheless, the other big single, "Engel," carries many elemental images. One might expect lots of air imagery, in light of the song's title and the band's intensive use of fire, water, earth and air in their first album. Yet the first line of the song contains a mention not of air, but of "Erden" [earth]. The air imagery does however soon appear with "Himmel"[4] [heaven], a word which occurs frequently throughout the song, in the chorus as well as in both verses. The lyric supports the dominant air imagery with (the mixed water/air image) "Wolken" [clouds] in the chorus.

The visuals in the music video for "Engel" accomplish a maneuver similar to the lyric: whereas the lyric begins with an earth symbol before establishing the primacy of air imagery, the video starts with the air before another element takes over. The video begins and ends with the same low-angle shot, with the camera aimed toward the sky. Yet air is not the main visual element, as one would expect from the song's title or lyrics, or the video's opening shot. Fire dominates the rest of the video, climaxing with machine guns and guitars shooting flames in the hellish club which serves as the setting.[5] So thorough is the domination of fire during the body of the video that even the angels do not have wings, which would suggest flight and air. As with the music video for "Seemann" mentioned above, the images in the "Engel" video subvert the elemental images as they appear in the song lyrics.

The two songs from *Sehnsucht* which most prominently feature the elements are "Alter Mann" and the opening, title track. Water, in many different forms, clearly dominates the imagery in "Sehnsucht." "Alter Mann," on the other hand, is another Rammstein songs which contains all four elements. Water and air are most prominent in this track, the former slightly more so, as the German word for water [*Wasser*] appears in each of the first three verses as well as the chorus.

While water, fire, earth and air all appear repeatedly in these two albums, water clearly dominates the elemental imagery of *Sehnsucht*, as it does *Herzeleid*. Indeed, water finds itself even more dominant on their second album. On *Herzeleid*, Rammstein sings iconic fire lyrics in opening track "Wollt ihr das Bett in Flammen sehen?" and album closer "Rammstein." The strength and placement of these lyrics bolster the element fire, though it does not otherwise appear as prominently or as often as water. No similarly powerful fire imagery on *Sehnsucht* comes close to the status of these earlier texts. As a result, the lyrical saturation of water on the band's second album appears even greater than it already is from its sheer numbers.

Sehnsucht's international success prompted the release of two stand-alone singles in the late 1990s. After the album reached the top of the German charts and yielded two consecutive top-five singles, "Das Modell" [The Model, 1997], a cover of Kraftwerk's *Mensch-Maschine* classic, continued this streak. The band produced a video for "Das Modell," though they ultimately decided against using it. "Das Modell" achieved very good sales despite a lack of video and despite the dubious quality of the track — it conveys neither the elegance and novelty of the original, nor the power and instrumental interplay already apparent in Rammstein's work — which demonstrates the level of Rammstein's popularity at that time. The song contains no significant reference to the four elements[6] and, unfortunately for the present study, one cannot examine the video to this rare non-album single to see if and how it treats the elements.

"Das Modell" and the next single, "Stripped" (1998), exist as oddities in the Rammstein oeuvre. They are the band's only non-album singles,[7] and — unlike the music on their albums — these two songs were not written by the band. The cover of Depeche's Mode's "Stripped" proves a particular departure. This track compels/allows the band to record the song in a language besides their native German, another rarity. "Stripped" claims a prominent, if not necessarily positive, place in Rammstein's history. Few critics or reviewers hail the merits of this track — quite the opposite in fact (Gerbert). The band itself does not seem to esteem "Das Modell" or "Stripped" highly, as neither song appears on the standard edition of their greatest hits collection *Made in Germany*. "Stripped" does show up in the Deluxe and Super Deluxe editions of this collection, but only in a remixed version.

More prominent than the actual merits of the song has been its music video,[8] which draws generously from Leni Riefenstahl's 1938 film *Olympia*. Due to its use of clips from this Nazi-era film, by the director most intimately associated with National Socialism, the video received great condemnation. The video itself is beautiful, because Riefenstahl created gorgeous images in her films. Her artistry has never seriously come into question. And the video embodies a clever idea: just as "Stripped" is a cover of another group's song, the video is a cover — perhaps a remix — of another artist's film.

The song contains little elemental imagery, but the video more than makes up for that relative paucity. Fire takes over about 90 seconds into the clip, and that fire becomes the Olympic torch. We then follow runners carrying the torch to the Olympic stadium. One athlete runs with the torch on the beach, first on the land at the edge of the water, and then in the water. Three of the elements combine here in a conspicuous manner. The fourth element, air, is obviously the element most difficult to emphasize on film, yet the video soon does just that. In the diving segments near the end of the "Stripped" video, athletes dive in both reverse and forward motion, something Riefenstahl had spoken about just a few years earlier for the 1993 documentary *The Wonderful, Horrible Life of Leni Riefenstahl*.[9] The effect of these scenes is that of Olympians diving out of the water and into the air.

Though only two years passed between the first two studio albums, it took Rammstein another four years before they released their third. In the meantime came the singles for "Das Modell" and "Stripped," the live album *Live aus Berlin* (Live from Berlin, 1999), and well over 100 live performances. *Mutter* [Mother] reached the market in 2001. The group infused its first two albums with elemental imagery, with water overwhelming earth, air and even fire. One might naturally expect that Rammstein would continue to point to the four elements in its imagery, and that water would continue its dominance. While *Mutter* clearly and immediately affirms the first expectation, water loses its foothold. That comes as a particular surprise, considering that at least one member of the band has directly connected the title with this element. Kruspe notes, "Our album is called Mutter-'mother'-and you think of birth ... and birth, after all, has something to do with water" (Marshall). The cover booklet for the *Mutter* CD further develops the expected water imagery, inasmuch as it depicts the members of Rammstein floating in some form of liquid. Yet the band dashes those expectations.

Rammstein begins *Mutter* with "Mein Herz brennt" [My heart is burning]. Though this title starts the album off with the fire, the lyrics provides little or no support for this element, apart from the statement of the title at the chorus. When Lindemann sings "Mein Herz brennt" at that point, these words seem only minimally connected to the rest of the lyrics or to the music, with its nod to Led Zeppelin's "Kashmir." One may trace this tenuous connection to the origin of the song, whose working title was "Sandmann" (Williams, "What"). Even in the finished version, Rammstein famously retains borrowings from the children's television show *Das Sandmännchen* [The Little Sandman].[10]

With the original title and the lyrics from the children's program, along with the mythological and popular cultural weight of the sandman figure,[11] *Mutter*'s opener could easily have been a much stronger elemental anchor — though not one for fire, but for earth, because of the sand. As it stands, "Mein Herz brennt" bears importance for the element fire mainly — and perhaps solely — for its title and its position in the album.

Though not as powerful an opening salvo as it could have been, the position of "Mein Herz brennt" as first song in the album is not inconsequential. Fire is an important theme on *Mutter*. The release of the album's first single, "Sonne" [Sun], and final single "Feuer frei!" [Fire at Will!] attest to that. The lyrics to "Sonne" make a nod to the element fire, yet the music video de-emphasizes that theme. The video mostly takes place in a mine underground and, at the end, on top of a mountain. While fire in the form of sparks does appear when the miners — the members of Rammstein — strike with their hammers, the ground indubitably dominates the video. Thus both "Mein Herz brennt" and "Sonne" present the fire element on the surface, yet the earth element undermines them — through strong intertextual allusions in the former and through the video for the latter.

Whereas those two works offer only muted support for the element of fire inherent in their titles, "Feuer frei!" more than lives up to its name. The German word for fire appears in the song's name, in its chorus and in each individual verse, while the song contains a great amount of additional language which supports that element. The video plays up the fire angle. The "Feuer frei!" clip is a performance video, with the band playing in a crowded hall. Fire lights up the walls of the hall, and fire burns on the stage. Flames surge with the music. Kruspe shoots fire from a mask. Scenes of fire and explosions from the movie *XXX*— "Feuer frei!" is the lead track off the *XXX* soundtrack — are interspersed throughout the video. "Feuer frei!" — the track and its video — provides a fire thematic both strong and unadulterated.

While fire gains in prominence on *Mutter*, the title track focuses primarily and powerfully on water imagery. Other elements appear in "Mutter," but they do so only briefly. The text even negates its sole fire image: "keine Sonne" [no sun]. Lindemann saturates this song with water vocabulary, including one of his more memorable images: breasts (not) weeping milk. As "Mutter" serves as the fourth single off this album, Rammstein also released a video for this song. The video begins in the water, with a man (played by Lindemann) dragging a boat through reeds. Then a caged man, also played by Lindemann, begins to sing. The audience later sees the first man row the boat in the night. The boatman comes to the caged man and gives him a cup of water before taking to his boat once again at the end of the video. In the middle of the video, the boatman drowns (or appears to do so), a sequence which not only hearkens back to a line in the song, but also, as Lindemann mentions, to the photos on the album cover ("Making of Mutter"). Clearly, this video intensifies the prominence of the element water already so important in the song.

Water is the element which most strongly marks the first two Rammstein albums, and it also holds a prominent position on this album. "Mutter" provides the strongest thematic use of water in terms of both the lyrics and the video, and by dint of being the title song and central track on the album carries great significance. And as with "Feuer frei!," the "Mutter" video greatly supports the song's main element. Fire varies in importance across these first three albums. It is a very strong secondary element in *Herzeleid*, then the band uses it significantly less on *Sehnsucht*, yet on *Mutter* fire features as the foremost element. "Mein Herz brennt" and "Sonne," although the fire is undermined in both these works, carry import as the opening track and opening single, respectively, and "Feuer frei!" bears fire vocabulary as robustly as "Mutter" uses water imagery. Looking at the *Mutter* album in conjunction with the works which preceded it, it becomes clear that water and fire dominate Rammstein's early work.

Reise, Reise, Rammstein's 2004 fourth album, displays the group's interest in the elements as vividly as the earlier ones, with fire, water, earth and/or air appearing in all but one song, more than either *Sehnsucht* or *Mutter*. The singles from *Reise, Reise* do not however convey the great amount of elemental imagery that most of those from the previous album exhibited. In fact, the second single, "Amerika," is the one track on the album which lacks any real elemental vocabulary.[12] Nonetheless, the album's first single "Mein Teil" is part of an opening trio of songs that frontloads the album with an immense amount of elemental imagery.

The lyrics to "Mein Teil" contain multiple words pointing to air and fire. The vocabulary for these elements comes together in clusters: the middle eight contains both of the words referring to fire, while the last verse has all the three air images. Though "Mein Teil" does not have the sheer number of an individual elemental references that many other Rammstein songs have — including the two tracks surrounding it on the *Reise, Reise* album — the concentration bolsters the effect.

The videos for many earlier singles fail to bolster — and often subvert — the elemental emphases in the lyrics, though clearly that is not always the case, as the videos for the previous two singles, "Mutter" and "Feuer frei!," demonstrate in spades. The "Mein Teil" clip prominently reflects an image from the song's lyrics: the angels and the feathery flesh from the last verse appears in the video when an angel — or a woman wearing angel's wings — consumes and/or fellates the singer, who later begins to eat her in turn.[13] This image runs throughout the music video and counts among the most memorable parts of this clip. Yet the video depicts no other imagery for air in the clip, and none whatsoever for fire, the other element which appears in the song. Water features more prominently here than either fire or air. The beginning of the video show scenes of a woman — actually drummer Christoph Schneider, dressed up to look like the mother of cannibal Armin Meiwes ("Making of Mein Teil [2]") — interspersed with shots of the legs of several men as they stand in muddy water. This beginning sets the viewer up for the climactic scene in which members of Rammstein fight each other in the mud and rain, a sequence which takes up over twenty seconds of the video's 4:24. Because of the stagnant water and the rain on the one hand and the angel's wings on the other, water and air share symbolic prominence in the video. As in the lyrics for "Mein Teil," mixed elemental imagery proves important to the song's video, though the combination of air and fire has been replaced by air and water. The reduction in prominence of fire to the benefit of water would put "Mein Teil" as a whole more in line both with the rest of the album, where fire imagery does not dominate any single song, and with the two tracks surrounding it on the album. Water dominates "Reise, Reise" and air "Dalai Lama."

"Reise, Reise" [Arise, Arise], the title of the opening, title track — and, of course, the entire album — is a sailor's wake-up call (Burns, 461). When the song begins, one can hear "...the sound of lonely waves and seagulls, an ominous warlike pounding, and the primitive chanting of sailors on a galley" (Berlinski, 68). Furthermore, Rammstein based the song on a German sea chantey (Berlinski, 68). Water-related nouns and verbs abound, and a sailor and common sailor's vocabulary appear. "Reise, Reise" features prominently both as the title track and album opener, and the strong water message it carries is not to be overlooked. This song has much more imagery connected with the element water than the first album's similarly-themed —

yet stylistically very different — "Seemann." Indeed, up to this point in the band's career, "Reise, Reise" is the Rammstein track carrying the greatest number of references to a single element.

The third track on *Reise, Reise*, "Dalai Lama," proves the equal to the opener in terms of elemental imagery. In what amounts to a break with earlier albums, where the songs containing significant amounts of elemental imagery mainly focused on fire or water, Rammstein places "Dalai Lama" firmly in the realm of air. Air imagery abounds. The focus on air should not, however, come as a great surprise, as the song is set in an airplane. "Dalai Lama" serves as a variation on Goethe's "Erlkönig," one of the most famous of all German poems, and one which has been set to music by several composers, perhaps most famously by Schubert.[14] The first line of Erlkönig reads: "Wer reitet so spät durch Nacht und Wind" [Who rides so late through night and wind], while "Dalai Lama" similarly opens with an airplane in the evening wind. With its air imagery, "Dalai Lama" stays true to its setting, while it also plays upon a theme present in the opening line of its source material. This stands in opposition to a song like "Mein Herz brennt" which has a large amount of background in the element earth, yet presents a surface which focuses on the element of fire.

Though the opener "Reise, Reise" features as the literal title track, "Dalai Lama" turns out to be the more representative song for the album whose cover bears the wording "Flugrekorder nicht öffnen" [Flight recorder. Do not open]. The use of air in this song matches the preeminence of that element throughout the album. *Reise, Reise* appears as the first Rammstein album to feature such a pronounced use of air. The elements which were so key on the first three albums, water and fire, feature less prominently here. Fire in particular retreats in significance; it appears less than any of the other elements on *Reise, Reise*.

The cover art for Rammstein's next album, *Rosenrot* [Rose-Red], depicts a ship in the ice, an image which immediately brings to mind the element water.[15] In part because it was released barely a year after *Reise, Reise* (easily the shortest stretch between album releases for the group) one might view it as a continuation of that earlier album.[16] As if to counter that assumption, the first track on the *Rosenrot* — and the song which also serves as the album's first single — is titled "Benzin" [gasoline]. In light of the band's famously fiery live show, the title brings to mind fire and explosions. With vocabulary such as "Explosiv" and "Dynamit" — two of the many words in the song with English cognates that even a non–German speaking international audience could understand — this track supports that line of thinking. Nonetheless, the song also underscores the liquid nature of gasoline. Terminology such as "flows" [fließt] and "swimming" [schwimmen] pulls the text away from fire and brings it closer to water, something which jibes with the cover art. The video, in which members of the band portray firemen, actually does little to push the overall work toward either of these elements. There is much smoke, but little or no fire. According to Paul Landers in the "Making of Benzin" video, this was an aspect of the video that he particularly enjoyed: "The good thing about this video, and the reason I liked the treatment, is that there is no fire and no petroleum featured. When you hear the track you think: Everything is on fire, even the TV could be on fire. I like the fact that nothing burns." No water appears in the video either, although the camera lingers briefly on a firehose. The emergency to which the firemen race is not a fire, but rather a suicide jumper on top of a tall building.[17] The repeated shots of windmills (which fits the anti-carbon-fuel message of the song) add air to the mixture of elements associated with the overall work "Benzin." The band self-consciously works against the song's imagery. Rammstein revels in flipping the messages in their text, as one can see from Landers' remarks above. One can find further evidence of the intentional undercutting of imagery in other band member's statements on the "Making of Haifisch" video, where they tell how "Haifisch" is about the band sticking together, and they enjoy how the song's video depicts the exact opposite. "Haifisch" comes from their latest studio album, but the trend had been apparent since the their debut; one can see it in the "Seemann" video, where the band almost totally removes the song's strong water imagery, to the degree that they put a boat in sand instead of water.

Elemental symbolism presents itself strongly in three other songs on *Rosenrot:* the title track, "Hilf Mir" [Help Me] and, naturally, "Feuer und Wasser" [Fire and Water]. "Rosenrot" was the second single issued off the album. Like "Dalai Lama" and to some extent "Amerika" from the previous album, the song serves as a variation on a Goethe poem, in this instance "Heidenröslein."[18] The song also alludes to the Grimm brothers' fairy tale "Schneeweißchen und Rosenrot" [Snow-White and Rose-Red] (Lüke, 17).[19] The element with the most varied vocabulary in "Rosenrot" proves to be earth. This song thereby holds a unique place among those Rammstein songs which feature elemental imagery to such a prominent degree. With "Wasser" appearing twice in the chorus — once singular and once plural — water offsets earth and appears as a strong secondary element in the song overall. The use of these two elements in "Rosenrot" proves characteristic for the album as a whole: water is once again well represented (it is the main element in many songs), and earth manifests itself more noticeably here than on any other Rammstein album.

The "Rosenrot" video supports the earth imagery. The clip begins with a long shot of the landscape where the members of Rammstein are dwarfed by mountains and rocks, and it ends with another landscape. The video has many overhead shots (both interior and exterior), including several shots of the band in a circle flagellating themselves, centered not on any one of them, but rather on the ground. Water also comes up in the video, with multiple shots of a brook in the countryside and, arguably, the fog rolling so quickly over the mountains near the start just as the lyrics begin. However, water plays a relatively minor role compared to fire which, though absent in the lyrics, plays an important part in the video: the singer is burned at the stake after committing a murder because of his blind love. As is the case with "Benzin," a third element plays a role in the video at least as significant as the two elements which dominate the song's lyrics.

"Hilf mir," the eighth track on the album, is based on "Die gar traurige Geschichte mit dem Feuerzeug" [The Dreadful Story of the Matches][20] from Heinrich Hoffmann's 1845 collection of stories entitled *Der Struwwelpeter*. The story of the song (and the tale on which it is based) concerns a child who plays with fire. Some of the lyrics are taken directly from the story, while Lindemann shifts the third person of the story into the first person, and changes the wording to fit the shift. Because the story to "Hilf mir" so closely resembles that of the *Struwwelpeter* tale, the dominant element remains the same: fire. By retaining the most prominent element of the story for this song, "Hilf mir" stands in contrast to "Mein Herz brennt," where the earth imagery inherent in its background is replaced — if only on the surface level — with that of fire.

It should come as no surprise that "Feuer und Wasser" displays the most elemental language of any song off *Rosenrot*, indeed of any song in Rammstein's catalogue. Fire and water are the two elements which appear most prominently in Rammstein's work. They far outdistance earth and air on their early albums, and, despite the relative assertion of air in *Reise, Reise* and earth on this album, fire and water remain the dominant elements in the band's oeuvre. "Feuer und Wasser" naturally and overwhelmingly emphasize these elements. Even in light of the frequent and heavy use of the elements in Rammstein's oeuvre, the amount of fire and water language in this song is outstanding.

The chorus of "Feuer und Wasser" proves particularly enlightening for an examination of the four elements in Rammstein's work. The first line of the chorus claims that fire and water do not mix, they cannot be put together and they are not related. They immediately proceed to disprove that claim, twice. With the phrases "in Funken versunken" [sunken in sparks] and "im Wasser verbrannt" [burned in water], Rammstein and Lindemann provide images in which these elements are mixed. The images are furthermore complementary: water is in fire in the first image, while fire is in water in the second. The complementary nature of these two connects them on an even deeper level. Even before the chorus which claims that fire and water cannot mix — in fact, immediately before the chorus, on the last line of the first verse — Rammstein combined fire, water and earth in the phrase "Funkenstaub fließt" [spark dust flows]. The statement itself, that the song's titular elements "kommt nicht zusammen," linguistically renders the two elements as a single unit: "kommt" is the third-person singular conjugation of the verb "kommen" [to come]. If fire and water were two entities, the proper conjugation would be the plural form "kommen." One notes that the next line uses the correct plural form of another verb "sein" [to be] for fire and water. Using this plural here for the same subject confirms the band's realization of the proper form. At the same time, using this form of "sein" also excludes the only other grammatical possibility for the form "kommt" here: as a plural imperative. If that were the case, the singer would be addressing these two elements with the command: "Fire and water, don't come together."

As mentioned above, either earth or water serves as the main element in most of the songs on *Rosenrot*. Though air — the dominant element from *Reise, Reise*— is almost nowhere to be found on *Rosenrot*, fire makes a very strong appearance on the album. For those songs in which fire appears, fire vocabulary is plentiful. While fire symbolism proves consistently strong in the songs where it appears on *Rosenrot*, water appears as the main element of more songs than earth, fire or air. It is notable that the song in which these elements appear together and are at their strongest, "Feuer und Wasser," water symbolism has a distinct edge over fire imagery. Water appears first in the song, appears last in the song, and overall appears slightly more often than fire.

Liebe ist für Alle Da [Love Is There for Everyone, 2009] is Rammstein's last studio album to date. Upon first hearing the title, one can sense a difference in the group's language. *Liebe ist für Alle Da* is a much more expansive title than any of the previous five, which either consists of a single word — as is the case with *Herzeleid*, *Sehnsucht*, *Mutter*, and *Rosenrot*—or of one word repeated, as with *Reise, Reise*. One can also note a change in their elemental language usage as well: vocabulary relating to the four elements in *Liebe ist für Alle Da* is much more sparse than any of the previous albums. Whereas at least eight of eleven songs — and often more — on each of their earlier albums contained language clearly related to one or more or the elements, only six of the songs on *Liebe ist für Alle Da* contain any imagery related to fire, water, earth or air.

Just one of the eleven songs bears strong elemental content: "Haifisch." True to the title, which means shark, the main element proves to be water in the song. Oddly, however, the water images — though they clearly dominate the song — appear only in the chorus. In the fourth verse, as contrast, fire appears twice in the space of two lines. Because of these two lines, and despite the title and the repetition of all the water vocabulary in the chorus, the water imagery does not totally control this song.

"Haifisch" is the third single off *Liebe ist für Alle Da*, and the last single to stem from any of the group's studio albums to date. To a large extent, the song's video supports the water imagery apparent in the song. It rains in the video, and many people are holding umbrellas. One notes, incidentally, that the German word for umbrella, "Regenschirm," contains the word for rain [Regen] in it. Tears, mentioned so often in the song, flow again and again in the video. There is even a shot of a woman as she passes water. (The German idiom meaning "to pass water" likewise uses that element: "Wasser lassen.") At the end, singer Lindemann turns up on an island, so the audience sees beautiful shots of the ocean. The video ends on a shot of a postcard which depicts Lindemann with a shark. Once again the ocean is in the background.[21]

On the other hand, the video also features the other elements prominently as well. The clip's setting is (the supposedly dead) Lindemann's funeral and burial, the latter of which clearly focuses on earth. The German word "Beerdigung" [burial] contains a contracted form of the word for that element. Keyboardist Flake Lorenz falls into the open grave near the end of the video, which further emphasizes earth. And, just as the lines about fire are sung in the song, the video begins a fantasy sequence in which drummer Christoph Schneider sets a fire to kill Lindemann. Fire also shows up in the candles in the church, the candelabra on the dining table, and also in the cigarettes smoked by Kruspe. As with the fire Schneider starts, air also shows up in another of Lindemann's fantasy death scenes, when bassist Oliver Riedel lets the air out of the singer's space suit. Also, the first words the audience sees in the video appear on a funeral bouquet. One can make out "Worte ... frisst Wind," presumably a quotation from Rammstein's earlier song "Nebel."[22]

Several sequences in the "Haifisch" video feature elements mixed together. In yet another Lindemann murder fantasy, guitarist Richard Z. Kruspe kills the singer while mountain climbing in the snow: the earth of the mountain meets the water of the snow. Low angle shots of people walking through mud — as with the previous example a mixture of earth and water, and perhaps the most common of all elemental mixtures — appear in the video just before the point where the album version of the song begins. The stone angels in the churchyard supply yet another mixture: earth and air.

Liebe ist für Alle Da has by far the lowest use of the four elements of all Rammstein albums. This latest studio album furthermore does not load the album opener (like *Herzeleid*), the title track (as on *Mutter*), or both (as with *Sehnsucht, Reise, Reise* and *Rosenrot*) with this imagery, which would emphasize the elemental influence on that album. Neither does the title or album art help convey any particular element or constellation of elements. *Liebe ist für Alle Da* therefore presents a break from earlier albums, though the song "Haifisch" and its video nevertheless reveals the group's continued fascination with the four elements as thematic tools.

Rammstein has only released one new track since *Liebe ist für Alle Da*. "Mein Land" (2011), the last of the three singles not appearing on any of Rammstein's studio albums, serves as the lone new track on Rammstein's greatest hits collection *Made in Germany*. The title means "my land," and the song provides lyrics which support the element earth inherent in this title. "Mein Land" also includes water and air language which staves off the one-sided pull of earth. Furthermore, the word "Horizont" [horizon] appears in the track's middle eight. As the meeting of sky with either the land or the sea, the horizon brings to mind the combination of multiple elements.

The video for "Mein Land" contains one of the largest amounts of element imagery of any of Rammstein's music videos, and it is perhaps the best at including and amplifying the varied imagery contained in the lyrics. Animated sea creatures — dolphins and a crab, respectively — begin and end this video. Seconds after the dolphin appears at the beginning, the U.S. flag flies in the wind, an image followed by that of breaking waves; flags and waves, both plucked from the lyrics, appear on the screen in short succession. The American flag appears, often in reflection, several times behind Lindemann as he lip-syncs the song. As the setting is a beach, the waves also reappear throughout the video. The beach setting proves appropriate for a band which repeatedly invokes the elements in its music and videos, and especially for a song like "Mein Land" which invokes air, water, and earth: everyone is on the sand near the ocean in the open air. While most of the song focuses abundantly if implicitly on these three elements, the last fifty seconds explicitly and no less abundantly feature fire. Flames burn the band's keyboards, guitars and drums with the band still playing them, while fire shoot out from flame throwers and from Lindemann's mouth. Other actors perform various circus pyrotechnics, such as eating fire and twirling in burning hula hoops. An explosion serves as the video's denouement. So overwhelming is the fire in this last quarter of the video that one barely notices the sand, which is obscured by darkness, by the video's focus on fire, sex and violence, and by the rapid-paced editing. One also notices a flag in this last section, though, like the sand — the other major elemental holdover from the main part of the video — it proves relatively obscure here. This time the audience sees a flag of the band's native Germany instead of the U.S. flag. Water is the only element which does not make an appearance in the video's last section.

During the song's middle eight, the "Mein Land" clip shows Lindemann running on the beach. He wears red swim trunks and carries a life preserver in his hand in a clear homage to Baywatch. The same scene also serves as an homage to the band's earlier video for "Stripped." Lindemann runs in the water and next to the water in this section, combining the two elements water and earth as the Olympic torch carrier in that earlier video did. In his right hand, Lindemann carries the red life preserver, which takes the place of the torch. A certain biographical logic exists here, inasmuch as the singer had previously been an Olympic-caliber swimmer. This fact, which would explain Lindemann's interest in the Olympic games and the movie which supplied the source for the "Stripped" video, largely if not completely escaped the notice of the press at the time of the earlier video — perhaps because the press was so taken aback by the use of Riefenstahl's material or because the public did not know the band and its individual members as well as it does today. The image of Lindemann as torch carrier works thematically as well: through this act Lindemann brings fire into the final segment. This visual signal combines and strengthens the musical and lyrical signals already apparent: Lindemann's elongated cries and especially the drum roll which precede this last section.

This examination of the elemental imagery in Rammstein's work reveals the band's long-term fascination with fire, water, earth and air. From the band's first album *Herzeleid* through to its fifth album *Rosenrot* almost a decade later, at least eight of each album's eleven tracks have some explicitly elemental imagery. Each of these albums contains multiple songs so replete with this imagery that any (German-speaking) listener would almost immediately perceive it. Even the latest studio album, *Liebe ist für Alle Da*, where Rammstein uses the elements much less than on their earlier albums, elemental imagery appears in just over half the songs, and this album still contains one song, "Haifisch," where the use of the elements appears as strongly as songs from earlier albums.

Rammstein's use of the four elements is not only copious, but also complex. On occasion, they will emphasize a single element to the exclusion of all others, while in other instances they craft songs which contain all four of Empedocles' elements. Rammstein uses its German literary and cultural inheritance repeatedly in their song lyrics e.g., the borrowings from Brecht's *Dreigroschenoper* in "Haifisch," or the reworkings of Goethe in "Dalai Lama" and "Rosenrot." But the band does not only invoke its cultural heritage to strengthen their elemental message, as in "Dalai Lama." On occasion, as with

"Mein Herz brennt," the band undermines the element prominent at the surface by intertextually favoring another element. The band uses a similarly diverse set of strategies in its music videos. While a few videos strongly support the dominant element of the song — "Feuer frei" being perhaps the best example — other videos such as "Seemann" actively undermine that dominant element. Still others alter the song's existing constellation of elements. Rammstein has also used its album covers to support its elemental imagery, with the run of albums from *Mutter* to *Rosenrot* each having cover art which gives an indication of the dominant element inside each cover. Only with *Liebe ist für Alle Da*, a departure for the band in many ways, does Rammstein cease this practice.

Despite the infamy which Rammstein has earned for its fiery performance, fire does not dominate the elemental imagery in the song texts and other aspects of the band's work. Rammstein does use fire imagery in many of its songs — and indeed, some of its most famous songs — yet on one album, *Reise, Reise*, fire is the least used of the four elements. Water appears more often and more prominently than fire on almost every album, and is by far the most dominant element in Rammstein's texts to date.

Any number of reasons exist why the fire so evident onstage is not mirrored in the lyrics. The sheer amount of fire the band so regularly faces may work against the need for this element to dominate in the actual songs. Also, one must consider that Lindemann's background — training for years to develop into an Olympic-caliber swimmer — could explain the surprising dominance of water in Rammstein's lyrics. Lindemann has also stated that he works on texts while swimming (Haack et al), which could also influence their contents. Lindemann offers "Feuer und Wasser" as an example of a song he has composed while swimming (Haack et al), which bears this point out. There exists another clear example where Lindemann's surroundings have influenced his writings: he began work on the text to "Mein Land" at the beach ("Making of Mein Land"), resulting in lyrics which mention both waves and the beach.

Future research should delve into the interplay between water's preeminence in Rammstein's texts and the dominance of fire in their live performance of those texts. Researchers should also consider how the tension between water/fire and text/performance corresponds to other prominent contrasts which inform the band's works. Scholars have already examined Rammstein's play with some of these contrasts, e.g., left-wing and right-wing politics (Weinstein), the Communist past and Capitalist present (Littlejohn and Putnam; Henry and Schicker), and modernism and post-modernism (Robinson), and further observation will surely uncover more.

It is by no means certain that Rammstein will release any new original material. Rumors of the band's dissolution go back several years, well before their greatest hits album *Made in Germany* was released (Kara). Drummer Christoph Schneider, in the "Making of Mein Teil" [part 3 of 3] video, confirms that internal conflicts made breaking up Rammsteina real possibility before their fourth album, 2004's *Reise, Reise*. The pressures of being in a successful band have not diminished over time; Kruspe claimed in late 2009 that he could not at the time imagine going back into the studio with the band after the experiences recording *Liebe ist für Alle Da* (Ewert). Rammstein only recorded one new song for *Made in Germany*, "Mein Land," and this song had been around at least since the time of that previous studio album ("Making of Mein Land"). The single to "Mein Land" furthermore contains the song "Vergiss Uns Nicht" [Don't Forget Us], a title which indicates — or, in the best Rammstein style, teases — that the end is near for the group. If Rammstein does in fact release new material in future, one has to be curious whether the patterns of elemental usage remains relatively consistent with their past work, or whether the band will find new ways to express their clear interest in fire, water, earth and air.

Notes

1. One of the group's two guitarists, Paul Landers, reveals that the band had first come up with "Rammstein-Flugschau" [Rammstein air show] for the band's name before deciding on the shortened version (Hof, 34).

2. "Vorsprung durch Technik" [Advancement through technology], the Volkswagen slogan on which this headline plays, is also quoted by U2 in the title song from their 1993 *Zooropa* album.

3. Due to copyright laws, the author must greatly limit his citation of Rammstein lyrics. As this essay focuses on the more obvious references to the elements, the reader should be able to identify these references while listening to the songs or reading the lyrics.

4. Like its English counterpart, *Himmel* carries the double meaning of (Judeo-Christian) "paradise" as well as "sky."

5. The club scene from *From Dusk Till Dawn*, the film written by and co-starring Quentin Tarantino, clearly serves as the model for this video's setting. The video for *Sehnsucht's* other best-selling single, "Du Hast," is similarly a take on Tarantino's *Reservoir Dogs*.

6. The lyrics mention the titular model drinking sparkling wine "*Sekt*" [sparkling wine]. One could argue that sparkling wine represents water in this song, because it is a liquid. In the author's opinion, however, this should lie outside the narrow boundaries of this present paper, which for clarity's sake focuses on the most basic or obvious elemental images.

7. "Stripped" has only appeared on some special/limited editions of *Sehnsucht*. It also shows up on the Depeche Mode compilation *For the Masses*.

8. The single did not sell that well, especially in contrast to the band's previous run of successes, until the video caught the attention of the public and the media (Weinstein, 133).

9. Original title: *Die Macht der Bilder: Leni Riefenstahl*.

10. There were two German children's Sandman programs during the Cold War: West German television had *Das Sandmännchen*, while East Germany produced *Unser Sandmännchen* [Our Little Sandman]. Though Rammstein come from the former East Germany,

they use the opening from the West German program. This is doubly notable inasmuch as the East German Sandmännchen proved more popular. West Germans, who could receive both East and West German stations, often chose *Unser Sandmännchen*, and indeed, it was the East German version of the show which survived the Reunification. (Martin, 42). It is still running today.

The use of the less popular West German Sandmännchen may shine a new light on the "Ostalgie" element in Rammstein's work noted by scholars such as Adelt and Littlejohn and Putnam. Ostalgie refers to the nostalgia — often for consumer goods no longer available — many former East Germans experienced after the Reunification. Rammstein's quotation of the West German Sandmännchen emphasizes a rare counterpoint of Ostalgie: here, the popularity of the East German Sandmännchen drove the other out of existence, just as many Western food, drinks, and car brands, for instance, soon eradicated their East German counterparts.

11. The sandman is mythological figure who brings children sweet dreams with his magical sand. The sandman has been immortalized in literature by E.T.A. Hoffmann, and in song ("Mr. Sandman") by The Chordettes. A character with the name of the Sandman has appeared in comic strips and in the movies as a villain for Spiderman, while a version of the mythical sandman appeared in a KIA commercial in 2012. Die Prinzen, a band which, like Rammstein, was comprised of former East Germans, produced a song entitled "Sandmännchen" in the 1990s.

12. Similar to the sparkling wine of "Das Modell," one could argue that, as a liquid, Coca-Cola represents the element water in this song. The author of this paper contends that Coca-Cola, like sparkling wine, lies outside the narrow parameters of this paper, particularly as the band is pointing out Coca-Cola more as a brand than as an actual drink.

13. The song "Mein Teil" [my part/penis] refers to an actual incident in Germany in which Armin Meiwes ate and killed Bernd Brandes, whom he met through an internet ad Meiwes had placed. Meiwes' actions were done with Brandes' consent. While Brandes was still alive, Meiwes cut off the other's penis and the two men tried, unsuccessfully, to eat it (hence the name of Rammstein's song). Meiwes soon thereafter killed Brandes. He was initially convicted of of manslaughter and later received a life sentence for murder.

14. Littlejohn and Putnam note a less explicit, but still palpable, connection to "Erlkönig" in the song "Amerika," another track on the *Reise, Reise* album (39).

15. The picture of the two people standing next to the ship also proves reminiscent of the video for "Seemann," where the ship stands lodged in sand while band members attempt to pull it.

16. Several of the songs on *Rosenrot* were written for *Reise, Reise*, and the album was initially to be called *Reise, Reise vol. 2* (Williams, "Reise").

17. In the song "Spring," from *Rosenrot*, another character contemplates jumping to his death, in this instance from the top of a bridge. Both jumpers are doomed: in the "Benzin" video the safety net rips after he jumps, the jumper in "Spring" is pushed off the bridge after deciding to climb down.

18. Like "Erlkönig," "Heidenröslein" has been set to music by Schubert and many other composers.

19. This fairy tale is different from the "Schneewittchen" [Snow White] tale with which most Americans are familiar, and which Rammstein used as a basis for their video to "Sonne."

20. Other English titles for this story include "The Dreadful Story about Harriet and the Matches" and "The Tragic Tale of Pauline."

21. In concert, keyboardist Flake Lorenz or bassist Ollie Riedel climbs into a raft and floats across the audience. This novel take on crowd surfing sharpens the image of the audience as a body of water in contrast to the fire onstage.

22. Quotations from the songs "Ohne dich" and "Seemann" also appear on bouquets.

Works Cited

Adelt, Ulrich. "Ich bin der Rock'n'Roll Übermensch: Globalization and Localization in German Music Television." *Popular Music and Society* 28, no. 3 (July 2005): 279–295.

Berlinski, Claire. "Rammstein's Rage." *Azure: Ideas for the Jewish Nation* 20 (Spring 2005): 63–96.

Burns, Robert G.H. "German Symbolism in Rock Music: National Signification in the Imagery and Songs of Rammstein." *Popular Music* 27, no. 3 (October 2008): 457–472.

Cole, Paul. "Rammstein: Vorsprung durch Pyrotechnik NEC Arena." *Sunday Mercury* 17 July 2005: 5. http://www.lexisnexis.com/lnacui2api/api/version1/getDocCui?lni=4GNJ-9CR0-00GG-M3GW&csi=167742&hl=t&hv=t&hnsd=f&hns=t&hgn=t&oc=00240&perma=true (accessed August 6, 2012).

Ewert, Laura. "Gitarrist Richard Kruspe: 'Rammstein sind zu schlau, um rechts zu sein.'" *Welt Online* 19 October 2009: [n.p.]. http://www.lexisnexis.com/lnacui2api/api/version1/getDocCui?lni=7X33-X3G1-2SKV-410G&csi=353180&hl=t&hv=t&hnsd=f&hns=t&hgn=t&oc=00240&perma=true (accessed August 6, 2012).

Gerbert, Frank. "Deutschrock: Im Banne der Teutonen." *Focus Magazin* 18 January 1999: 166–168. http://www.lexisnexis.com/lnacui2api/api/version1/getDocCui?lni=3VS1-80T0-009M-T3CN&csi=147879&hl=t&hv=t&hnsd=f&hns=t&hgn=t&oc=00240&perma=true (accessed August 6, 2012).

Haack, Melanie, Robert Dunker and Petra Schurer. "Doppel Interview: Biedermann und Lindemann über Musik und Sport." *Die Welt* 23 November 2009: [n.p.]. http://www.lexisnexis.com/lnacui2api/api/version1/getDocCui?lni=7X58-6VS1-2PFJ-102H&csi=268994&hl=t&hv=t&hnsd=f&hns=t&hgn=t&oc=00240&perma=true (accessed August 6, 2012).

"Having a Blast with Rammstein: German Powerhouse Fills ACC with Pyro, Keeps Tongue in Cheek." *Toronto Star* 10 May 2011: E2. http://www.lexisnexis.com/lnacui2api/api/version1/getDocCui?lni=52TV-N171-DY91-K380&csi=8286&hl=t&hv=t&hnsd=f&hns=t&hgn=t&oc=00240&perma=true (accessed January 8, 2012).

Henry, Nick, and Juliane Schicker. "Heimatsehnsucht: Rammstein and the Search for Cultural Identity." This volume.

Hof, Gerd. *Rammstein.* Berlin: dgv, 2001.

Kara, Scott. "Rammstein: Reise, Reise." *New Zealand Herald* 16 October 2004: [n.p.] http://www.lexisnexis.com/lnacui2api/api/version1/getDocCui?lni=4DJH-P4J0-01K9-43SX&csi=257912&hl=t&hv=t&hnsd=f&hns=t&hgn=t&oc=00240&perma=true (accessed August 6, 2012).

Littlejohn, John T. and Michael T. Putnam. "Rammstein and *Ostalgie*: Longing for Yesteryear." *Popular Music and Society* 33, no. 1 (February 2010): 35–44.

Lüke, Martina. "Modern Classics: Reflections on Rammstein in the German Class." *Die Unterrichtspraxis/Teaching German* 41, no. 1 (Spring 2008): 15–23.

"Making of Benzin." Dir. Bobby Good and Fubbi Karlsson. [n.d.] YouTube. http://www.youtube.com/watch?v=WWk7kVAjxb8 (accessed May 11, 2012).

"Making of Haifisch." Dir. Jürgen Schindler. 2010. YouTube. http://www.youtube.com/watch?v=5UqbPDUgcU0 (accessed May 11, 2012).

"Making of Mein Land." Dir. Jürgen Schindler. 2011. YouTube. http://www.youtube.com/watch?v=Vj5VUl7FYb0&feature=fvsr (accessed May 11, 2012).

"Making of Mein Teil [part 2 of 3]." [n.d.] YouTube. http://www.youtube.com/watch?v=gOhEI3sxfQs&feature=relmfu (accessed May 12, 2012).

"Making of Mein Teil [part 3 of 3]." [n.d.] YouTube. http://www.youtube.com/watch?v=3Q5syWZqC74&NR=1&feature=endscreen (accessed May 11, 2012).

"Making of Mutter." Dir. Jürgen Schindler. 2011. YouTube. http://www.youtube.com/watch?v=ASI-TNKJdog (accessed May 11, 2012).

Marshall, Clay. "Germany's Rammstein Hopes 'Mutter' Helps Cross Borders via Republic." *Billboard* 14 April 2001. http://www.lexisnexis.com/lnacui2api/api/version1/getDoc Cui?lni=42SP-HGR0-00T0-B3MK&csi=5545&hl=t&hv=t&hnsd=f&hns= t&hgn=t&oc=00240&perma=true (accessed August 6, 2012).

Martin, Terry. "Sandman's Success Transcends Politics." *Europe* (July/August 2001): 41–42.

Pearson, Beth. "Twisted Firestarters Rammstein." *Herald (Glasgow)* 14 July 2005: 6. http://www.lexisnexis.com/lnacui2api/api/version1/getDocCui?lni=4GMG-V740-TWTX-52JS&csi=142728&hl=t&hv=t&hnsd=f&hns=t&hgn=t&oc= 00240&perma=true (accessed August 6, 2012).

Raihala, Ross. "Rammstein Fires up the Target Center — Literally." *St. Paul Pioneer Press (Minnesota)* 7 May 2012: [n.p.]. http://www.lexisnexis.com/lnacui2api/api/version1/get DocCui?lni=55KP-PK61-DYT4-V549&csi=313961&hl=t&hv=t&hnsd= f&hns=t&hgn=t&oc=00240&perma=true (accessed August 6, 2012).

Ratliff, Ben. "Beware of Flaming Germans." *New York Times* 8 May 1998, late ed.: E24. http://www.lexisnexis.com/lnacui2api/api/version1/getDocCui?lni=3SMX-DR70-007F-G31H&csi=6742&hl=t&hv=t&hnsd=f&hns=t&hgn=t&oc=00240&perma=true (accessed August 6, 2012).

Robinson, David A. "Metamodernist Form, 'Reader-Response,' and the Politics of Rammstein: What Rammstein Means When You Don't Understand the Lyrics." This volume.

Weinstein, Valerie. "Reading Rammstein, Remembering Riefenstahl: 'Fascist Aesthetics' and German Popular Culture." In *Riefenstahl Screened: An Anthology of New Criticism*, edited by Neil Christian Pages, Mary Rhiel, and Ingeborg Majer-O'Sickey, 130–148. New York: Continuum, 2008.

Williams, Jeremy. "What does 'Mein Herz brennt' have to do with Das Sandmännchen?" Herzeleid.com. http://herzeleid.com/en/faq/mutter#faq4 (accessed February 26, 2012).

Williams, Jeremy. "Reise, Reise (Vol. 2)." Herzeleid.com. http://herzeleid.com/en/news /*/archive/2005-06 (accessed March 12, 2012).

Discography

Rammstein. "Das Modell." *Das Modell*. Motor. CD. 1997.

_____. *Herzeleid*. Slash. CD. 1995.

_____. *Liebe ist für Alle Da*. Vagrant. CD. 2009.

_____. "Mein Land." *Made in Germany 1995–2011*. Universal. CD. 2011.

_____. *Mutter*. Republic. CD. 2001.

_____. *Reise, Reise*. Republic. CD. 2004.

_____. *Rosenrot*. Republic. CD. 2006.

_____. *Sehnsucht*. Slash. CD. 1997.

_____. "Stripped." *For The Masses*. Various Artists. A&M. CD. 1998.

Videography

Rammstein. "Benzin." 2005. iTunes (accessed March 11, 2012).

_____. "Du hast." 1997. iTunes (accessed May 14, 2012).

_____. "Engel." 1997. iTunes (accessed February 26, 2012).

_____. "Mein Land." 2011. iTunes (accessed April 6, 2012).

_____. "Mein Teil." 2004. iTunes (accessed March 4, 2012).

_____. "Mutter." 2002. iTunes (accessed March 1, 2012).

_____. "Rosenrot." 2005. iTunes (accessed March 13, 2012).

_____. "Seemann." 1996. iTunes (accessed February 26, 2012).

_____. "Sonne." 2001. iTunes (accessed February 26, 2012).

13

Discipleship in the
Church of Rammstein[1]

MICHAEL T. PUTNAM

According to their own admission, the band members of Rammstein are self-proclaimed agnostics (if not full blown atheists) when it comes to religious beliefs. Consider the following comments by band members Flake and Paul on the topic of religion in an interview that took place in 2001 (*http://www. rammsteinniccage.com/media/interviews/rammcomjan01en.html*):

FLAKE: I disapprove of religions which are made into rigid institutions. I also think that religious fanaticism and missionary work are dangerous.

PAUL: I am not really concerned with religion and believe more in ourselves.

In spite of these comments, the lyrics and videos of Rammstein's entire catalogue of music are rife with allusions to angels, the afterlife, ritual, and religious ceremony. The prime aim of this essay is to attempt to shed some light on these persistent motifs in Rammstein's music. To address this complex topic, I provide a novel sketch of what discipleship in the Church of Rammstein would entail, i.e., would there be some sort of loose creed and accompanying doctrine that we should adhere to? In spite of Flake and Paul's comments to the contrary, and perhaps beyond their own recognition, the role of religious belief, motif, and ritual in the music and videos of Rammstein opens a fascinating realm of their identity that, at least to the best of my knowledge, has been unexposed and under-researched until now. Given that this topic is virgin territory, my humble goal here is to scratch the surface of this interesting theme while raising pertinent questions that will guide future explorations on this subject. This caveat notwithstanding, what I hope to show in this essay is that once again the views of the band members towards "religion" are directly impacted by their East German heritage (see e.g., Bettendorf, Littlejohn & Putnam, Henry & Schicker). What emerges from this discussion is the observation that although Rammstein's distrust of and disdain for totalitarian institutions (such as the former socialist German Democratic Republic (hereafter GDR), where the church functioned as a centerpiece of refuge and revolution against the ruling party of the GDR, the *Sozialistische Einheitspartei Deutschlands* [SED]) undoubtedly shapes their negative view of "religions which are made into rigid institutions," there remains not only an acknowledgement that life beyond the veil of death is not only a possibility, but also the responsibility of exploring exactly what this post-mortem existence consists of. As one might expect, although there is a recognition of the possibility of some form of afterlife, it isn't necessarily the rosy paradisiacal end that is promised in Judeo-Christian tradition. Rather, the references to angels and spiritual belief handed down to us by Rammstein's "canon of scripture" (i.e, their music and videos) paints a picture for disciples like us of an afterlife where we long to be mortal once again. As I will discuss throughout this paper, this view of the afterlife is also shared by a strong tradition of philosophers such as Nietzsche, Voltaire, Hume, Lucretius, Socrates, and Xenophanes, as well as modern German cultural and literary movements (as pointed out by Fosl).

Equipped with this preliminary background, the remainder of this essay discusses and critiques these religious motifs present in Rammstein's canon of scripture, providing both fan and scholar alike with an ancillary background on this topic to arrive at a better understanding of what the afterlife holds for us according to the Church of Rammstein. Following the suggestion of Irwin in his enlightening study of Metallica's religious references, although both Rammstein and Metallica appear at first glance to reject traditional Judeo-Christian values, it appears that both of these bands have moved closer towards embracing a belief system that resembles Buddhism in some respects. As I will discuss in this essay, however, although Rammstein has some tangential connection with contemporary Buddhist beliefs, there are some pronounced areas where this system is incompatible with what is found in Rammstein's canon. Fosl (2007) also points out that what is commonly interpreted as immoral from a Judeo-Christian perspective can, and in many instances, should be viewed as moral outside of the "slave mentality" (à la Nietzsche) that abounds in this religious tradition. With numerous references to sadomasochism, incest, necrophilia and other alleged "taboo" topics in Western culture, it appears that Rammstein is once again just attempting to engage in some form of shock therapy. This, unfortunately, represents an easy way out and fails to acknowledge the depth and craft of Rammstein's overall message regarding societal norms and religious belief. These actions are a result of the human condition of desire, and, as the second tenet of Buddhism instructs us, "all desire leads to suffering" (Irwin, 26).

In what remains, I will attempt to provide working answers to the following questions, which will shape the content and structure of this essay:

Q1: What is the nature of deity in the canon of Rammstein? What disposition do these figures have? Can a deity capable of saving the human race be established?

Q2: What role do angelic entities play in the canon of Rammstein?

Q3: What role do religious rituals (such as marriage) and institutions (formal churches and religious institutions) play here?

Q4: To what extent can we project that religious motifs in the canon of Rammstein are (directly) affected by their (East) German background?

The result of this query into the doctrines and beliefs of the Church of Rammstein reveals a complex system that provides as many questions as it does answers. Rammstein's failure to merely conform to societal norms and to continually question all aspects of our existence — even our existence beyond the grave — leads to enlightenment, similar in many respects to the philosophical work of Nietzsche in this regard.

Don't F*ck with Deity — It Will Kick Your Ass

First things first; in any sort of church or structured belief system, we need to have a clear understanding of the figure(s) that we are subordinate to in a traditional Judeo-Christian belief system. Simply put, who is our God in this system, what ontological attributes does he/she/it/they possess, and what is our relationship to this/these entity(ies)? In the song "Bestrafe mich" (punish me), we receive our first clues as to the nature of our relationship with deity. As could be expected, it's a pretty one-sided affair. The allusion to prayers and various Bible verses show that individuals are rendered powerless to the wills and whims of a distant, disconnected deity. The lyrics seem to indicate that the sheer size and power of this deity imposed majesty and dominion upon mere mortals. In this respect, Rammstein makes the allusion that the relationship between deity and its subordinate creatures strongly resembles a sadomasochist hierarchical relationship between the dominator (God) and the dominated (mortals). As a matter of fact, the deity is rendered a rather sinister disposition in the inversion of the Bible verse found in Job 1:21, where we are instructed that the "the Lord giveth, and the Lord taketh away." In "Bestrafe mich," we see a God who takes pleasure in taking first and giving later (on his/her terms, of course) and only providing to those whom he (God) loves.[2] A similar uneven relationship can be seen in the video to "Sonne," where the band (portrayed as dwarfs) await the return of Snow White. In many respects, Snow White represents some form of deity in this video, given her golden appearance and the cadaver-like, unyielding obedience on the part of the dwarfs towards Snow White. She beats them and has relegated them to the role of slaves. Upon the death of Snow White, the dwarfs appear to have lost all sense of belonging and identity, unsure of their raison d'être from this moment forward. In sum, God in this system is not someone to fuck with, and, in some respects, represents a very Old Testament vengeful God that wrought pestilence and plagues upon those who would not succumb to his power and majesty.[3]

The New Testament ushered in a different view of the Judeo-Christian God, one where God so loved mankind that he provided His Only Begotten Son as a sacrifice to reconcile sinful man with Himself (John 3:16). Rammstein seems to acknowledge the potential existence of a Savior/Christ-figure in the song "Asche zu Asche" (ashes to ashes) to the extent that death, crucifixion, and resurrection are mentioned in this song. The version of Rammstein's Savior is one who returns ten days after his resurrection seeking revenge on those who performed this heinous act. This Savior does not waste time hunting down these wrongdoers and bringing them to justice. In this respect, it is difficult to find any sort of notion of reconciliation (and sin for that matter) in this portrayal of Rammstein's Savior. What is present, however, is the notion of an afterlife and some form of resurrection — something that one would not expect from a purely atheist interpretation of religion. In this regard, Rammstein's Savior in some respects resembles some of the warrior attributes found in the heroic epic poem *The Heiland*.

In spite of this warrior image of a Savior embraced in Rammstein's lyrics, the concept of salvation (Erlösung) does play a prominent role in the song "Alter Mann" (old man). The song is somewhat out of character when compared with most songs in Rammstein's canon, involving a complex allegory involving a young man, an older man, water, and a fan. One possible interpretation of this allegory takes on a strong traditional Judeo-Christian understanding of wisdom and salvation:[4] The water can be understood as the souls of men, with the younger man unaware of the impact of his deeds (thus a tangential reference to some form of sin?). The old man represents God and His Wisdom; i.e., he is omnipotent. The "fan" which the old man possesses is some form of Holy Writ (perhaps the Bible?). The old man knows how to calm the waters with his fan, which is a symbol of his wisdom and omnipotence. At first, the young man does not comprehend the power and wisdom of the old man and throws rocks across the water, thus disrupting the harmony of the water. The old man provides sound advice to the young man, and even delivers council to him from beyond the grave. Although the old man passes away, his "wisdom" lives on to the extent that the young man now possesses the wisdom and the ability to calm the waters with the aid of the fan (again, likely some form of Holy Writ). It is here that the concept of salvation (Erlösung) is referenced, however, it remains unclear exactly what sort of "salvation" is to be understood in this context. Two possibilities come to the forefront: One reading of this passage sees the young man hoping for the eventual release/salvation from the trials and tribulations of this life. Although such an interpretation is indeed possible, as we shall see in our discussion regarding the role of angels in Rammstein's canon, it appears that upon death, we (assuming we return as angels or some other creatures) will dearly miss our probationary mortal existence. Therefore, although a desire for a release from some of the temporal trials and tribulations of mortality is indeed a licit possible interpretation here, it remains highly unlikely that the release sought here is a request to end one's mortal state altogether.

A second interpretation is more likely here, one in which the young man wishes for a caring God and an afterlife that might exist, but tragically does not. Such a view is reminiscent of Metallica's "The God That Failed," a song in which the desire for the loving Judeo-Christian God is abandoned. As pointed out by Fosl, even if we buy into this "God is dead" ideology, we still have the desire to fill this void "like addicts suffering from withdraw" (81). Unable to find value in mortal existence, we construct a culture of fear and death, which is prevalent not only in rock music, but also can easily be found whenever we watch the 6 o'clock news. It is important to realize at this juncture, that we are not dealing with any outright rejection of God or Judeo-Christian values here; the apparent message here is an expression of sadness lamenting the failure of this God and a sincere hope that He who embodies hope and salvation were true. This viewpoint expresses something much deeper than a cheap cynical version of nihilism; it's an expression of a sincere hope for something that (unfortunately in the eyes of Rammstein) doesn't exist. In other words, even if we kill God, this doesn't necessarily make our lives any easier.

What have we learned thus far about the ontology of Deity and its attributes? What we have at hand is a complicated, and in some respects, paradoxical depiction of Deity. On the one hand, we see a God who is vengeful and outright neglects the needs of those who depend on His very existence. It is difficult to envisage any form of sin and necessity of salvation in this system. From another perspective, we must cope with a version of Deity that is a sage mentor that can teach us the way to "calm the waters" of life if we will listen and harken to His council. In this respect, the role and attributes of Deity in this system are quite complex, although, it appears that there is an expression of a sincere hope for things that might/could be (but likely do not exist) and the hope for the existence of a wise Deity who can grant some form of salvation either in this life or the next. It is important to mention here that in this discussion of Deity we are still without any mentioning of institutional religion, which leads us to conjecture that if some version of God is found to exist, he likely will not be found in any man-made institutions.

Being an Angel Ain't Everything It's Cracked Up to Be

After attempting to come to grips with the Deity that holds power over us, the next question involves our post-mortem fate; i.e., what happens to us after we die? For all intents and purposes, it appears that we either become angels or "something else" (although it isn't quite clear exactly what "something else" is). In the canon of Rammstein we are once again confronted with an image of angels that is somewhat contradictory to what we would commonly expect approaching angels from a traditional Judeo-Christian perspective. Perhaps in no song is this more prevalent than "Engel" (angel), which involves a narrator describing the conditions of existence of angels as well as the angels themselves expressing fear and loneliness. Although it is generally considered to be a "reward" to become an angel upon the successfully completion of our mortal sojourn, things aren't as wonderful as advertised. The angels in this song are virtually powerless; they exist completely removed from other forms of life and their existence is masked by clouds. Their very ability to move is hampered as they must crawl on the stars to keep from falling. Even worse, they profess that they are alone and live in a constant state of fear. The narrator's proclamation that he never wants to become an angel is a telling one; it is an acknowledgement of life after death, but it simultaneously expresses a desire to continue to exist on one's own terms. The transition from life to death is an unavoidable event that all mortals must pass through; however, why must we exist as angel in a constant state of fear, removed from those we love and the experiences that have shaped us thus far in our existence? The narrator challenges God to allow him to exist in the afterlife on his terms.

This less-than-glorious image of angels and their role in the afterlife is reminiscent to the depiction of angels in director Wim Wenders' 1987 film *Der Himmel über Berlin* (Wings of Desire). The central theme of the film revolves around two immortal angels, Damiel and Cassiel, who populate West Berlin, listening to the thoughts of humans and comforting those in need. Although the film exists as a mediation on the city of Berlin's past, present, and future, these angels exist to "assemble, testify, and preserve" reality. They exist, yet they do not live. They merely "assemble, testify, and preserve" and are not supposed to intermingle with human inhabitants. A subplot of the film involves the character Peter Falk, a filmmaker, who was once an angel who grew tired of always observing and never experiencing. Falk renounced his immortality to join the ranks of those he once only observed. Damiel follows this same path of Peter Falk, renouncing his immortality and is able to bleed, see colors, and enjoy food and drink coffee. Cassiel, who remains an angel, fails in an attempt to prevent a young man from committing suicide from jumping from a tall building; he is haunted by his failure to stop this tragedy. The angels in Rammstein's "Engel" as well as Wenders' *Der Himmel über Berlin* bear a striking resemblance to one another; in both of these works angelic creatures envy their mortal counterparts and long to become one of them (once again). In Wenders' film, whereas Damiel's new found mortality is celebrated, Cassiel must face the eternal punishment of failure in saving the man from attempting suicide. As pointed out by Adney (this volume), this "twisting of the glorious and profane" is also found in the video for "Mein Teil" (my part), where Till Lindemann receives oral sex from an angelic figure. One can interpret this scene as a desire on the part of the angel to once again engage in sexual acts. In all of these works, the powers and privileges of angels are severely limited. These beings are not to be envied, but rather pitied, because they have been sentenced to an eternal prison sentence where they must watch existence pass them by, yet they are unable to participate and to feel.

It is unclear exactly what angels do and who becomes an angel in the canon of Rammstein. For instance, consider the account of angels in the song "Spieluhr" (music box). The lyrics focus on a deceased young girl who continues to sing the chorus of a familiar child's song from beyond the grave ("Hoppe, hoppe, Reiter"). Here we are told that she does not transform into an angel from the grave and that the only element that could be construed as "tears" on the gravesite are nothing more than rain. Again, although there seems to be confirmation of life beyond the grave (since the child is still singing), she does not become an angel nor is there any angel present at her gravesite. Due to their limited power and depressing existence, perhaps we should consider it a happy ending that the girl continues to exist as a non-angel. Finally, it is unclear to what extent angels function in the role as some sort of guardian figure that can protect mankind. Case in point, consider the song "Morgenstern" (morning star) where the protagonist expresses the hope for a caring God and one of His angels for guidance and protection. In the next verse, we learn that this wish remains unfulfilled as she goes off alone into the night.

Finally, in "Der Meister" (the master), the protagonist sings from the perspective of an apocalyptic messenger pronouncing imminent doom on the inhabitants of the earth. They have been commissioned by "the master" himself to deliver this proclamation of doom and they are unable to avenge humankind. Although it is clearly more acceptable to be an angel announcing doom and despair rather than one that merely observes and reports like a mall security guard, angels are nothing more than foot soldiers and carrier pigeons to this all-powerful Deity who calls all of the shots. In addition to this apocalyptic message, an additional stipulation included in this proclamation is that there are no angels available to avenge mankind at this hour of tribulation. Angels come in different shapes and sizes and obviously have different roles and responsibilities, but the fact that any sort of avenging angels are completely void here is quite telling.[5]

Although it clearly is highly undesirable to become an angel robbed of all of the awesome experiences that one participates in during one's mortal existence, there's something more at stake here than a depressing tale of "being an angel really, really sucks." Two fundamental aspects of the "belief system"— doctrine, if you will — of the Church of Rammstein come to the forefront here: First, similar to Nietzsche and Marx, there is a call for the abandonment of any sort of "slave morality" found in Christianity. This rejection of Christian virtue and value can be seen in Rammstein's depiction of a Savior-figure in "Asche zu Asche," but it shines through most clearly in their negative description of angels. Secondly, and related to the first point, is the blatant defiance of accepting the role of a passive angel at the conclusion of one's life. In "Engel," the denouncement of wanting to be any sort of underling that lives in constant fear and isolation is boldly set forth. Rammstein calls for a revolution on the part of us, as mortals, against the tyranny of Deity who forces us into these servant roles once we pass on. In this respect, Rammstein wants to renegotiate our contract with God, the punisher and dominator.

Rammstein's coming to grips with the relationship between God and humankind is not unique in German-speaking art and culture. In her excellent dissertation, Kita (2011) explores the meaning of art and religion in fin-de-siècle Vienna through the symphonies of the composer Gustav Mahler (1860–1911) and the philosophical and dramatic works of the poet Siegfried Lipiner (1856–1911). Lipiner's translation of Mickiewicz's *Todtenfeier* (celebration of the dead), completed in 1887, and his publication of *Der entfesselte Prometheus* (the unleashed Prometheus) in 1877 relay parallel stories of heroes (Prometheus and Konrad respectively) who are "both heroic characters that see themselves as possessing creative powers rivaling those of God" (Kita, 70). Both heroes challenge God, whom they revere as a tyrannical dictator, who, like the angels in Rammstein's "Engel," remains distant and disconnected from his creations. For example, in Todtenfeier, Konrad insults God by comparing him to the foreign rulers of Poland during the time Mickiewicz original wrote this work, "Dass du der Vater nicht der Welt, dass du ihr — Zar!" (Mickiewicz, 152).[6] Taken together, both of the heroes in these works are figures who demand more from their Gods and confront them directly (although they admittedly eventually succumb to the Will of God and become martyrs for the sake of their people). In chapter 4 of her dissertation, Kita discusses the "redemption" of the Volk — which focuses more on bringing our earthly existence closer in line with any sort of celestial existence that may exist (which contrasts with Wagner's contemporary work in the 19th century).

It comes as little surprise that Mahler, Lipiner, and Mickiewicz were ardent scholars of Nietzsche's writings. In many respects, one could issue the same reproach to Rammstein with respect to their abandonment of the "slave morality" of Christian doctrine and ethics. Although it is a bit of a stretch to assert that Rammstein overtly portrays Christianity and organized religion in general as "the opium of the people" in a Marxian sense, the portrayal of angels in such a negative light as slaves to an oppressive Deity at the very least signifies that the value system in Judeo-Christian tradition is flawed. As pointed out by Fosl (74), what is morally "good" is actually "corrupt"; i.e., truth is really deceit, which is a philosophical view that goes back to philosophers such as Voltaire, Hume, Lucretius, Socrates, and Xenophanes. Fosl comments further on how Christianity and its structure of virtue (embedded in its notion of "sin") eventually lead to an enslavement of its followers:

> But it wasn't nearly enough for early Christians simply to defy Roman rule. They also produced their own distinctive way of ruling, of exerting power over others. Perhaps the move effective way Christians exerted their power was by collecting the faithful into a docile "herd" through the idea that we all carry internal debt called "sin." Having convinced people of this, Christian priests proclaimed that they alone could forgive the debt, that only through the authority of their religion could human beings find consolation and salvation (John 14:6, 10:9). It was a wildly successful technique [75].

This worldview leads to a complete devaluation of the present transient world in which we currently reside. Christianity in this respect leads to nihilism, as explained by Fosl:

> It's bad that everything changes, that nothing lasts forever, and that we die. It's bad that we must labor and struggle and exert ourselves in contests of power. It's bad that we don't know everything and that people hold different opinions and values. In place of this inferior world, the Christian-Platonic tradition promises a better, transcendent world beyond it [79].

Rammstein falls prey to this in their portrayal and, in some respects, the celebration of morbid and tragic aspects of human existence; however, in light of this current discussion, it would seem that tragic and grotesque elements in their lyrics and videos are as much a result of this nihilist state of mind than anything else. Just like everyone else, Rammstein is looking to fill this incredible void when one discovers that their God is truly dead (à la Nietzsche). This interpretation brings a new, ambiguous meaning to the title of their second album, *Sehnsucht* (desire, longing), which can now be seen as a longing not only for understanding our temporal condition, but also our eternal destiny. Although it remains unclear whether or not there is some form of an afterlife in the Church of Rammstein, it does appear from the evidence discussed in this essay that we are admonished to make the most of our lives in the present, and that we should hope for a renegotiation of the terms of our role in the Kingdom of God after this life. This view is in line with Mahler's 2nd and 4th symphonies, particularly the latter where he suggests that life after death is very similar to life before death, where human life in heaven appears to be quite similar to life on earth; where food, drink, and the simple joys of life are maintained (see e.g., especially stanzas 2–4) (Niekerk, 120).[7] Martha Nussbaum elaborates further on the 5th movement, stating that the portrayal of the hereafter is "distinctively [the] Jewish picture of [the] afterlife" in that it "mirrors Judaism's insistence on finding the worth and meaning of a life within history in its choices and striving in this life" (Niekerk, 97). Worth and meaning and existence are confined to the here and now; and have eternal consequences in the afterlife.

Are You Sure You Want to Get Married?

As is customary in Rammstein's lyrics and videos, large-scale institutions that enforce their own moral code on the masses are to be feared and abhorred and, if at all possible, destroyed. When it comes to religious institutions, it comes as little surprise that Rammstein openly mocks them in their music. For example, in the videos for "Haifisch" (shark) and "Hallelujah" we observe direct criticism of organized religion. In the video for "Hallelujah," we see an overt rejection of the church as a holy institution with pious clergy. Here we see a priest, who, representing an institution, represents an abuse of power and trust of those whom he shepherds, which is present in the lyrics with the ambiguous use of the verb *drehen* "to turn" (i.e., in the sense of turning one's back on someone) in the first verse. In other words, hypocrisy in these institutions abounds, which is omnipresent in Rammstein's music declaring an inevitable distrust in hierarchical institutions. Although this does not appear at first glance to be anything new and is something we should come to expect, the question remains whether large-scale institutions serve any (positive) function in the Church of Rammstein. In other words, even though hypocrisy reigns in organized religion, are all-encompassing institutions and dogmatic rules still to some extent a necessary evil? In an attempt to arrive at a working answer to this puzzling question, let's take a closer look at the role of ritual—in particular, marriage—in the canon of Rammstein. The lyrics to "Heirate Mich" (Marry Me) and "Du Hast" (You Have) immediately come to mind. In "Heirate mich," we are invited into the psyche of a lonely widower who is driven to the brink of insanity after losing his beloved wife. His continued devotion is unwavering (he spends every night sleeping by her tombstone), which establishes the deep level of commitment on the part of this man and the solemnity of the ritual (sacrament?) of marriage. In the second verse of the song, the widower gives in to his carnal desires and has sex with his wife's corpse, which is accompanied with graphic images of her skin ripping like paper. His love for this woman transcends beyond the grave, but his carnal desire to unite with her physically once again does not quench his insanity, for at the end of the song he decapitates a rooster who announces the break of a new day. The killing of the rooster perhaps embodies an ambiguous expression of disappointment on the part of the protagonist; on the one hand the rooster announces the end of the night, which is the time that he can be close to his beloved. At the same time, the announcement of the break of a new day reveals the destruction (and desecration) of his bride's corpse. In "Du Hast," we are confronted with wedding vows in the chorus and the strong negative reaction of the protagonist are a clear indication of the severity of these vows in this life. After all, if this were not the case, why would they go to such lengths to make such a big deal about marriage?

The institution of marriage and its demands of an unwavering commitment to one's partner seems to be an undisputed truth in the Church of Rammstein. The *Nein!*-cry of the protagonist in "Du Hast" as well as the lyrics of "Stein um Stein" (Stone upon Stone) relay a sense of being trapped through marriage. It appears as if there is no escape from this institution, which due to the fact that it is mandated through a larger centralized institution (i.e., organized religion), should be distrusted. The lyrics to "Stein um Stein" tell the story of a man who is trapped within a structure that is being built around him "stone upon stone."[8] Although they are mum on the facts regarding who can officiate the ceremony/ritual and whether or not anything of this nature is required in the first place, the emotional commitment of two united souls transcends the grave. It is here that we see traces of Buddhist thought in Rammstein's treatment of marriage, for, as pointed out by Irwin (26), that in Buddhism carnal craving and desire are at the heart of all human suffering. Buddhism denies the existence of any gods and the eternal nature of the soul; Buddha himself focused on achieving enlightenment and Nirvana in this life. In this respect, we must be like Nietzsche's Zarathustra and "stay true to the earth," living life for the here and now. Of course, here we see only tendencies towards Buddhist thought, because up to this point Rammstein has not openly embraced the message of compassion, ego deflation, and acceptance that can bring about this freedom from suffering. At this point, there is simply an acknowledgement that carnal desire is the root of most (if not all) problems. Rammstein issues us this warning in the title track of this debut album *Herzeleid* (heartache). Here we are warned that even if we are united (in marriage), one day our many years together will seem like mere minutes; i.e., all true love ends in heartache and despair (see also Lüke this volume). This nihilistic outcry embodies the yearning and desire to enjoy life to its fullest while we can, but at the same time it expresses the ultimate disappointment that one day it will all end.

A Product of Their Own Environment (Again)

A recurrent theme in the academic literature on Rammstein is how their East German heritage has played a substantial role in shaping the context of their lyrics and on stage performances (see e.g., especially previous work by Bettendorf, Littlejohn & Putnam, and Henry & Schicker). Their strong distrust and adamant fear of oppressive governing systems (as was in place in the former GDR) can easily be transferred to their views of clergy and religious doctrine and dogma that leads to any form of fanaticism. In many respects, Rammstein appears to once again harken back to the council of Nietzsche's Zarathustra, especially concerning his "transvaluation of all values." The notion of focusing your efforts on this life (for the sake of the welfare and prosperity of the State) clearly finds roots in socialist East German rhetoric. Once again we see a celebration of "dead" Christian morals that don't advance society or the well-being of individuals. "God" in this context is similar to the "God" described in "Bestrafe mich," who can freely give and take as it pleases. Subordination is imminent under these conditions. Rammstein's key message here — from a temporal and a spiritual sense — is to avoid enslavement from oppressive systems (be they governments, organized religions, or marriage) that prevent one from experiencing life to its fullest. Similar to Tool's "Lateralus," which commissions us to expand our boundaries of knowledge and experience and to simply "spiral out," Rammstein's use of militaristic and sadomasochist themes serve as a quasi-warning to all of us; this is the fate that awaits us if we engage in blind faith in oppressive systems. The key doctrine of the Church of Rammstein is one of enlightenment that loosens the binds of mental, physical, and spiritual slavery that threatens us all.

Before moving to the conclusion, we must return to the concept of angels once more. Mühlmann's (1999) comprehensive overview of the *Neue Deutsche Härte* (New German Hardness) of which Rammstein was a key member illuminates the fact that many of Rammstein's earliest contemporaries were fascinated with death, angels and, to a slightly lesser extent, deity and (some form of "salvation"). Another contemporary, namely Blixa Bargeld and Einstürzende Neubauten (EN), have a long standing connection with angels and the city of Berlin. Shrayane's (2011) comprehensive study of Blixa Bargeld and EN explores the connection between the destructive character of the angel and its connection with Berlin and EN's music. The purpose of mentioning Shrayane's analysis of EN's treatment of angels is to draw parallels between EN and Rammstein in this work that are difficult to pass over. According to Shrayane, the writings of Walter Benjamin (1892–1940) had a strong influence on their work. For Benjamin, his "ideal Mensch as the Destructive Character is cheerful in the knowledge that everything deserves to perish" (Shrayane, 16–7). Shrayane further explicates that "this Destructive Character must be a new Unmensch" (17), whose task, according to Hanssen is "to bring on the dawning of a new humankind that would prove itself by destruction" (123). As pointed out by Shrayane (18), this shift in values has resulted in a shift of the role that angels play in the afterlife and what their existence represents for the new *Unmensch*: "Through Benjamin's literary intervention, this angel has come to represent the presence of the burden of history and the loss of faith in progress. No longer a messenger of hope, he is a melancholic witness (in a godless age) to man's lost stories 'from the failed French Revolution to the successful mass-murders at Auschwitz.'" Perhaps nowhere is this image more prevalent than in Wim Wenders' *Der Himmel über Berlin*, where Berlin, described as the "worst place in the world," is the place where the angel Damiel renounces his immortality to join the ranks of temporal beings. We are also reminded of the incredible and terrifying burden the angel Cassiel must face due to his inability to prevent a man from committing suicide. According to Shrayane, angels in EN's texts are "initially both challenging children and useless or dead relics; later, there is a sense of hope in renewed flight and an angel's-/bird's-eye view of the land" (20). In "Engel der Vernichtung" (exterminating angel), angels appear as disturbing figures of childhood described as "eingeschlossen in Schlafträume" (locked inside dormitory dreams). Their eventual goal in the song, with the aid of their Angelus Novus, is to abolish God. The characteristics of the angels in EN's "Engel der Vernichtung" are strikingly similar to Rammstein's angels in "Engel."[9] In both of these works,

angels are tortured by the images they can only witness and feel helpless in
not being able to have an effect on the outcome of human events. Their fate,
similar to the man imprisoned in Metallica's "Trapped Under Ice," is one who
is struggling to survive and must reluctantly observe "hell, forevermore."

In chapter 2 of Shrayane's study, she discusses the concept of "divided
music," focusing on the divergent paths that East and West German popular
music developed. Due to the fact that the band members of EN grew up in
West Berlin, the predominant focus is on the development of culture and art
in the Western sector of the city. According to Shrayane, EN's struggle to
develop of sense of identity can be traced to those born after 1945, or *Stunde
Null* (hour zero). Simon Frith (1998) addressed this issue in an editorial in
Popular Music:

> ...there is an important reason why German popular music has to be understood
> differently to popular music elsewhere; twentieth century German history has
> posed German musicians and audiences particular problems of national identity.
> On the other hand, the question has to be asked: what is the relationship of
> popular German music tradition, of the Schlager, to the Nazi period, to
> 'National Socialism,' anti-Semitism and Aryanism?

West Germany, and West Berlin, became a symbol of capitalist decadence,
whereas East Germany, and East Berlin, found its cultural and financial support from the Soviets. In both spheres, the second (and third) generation(s)
of East and West German grew dissatisfied with the delusion of a promised
utopia that never materialized. For EN, it was the architecture of Berlin and
a large scale disregard for the unique history of Berlin embedded in its buildings and landscape that motivated a great deal of their music throughout their
career. Eventually, EN would once again be involved in a movement that criticized the *Rückbau* (re-building) that took (and is unfortunately still taking
place) place in East Berlin during the 2000s. As buildings such as the former
GDR's politburo *Palast der Republik* were set to be demolished and other
buildings (both new and old) of Berlin continued to be discussed and rein-
terpreted for their history and associations, it was often the empty spaces, the
voids and the missing buildings that drew the attention of EN. Here we see
another strong correlation between EN and Rammstein in their disdain for
the reinterpretation of German history—both East and West German history—and the disassociation with the past. As Littlejohn & Putnam (2010)
discuss, the contrast between the songs "Moskau" and "Amerika" show that
Rammstein is still collectively coming to terms with its (East) German past.
The Reunification is in many respects a symbol of a failed utopia, with
reunified Germany still facing many of the issues that also burdened previous
generations.[10] Berlin, as the City of Angels, naturally had an impact on Ramm-

stein's worldview, and it also appears to have played a decisive role in shaping their views of angelic creatures in the afterlife. In this regard, their (East) German heritage did influence their outlook on religion; however, their search for identity, as is/was the case for many former East Germans, is a complex problem that West Germans must also confront in a Reunified Germany. On both sides of the Wall, angels in Berlin lore are creatures to pity rather than worship and respect.

The Church of Rammstein

As shown in this essay, concepts associated with religion (e.g., deity, afterlife, angelic creatures, salvation) in the canon of Rammstein represents an extremely complex system. Be that as it may, at the very least I hope to have scratched the surface on this topic and to have provided some ample food for thought on the subject matter. As far as the Church of Rammstein is concerned, the key doctrine in my view is to live life to its fullest in the here and now, for any sense of "salvation" that can be granted after this life is not what is expected in the traditional Judeo-Christian sense. There is no place for a passive Savior in this belief system, as insinuated in the lyrics of "Bestrafe mich" and "Asche zu Asche." According to Rammstein, the existence of angels is roughly equivalent to being a spectator of an intense tragic drama — one where the spectator (angels) is/are in a constant state of fear and isolation. Rammstein calls us to be more like epic heroes such as Prometheus and Konrad and challenge God for our role in the afterlife. Again, there doesn't appear to be an outright rejection of an afterlife, but rather a call for a renegotiation of the terms of our post-mortem existence. Organized religion is viewed on par with oppressive government systems; those in power exert their will on their subjects. Rather than rendering ourselves powerless to the whims of tyranny, we are called to take charge of our lives.

With respect to eternal salvation, there appears to be a sincere hope for something better beyond the veil of death and a respect for accumulated wisdom in the lyrics of "Alter Mann." It remains a matter of debate as to whether or not the strong Christian overtones with allegorical reference to Holy Writ and the submission of the will of the young man to the ways and wisdom of the old man (God?) can be extended to Rammstein's message here; however, the mere recognition of this possibility seems to indicate that the Church of Rammstein offers hope for its disciples in leading a better earthly existence if we adhere to the "wisdom of the ages." Therefore, the debate isn't whether or not there is some sort of teaching and principles that bring peace in this life (and possibly the next), but exactly what these teachings are and their origin.

As a disciple in the Church of Rammstein, I have come to admire and respect the complex themes interwoven throughout aspects of their music and performance. Their treatment of religion and metaphysics discussed in this essay are yet another example of how the aspects of the seemingly mundane in Rammstein can unlock numerous mysteries that remain unexplored. Here we are called to continue to develop, flourish and enjoy our existence as much as possible. The instructions that we are given are those that seek to help us avoid hierarchical systems that will only repress us and bring us pain during our earthly sojourn. In the end, we are admonished to seek wisdom much like the young man in "Alter Mann;" we are called to find the path that leads to peace in this life. Any true fan of Rammstein knows that the band has been trying to do this for themselves from the beginning of their journey, and they are calling us to do the same on our own terms at our own pace. Discipleship in the Church of Rammstein requires continued intellectual growth, a curbing of natural, carnal desires, and a sincere thirst for knowledge and wisdom. The Church of Rammstein cannot promise a glorious afterlife where one enters into enter rest in the presence of (some form of) deity, but given the depiction of angels in their canon, one has to question whether this is a desirable outcome worthy of the description of "salvation." In many respects, we are called to believe in ourselves in an almost Buddhist-esque approach to this life and the hereafter a striving to achieve Nirvana in this life rather than viewing this world as inferior as in Christian-Platonic tradition.

Notes

1. I am particularly grateful to Nick Henry, John Littlejohn, and Juliane Schicker for countless discussions on the ideas presented here. Their critical feedback on earlier versions of this manuscript provided invaluable criticism that helped me strengthen this manuscript. Lastly, I would like to dedicate this essay to my former students at Carson-Newman College who participated in my seminar where we investigated and explored the depth of Rammstein's lyrics. All remaining shortcoming and inconsistencies are solely the fault of the author.

2. Mühlmann (1999) points out numerous parallels between the band Oomph!'s "Sex," "Mitten ins Herz," and "Das ist Freiheit" and Rammstein's "Bestrafe mich" and "Asche zu Asche." What this indicates, as mentioned later in this essay, is that a larger scale investigation of the notion of religion in the music of *Neue Deutsche Härte* (NDH) musicians is necessary to gain a more comprehensive understanding of this complex theme. Due to time and space restrictions, I leave this fascinating topic for future research.

3. Another form of potential "heresy" on the part of Rammstein here is the association of God with a female entity, which contradicts the traditional understanding of God. Although it is possible to interpret this tyrannical female figure as nature, this seems unlike due to the way the dwarfs (i.e. members of the band) worship her in adoration.

4. The origin of this interpretation comes from the contributor DasModell on 02/17/2007 on the website http://www.dasschoenstekind.de/forum/showthread.php?t=299. Although I have adapted this original interpretation here to conform to the discussion at hand, I recognize that my ideas stem from this entry.

5. Nick Henry (p.c.) brings up an excellent point that the figures delivering the apocalyptic message may be mortal prophets rather than angelic creatures.

6. "You are not the father of this world — you are her Czar!"

7. Thanks to Juliane Schicker (p.c.) for bringing this similarity to my attention.

8. As a matter of fact, Till Lindemann indicates that this song came about after his then girlfriend began seriously discussing the possibility of marriage with him.

9. See also EN's "Haus der Lüge" (house of lies) for a similar treatment of angels.

10. This expressed disappointment in the portrayal of East German history is also present in contemporary hip hop lyrics from artists hailing from the former GDR (see e.g., Putnam and Schicker [forthcoming] for a detailed discussion and analysis of this topic).

Works Cited

Adney, Karley K. "A Carnivalesque Cannibal: Armin Meiwes, 'Mein Teil,' and Representations of Homosexuality." This volume.

Bettendorf, Michele. *Ursprung Punkszene. Oder Rammstein hätte es im Westen nie gegeben.* Books on Demand GmbH, 2002.

DasModell. Comment on Rammstein Alter Mann — Interpretation. February 17, 2007 (9:03pm). http://www.dasschoenstekind.de/forum/showthread.php?t=299.

Hanssen, Beatrice. *Walter Benjamin's Oral History.* Berkeley: University of California Press, 2000.

Henry, Nick, and Juliane Schicker. "Heimatsehnsucht: Rammstein and the Search for Cultural Identity." This volume.

Fosl, Peter S. "Metallica, Nietzsche, and Marx: The Immorality or Morality." *Metallica and Philosophy: A Crash Course in Brain Surgery*, edited by William Irwin, 74–84. Malden, MA: Blackwell-Wiley, 2007.

Frith, Simon. *Performing Rights: On the Value of Popular Music.* Cambridge: Harvard University Press, 1998.

Irwin, William. "The Search Goes On: Christian, Warrior, Buddhist." *Metallica and Philosophy: A Crash Course in Brain Surgery*, edited by William Irwin, 16–28. Malden, MA: Blackwell-Wiley, 2007.

Kita, Caroline A. "Jacob Struggling with the Angel: Siegfried Lipiner, Gustav Mahler, and the Search for Aesthetic-Religious Redemption in Fin-de-siècle Vienna." Ph.D. diss., Duke University, 2011.

Littlejohn, John T., and Michael T. Putnam. "Rammstein and Ostalgie: Longing for Yesteryear." *Popular Music and Society* 33, no. 1 (2010): 35–44.

Lüke, Martina. "Love as a Battlefield: Reading Rammstein as Dark Romanticists." This volume.

Mickewicz, Adam. *Todtenfeier* (Dziady). Translated by Siegfried Lipiner. Leipzig: Breitkopf & Härtl, 1887.

Mühlmann, Wolf-Rüdiger. *Letzte Ausfahrt: Germania — Ein Phänomen namens Neue Deutsche Härte.* Berlin: Verlag Jerske, 1999.

Niekerk, Carl. Reading Mahler. *German Culture and Jewish Identity in Fin-de-Siecle Vienna.* Rochester: Camden House, 2010.

Putnam, Michael, and Juliane Schicker. "Straight Outta Marzahn: (Re)constructing Communicative Memory in East Germany through Hip Hop." *Popular Music and Society.* Forthcoming.

Rammstein.com interview with Paul, Flake, Christoph, and Richard. http://www.rammsteinniccage.com/media/interviews/rammcomjan01en.html. Last updated October 19, 2009.

Shrayane, Jennifer. *Blixa Bargeld and Einstürzende Neubauten: Germanic experimental music — Evading do-re-mi.'* London: Ashgate, 2010.

Discography

Einstürzende Neubauten. "Engel der Vernichtung." *Zeichnung des Patienten O.T.* Some Bizarre Records. CD. 1983

Metallica. "The God That Failed." *Metallica.* Elektra. CD. 1991.

_____. "Trapped Under Ice." *Ride the Lightning.* Megaforce. CD. 1984.

Rammstein. "Alter Mann." *Sehnsucht.* Motor. CD. 1997.

_____. "Amerika." *Reise, Reise.* Motor. CD. 2004.

_____. "Asche zu Asche." *Herzeleid.* Motor. CD. 1995.

_____. "Bestrafe mich." *Sehnsucht.* Motor. CD. 1997.

_____. "Engel." *Herzeleid.* Motor. CD. 1997.

_____. "Haifisch." *Liebe ist für Alle Da.* Universal. CD. 2009.

_____. "Heirate mich." *Herzeleid.* Motor. CD. 1995.

_____. "Herzeleid." *Herzeleid.* Motor. CD. 1995.

_____. "Mein Teil." *Reise, Reise.* Motor. CD. 2004.

_____. "Der Meister." *Herzeleid.* Motor. CD. 1995.

_____. "Morgenstern." *Reise, Reise.* Motor. CD. 2004.

_____. "Moskau." *Reise, Reise.* Motor. CD. 2004.

_____. "Sonne." *Herzeleid.* Motor. CD. 1997.

_____. "Spieluhr." *Mutter.* Motor. CD. 2001.

_____. "Stein um Stein." *Reise, Reise.* Motor. CD. 2004.

Tool. "Lateralus." *Lateralus.* Volcano. CD. 2001.

Filmography

Wenders, Wim. *Der Himmel über Berlin.* Basis-Film-Verleih, 1987.

About the Contributors

Karley K. Adney is the senior faculty manager at ITT Technical Institute Online. She received her Ph.D. in 16th- and 17th-century British literature from Northern Illinois University. Her primary research interests include adaptations of Shakespeare's plays for children, the Harry Potter series, and representations of women in popular culture.

Robert G. H. Burns became a professional musician in the early 1970s and has been a touring and recording bass guitarist for American soul artists such as Sam and Dave, Isaac Hayes, The Stylistics and Edwin Starr. In the late 1970s he performed in the rock opera *Tommy* with its composer, Pete Townsend of The Who. Since 2001, Robert has lectured in music at the University of Otago and has published on progressive rock music, iconography in rock music, and national identity in folk and rock music.

Nick Henry is a Ph.D. candidate in German applied linguistics and language sciences at Penn State. He received his bachelor's degree in German from Texas Tech University, where he also earned master's degrees in applied linguistics and German. His research interests include second language acquisition, psycholinguistics and sentence processing, second language pedagogy, East German studies, and reflections of German culture in popular music.

Corinna Kahnke received her Ph.D. in modern German literature and culture with a minor in cultural studies from Indiana University, Bloomington, in 2007. She directed the German program at the California Polytechnic State University in San Luis Obispo from 2007 to 2010. Since the fall of 2010 she has been an assistant professor of German and director of Germanic languages and literatures at Duke University. She has published on contemporary pop literature, musical subcultures in pedagogy, and gender studies.

Brad Klypchak teaches courses in liberal studies at Texas A&M University, Commerce. While he has published and presented on topics across film, theatre, sport, performance, cultural, and mass media studies, his particular research emphasis has been on heavy metal music.

John T. Littlejohn is a lecturer of German at Coastal Carolina University, where he teaches classes on German language, literature and culture. After earning his Ph.D. at the University of Kansas, he became fascinated with the musician's role and self-representation within a changing German society, and increasingly focused his research on German rock and hip-hop music. He has also published on post-reunification German film and interwar German drama.

Martina Lüke is an assistant professor in residence for German and comparative literature and cultural studies and research associate at the University of Connecticut. Her research and publications focus on German Romanticism and Expressionism literature; modern history (18th to 21st century); philosophies and theories on war and violence; history of pedagogy; business German; and German film. She is also the author of two monographs.

Daniel Lukes is a postdoctoral fellow in the Morse Academic Plan at New York University. He received his Ph.D. in comparative literature from New York University in 2012. His research primarily deals with representations of masculinity and failure in twentieth century and contemporary British, North American and European literature, theory, and culture. He has published articles on music since 1999.

Michael T. Putnam is an assistant professor of German and linguistics at Penn State University. Aside from his research in theoretical linguistics, he has published extensively on German popular music and its connection to sociolinguistics and contemporary cultural and literary developments in German-speaking Europe. His research explores the connections between collective and cultural memory in East German hip-hop (with Juliane Schicker) and *Ostalgie* in the lyrics of Rammstein (with long-time collaborator John T. Littlejohn).

Simon Richter is a professor of German literature at the University of Pennsylvania. He is the author of *Laocoon's Body and the Aesthetics of Pain*; *Missing the Breast: Gender, Fantasy and the Body in the German Enlightenment*; and *Women, Pleasure, Film: What Lolas Want*. He is the past president of the Goethe Society of North America and past editor of the *Goethe Yearbook*.

David A. Robinson is a lecturer of history at Edith Cowan University, Western Australia, where he teaches courses on global history, war and conflict, human rights, and genocide. His research interests include African history, international relations, contemporary social movements, Marxist political economy, and Žižekian social theory. Recent projects are research on Sigmund Freud's cocaine use and the politics and lyrical references of the radical rap-metal band Rage Against the Machine.

Juliane Schicker is a Ph.D. candidate in German at Pennsylvania State University. She received her teaching certification from the Otto-von-Guericke-Universität Magdeburg and a master's degree in German from Texas Tech University. She has published and presented on linguistic and literary aspects of songs of the Hitler Youth, the band Rammstein, the composer Kurt Weill, and music and trauma in the GDR.

Patricia Anne Simpson is a professor of German studies at Montana State University in Bozeman, where she chairs the Department of Modern Languages and Literatures. Simpson has published widely on the erotics of war in German romanticism, cultures of violence in German-speaking Europe, and on contemporary film, music, and literature. Her research focuses on changing representations of the European family in the age of immigration, epistemologies of the playroom and playground, and public art/anti-violence campaigns.

Erin Sweeney Smith is a Ph.D. candidate in musicology at Case Western Reserve University. Her research areas include music video, the cultural interactions between music and imaginary geographies, and musical representations of the New Woman at the turn of the century. She also holds degrees in vocal performance and collaborative piano.

Index

273

Milton Keynes UK
Ingram Content Group UK Ltd.
UKHW031148121124
451045UK00015B/300